Beyond Boundaries
The Manning Marable Reader

MANNING MARABLE

Edited by
RUSSELL RICKFORD

Paradigm Publishers
Boulder • London

Copyright © 2011 Paradigm Publishers

Published in the United States by Paradigm Publishers, 2845 Wilderness Place, Suite 200, Boulder, CO 80301 USA.

Paradigm Publishers is the trade name of Birkenkamp & Company, LLC, Dean Birkenkamp, President and Publisher.

Library of Congress Cataloging-in-Publication Data for this book is available from the Library of Congress

ISBN 978-1-59451-861-4 (hardcover : alk. paper)
ISBN 978-1-59451-862-1 (paperback : alk. paper)

Printed and bound in the United States of America on acid-free paper that meets the standards of the American National Standard for Permanence of Paper for Printed Library Materials. Designed and Typeset by Straight Creek Bookmakers.

15 14 13 12 11   1 2 3 4 5

Contents

Preface by Manning Marable   v

Introduction by Russell Rickford   ix

SECTION I. ON RACE AND RACIALIZATION   1

    Introduction: The Prism of Race, 3
    History and Black Consciousness:
       The Political Culture of Black America, 11
    On Being Black: The Burden of Race and Class, 22

SECTION II. ON BLACK PROTEST AND POLITICS:
THE 1970s AND 1980s   31

    Anatomy of Black Politics, 33
    Reaganism, Racism, and Reaction:
       Black Political Realignment in the 1980s, 44
    The Unfinished Revolution, 57
    African Links, 62
    Black Politics in Crisis, 68

SECTION III. ON BLACK PROTEST AND POLITICS:
THE 1990s TO THE PRESENT   79

    Black Politics and the Challenges for the Left, 81
    Eurocentrism vs. Afrocentrism: The Impasse of Racial Politics, 87
    A New Black Politics, 91
    Black America in Search of Itself, 102
    African-American Empowerment in the Face of Racism:
       The Political Aftermath of the Battle of Los Angeles, 113
    After the March, 120
    Facing the Demon Head On: Race and the Prison Industrial Complex, 126

SECTION IV. ON THE SOUTHERN QUESTION   137

Tuskegee and the Politics of Illusion in the New South, 139
The Land Question in Historical Perspective:
   The Economics of Poverty in the Blackbelt South, 1865–1920, 153
The Tchula 7: Harvest of Hate in the Mississippi Delta, 166

SECTION V. ON BLACK LEADERSHIP   173

A. Philip Randolph and the Foundations of Black American Socialism, 175
King's Ambiguous Legacy, 194
Kwame Nkrumah and the Convention People's Party:
   A Critical Reassessment, 201
Rediscovering Malcolm X's Life:
   A Historian's Adventures in Living History, 215
Racializing Obama: The Enigma of Post-Black Politics and Leadership, 232

SECTION VI. ON BUILDING A SOCIAL JUSTICE MOVEMENT   245

Socialist Vision and Political Struggle for the 1990s, 247
Multicultural Democracy, 255
9/11 Racism in the Time of Terror, 262
The Political and Theoretical Contexts of the Changing Racial Terrain, 279
Interview with Former Jamaican Prime Minister Michael Manley, 293

Notes   *317*

Credits   *337*

Index   *341*

About the Author and Editor   *351*

Preface

The black intellectual tradition is the body of critical analysis and scholarly commentary about the people of African descent, over the past several centuries. At the core of this tradition is black history—the study and documentation of the black experience over time. In traditional West African societies, local historians who had memorized the sagas of their people were called *griots*. In the United States, for many years the enterprise of black history was suppressed and distorted. White historians for many years discounted oral histories or testimonies from slave *griots* about their lives in bondage, for example, because such evidence was deemed biased. It was only within the black intellectual tradition that scholars placed at the center of their work the perspectives and voices of African-American people. These intellectuals understood that history's power was rooted not simply in memory but also in possibility. A clear vision of the future begins with an understanding of the past.

My introduction to the black intellectual tradition came initially from my mother, June Morehead Marable. During World War II my mother worked as a secretary at a military installation. Saving her money, in the fall of 1944, June matriculated at historically black Wilberforce University in Ohio. She was subsequently employed as a housekeeper for several years in the home of Wilberforce college president, Dr. Charles H. Wesley. A noted historian of the African-American experience, Wesley made history accessible to everyday people through his popular writings and lectures. After his presidencies at Wilberforce and Central State University, Wesley went on to lead the Association for the Study of Negro Life and History. When my mother graduated in 1948, she promised that one of her children would become a black historian, in honor of Wesley. Two years later, on May 13, 1950, I was born in Dayton, Ohio. My mother, a public school teacher, organized a regime of obligatory books to read, covering US and world history. Every summer I wrote dozens of book reviews analyzing increasingly complex studies. And I loved all of it. I found freedom within the historical imagination, the search for meaning in our past. My life and career as a historian had been determined before I was born.

Consequently, from the beginning of my academic life I viewed being a historian of the black experience as becoming the bearer of truths or stories that had been suppressed or relegated to the margins. Following the models of W. E. B. Du Bois and Wesley, I came to understand that history itself could empower the oppressed; that history always had a point of view, and the perspectives we assume inevitably shape the outcomes of our inquiry. I came to recognize the complicated dialectics of history: that all people make history, but not in ways they choose, to paraphrase Marx. History, to the disadvantaged, can become a site of resistance and cultural renewal. It forms the foundations necessary for an alternative consciousness.

Beyond Boundaries presents an outline of my life and adventure as a public historian and radical intellectual in the final decades of the twentieth century and the dawn of the twenty-first century. There have been several central themes that have defined nearly all of my work. The first and foremost is a question—which also preoccupied Frantz Fanon and Malcolm X—the nexus between history and black consciousness: what is the meaning of black group identity as interpreted through the stories of African-American people, over time? How do oppressed people create the tools and language of resistance? I have tried to answer these questions by examining the rise and fall of different sorts of black social movements within the United States, the Caribbean, and Africa. Each struggle is unique, yet there are also general lessons that can be taken from these experiences as a whole. Consciousness also involves the question of how people define "leadership"—the capacity of any group to realize its interests and visions. Because African Americans were denied voting rights and full political representation for hundreds of years, they evolved attitudes about politics and leadership that most white Americans did not share.

I was also fortunate to come to maturity at a time when the Black Freedom Movement in the United States emphasized the connections and commitments with Africa, other parts of the African diaspora, and other international populations. There has always been a long history of internationalism, of course, within the African-American political culture. Henry Highland Garnet, Edward Wilmot Blyden, W. E. B. Du Bois, Marcus Garvey, Paul Robeson, and Ralph Bunche all in different ways expressed internationalism. In the early 1970s, an intellectual commitment to Pan-Africanism meant, to me, that it was impossible to be a serious, well-grounded student of black American history without also knowing a good deal about Africa and the Caribbean as well. Consequently, my doctoral dissertation was a biographical study of John Langalibalele Dube, the first president and cofounder of the African National Congress (ANC). Although the primary focus of my writing from the late 1970s on was devoted to black America and the United States, I continued to analyze events and struggles across the African diaspora. I wrote extensively, for example, about the anti-apartheid movement, the triumph of the ANC, and the difficulties and challenges of post-apartheid society. I developed political and academic contacts across the black world, but especially in Jamaica, Cuba, and Great Britain. My conversations and debates with the Cubans and Jamaicans in the 1980s, for example, deeply influenced my 1987 book *African and Caribbean Politics*.

Finally, I have long been preoccupied with studying the role of intellectuals in the remaking of racialized societies. Theoretically, my points of reference were provided by the writings and lives of Du Bois, C. L. R. James, and Antonio Gramsci. Du Bois was the consummate Renaissance man, a genius in the arts, literature, sociology, and historical writing. But he was never content just to interpret the world. So he also helped to establish the Niagara Movement in 1905 and the National Association for the Advancement of Colored People five years later. James continually linked theoretical work to political practice, from his involvement in the international Trotskyist movement during the 1930s, to his leadership role in Trinidad and Tobago's independence movement, and subsequently in the Federation movement in the English-speaking Caribbean in the late 1950s–early 1960s. Gramsci provides the great example of how a critically engaged mind can overcome even the draconian power of prisons. I have learned from each of them and have tried to apply the same discipline and passion they embody to my own endeavors.

The most rewarding aspect of my intellectual life has been to work with young scholars, who are defining the new directions of the black intellectual tradition. One of the most talented and insightful intellectuals of this new generation is Russell Rickford. He has already produced several outstanding, scholarly studies, and his Ph.D. dissertation was a critical historical interpretation of independent and alternative educational institutions during the black power period of the 1970s. Rickford possesses a deep knowledge of the freedom struggle, as well as a Pan-Africanist's appreciation for the connections between the various leaders and resistance movements throughout the African diaspora.

Rickford has thoughtfully reviewed my historical and political essays on many different topics, produced over thirty-five years. What is really impressive is how he has focused on themes that are central to all of the works, regardless of the particular topics they may address. The collection title, *Beyond Boundaries*, is an acknowledgment of my intellectual debt to and kinship with James, author of *Beyond a Boundary*. It is a metaphor for what social history and critical theory must accomplish: the shattering of barriers that divide people into social hierarchies, that condemn human beings to lives of inequality due to their color, class, or gender. Another way of life is possible, and critical reconstructions of the past are essential in creating such futures.

Manning Marable
June 21, 2010

Introduction

Russell Rickford

I first came to Harlem, the Upper Manhattan neighborhood that would provide the backdrop for some of my most significant political awakenings, to join a protest. Well, actually, it was to interview a subject for a book project I was working on, but the interview was to take place amid a sidewalk demonstration in which said subject—controversial City College of New York black studies professor Leonard Jeffries—was participating. This was around 2000, and a 6,000-square-foot Disney retail store had just opened on the corner of 125th Street and Frederick Douglass Boulevard in the heart of black Harlem. Disney's arrival on 125th, the storied thoroughfare upon which the great platform speakers—Marcus Garvey, Adam Clayton Powell, Jr., and Malcolm X—had once exhorted, and which urban decay had long since blighted, was being touted by private developers as a centerpiece of a larger Harlem revitalization. That economic revival, bolstered by the area's designation as a federal empowerment zone, would bring an Old Navy and a Magic Johnson Theater to the once-shabby block that Disney now anchored, and ultimately would clog much of "'Two-Fifth" (as some black New Yorkers call Harlem's major artery) with national outlets, including H&M, Blockbuster, and, inevitably, Starbucks.

Back in 2000 some Harlemites welcomed early signs that 125th might become an overgrown strip mall. Ritualized consumerism, after all, is as much a cultural tradition—and as much a spectacle—in the largely poor, uptown community as it is on Rodeo Drive in Beverly Hills. But other locals saw the coming of big chains to their neighborhood as a kind of recolonization of the capital of black America, a takeover that would bring few jobs and the scourge of gentrification, displacing residents and small, black-owned businesses. Especially galling to foes of Harlem's corporate redevelopment was the incursion of Disney—a brand associated with a long history of stereotypical and racist characters and plots— just paces from the famous Apollo Theater and other sacred landmarks. Black nationalists shared the impulse to defend black cultural space and the tenuous, petty bourgeois privileges of African-American storeowners against the onslaught of white capital. And so it was that sometime in 2000, having driven up from Philadelphia to interview Jeffries, I found myself tromping back and forth between police barricades on the corner of 125th and "Freddy-D," a cassette recorder in hand, questioning the handsome professor as he strode alongside other picketers urging a boycott of the Disney store.

At the time I thought the protest entirely appropriate. I knew that Harlem had long resisted the exploitation of the non-African-American merchants, big and small, who control much of the commerce north of 110th Street. Their businesses, which often dispensed low-quality food and overpriced products to poor residents, had been targeted during spontaneous uprisings (or "race riots") in the 1940s and 1960s, and had drawn the condemnation of the redoubtable stepladder preacher Carlos A. Cooks, whose African Nationalist Pioneer Movement had pressed Harlemites to "Buy Black." Back in 2000 I viewed economic exploitation in much the same manner that Cooks and other Garveyites had: primarily in racial terms. To me, Harlem represented the black proletariat, and its oppression came inexorably at the hands of white rulers. It was only after I moved to the neighborhood in 2002 to attend graduate school that my critique of capitalism moved decisively beyond black and white.

In a sense, it was my ideological journey from conservative nationalism to socialism that catapulted me to Harlem in the first place. As an adolescent attending affluent, predominantly white schools in Palo Alto, California, during the 1980s and early 1990s, I had become an unabashed black nationalist. By high school I had utterly rejected the creed of liberal integration conveyed through the mushy idiom of "multiculturalism" and reinforced by triumphalist narratives of the civil rights movement of the 1950s and 1960s. Imbibing the neo-black nationalist themes of the ascendant hip-hop movement, I unquestioningly embraced racial solidarity as the exclusive path to black liberation. I idolized Malcolm X (whose uncompromising image contemporary rappers, filmmaker Spike Lee, and a host of commercial interests had recently resurrected) as an icon of black manhood and cultural authenticity.

My nationalism remained patriarchal and bourgeois as I matriculated at Howard University, Washington, D.C.'s historically black mecca, in the mid-1990s. I vividly recall the collective euphoria of the Million Man March of October 16, 1996, an event that coincided with my senior year. As I communed with thousands of black men on the National Mall that day, the deeply conservative implications of our gathering in the nation's capital to "atone" for our failure to adequately provide for, protect, and control the heterosexual, patriarchal family simply did not cross my mind. To me, the peaceful congregation of so many brothers was evidence in itself of black progress. Clearly we were "getting ourselves together."

As I graduated from Howard in 1997 and went to work for a Philadelphia newspaper, the assumption that the struggle against white supremacy meant fighting for black advancement within the existing capitalist order continued to largely define my political outlook. In subsequent years, however, as I began to read more seriously black thinkers whose radicalism combined racial and class analyses (including C. L. R. James, Frantz Fanon, Walter Rodney, Huey P. Newton, Angela Davis, Assata Shakur, and Malcolm himself), critiques of global capitalism as the author of the most brutal forms of racial exploitation began to pierce my consciousness. Finally, around 2001, I read Manning Marable's *How Capitalism Underdeveloped Black America.*

It's funny how books find you when you're ready for them. I can't remember precisely how I got my hands on that copy of Marable's classic study of racism and political economy, originally published in 1983. I do recall that the slim volume, which takes its title from Rodney's magisterial *How Europe Underdeveloped Africa,* helped cement the fragments of class analysis that had been bobbing on the sea of my racial awareness without a body of theory upon which to fasten themselves. I did not immediately become a socialist. Pan-Africanism, which I considered the most enlightened form of black nationalism, continued to shape my political sensibilities. But I knew that I had to apprentice myself to this Marable. You can imagine how delighted I was when the scholar phoned in the spring of 2002 to tell me that I had been accepted to the master's program at Columbia University's Institute for Research in African-American Studies (IRAAS), which he had founded in 1993 and now directed.

Columbia, which perches atop the Upper West Side of Manhattan, calls its surrounding neighborhood "Morningside Heights." But the instant I got Marable's call I knew where I was headed: I would live and study just north of that Ivy League behemoth in the historic village of "Harlem, USA!"

When I finally arrived in Harlem in the fall of 2002, the changes that I had first glimpsed two years earlier while shuffling around the new Disney store were gaining momentum. Condominiums continued to shoot up, their glass facades a rebuke to the brick housing projects that had long towered over much of the neighborhood. More big chain stores had appeared, and Bill Clinton had moved his headquarters into the massive State Office Building at 125th and Adam Clayton Powell Boulevard.

Some of these developments brought real benefits and convenience to local residents eager to hunt for discount clothing at the new Marshalls or pay a phone bill at the Sprint store. Many Harlemites welcomed the returning prestige of a community that, despite the glamorous episodes of its past, had for decades been associated with drugs and crime. It was this promise of continued renaissance (and, I would argue, a psychic need for white affirmation) that generated the ecstatic black crowds that greeted Clinton as he moved into his uptown office in 2001. Long before the recession began to slow the uneven development that had brought new sidewalk cafes and bank branches to some sections of Harlem, however, it was obvious that poverty remained as omnipresent in the neighborhood as the liquor stores, pawn shops, and check-cashing joints cluttering many of its corners.

Some symbols of Harlem's economic oppression clearly reflected the domination of white elites. White absentee landlords jacked up already criminally high rents, ensuring that the gears of gentrification continued to churn. Despite Clinton's rapturous welcome to the 'hood (I was scandalized to see a 125th Street mural depicting the former president paternally holding aloft portraits of Martin Luther King, Jr., and Malcolm X), the man who had overseen welfare "reform" in the 1990s was himself responsible for curtailing the meager supplemental income upon which many of the community's working families depended. Even Harlem's tourist influxes, which every Sunday morning filled black storefront churches with Europeans toting expensive cameras, seemed to highlight the color line dividing affluence and need.

It soon grew apparent, however, that class inequity in Harlem was not merely a matter of color. Many of the young professionals moving into condos and refurbished brownstones (and thus driving up rent) were black. (Though I complained as bitterly as other tenants about soaring bills, I came to recognize that as a Columbia grad student living in an overpriced one-bedroom in Central Harlem, I was as much the face of gentrification as anyone else.) In time, African-American entrepreneurs opened an incongruous caviar store near Marcus Garvey Park. When a black-owned Lamborghini and exotic car dealership favored by bling-bling rappers appeared on Malcolm X Boulevard in an area that had seen a resurgence of homelessness, heroin addiction, and hungry children, I lost it. "This society is insane!" I thought. Some black capitalists, it seemed, were as eager as their white counterparts to exploit Harlem's renewed cultural cachet, no matter what the social cost.

My old political assumptions—that black Americans represent a nation within a nation, share a more or less uniform experience of cultural, economic, and political oppression, and can resist white subjugation only by building strong, internal institutions—seemed increasingly inadequate for comprehending Harlem realities. Meanwhile, my formal education (both at IRAAS and within Columbia's history department, where I went on to pursue a doctorate) and involvement in radical study groups exposed me to more Marxist and black feminist critiques of bourgeois nationalism. I knew that I was not becoming a doctrinaire Marxist-Leninist. Though third world anti-imperialism powerfully informed my emerging, materialist visions of social justice, narrow economic determinism seemed to me as shortsighted and reductionist as rigid black chauvinism. The virulent racism historically exhibited by white workers, moreover, left me suspicious of theories of multiracial class alliances. And the noisy sectarianism I encountered at radical conferences made me wary of the Left's belligerent orthodoxies.

The more progressive and leftist my democratic principles became, however, the more reactionary Harlem's black nationalists (as represented by self-styled fundamentalists such as the Black Israelites) began to seem. One afternoon while dining at the Uptown Juice Bar, a local vegetarian joint, I overheard a streetwise young brother, perhaps a member of the breakaway Nation of Islam faction known as the Five Percenters, railing against black lesbianism at a nearby table. According to this guy, who like me was in his thirties, homosexuality in the 'hood was just another sign of the disintegration of the "traditional" African family, the principal cause, he argued, of much of black America's crises. Despite my better instincts, I spoke up.

Actually, I volunteered, the main source of black suffering was a devastating matrix of discrimination in areas such as housing, employment, health, education, and criminal justice rooted in a bitter history of capitalist exploitation. What black America truly needed was an end to structural racism and a massive Marshall Plan for the inner city. Besides, I concluded, how did banishing African-American gays, lesbians, and feminists from the sanctuary of authentic "blackness" empower working-class and poor black folk? The brother paused, then leaned in close, eyeing me warily. "Brother," he asked solemnly, "are you a homo?"

During my tenure in Harlem, I grew convinced of the futility of trying to dismantle white supremacy with the tools of the white supremacist—i.e., racial chauvinism, militarism, sexism, homophobia, and the unrestrained ethic of private wealth accumulation. As I continued to study and evolve, struggling to devise a political framework that could accommodate both my deep belief in the necessity for black political and cultural self-determination and my newer emphasis on the material realities of workers and the poor, I came to adopt a rather complex political identity. I was, I finally decided, a progressive black nationalist-feminist driven by the radical ethics of the Marxist-Leninist and the pragmatism and anti-authoritarianism of the social democrat.

Oddly enough, rather than segmenting my political philosophies, this approach synthesized my evolving beliefs. I still insisted upon the inalienable right, under the principle of self-government, of black folk to gather *as black folk* to address certain issues, such as affirmative action or reparations for slavery, even as we coordinate with progressive whites and others on behalf of such causes. On the other hand, I came to believe that for black workers, progressive racial consciousness and class consciousness could be symbiotic (though I recognized that all people must guard against racial essentialism and its tendency to obscure class interest). In time I also witnessed the profound power of multiracial organizing, which strengthened opposition to the American invasion of Iraq and the fascist assault on black New Orleans after Katrina. I began to understand women's liberation and gay rights as crucial weapons in the fight against racism and capitalism. I grasped the vital link between democracy and socialism—the need to place human need before private profit, distribute capital more evenly, and reorganize society along cooperative lines—and I embraced both strategic reform and rebellion as paths to social change,

In retrospect, what I was struggling toward during my sojourn in Harlem was a viable praxis—a way of translating my political revelations into a coherent system of thought and practice. How could my life and work more fully embody the expansive visions of social justice that inspired me? How could I scientifically critique corrupt political economies while defending human individualism, creativity, and joy? How could I build socialism and express solidarity with workers and the poor while draw-ing my livelihood from large, private universities that themselves reinforce capitalist hegemony? Ultimately I decided that I would reject dogma, orthodoxy, and static theories in my personal and professional lives, even as democracy and economic justice remained constant ideals in my political imagination. It is this awareness and commitment to self-criticism that finally made me a true child of Malcolm, who never stopped evolving, though it cost him his life. And it is this adaptability, as much as a fundamental devotion to socialism and black freedom, that has made me a spiritual son of Manning Marable.

Marable represents the best tradition of the public intellectual. For four decades he has exemplified the principle that knowledge is communal, that it ought to be widely disseminated as a weapon of the masses rather than hoarded as the private prerogative of elites. Indeed, he has defended that old, venerable idea that non-elites— workers, prisoners, and the poor—generate their own revolutionary knowledge, and that any sound endeavor to redeem American democracy must bear in its soul the lessons of their lived experience.

Marable is a custodian of the belief that radical intellectuals must practice their craft in the scrum of political debate, alongside (and not merely on behalf of) the oppressed. Their lifestyles, in other words, must be a bit frenetic, a bit uncomfortable. At all times, in every possible way, they must struggle to place their interpretive energies at the disposal of the people. Marable inherited this sense of duty early in his career from figures like Walter Rodney, the leftist Guyanese historian and Pan-African theorist, who prior to his 1980 assassination, in the service of workers and the poor in Jamaica, Tanzania, and Guyana, essentially committed what Guinean revolutionary Amilcar Cabral called "class suicide."

Marable met Rodney during the 1970s when both scholars were associated with Atlanta's Institute of the Black World, an extraordinary collection of black intellectuals dedicated to cultivating the internationalist, progressive, and emancipatory impulses within the black studies movement. Though it is easy to forget today, that movement emerged during the 1960s from the basic conviction that black scholarship should respond to the total needs of black communities. This radical vision still propels Marable, whose accessible, astonishingly profuse publications and lectures (a remarkable portion of which are dispatched to popular audiences) have long nourished "the grassroots" while edifying the "ebony tower" of the academy.

As an exuberant graduate student, I sat in Marable's seminars and listened to him passionately extol the activist concept of black studies. He continually stressed the corrective, descriptive, and prescriptive functions of the field. Our task was to correct distortions of black heritage, describe the African diasporic experience, and prescribe solutions for enduring racial inequality and subjugation. In conveying this charge, Marable often cited the example and wisdom of his personal heroes, especially the distinguished Marxist theorist C. L. R. James (whose affectionate moniker, "Nello," he invariably used), and Du Bois, father of all black intellectuals.

Marable's writing crackles with the energy of these two titans. Its breadth and multidisciplinary nature recall their fiercely incisive political critiques and that of other black radicals who have helped sustain democratic and anticolonial movements throughout the world. Indeed, Marable's criticism, in which the disciplines of political science and history commingle, reflects a similar long-term preoccupation with social justice. His central mission as social scientist and humanist has been to map out tactical, progressive, and leftist responses to shifts in political economy (the link between economic relations and the organization of politics), even as corporate capital has consolidated its global hegemony over the course of his professional life, especially during the final quarter of the twentieth century and the first decade of the new millennium.

Marable has consistently promoted the ideal of a supple, ecumenical, internationalist, and multiracial American Left, alert to the illusions of liberal reform; willing to cooperate with progressives for genuine social democratic change; responsive to the day-to-day struggles of minorities, immigrants, and the poor; imbued with the transformative, egalitarian spirit of the black freedom struggle. At the same time, he has agitated for a more radical, inclusive, independent, and proletarian black political agenda committed to liberating women and homosexuals, building progressive alliances across racial lines, ending the mass imprisonment for corporate profit of African Americans and Latinos, and seeking wholesale economic justice rather than the chimera of pluralist capitalism.

Throughout the backlash against black freedom, the long midnight of Reaganism, the destruction of the social wage, the horror of apartheid and genocide, the evisceration of the inner city, the betrayal of liberal complacency, the menace of corporate globalism, and the specter of imperialist war, Marable's devotion to these values has proven steadfast. He has encouraged black folk and people of conscience to remain hopeful and determined, urging us to seek strategic social reform while working to topple the leviathan of capitalism. This message, elegantly represented in the contents of this volume, may yet rescue us from cynicism, dogma, and despair, laying before us a course of radical resistance.

The articles that follow, culled from the best of Marable's popular and scholarly writing over the last thirty years, reflect the urgency, insight, and diversity of the intellectual's work. They are presented here in six interrelated sections: On Race and Racialization; On Black Protest and Politics (1970s and 1980s); On Black Protest and Politics (1990s to Present); On the Southern Question; On Black Leadership; On Building a Global Justice Movement. Taken as a whole, the pieces reveal an abiding concern with political economy, the persistence of structural racism, and the evolution of black political culture. Their most salient theme is the vortex of race and class—the historically specific manner in which systemic racism and class exploitation have conspired to stifle human progress, and the strategic ways that we can help reverse the resulting devastation.

It is this emphasis on strategy that lends this volume its striking timeliness. Whether discussing black land tenure after Reconstruction or racial profiling after the 9/11 attacks, the articles collected here forcefully argue that only the coordinated, sustained response of coalitions of people of color, workers, the poor, young people, and progressives can prevent the consolidation of a world order based on imperialism, capitalism and militarism, a project that caused profound suffering in the twentieth century and that now threatens to outdo itself in the twenty-first.

Readers will discover in these pages brisk accounts of the rise of contemporary political reaction, especially as it has devoured the moral energy of black insurgency during the "post–civil rights" era of the last four decades. The suppression and distortion of the black freedom struggle, a movement that produced one of the greatest challenges to entrenched social inequality that the modern world has known, helped transform the flawed but hopeful War on Poverty into the social chaos and racism of the War on Drugs and the War on Crime, setting the stage for today's jingoistic War on Terror. At the same time, the forces of reaction have waged war on social welfare, civil liberties, workers, organized labor, the poor, immigrants, women, minorities, gays, and lesbians in the name of that most patriotic American mission: subsidizing the expansion of corporate capital and expropriating wealth for the ultrarich.

While the essays featured here soberly indict the state apparatus for its role in these crimes, their primary analytic subject is us. Marable demonstrates that the internal contradictions and theoretical weaknesses of progressives and people of color are as responsible for the failures of democracy as is any onslaught from the Right. He reserves his most trenchant critiques for the shibboleths of black politics and protest. He argues, for example, that by substituting incremental reformism, accommodationism, and their own petty bourgeois class interests for more thoroughgoing definitions of black freedom, African-American leaders (from moderate leftists like A. Philip Randolph to centrists like Barack Obama) have consistently failed to fulfill their own progressive potential.

Moving beyond a narrow focus on elites, Marable invites all dissenters from the traditions of racist capitalism to help rewrite black and antiracist politics from the ground up. Doing so, he suggests, will require a bold expansion of our radical imagination. We must acknowledge the futility of bourgeois reformism and "black capitalism" as paths to racial equality. (A social structure predicated upon unemployment and severe labor exploitation can never offer the black masses full inclusion.) We must end our slavish devotion to the Democratic Party. (Genuine political dissent cannot mean sacrificing principle for vain promises or marginal gains.) Indeed, we must act within and beyond the electoral realm, resisting the delusion that Obama's ascent to the White House signals the advent of postracial politics and the decline of institutional racism as a target for agitation and legislation.

The vision of social justice that emerges from this collection empowers us to reject elitism, dogma, and mechanistic theories while fighting for full employment, a guaranteed income, quality education and housing, universal health care, the nationalization of industries vital for human survival and prosperity, and the ethical reconstruction of our political economy. As Marable reminds us, this mandate for sweeping social change has drawn its most powerful historical impetus from the black freedom struggle's spirit of radical egalitarianism. Today it falls to us to fulfill the movement's largely forgotten materialist ethos and revive the dream of economic democracy.

As we embark on this mission, the moral clarity of this text may prove indispensable. Its title, borrowed from *Beyond a Boundary,* C. L. R. James's brilliant essay on cricket and colonialism, seems especially apt. Now more than ever, drafting a new lexicon of radical struggle means traversing boundaries of race, gender, nation, religion, and ideology. By crossing these divides we may yet free our consciousness, decolonize our neighborhoods, and finally liberate Harlem.

SECTION I

On Race and Racialization

~

INTRODUCTION

The Prism of Race

Black and white. As long as I can remember, the fundamentally defining feature of my life, and the lives of my family, was the stark reality of race. Angular and unforgiving, race was so much more than the background for what occurred or the context for our relationships. It was the social gravity which set into motion our expectations and emotions, our language and dreams. Race seemed far more powerful than distinctions between people based in language, nationality, religion or income. Race seemed granite-like, fixed and permanent, as the center of the social universe. The reality of racial discrimination constantly fed the pessimism and doubts that we as black people felt about the apparent natural order of the world, the inherent unfairness of it all, as well as limiting our hopes for a better life somewhere in the distant future.

I am a child of Middle America. I was born in Dayton, Ohio, on 13 May 1950, at the height of McCarthyism and on the eve of the Korean conflict. One of the few rituals I remember about the anti-Communist hysteria sweeping the nation in the fifties were the obligatory exercises we performed in elementary school, "ducking and covering" ourselves beneath small wooden desks in our classroom to shield ourselves from the fallout and blast of a nuclear explosion. Most of what I now recall of growing up in south-central Ohio had little to do with nuclear war or communism, only the omnipresent reality of race.

In the 1950s, Dayton was a predominantly blue-collar, working-class town, situated on the banks of the Great Miami River. Neighborhoods were divided to some extent by class. Oakwood was the well-to-do, WASP-ish community, filled with the corporate executives and professionals who ran the city's enterprises. Dayton View on the northwest side was becoming increasingly Jewish. Kettering and Centerville were unpretentiously middle class, conservative and Republican. But beneath the divisions of income, religion and political affiliation seemed to be the broad polarization rooted in race. There appeared to be two parallel racial universes which cohabited the same city, each with its own set of religious institutions, cultural activities, social centers, clubs, political organizations and schools. African-Americans generally resided west of the Great Miami River. The central core of the ghetto was located along the corridors of West Third and West Fifth Street. With the great migration of southern blacks to Dayton immediately following World War II, the African-American population became much more dense, and began to spread west, out to the city's farthest boundaries.

The black community existed largely in its own world, within the logic of institutions it had created to sustain itself. We were taught to be proud of our history and literature. Every day, on the way to Edison Elementary School, I would feel a surge of pride as we drove past the home of celebrated African-American poet Paul Lawrence Dunbar. My parents, James and June Marable, were school teachers, a solidly middle-class profession by the standards of the status-conscious Negro elite. During the fifties, my father taught at predominately black Dunbar and Roosevelt high schools during the day; after school was dismissed, he worked as a laborer in the second shift at Dayton tire factory. Although my father had a principal's certificate and a Master's degree, which qualified him to be appointed as a principal, he was constantly passed over by white administrators because of his fiercely independent spirit and self-initiative. Frustrated, my father eventually went into business for himself, borrowing the money to build a private nursery and daycare center for black children on the city's West Side.

Because of my parent's education and jobs, we were part of Dayton's Negro middle class. Our family attorney, James McGee, was elected the city's first black mayor after the successes and reforms in the wake of the civil-rights movement. Most of my parents' friends were physicians, dentists, lawyers, school teachers, entrepreneurs and professionals of various types. Despite their pretensions, most middle-class Negroes were barely two or three paychecks from poverty. Many of the businesses that sold consumer goods to blacks, which were located on West Third Street, were white-owned. Our own business sector consisted chiefly of funeral parlors, beauty salons, auto repair shops and small restaurants.

The college-educated Negro middle class had begun purchasing comfortable, spacious homes clustered high on the ridge which overlooked the West Side, not far from the mostly German farm families who lived in Jefferson Township. Poorer black families lived closer to the factories and foundries, near the dirt, smoke and industrial stench I vividly recall even today. Social class and income stratification were not unimportant. There seemed to be striking similarities between the houses and the manner in which working and poor people were dressed on "our" side of town and in "their" working-class neighborhoods. But color was the greatest denominator of all.

On Gettysburg Avenue there were a group of small rental properties and boarding houses which were within walking distance of the Veteran's Administration Hospital on the far West Side. In the front windows of most of these buildings were small cardboard signs, reading simply "No Colored." Blacks legally could not be denied entrance into the hotels or best restaurants downtown, but they were certainly not welcomed. White taxicab drivers often avoided picking up black passengers at the train station. Very few blacks were on the local police force. Black children weren't permitted to use the public swimming pool on Germantown Pike. In most aspects of public and private life, whites acted toward African-Americans as "superiors," and usually expected to be treated deferentially. There were exceptions, certainly. At my elementary school, there were white students who were friendly. There were white teachers who displayed kindness and sincerity toward their black students. But there was always an unbridgeable distance separating us. No white students with whom I attended school ever asked to come to my home. Although my parents taught in the Dayton Public School system, most white teachers and administrators maintained a strictly professional rather than personal relationship toward them. Whites were omnipresent in our lives, frequently as authority figures: politicians, police officers, bank-loan officers, school administrators, tax auditors, grocery-store managers. Race existed as a kind of prism through which we understood and saw the world, distorting and coloring everything before us.

Despite these experiences and numerous examples of discrimination, Dayton, Ohio, was never the Deep South. Although the largest department stores downtown rarely employed Negroes, I recall that black customers were usually treated with courtesy. Whites were enrolled in every school I attended. Occasionally, whites attended our black church. Public institutions were largely desegregated. The color line was at its worst where it converged with the boundaries of class inequality. Blacks were treated most differently, for example, when it was also clear that they lacked money or material resources. Conversely, middle-class African-Americans certainly experienced prejudicial behavior by whites, but often encountered a less virulent form of hatred than their sisters and brothers who were poor. The recognition of class mobility and higher education gave a small number of blacks a buffer status from the worst forms of discrimination at a day-to-day level. But despite this relative privilege, we never forgot that we were black.

Every summer we had the opportunity to encounter a far more racially charged society. At the end of the school year, my family packed our 1937 Chevrolet and traveled south, through Cincinnati and Nashville, along highways and narrow, two-lane country roads. Often at night we were forced to sleep in the cramped confines of the automobile, because we could find no motel which permitted black people to stay overnight. We would stop along the highway to purchase gasoline, never knowing in advance whether we would be allowed to use the gas station's toilet facilities. If we were stopped for any reason by a highway patrol officer, we had to be prepared for some kind of verbal, racist abuse, and we had absolutely no recourse or appeal against his behavior or actions. Finally, we would arrive at my father's family home, Tuskegee, Alabama, where the sense of racial hostility and discrimination against African-Americans was the central theme of local life. I knew that Tuskegee then was in the midst of a major legal struggle initiated by blacks to outlaw the political gerrymandering of the city that had in effect disfranchised African-Americans. We were taught that any open protest or violation of the norms of Jim Crow segregation was to court retaliation and retribution, personally and collectively. We learned that whites, with few exceptions, saw us as subhuman, without the rights to economic development, political expression and participation, and public accommodation which whites accepted and took for granted for themselves.

It was in Tuskegee, during my long visits to Alabama's Black Belt as a child, that many of my basic impressions concerning the relative permanence and inflexibility of race were formed. Part of that consciousness was shaped by the experiences and stories of my father. James Marable was the grandson of slaves, and the second son of thirteen children. His father, Manning Marable, had owned and operated a small sawmill, cutting pulpwood for farm households. Along with other black rural families, they experienced the prism of race in hundreds of different ways, which formed the basic framework of their existence. From being denied the right to vote to being confined to unequal, segregated schools; from being harassed and intimidated by local white police officers to being forced to lower one's eyes when being directly addressed by a white man, "race" was ingrained in the smallest aspects of Southern daily life.

My father rarely talked at length about growing up black in the Deep South. But occasionally, and especially when we were visiting his large, extended family in Tuskegee, he would reflect about his own history, and recall the hostility and rudeness of whites toward himself, his family and his people. He was trying to prepare me for what I would surely experience. One of my father's stories I remember best occurred on a cold, early winter day in 1946. World War II had ended only months before, and millions of young people were going home. My father had served as a master sergeant in a segregated unit in the US Army Air Corps. Arriving in the Anniston, Alabama, bus station, he had to transfer to another local bus to make the final forty-mile trek to his family's home outside Wedowee, Alabama.

My father was wearing his army uniform, proudly displaying his medals. Quietly he purchased his ticket and stood patiently in line to enter the small bus. When my father finally reached the bus driver, the white man was staring intensely at him. With an ugly frown, the driver took a step back. "Nigger," he spat at my father, "you look like you're going to give somebody some trouble. You had better wait here for the next bus." My father was immediately confused and angry. "As a soldier, you always felt sort of proud," my dad recalls. This white bus driver's remarks "hit me like a ton of bricks. Here I am, going home, and I'd been away from the South for four years. I wasn't being aggressive."

Dad turned around and saw that he was standing in front of three whites, who had purchased tickets after him. James Marable had forgotten, or had probably repressed, a central rule in the public etiquette of Jim Crow segregation. Black people had to be constantly vigilant not to offend whites in any way. My father was supposed to have stepped out of line immediately, permitting the white patrons to move ahead of him. My father felt a burning sense of rage, which he could barely contain. "You get there some other way, nigger," the driver repeated with a laugh. The bus door shut in my father's face. The bus pulled away into the distance.

There was no other bus going to Wedowee that afternoon. My father wandered from the station into the street, feeling "really disgusted." Nothing he had accomplished in the previous four years, the sacrifices he had made for his country, seemed to matter. The rhetoric of democracy and freedom which had been popularized in the war against fascism rang hollow and empty. Although he eventually obtained a ride home by hitchhiking on the highway, my father never forgot the bitterness and hatred in the bus driver's words. Years later, he still felt his resentment and rage of that winter afternoon in Alabama. "When you go against the grain of racism," he warned me, "you pay for it, one way or another."

For both my father and myself, as well as for millions of black people for many generations, the living content of race was simultaneously and continuously created from within and imposed from without. That is, "race" is always an expression of how black people have defined themselves against the system of oppression, as well as a repressive structure of power and privilege which perpetuates an unequal status for African-Americans within a stratified social order. As an identity, race becomes a way of perceiving ourselves within a group. To be black in what seems to be a bipolar racial universe gives one instantly a set of coordinates within space and time, a sense of geographical location along an endless boundary of color. Blackness as a function of the racial superstructure also gives meaning to collective memory; it allows *us* to place ourselves within a context of racial resistance, within the many struggles for human dignity, for our families and for material resources. This consciousness of racial pride and community awareness gave hope and strength to my grandfather and father; it was also the prime motivation for the Edward Wilmot Blydens, Marcus Garveys and Fannie Lou Hamers throughout black history. In this way, the prism of race structures the community of the imagination, setting parameters for real activity and collective possibility.

But blackness in a racially stratified society is always simultaneously the "negation of whiteness." To be white is not a sign of culture, or a statement of biology or genetics: it is essentially a power relationship, a statement of authority, a social construct which is perpetuated by systems of privilege, the consolidation of property and status. There is no genius behind the idea of whiteness, only an empty husk filled with a mountain of lies about superiority and a series of crimes against "nonwhite" people. To be black in a white-dominated social order, for instance, means that one's life chances are circumscribed and truncated in a thousand different ways. To be black means that when you go to the bank to borrow money, despite the fact that you have a credit profile identical to your white counterpart, you are nevertheless two or three times more likely to be denied the loan than the white. To be black means that when you are taken to the hospital for emergency health-care treatment, the quality of care you receive will be inadequate and substandard. To be black means that your children will not have the same academic experiences and access to higher learning resources as children in the white suburbs and exclusive urban enclaves. To be black means that your mere physical presence and the reality of your being can trigger surveillance cameras at shops, supermarkets, malls and fine stores everywhere. To be black, male, and to live in central Harlem in the 1990s, for example, means that you will have a life expectancy of forty-nine years of age—less than in Bangladesh. Race constantly represents itself to black people as an apparently unending series of moments of inequality, which constantly challenge us, sapping and draining our physical, mental and moral resources.

Perhaps this is what most white Americans have never fully comprehended about "race": that racism is not just social discrimination, political disfranchisement and acts of extra-legal violence and terror which proliferated under the Jim Crow segregation of my father's South. Nor is racism the so-called "silent discrimination" faced by my generation of African-Americans raised during the civil-rights era, who are still denied access to credit and capital by unfair banking practices, or who encounter the "glass ceiling" inside businesses which limits their job advancement. At its essential core, racism is most keenly felt in its smallest manifestations: the white merchant who drops change on the sales counter, rather than touch the hand of a black person; the white salesperson who follows you into the dressing room when you carry several items of clothing to try on, because he or she suspects that you are trying to steal; the white teacher who deliberately avoids the upraised hand of a Latino student in class, giving white pupils an unspoken yet understood advantage; the white woman who wraps the strap of her purse several times tightly around her arm, just before walking past a black man; the white taxicab drivers who speed rapidly past African-Americans or Latinos, picking up whites on the next block. Each of these incidents, no matter how small, constructs the logic for the prism of race for the oppressed. We witness clear, unambiguous changes of behavior or language by whites toward us in public and private situations, and we code or interpret such changes as "racial." These minor actions reflect a structure of power, privilege and violence which most blacks can never forget.

The grandchildren of James Marable have never encountered Jim Crow segregation. They have never experienced signs reading "white" and "colored." They have never been refused service at lunch counters, access to hotel accommodation, restaurants or amusement parks, or admission to quality schools. They have never experienced the widespread unemployment, police brutality, substandard housing and the lack of educational opportunity which constitute the everyday lives of millions of African-American youth. For my children—eighteen-year-old Malaika and sixteen-year-old twins Sojourner and Joshua—Martin Luther King, Jr., Medgar Evers, Fannie Lou Hamer and Ella Baker are distant figures from the pages of black history books. Malcolm X is the charismatic image of Denzel Washington from Spike Lee's film, or perhaps the cinematic impression from several recent hip-hop music videos. "We Shall Overcome" is an interesting but somewhat dated melody of the past, not a hopeful and militant anthem projecting an integrated America.

Yet, like my father before them, and like myself, my children are forced to view their world through the racial prism. They complain that their high-school textbooks don't have sufficient information about the activities and events related to African-Americans in the development of American society. In their classrooms, white students who claim to be their friends argue against affirmative action, insisting that the new "victims" of discrimination are overwhelmingly white and male. When Joshua goes to the shopping mall, he is followed and harassed by security guards. If he walks home alone through an affluent white neighborhood, he may be stopped by the police. White children have moved items away from the reach of my son because they have been taught the stereotype that "all blacks steal." Sojourner complains about her white teachers who have been hostile and unsympathetic toward her academic development, or who have given her lower grades for submitting virtually the identical level of work turned in by her white friends. As my daughter Malaika explains: "White people often misjudge you just by the way you look, without getting to know you. This makes me feel angry inside."

A new generation of African-Americans who never personally marched for civil rights or Black Power, who never witnessed the crimes of segregation, feel the same rage expressed by my father half a century ago. When they watch the beating of Rodney King on television or the trial of O. J. Simpson, they instantly comprehend the racism of the Los Angeles police officers involved in each case, and the larger racial implications of both incidents. When they listen to members of Congress complain about "welfare dependency" and "crime," they recognize the racial stereotypes which are lurking just behind the code words. They have come to expect hypocritical behavior from the white "friends" who act cordially toward them at school but refuse to acknowledge or recognize them in another context. Race is a social force which still has real meaning to the generation of my children.

But the problem with the prism of race is that it simultaneously clarifies and distorts social reality. It both illuminates and obscures, creating false dichotomies and distinctions between people where none really exists. The constructive identity of race, the conceptual framework which the oppressed create to interpret their experiences of inequality and discrimination, often clouds the concrete reality of class, and blurs the actual structure of power and privilege. It creates tensions between oppressed groups which share common class interests, but which may have different physical appearances or colors. For example, on the recent debates concerning undocumented immigrants, a narrow racial perspective could convince African-Americans that they should be opposed to the civil rights and employment opportunities of Mexican Americans, Central Americans and other Latino people. We could see Latinos as potential competitors in the labor market rather than as allies in a struggle against corporate capital and conservatives within the political establishment. On affirmative action, a strict racist outlook might view the interests of lower-class and working-class whites as directly conflicting with programs which could increase opportunities for blacks and other people of color. The racial prism creates an illusion that "race" is permanent and finite; but, in reality, "race" is a complex expression of unequal relations which are dynamic and ever-changing. The dialectics of racial thinking pushes black people toward the logic of "us" versus "them," rather than a formulation which cuts across the perceived boundaries of color.

This observation is not a criticism of the worldviews of my father, my children, or myself as I grew up in Dayton, Ohio. It is only common sense that most African-Americans perceive and interpret the basic struggle for equality and empowerment in distinctly racial terms. This perspective does speak to our experiences and social reality, but only to a portion of what that reality truly is. The parallel universes of race do not stand still. What was "black" and "white" in Booker T. Washington's Tuskegee of 1895 was not identical to categories of color and race in New Orleans a century ago; both are distinctly different from how we perceive and define race in the USA a generation after legal segregation. There is always a distance between our consciousness and the movement of social forces, between perception and historical reality. "Blackness" must inevitably be redefined in material terms and ideologically, as millions of black and Hispanic people from the Caribbean, Africa and Latin America immigrate into the USA, assimilating within hundreds of urban centers and thousands of neighborhoods with other people of color. As languages, religions, cultural traditions and kinship networks among blacks in the USA become increasingly diverse and complex, our consciousness and our ideas of historical struggle against the leviathan of race also shift and move in new directions. This does not mean that "race" has declined in significance; it does mean that what we mean by "race" and how "race" is utilized as a means of dividing the oppressed are once again being transformed in many crucial respects.

At the beginning of the African presence in the Americas, an African-American culture, nationality and consciousness was constructed. Against great odds, inside the oppressive context of slavery and later racial segregation, the racial identity and perspective of resistance, a community empowered by imagination, was developed against the weight of institutional racism. That historic leap of collective self-definition and inner faith must once again occur, now inside the very different environment of mature capitalism. We must begin the process of redefining blackness in a manner which not only interprets but also transforms our world.

~

HISTORY AND BLACK CONSCIOUSNESS
The Political Culture of Black America

The central theme of black American history has been the constant struggle to overcome the barriers of race and the reality of unequal racial identities between black and white. This racial bifurcation has created parallel realities or racial universes, in which blacks and whites may interact closely with one another but perceive social reality in dramatically different ways. These collective experiences of discrimination, and this memory of resistance and oppression, have given rise to several overlapping group strategies or critical perspectives within the African-American community, which have as their objective the ultimate empowerment of black people. In this sense, the contours of struggle for black people have given rise to a very specific consciousness: a sense of our community, its needs and aspirations for itself. The major ideological debates which map the dimensions of the political mind of black America have always been about the orientation and objectives of black political culture and consciousness. The great historical battles between Booker T. Washington, the architect of the "Atlanta Compromise" of 1895, and W.E.B. Du Bois, the founder of the NAACP, and the conflicts between Du Bois and black nationalist leader Marcus Garvey were fought largely over the manner in which the black community would define for itself the political and economic tools necessary for its empowerment and future development. Sometimes the battle lines in these struggles for black leadership and for shaping the consciousness of the African-American community were defined by class divisions. More generally, the lines of separation had less to do with class than with the internalized definitions of what "race" meant to African-Americans themselves in the context of black political culture.

Ironically, the historical meaning and reality of race was always fundamentally a product of class domination. Race, in the last analysis, is neither biologically nor genetically derived. It is a structure rooted in white supremacy, economic exploitation and social privilege. It evolved in the process of slavery and the transatlantic slave trade. Racism has power only as a set of institutional arrangements and social outcomes which perpetuate the exploitation of black labor and the subordination of the black community's social and cultural life. But all of this is masked by institutional racism to those who experience the weight of its oppression. The oppressed perceive domination through the language and appearance of racial forms, although such policies and practices always served a larger class objective. As a result, the political culture of black America is organized around racial themes, either an effort to overcome or escape the manifestations of institutional racism or to build alternative institutions which empower black people within environments of whiteness. The approach of political empowerment is distinctly racial, rather than class-oriented.

Most historians characterized the central divisions within black political culture as the 150-year struggle between "integration" and "separation." In 1925, this division was perceived as separating Du Bois and the NAACP from the Garveyites. In 1995, the division is used to distinguish such pragmatic multicultural liberals as Henry Louis Gates, director of Harvard University's Afro-American Studies department, from the architect of Afrocentrism, Temple University professor Molefi Asante. However, this theoretical model has serious limitations. The simple fact is that the vast majority of African-American people usually would not define themselves as either Roy Wilkins–style integrationists or black separatists like City University of New York Black Studies director Leonard Jeffries. Most blacks have perceived integration or black nationalism as alternative strategies which might serve the larger purpose of empowering their community and assisting in the deconstruction of institutions perpetuating racial inequality. As anthropologist Leith Mullings and I have argued (Chapter 17, *Beyond Black and White*), a more accurate description of black political culture would identify three strategic visions; these can be termed "inclusion" or integration, "black nationalism," and "transformation."

Since the rise of the free Negro community in the North during the antebellum era, inclusion has been the central impulse for reform among black Americans. The inclusionists have sought to minimize or even eradicate the worst effects and manifestations of racism within the African-American community. They have mobilized resources to alter or abolish legal restrictions on the activities of blacks, and have agitated to achieve acceptance of racial diversity by the white majority. Essentially, the inclusionists have operated philosophically and ideologically as "liberals": they usually believe that the state is inherently a "neutral apparatus," open to the pressure and persuasion of competing interest groups. They have attempted to influence public opinion and mass behavior on issues of race by changing public policies and educational and cultural activity. But the theoretical guiding star of the inclusionists has been what I term "symbolic representation." They firmly believe that the elevation and advancement of select numbers of well-educated, affluent and/or powerful blacks into positions of authority helps to dismantle the patterns and structures of racial discrimination. The theory is that if blacks are well represented inside government, businesses and social institutions, then this will go a long way toward combatting the traditional practices of inequality and patterns of discrimination. Black representatives within the system of power would use their leverage to carry out policies that benefited the entire African-American population.

Embedded deeply within the logic of inclusionism were two additional ideas. First, the intellectual foundations of inclusionism drew a strong parallel between the pursuit of freedom and the acquisition of private property. To unshackle oneself from the bonds of inequality was, in part, to achieve the material resources necessary to improve one's life and the lives of those in one's family. This meant that freedom was defined by one's ability to gain access to resources and to the prerequisites of power. Implicitly, the orientation of inclusionism reinforced the logic and legitimacy of America's economic system and class structure, seeking to assimilate blacks within them. Second, inclusionists usually had a cultural philosophy of integration within the aesthetic norms and civil society created by the white majority. Inclusionists sought to transcend racism by acting in ways which whites would not find objectionable or repulsive. The more one behaved in a manner which emulated whites, the less likely one might encounter the negative impact and effects of Jim Crow. By assimilating the culture of whites and by minimizing the cultural originality and creativity of African-Americans, one might find the basis for a "universalist" dialogue that transcends the ancient barriers of color. Historically, the inclusionists can be traced to those groups of former slaves in colonial America who assimilated themselves into majority white societies, who forgot African languages and traditions and tried to participate fully in the social institutions that whites had built for themselves. In the nineteenth century, the inclusionists' outstanding leader was Frederick Douglass. Today, the inclusionists include most of the traditional leadership of the civil-rights organizations such as the National Association for the Advancement of Colored People and the National Urban League, the bulk of the Congressional Black Caucus and most African-American elected officials, and the majority of the older and more influential black middle class, professionals and managerial elites.

On balance, the inclusionists' strategy sought to transcend race by creating a context wherein individuals could be judged on the basis of what they accomplished rather than on the color of their skin. This approach minimized the extensive inter-connectedness between color and inequality; it tended to conceive racism as a kind of social disease rather than the logical and coherent consequence of institutional arrangements, private property and power relations, reinforced by systemic violence. The inclusionists seriously underestimated the capacity and willingness of white authorities to utilize coercion to preserve and defend white privilege and property. Integration, in short, was a strategy to avoid the worst manifestations of racism, without upsetting the deep structures of inequality which set into motion the core dynamics of white oppression and domination.

Although the inclusionist perspective dominates the literature that interprets black history, it never consolidated itself as a consensus framework for the politics of the entire black community. A sizable component of the African-American population always rejected integration as a means of transcending institutional racism. This alternative vision was black nationalism. Black nationalism sought to overturn racial discrimination by building institutions controlled and owned by blacks, providing resources and services to the community. The nationalists distrusted the capacity of whites as a group to overcome the debilitating effects of white privilege, and questioned the inclusionists' simple-minded faith in the power of legal reforms. Nationalists rejected the culture and aesthetics of white Euro-America in favor of what today would be termed an Afrocentric identity. Historically, the initial nationalist impulse for black group autonomous development really began with those slaves who ran away from the plantations and farms of whites, and who established "maroons," frontier enclaves or villages of defiant African-Americans, or who mounted slave rebellions. Malcolm X and Marcus Garvey, among others, are within this cultural, intellectual and political tradition. However, like the inclusionists, the nationalists often tended to reify race, perceiving racial categories as static and ahistorical, rather than fluid and constantly subject to renegotiation and reconfiguration. They struggled to uproot race, but were frequently imprisoned themselves by the language and logic of inverted racial thinking. They utilized racial categories to mobilize their core constituencies without fully appreciating their own internal contradictions.

The black nationalist tradition within black political culture was, and remains, tremendously complex, rich and varied. At root, its existential foundations were the national consciousness and collective identity of people of African descent, as they struggled against racism and class exploitation. But, as in any form of nationalism, this tradition of resistance and group consciousness expressed itself politically around many different coordinates and tendencies. Within black nationalism is the separatist current, which tends to perceive the entire white community as racially monolithic and articulates racial politics with starkly confrontational and antagonistic overtones. Today, one could point to educator Len Jeffries' controversial descriptions of European Americans as "ice people"—cold, calculating, materialistic—and African-Americans as "sun people"—warm, generous, humanistic—as a separatist-oriented, conservative social theory within the nationalist tradition. The Nation of Islam's theory of Yacub, first advanced under the leadership of Elijah Muhammad, projected an image of whites as "devils," incapable of positive change. At the other end of the nationalist spectrum were radicals like Hubert H. Harrison, Cyril V. Briggs and Huey P. Newton, and militant groups such as the League of Revolutionary Black Workers from the late 1960s, who incorporated a class analysis and the demand for socialism within their politics. To this radical tendency, black nationalism had to rely on the collaboration of other oppressed people regardless of the color of their skin, languages or nationalities. Between these two tendencies is the black nationalism of the rising black petty bourgeoisie, which utilizes racial segregation as a barrier to facilitate capital accumulation from the mostly working-class, black consumer market. Nationalist rhetoric such as "buy black" becomes part of the appeal employed by black entrepreneurs to generate profits. All of these contradictory currents are part of the complex historical terrain of black nationalism.

The basic problem confronting both inclusionism and black nationalism is that the distinct social structure, political economy and ethnic demography which created both strategic visions for black advancement has been radically transformed, especially in the past quarter of a century. Segregation imposed a kind of social uniformity on the vast majority of black people, regardless of their class affiliation, education or social condition. The stark brutality of legal Jim Crow, combined with the unforgiving and vicious character of the repression that was essential to such a system, could only generate two major reactions: a struggle to be acknowledged and accepted despite one's racial designation, or a struggle to create an alternative set of cultural, political and social axioms which could sustain a distinctly different group identity against "whiteness." But as the social definition of what it means to be "different" in the USA has changed, the whole basis for both of these traditional racial outlooks within African-American society becomes far more contentious and problematic.

Many people from divergent ethnic backgrounds, speaking various languages and possessing different cultures, now share a common experience of inequality in the USA—poor housing, homelessness, inadequate health care, underrepreesentation within government, lagging incomes and high rates of unemployment, discrimination in capital markets, and police brutality on the streets. Yet there is an absence of unity between these constituencies, in part because their leaders are imprisoned ideologically and theoretically by the assumptions and realities of the past. The rhetoric of racial solidarity, for instance, can be used to mask class contradictions and divisions within the black, Latino and Asian-American communities. Symbolic representation can be manipulated to promote the narrow interest of minority elected officials who may have little commitment to advancing the material concerns of the most oppressed sectors of multicultural America.

What is also missing is a common language of resistance. Race as a social construction generates its own internal logic and social expressions of pain, anger and alienation within various communities. These are often barriers to an understanding of the larger social and economic forces at work which undermine our common humanity. From the cultural threads of our own experiences, we must find parallel patterns and symbols of struggle which permit us to draw connections between various groups within society. This requires the construction of a new lexicon of activism, a language which transcends the narrow boundaries of singular ethnic identity and embraces a vision of democratic pluralism.

The immediate factors involved in a general strategic rethinking of the paradigms for black American struggle are also international. A generation ago, black Americans with an internationalist perspective might see themselves as part of the diverse nonaligned movement of Third World nations, strategically distanced between capitalist America and Communist Russia. Like legal racial segregation, the system of Soviet Communism and the Soviet Union itself no longer exist. Apartheid as a system of white privilege and political totalitarianism no longer exists, as the liberation forces of Nelson Mandela and the African National Congress struggle to construct a multiracial democracy. The Sandinistas of Nicaragua lost power, as their model of a pluralistic, socialist-oriented society was overturned, at least for the time being. Throughout the rest of the Third World, from Ghana to Vietnam, socialists moved rapidly to learn the language of markets and foreign investment, and were forced to curtail egalitarian programs and accommodate themselves to the ideological requirements of the "New World Order" and the demands of transnational capital. Millions of people of color were on the move, one of the largest migrations in human history. Rural and agricultural populations migrated to cities in search of work and food; millions traveled from the Third World periphery to the metropolitan cores of Western Europe and North America to occupy the lowest levels of labor. In many instances, these new groups were socially stigmatized and economically dominated, in part by the older categories of "race" and the social divisions of "difference" which separated the newest immigrants from the white "mainstream."

Nevertheless, within this changing demographic/ethnic mix which increasingly characterizes the urban environments of Western Europe and North America, the older racial identities and categories have begun in many instances to break down, with new identities and group symbols being formulated by various "minorities." In the United Kingdom by the 1970s, immigrants—radically divergent ethnic backgrounds and languages—from the Caribbean, Asia and Africa began to term themselves "black" as a political entity. In the US, the search for both disaggregation and rearticulation of group identity and consciousness among people of color is also occurring, although along different lines due to distinct historical experiences and backgrounds. In the Hawaiian islands, for example, many of the quarter of a million native Hawaiians support the movement for political sovereignty and self-determination. But do native Hawaiians have more in common culturally and politically with American Indians or Pacific islanders? What are the parallels and distinctions between the discrimination experienced by Mexican-Americans in the US Southwest, and African-Americans under slavery and Jim Crow segregation? Do the more than five million Americans of Arab, Kurdish, Turkish and Iranian nationality and descent have a socioeconomic experience in the USA which puts them in conflict with native-born African-Americans, or is there sufficient commonality of interest and social affinity to provide the potential framework for principled activism and unity?

Similar questions about social distinctions rooted in mixed ethnic heritages and backgrounds could be raised within the black community itself. At least three out of four native-born Americans of African descent in the USA have to some extent a racial heritage which is also American Indian, European, Asian and/or Hispanic. Throughout much of the Americas, racial categories were varied and complex, reflecting a range of social perceptions based on physical appearance, color, hair texture, class, social status and other considerations. In the USA prior to the civil-rights movement, with a few exceptions, the overwhelmingly dominant categorization was "black" and "white." In the late 1970s, the federal government adopted a model for collecting census data based on four "races"—black, Asian, American Indian and white—and two ethnic groups, Hispanic and non-Hispanic, which could be of whatever "racial" identity. Today, all of these categories are being contested and questioned. Some of the hundreds of thousands of African-Americans and whites who intermarry have begun to call for a special category for their children—"multiracial." By 1994, three states required a "multiracial" designation on public-school forms, and Georgia has established the "multiracial" category on its mandatory state paperwork. The "multiracial" designation, if popularized and structured into the state bureaucracy, could have the dangerous effect of siphoning of a segment of what had been the "black community" into a distinct and potentially privileged elite, protected from the normal vicissitudes and ordeals experienced' by black folk under institutional racism. It could become a kind of "passing" for the twenty-first century, standing apart from the definition of blackness. Conversely, as more immigrants from the

African continent and the Caribbean intermarry with native-born black Americans, notions of what it means to be "black" become culturally and ethnically far more pluralistic and international. The category of "blackness" becomes less parochial and more expansive, incorporating the diverse languages, histories, rituals and aesthetic textures of new populations and societies.

Inside the United States, other political and social factors have contributed to the reframing of debates on race and our understanding of the social character of the black community. In just the past five years, we have experienced the decline and near-disappearance of Jesse Jackson's Rainbow Coalition and efforts to liberalize and reform the Democratic Party from within; the explosive growth of a current of conservative black nationalism and extreme racial separatism within significant sections of the African-American community; the vast social uprising of the Los Angeles rebellion in April and May 1992, triggered by a Not Guilty verdict on police officers who had viciously beaten a black man; and the political triumph of mass conservatism in the 1994 congressional elections, due primarily to an overwhelmingly Republican vote by millions of angry white males. Behind these trends and events, from the perspective of racial history, was an even larger dilemma: the failure of the modern black American freedom movement to address or even to listen to the perspectives and political insights of the "hip-hop" generation, those African-Americans born and/or socialized after the March on Washington of 1963 and the passage of the Civil Rights Act a year later. The hip-hop generation was largely pessimistic about the quality and character of black leadership, and questioned the legitimacy and relevancy of organizations like the NAACP. Although the hip-hop movement incorporated elements of black nationalism into its wide array of music and art, notably through its iconization of Malcolm X in 1990-93, it nevertheless failed to articulate a coherent program or approach to social change which addressed the complex diversities of black civil society. Both inclusionism and black nationalism had come to represent fragmented social visions and archaic agendas, which drew eclectically from racial memory. Both ideologies failed to appreciate how radically different the future might be for black people, especially in the context of a post-Cold War, postmodern, post-industrial future. The sad and sorry debacle surrounding the public vilification and firing of NAACP former national secretary Benjamin Chavis, for example, illustrated both the lack of internal democracy and accountability of black political institutions, as well as the absence of any coherent program which could speak meaningfully to the new social, political and cultural realities.

The urgent need to redefine the discourse and strategic orientation of the black movement is more abundantly clear in the mid 1990s than ever before. Proposition 187 in California, which denied medical, educational, and social services to undocumented immigrants, as well as the current national debates about affirmative action and welfare, all have one thing in common: the cynical and deliberate manipulation of racial and ethnic stereotypes by the Far Right. White conservatives understand the power of "race." They have made a strategic decision to employ code-words and symbols which evoke the deepest fears and anxieties of white middle-class and working-class Americans with regard to African-American issues and interests.

The reasons for this strategy are not difficult to discern. Since the emergence of Reaganism in the United States, corporate capitalism has attempted to restrict the redistributive authority and social-program agenda of the state. Many of the reform programs, from the legal desegregation of society in the 1960s to the Johnson administration's "War on Poverty," were created through pressure from below. The initiation of affirmative-action programs for women and minorities and the expansion of the welfare state contributed to some extent to a more humane and democratic society. The prerogatives of capital were not abolished by any means, but the democratic rights of minorities, women and working people were expanded. As capitalist investment and production became more global, the demand for cheap labor increased dramatically. Capital aggressively pressured Third World countries to suppress or outlaw unions, reduce wage levels, and eliminate the voices of left opposition. Simultaneously, millions of workers were forced to move from rural environments into cities in the desperate search for work. The "Latinization" of cities, from Los Angeles to New York, is a product of this destructive, massive economic process.

In the United States since the early 1980s, corporate capital has pushed aggressively for lower taxes, deregulation, a relaxation of affirmative action and environmental protection laws, and generally more favorable social and political conditions for corporate profits. Over the past twenty years, this has meant that real incomes of working people in the United States, adjusted for inflation, have fallen significantly. Between 1947 and 1973, the average hourly and weekly earnings of US production and nonsupervisory workers increased dramatically —from \$6.75 per hour to \$12.06 per hour (in 1993 inflation-adjusted dollars). But after 1973, production workers lost ground—from \$12.06 per hour in 1979 to \$11.26 per hour in 1989 to only \$10.83 per hour in 1993. According to the research of the Children's Defense Fund, the greatest losses occurred among families with children under the age of eighteen where the household head was also younger than the age of thirty. The inflation-adjusted income of white households in this category fell 22 per cent between 1973 and 1990. For young Latino families with children, the decline during these years was 27.9 per cent. For young black families, the drop was a devastating 48.3 per cent.

During the Reagan administration, the United States witnessed a massive redistribution of wealth upward, unequaled in our history. In 1989, the top 1 per cent of all US households received 16.4 per cent of all US incomes in salaries and wages; it possessed 48.1 per cent of the total financial wealth of the country. In other words, the top 1 per cent of all households controlled a significantly greater amount of wealth than the bottom 95 per cent of all US households (which controlled only 27.7 per cent). These trends produced a degree of economic uncertainty and fear for millions of households unparalleled since the Great Depression. White working-class families found themselves working harder, yet falling further behind. "Race" in this uncertain political environment easily became a vehicle for orienting politics toward the Right. If a white worker cannot afford a modest home in the suburbs such as his or her parents could have purchased thirty years ago, the fault is attributed not to falling wages but to affirmative action. If the cost of public education spirals skyward, white teenagers and their parents often conclude that the fault is not due to budget cuts but to the fact that "undeserving" blacks and Hispanics have taken the places of "qualified" white students.

As significant policy debates focus on the continuing burden of race within society, the black movement is challenged to rethink its past and to restructure radically the character of its political culture. Race is all too often a barrier to understanding the central role of class in shaping personal and collective outcomes within a capitalist society. Black social theory must transcend the theoretical limitations and programmatic contradictions of the old assimilationist/integrationist paradigm on the one hand, and of separatist black nationalism on the other. We have to replace the bipolar categories, rigid racial discourses and assumptions of the segregationist past with an approach toward politics and social dialogue which is pluralistic, multicultural, and nonexclusionary. In short, we must go beyond black and white, seeking power in a world which is increasingly characterized by broad diversity in ethnic and social groupings, but structured hierarchically in terms of privilege and social inequality. We must go beyond black and white, but never at the price of forgetting the bitter lessons of our collective struggles and history, never failing to appreciate our unique cultural and aesthetic gifts or lacking an awareness of our common destiny with others of African descent. We must find a language that clearly identifies the role of class as central to the theoretical and programmatic critique of contemporary society. And we must do this in a manner which reaches out to the newer voices and colors of US society—Latinos, Asian-Americans, Pacific Island Americans, Middle East Americans, American Indians, and others.

We have entered a period in which our traditional definitions of what it has meant to be "black" must be transformed. The old racial bifurcation of white versus black no longer accurately or adequately describes the social composition and ethnic character of the United States. Harlem, the cultural capital of black America, is now more than 40 per cent Spanish-speaking. Blackness as an identity now embraces a spectrum of nationalities, languages, and ethnicities, from the Jamaican and Trinidadian cultures of the West Indies to the Hispanicized blackness of Panama and the Dominican Republic. More than ever before, we must recognize the limitations and inherent weaknesses of a model of politics which is grounded solely or fundamentally in racial categories. The diversity of ethnicities which constitute the urban United States today should help us to recognize the basic common dynamics of class undergirding the economic and social environment of struggle for everyone.

Historically, there is an alternative approach to the politics and social analysis of black empowerment which is neither inclusionist nor nationalist. This third strategy can be called "transformationist." Essentially, transformationists within the racial history of America have sought to deconstruct or destroy the ideological foundations, social categories and institutional power of race. Transformationists have sought neither incorporation nor assimilation into a white mainstream, nor the static isolation of racial separation; instead they have advocated a restructuring of power relations and authority between groups and classes, in such a manner as to make race potentially irrelevant as a social force. This critical approach to social change begins with a radical understanding of culture. The transformationist sees culture not as a set of artifacts or formal rituals, but as the human content and product of history itself. Culture is both the result of and the consequences of struggle; it is dynamic and ever-changing, yet structured around collective memories and traditions. The cultural history of black Americans is, in part, the struggle to maintain their own group's sense of identity, social cohesion and integrity, in the face of policies which have been designed to deny both their common humanity and particularity. To transform race in American life, therefore, demands a dialectical approach toward culture which must simultaneously preserve and destroy. We must create the conditions for a vital and creative black cultural identity—in the arts and literature, in music and film—which also has the internal confidence and grace of being to draw parallels and assume lines of convergence with other ethnic traditions. But we must destroy and uproot the language and logic of inferiority and racial inequality, which sees blackness as a permanent caste and whiteness as the eternal symbol of purity, power and privilege.

The transformationist tradition is also grounded in a radical approach to politics and the state. Unlike the integrationists, who seek "representation" within the system as it is, or the nationalists, who generally favor the construction of parallel racial institutions controlled by blacks, the transformationists basically seek the redistribution of resources and the democratization of state power along more egalitarian lines. A transformationist approach to politics begins with the formulation of a new social contract between people and the state which asks: "What do people have a right to expect from their government in terms of basic human needs which all share in common?" Should all citizens have a right to vote, but have no right to employment? Should Americans have a right to freedom of speech and unfettered expression, but no right to universal public health care? These are some of the questions that should be at the heart of the social policy agenda of a new movement for radical multicultural democracy.

The transformationist tradition in black political history embraces the radical abolitionists of the nineteenth century, the rich intellectual legacy of W.E.B. Du Bois, and the activism of militants from Paul Robeson to Fannie Lou Hamer. But it is also crucial to emphasize that these three perspectives—inclusion, black nationalism, and transformation—are not mutually exclusive or isolated from one another. Many integrationists have struggled to achieve racial equality through the policies of liberal desegregation, and have moved toward more radical means as they became disenchanted with the pace of social change. The best example of integrationist transformationism is provided by the final two years of Martin Luther King, Jr.'s public life: anti–Vietnam War activism; advocacy of a "Poor People's March" on Washington, DC; the mobilization of black sanitation workers in Memphis, Tennessee; and support for economic democracy. Similarly, many other black activists began their careers as black nationalists, and gradually came to the realization that racial inequality cannot be abolished until and unless the basic power structure and ownership patterns of society are transformed. This requires at some level the establishment of principled coalitions between black people and others who experience oppression or social inequality The best example of a black nationalist who acquired a transformationist perspective is, of course, Malcolm X, who left the Nation of Islam in March 1964 and created the Organization of Afro-American Unity several months later. In the African diaspora, a transformationist perspective in politics and social theory is best expressed in the writings of Amilcar Cabral, C.L.R. James and Walter Rodney.

In the wake of the "failure" of world socialism, the triumph of mass conservatism in politics, and the ideological hegemony of the values of markets, private enterprise and individual self-interest, black politics has to a great extent retreated from the transformationist perspective in recent years. It is difficult, if not impossible, to talk seriously about group economic development, collective interests and the radical restructuring of resources along democratic lines. Yet I am convinced that the road toward black empowerment in the multinational corporate and political environment of the post–Cold War would require a radical leap in social imagination, rather than a retreat to the discourse and logic of the racial past.

Our greatest challenge in rethinking race as ideology is to recognize how we unconsciously participate in its recreation and legitimization. Despite the legal desegregation of American civil society a generation ago, the destructive power and perverse logic of race still continues. Most Americans continue to perceive social reality in a manner which grossly underestimates the role of social class, and legitimates the categories of race as central to the ways in which privilege and authority are organized. We must provide the basis for a progressive alternative to the interpretation of race relations, moving the political culture of black America from a racialized discourse and analysis to a critique of inequality which has the capacity and potential to speak to the majority of American people. This leap in theory and social analysis must be made, if black America has any hope of transcending its current impasse of powerlessness and systemic inequality. As C.L.R. James astutely observed: "The race question is subsidiary to the class question in politics, and to think of imperialism in terms of race is disastrous. But to neglect the racial factor as merely incidental is an error only less grave than to make it fundamental."

ON BEING BLACK
The Burden of Race and Class

I

At the dawn of the twentieth century, W.E.B. Du Bois predicted with grim accuracy that the central crisis facing the world during the next 100 years would be "the problem of the color line—the relation of the darker to the lighter races of men in Asia and Africa, in America and the islands of the *sea.*" A brilliant social scientist, reseacher and political activist, Du Bois devoted more than seven decades to patient investigation into what was once termed "The Negro Problem." Nearing the end of his long and productive career in 1953, he remarked that his initial research was deficient in two critical respects. The first was the omission of "the influence of Freud" and the factors of "unconscious thought and the cake of custom in the growth and influence of race prejudice." The second and more important omission was "the tremendous impact on the modern world of Karl Marx." Du Bois observed, "I still think today as yesterday that the color line is a great problem of this country. But today I *see* more clearly than yesterday that back of the problem of race and color, lies a greater problem which both obscures and implements it: and that is the fact that so many civilized persons are willing to live in comfort even if the price of this is poverty, ignorance and disease of the majority of their fellowmen." The burden of racial prejudice or racism was more fundamentally the problem of class exploitation.

The question of whether it is race or class that lies at the heart of the inferior status of blacks broke out most recently in the October 5, 1980, issue of *The New York Times Magazine.* Carl Gershman, vice chairman of Social Democrats, USA, and a resident at the neoconservative Freedom House, was assigned the task of presenting the case for a class analysis of black social conditions. Black psychologist Kenneth Clark, author of *Dark Ghetto,* was asked to discuss black socioeconomic inequality as a function of race prejudice. Despite the widespread comment that the debate subsequently received on university campuses, neither Gershman nor Clark added anything that had not been said many times.

22

Gershman's approach to the crisis of black unemployment and discrimination was not very different from that of Daniel Patrick Moynihan; indeed, he begins his article with a defense of Moynihan's 1965 report, *The Negro Family: The Case for National Action,* which suggested that there was a "tangle of pathology" in the social fabric of the ghetto underclass. Black intellectual and activist protests against the Moynihan thesis "were frequently couched in radical–sounding terms," Gershman observed. "The sad irony in all of this," he went on, "is that what appeared to be a form of racial militancy was, in reality, a policy of racial accommodation. The new approach both rationalized and subsidized the underclass's continued existence." Gershman argues that Black Power was in effect an elitist movement which allowed the new black professional and managerial elite to become power brokers between the state and the permanent black underclass. He applauds the thesis of University of Chicago professor William Julius Wilson "that in the modern industrial period, unlike the earlier periods of slavery and industrialization, class plays a more significant role than race in determining a black's position in society." He concludes by observing paternally that "the crisis within the black movement" is related to the utter failure of a generation of black activists to comprehend what basic economic problems exist within their own ghetto.

Ironically, Kenneth Clark in his "rejoinder" found that he had much in common with Gershman on the race/class issue. First, Clark warned blacks not "to dismiss (Gershman's) article as another example of whites exercising their power to define contemporary civil rights problems primarily in terms of their own aspirations and interests." Clark agreed with Gershman that the Black Power movement and demands for black community–controlled schools were strategies of "racial accomodation" and neo–Booker T. Washingtonism. "While having some temporary cathartic value," he noted, Black Power "did not improve by one iota the educational and economic status of ghetto-entrapped underclass blacks." In short, both authors were confirmed integrationists on the question of black-white alliances. Both rejected categorically the idea that an autonomous black political and social movement could bring about meaningful change in the black urban enclaves. Both Clark and Gershman saw racism as a pattern of biased social attitudes and intolerant behavior by white people, rather than as a systemic or structural part of modern capitalist political economy. In their only significant area of disagreement, Clark maintained that the ghetto was a product of racial oppression. But even here, Clark views racism as "a dangerous social disease" and not the logical outcome of consistent and coherent social structure, worldview and economic order. Both view "class" as a function of income or economic mobility, rather than as a group relationship to the means of production, distribution and ownership.

Black intellectuals had their own race/class debate during the years 1973 through 1975. Black Studies journals such as *Black World, The Black Scholar, Black Books Bulletin, The Journal of Black Studies* and others were filled with bitter polemics advancing either Marxist or black nationalist points of view. In the progressive wing of the modern Black Power movement, the debate began somewhat earlier in the late 1960s. Stokely Carmichael left the Black Panther Party in 1969, charging that

Eldridge Cleaver, then the party's Minister of Information, and the Panthers were too preoccupied with class alliances with the New Left. Cleaver retorted that Carmichael was caught up in a "skin game," and that white members of the Students for a Democratic Society who had read Marcuse, Fanon and Malcolm were appropriate allies in the struggle against the system.

In the late 1970s, the debate took a new turn to the right. Stanford professor Thomas Sowell used the pages of *Commentary* magazine to debunk affirmative action. In Sowell's view, affirmative action was based on the rather vague notion that blacks as a group had been historically oppressed and that massive federal intervention into the free market would halt racial discrimination. He ridiculed the idea that all blacks were equally oppressed and criticized the social democrat logic behind the legislation as harmful to both business interests and to unemployed blacks. William Julius Wilson went a step further in his controversial study *The Declining Significance of Race*. Wilson reviewed the political economy of black workers throughout US history, and argued that the civil rights movement and the progressive actions of corporate management had nearly created "the elimination of race in labor-managment strife." Wilson's basic thesis was that racial discrimination is no longer a major bar to economic security or upward mobility by most blacks. Since the majority of blacks were now in the middle class, the time had come to shift legislative priorities from racial questions to the more specific problems of the economic underclass.

Recent events within the political economy seemingly validate many of Wilson's conclusions. The percentage of black families below the poverty level dropped from 55.1 percent in 1959 to 32.2 percent in 1969, but since then has remained about the same level. Black family heads with four years or more college education, however, earn about 90 percent of their white counterparts. Black married couples below the age of 35 in the Northern and Western states who both work earn median incomes at the same level of white couples. This new black strata of upper middle to upper income earners have articulated a clearly more conservative, class-conscious politics than the majority of blacks. The evidence for this is seen in the surprisingly high percentage (15 percent) of black votes for Reagan—the largest black total for any Republican presidential candidate since the Nixon-Kennedy race in 1960. When the Reverend Ralph David Abernathy and other former associates of Martin Luther King, Jr. embraced Reagan, and after Leon Sullivan (the black director of the Opportunities Industrial Centers) endorsed the nomination of Alexander Haig as Secretary of State, a new political current was born—Black Reaganism. These "new accommodationists" exhibit the same electoral political behavior as white neoconservatives.

Actually, there have been two different debates on the race/class question over the last decade. White paternalists like Gershman and integrationist-oriented blacks like Clark and Wilson are asking a series of questions that are premised on the assumption that racial integration is a positive good and a worthy social ideal. Black nationalists and activists, both in the universities and in the streets, are raising a radically different series of theoretical and programmatic issues. From the white side, the concerns expressed include: Should public policy concentrate on racial problems and continue to use race as a central or critical variable? Should blacks concentrate their energies on matters of mutual racial interest, or should they begin to address the larger economic problems that transcend race entirely? From the black activist side, the questions include: What is white racism? Is it different from other "social diseases" like intolerance or bigotry? What is the relationship between racism as a system to the general economic order? What is the possibility of a political union or common program between black, Hispanic and progressive white groups, given the omnipresence of white racism and the disastrous history of multiracial alliance, from Populism to Black Power? Leaving aside the concerns of white social scientists for the moment, let us concentrate on the black side of the race/class dilemma.

II

There is a major difference between racial prejudice against blacks in the US and other forms of intolerance or persecution. Intolerance has existed as long as human beings have lived together in social units. The victims of intolerance are forced to give up their own group's belief systems, forms of cultural and social institutions, and so forth. The outsider must, for the good of the majority, renounce his differences and embrace those values defined as "normal" by those who control the social, cultural and economic hierarchies. Racial prejudice is radically different, developing gradually in the West as capitalism and nationalism emerged. Its purpose is to withdraw the dominant group's sympathy from an "inferior race," to facilitate its exploitation. Thus, some of the very goals of black liberation, which include the ability to control blacks' labor, the establishment of stable, independent communities and the opportunity to participate and to compete within the socioeconomic institutions of the dominant society according to our own self-interests, threaten white racist beliefs and social structures crucial to the continuation of white racial domination.

Black sociologist Oliver Cromwell Cox expressed the problem of racial prejudice succinctly by presenting the familiar analogies between blacks and Jews as victims in a new way. "The dominant group is intolerant of those whom it can define as antisocial, while it holds race prejudice against those whom it can define as subsocial. In other words, the dominant group or ruling class does not like the Jew at all, but it likes the Negro in his place." The function of white racist attacks against black children who are bused across town to attend a formerly all-white, suburban school is therefore fundamentally different from the bombing of a synagogue in Paris by neoNazis. Jews are objects of hatred for being different, e.g., non-Christian; blacks are hated for attempting to reverse the natural social order of things. Cox explains, "A Jewish pogrom is not exactly similar to a Negro lynching. In a pogrom, the fundamental motive is the extermination of the Jews; in a lynching, however, the motive is that of giving the Negro a lesson in good behavior."

A central theme in Frantz Fanon's *Peau Noire, Masques Blancs* is the examination of the similarities and differences between white anti-Semitism and white racism against the people of African descent. "No anti-Semite would ever conceive of the idea of castrating the Jew," Fanon observed. He is killed or sterilized. But the Negro is castrated. The penis, the symbol of manhood, is annihilated, which is to say that it is denied." The anti-Semite attacks the religious and cultural symbols that set Jews apart from other people within Western culture. This is a denial of history, as it were. But blacks *are assumed to have no history,* and are assaulted on radically different philosophical grounds. "All the same, the Jew can be unknown in his Jewishness." Fanon continued:

> One hopes, one waits. His actions, his behavior are the final determinant. He is a white man, and, apart from some rather debatable characteristics, he can sometimes go unnoticed. Granted, the Jews are harassed—what am I *thinking* of? They are hunted down, exterminated, cremated. But these are little family quarrels. The Jew is disliked from the moment he is tracked down. But in my case, everything takes on a *new* guise. I am given no chance. I am overdetermined from without. I am the slave not of the "idea" that others have of me but of my own appearance. I am *fixed.*

Thus, racism should be understood as an institutional process rather than a random pattern of intolerant collective behavior. Broadly defined, it is a process of persecution and violence in the service of white power; its purpose is the systemic exploitation of black life and labor. The key word here is *systemic.*

A social order can be characterized as distinctively racist if it exhibits the following characteristics. The most important of these is a political economy in which the surplus value produced by black workers is expropriated to a much greater degree than is that produced by white labor. In a precapitalist or primitive capitalist society, this exploitation usually takes the form of a system of compulsory black labor. W. Kloosterboer's *Involuntary Labour Since the Abolition of Slavery* defines compulsory labor "as that from which withdrawal from is generally considered a criminal offense, so that it engenders penal sanction, and/or for which (the laborer) has been accepted without his willing consent." Using this criteria, both chattel slavery (pre-1865) and sharecropping (post-1865) can be classified as kinds of involuntary labor exploitation in the black South. In advanced capitalist societies, black workers assume the role of a surplus labor pool which must be prepared to shift from one low-paying sector of the economy to another upon demand. Blacks are "the last hired, the first fired" under these unstable conditions. Moreover, since capitalism by its very nature cannot provide a full-employment economy, a permanent underclass of blacks is created, who are for all practical purposes outside the workplace. The managerial heights of the racist political economy are occupied almost totally by whites. Blacks as individuals may be appointed to managerial positions within the corporate hierarchy, but blacks as a group have absolutely no critical power other than as consumers.

Characteristic of any racist order is the historic and systemic pattern of physical isolation, exclusion and (in many cases) extermination of the oppressed race/class. This includes both *de facto* and *de jure* segregation, customary and legal forms of Jim Crow. To be sure, different cultural and social forms of racial isolation and exclusion have existed in the Americas. Brazilians have an obvious racial bias against people of African descent, but this has been muted and redirected in ways that a North American white could scarcely comprehend. The common saying in nineteenth century Brazil, "Money lightens the skin," shows that blacks were almost always poor, but that wealth induced virtually color blindness. This was far from the case in countries settled by the English and Dutch, who practiced a radical form of collective exclusion and social isolation from their African laborers. The largest settler regimes which these two European nations founded, the United States of America and the Republic of South Africa, are still objectively the most racist countries to this day.

The third factor, to use Italian Marxist Antonio Gramsci's concept, is the ideological hegemony of white racism. The ideological apparatuses of the state—the universities, public schools, media, theater and all creative arts, religion, civic associations, political parties—provide the public rationale to justify, explain, legitimize or tolerate the previous two characteristics. Hegemony is the ideological or cultural glue through which collective consensus is achieved within any social order. Within the United States, racist hegemony is achieved in part through the media, which play down potentially disruptive information on the race question; inferior schooling for black children, which denies them necessary information and skills; a rewriting of cultural and social history so that racial conflict and class struggle are glossed over and the melting pot ideal stressed; religious dogma such as those exposed by fundamentalist Christians which divert and reaffirm the conservative values on which white middle class's traditional illusions of superiority are grounded.

The fourth variable involves the relationship between black people and the coercive apparatuses of the State—the police, armed forces, prisons, the criminal justice system, and white vigilante hate-groups such as the Ku Klux Klan. In all racist states, blacks make up a disproportionately large percentage of the prison population compared with their numbers in the society as a whole. In the United States, studies have shown that black, Hispanic and poor defendants on the whole receive harsher sentences and more meager legal services than middle-class whites who commit identical crimes. The percentage of black policemen on metropolitan forces is almost always lower than the black urban population in the area. The percentage of blacks in managerial positions in any agency of coercion (the armed forces, police, penal systems) is always lower than the percentage of blacks who are employed in menial tasks. Generally, the coercive state apparatuses serve to disrupt, regulate and suppress the development of black social space—that is, the ability of blacks as a group to develop stable family units and neighborhoods, to construct social, cultural and alternative economic institutions, to strive for upward socioeconomic mobility within the predominantly white order of things.

The fifth category is philosophical—the redefinition of "blackness" in the light of the reality of "whiteness." As G.W.F. Heger s *Lordship and Bondage* points out, human identity, that is, critical self-consciousness, is directly related to ideas of reciprocity and recognition. Human beings exist only as they are recognized by others. The dialectics of recognition, however, usually do not occur on the basis of equality. Furthermore, an important source of identity for human beings is the labor they perform.

In at least three respects, the racist order transforms both the master and the slave. First, the oppressed are unable to acquire meaning or purpose from the compulsory labor that is invariably their lot; in a contemporary capitalist economy, they are denied the opportunity to work at meaningful jobs. Work as a creative, productive endeavor ceases to exist for blacks as a group, and whites draw the erroneous conclusion that blacks do not like to work simply because they are black. Second, the ideological and coercive apparatuses of the State block the struggles of blacks to attain full equality, and in so doing, disrupt the development of a positive black identity. The African socialist theorist Amilcar Cabral suggested that when colonialism or compulsory labor began, African history was frozen or "stopped." Black revolutions represented an attempt "to return to the source"; rejecting the inequality of the white world, they sought a renaissance of the precolonial, preracist black culture and society.

In order for the racist order to function, any prior claim to an alternate set of human values, customs, and institutions that the oppressed might have had in the preracist state must be suppressed. Whites as a group have historically approached blacks not in the light of their "blackness"—perhaps a better term would be "Africanness"—but in light of what whites believed that blacks must become from the vantage point of their own "whiteness." Racist societies must invent "the Negro."

This transormation of African peoples into the status of "Negroes" took place even before black chattel slavery was established as the dominant means of production in the Southern United States. For example, many colonial historians have observed that white settlers always referred to the Native Americans or Indians as members of certain nations or tribes, or at worst, as "savages" or "heathens." Other than the term "redskin" (which is not pejorative), Indians were not described on the basis of skin color. Among white colonists, the principle perceived distinctions were obviously religious or ethnic. Blacks alone were set apart because of their skin color. And as early as 1660 in the Virginia colony, blackness itself was identical with the status of a chattel slave. Negroes ceased to be Africans; blackness was an ascribed status rising out of whites' demands for black labor, not a distinctive culture or even a condition of humanity.

The sixth factor is sexual. A major force behind all anti-black restrictions and regulations has always been the irrational yet very real anxiety white males have expressed concerning black sexuality. In *The White Man's Burden,* historian Winthrop Jordan argues that the threat of black slave revolts in the seventeenth and eighteenth centuries was usually perceived in sexual terms. "The notion existed that black men were particularly virile, promiscuous and lusted after white women. It is apparent that white men projected their own desires onto Negroes: their own passion for black women was not fully acceptable to society or the self and hence, not readily admissible." Black women, however, were naturally lascivious and passionate, and thus were fair game for sexual predation. The sexual pathology of whites became public policy through legal castration. Colony after colony, from Quaker Pennsylvania to the Carolinas, sanctioned castration as a form of lawful punishment for a whole set of black male offenses. At the root of this cruel punishment, Jordan contends, was the white man's "racking fear and jealousy" of what black men could do if their relative positions and powers were reversed. Their mastery in the world of economics and politics meant little if the very black man they belittled and abused "performed his nocturnal offices better than the white man. Perhaps, indeed, the white man's woman really wanted the Negro more than she wanted him."

Here again, Fanon's commentary is critical. "The civilized white man retains an irrational longing for unusual eras of sexual license, of orgiastic scenes, of unpunished rapes, of unrepressed incest. Projecting his own desires onto the Negro," Fanon noted, "the white man behaves 'as if' the Negro really had them." For the racist, the black male represents or symbolizes the fundamental biological fear:

> On the genital level, when a white man hates black men, is he not yielding to a feeling of impotence or of sexual inferiority? Since his ideal is an infinite virility, is there not a phenomenon of diminution in relation to the *Negro,* who is viewed as a penis symbol? Is the Negro's superiority real? Everyone *knows* that it is not, But that is not what matters. The prelogical thought of the phobic has decided that such is the case.

Racism, then, is not merely intolerance toward blacks, or the "superstructural jus-tification" of the exploitation of black labor, or the collective projection of white psychosexual neuroses. All of these elements rise out of the social nexus of Western capitalist society and culture. Thus it seems unlikely that the simple transfer of state authority from one group of barbarous whites to another group of well-meaning whites (the Old Left, New Left, liberals or others) would change the basic dynamics of a system that is almost four centuries old.

III

Blacks, and blacks alone, must take the initial and decisive steps toward developing an adequate social theory to destroy white racism. This observation is not made out of black chauvinism, or disregard for the many sincere and dedicated white activists who gave their lives for the cause of black freedom—from John Brown and William Lloyd Garrison to Andrew Goodman and Michael Schwerner. It simply recognizes the fact that nothing in socialist or liberal political theory or practice to date indicates that white radicals and liberals have abandoned their respective infantile economic determinism and unrealistic belief in moral suasion. No long-range coalitions between white progressive organizations and black militant groups, such as the newly formed National Black Independent Political Party, can successfully mount a challenge to the New Right—a white social protest movement that is both intolerant and racist in character and intent—until this hard and painful theoretical work is done.

In *An American Dilemma,* Gunnar Myrdal observed that even during the Great Depression most blacks found it difficult to accept the Old Left's argument that socialism would quickly end the race problem. "When discussing communism in the Negro community," he wrote, "the most common black response was the com-ment, 'Even after a revolution, the country will be full of crackers.'" When American progressives, black and white, recognize the kernel of truth within this remark, and begin to construct a more realistic theoretical and programmatic response to white racism, can the promise of a truly nonracist society begin to be realized. The burden of race *and* class may be finally solved.

REFERENCES

Kenneth Clark and Carl Gershmann. "The Black Plight: Race and Class?" *New York Times Magazine* (October 5, 1980).

Oliver Cromwell Cox. *Caste, Class, and Race: A Study in Social Dynamics* (New York and London: Monthly Review, 1970).

W.E.B. Du Bois. *The Souls of Black Folk, Essays and Sketches* (Greenwich, Connecticut: Fawcett Publications, 1961).

Frantz Fanon. *Black Skin, White Masks* translated by Charles L. Markmann (New York: Grove Press, 1967).

H. Hoetink. *Slavery and Race Relations in the Americas: Comparative Notes on their Nature and Nexus* (New York: Harper and Row. 1973).

James Joll. *Antonio Gramsci* (New York: Penguin Books, 1978).

Winthrop D. Jordan. *The White Man's Burden: Historical Origins of Racism in the United States* (London and New York: Oxford University Press, 1974).

Manning Marable. *From the Grassroots: Social and Political Essays Towards Afro-American Liberation* (Boston: South End Press. 1980).

Edmund S. Morgan. *American Slavery, American Freedom: The Ordeal of Colonial Virginia* (New York: W. W. Norton. 1975).

Gunnar Myrdal. *An American Dilemma* (New York: Harper and Row. 1944).

Edward Peeks. *The Lone Struggle for Black Power* (New York: Charles Scribner's Sons, 1971).

SECTION II

On Black Protest and Politics:
The 1970s and 1980s

~

ANATOMY OF BLACK POLITICS

Historians will record that November 2, 1976, was an important date in the history of Afro-American politics. James Carter, a southern peanut farmer and one-term governor from Georgia, was elected president of the United States by a margin of less than two million popular votes over his Republican opponent, President Gerald R. Ford. Despite early predictions from political analysts that the election would "hardly be a contest," the electoral vote was quite close—297 to 241 votes. In at least 13 states, including Ohio, New York, Pennsylvania, Alabama, and Texas, the black vote proved to be the most decisive factor in providing Carter's margin of victory. In Mississippi, for example, Carter received 147,540 votes from Blacks, enough support to create a slim statewide majority of 11,537 votes over Ford. The largest number of black voters in history came to the polls; had the black vote been excluded or as divided as the white electorate, Carter would have been soundly defeated. The political message was clear: Jimmy Carter became president largely on the votes of the most oppressed sector of the American population. Black elected officials, intellectuals, and religious leaders had convinced Blacks that Carter's election was essential for their salvation.

Most black leaders had not anticipated that Carter would receive the Democratic party's nomination for president and were the last part of the old Franklin D. Roosevelt coalition to fully accept him. Many were suspicious of his record as governor of Georgia and of his reluctance to commit himself to a political platform throughout the state primaries. After August, black Democratic leaders began to promote the Carter candidacy. Early supporter Andrew Young spoke of Carter in glowing tones, insisting that he "is a product of the southern church and knows the language and culture of the black community." Atlanta's black congressman conceded that his man had none of the graces that "came from Ivy League colleges and liberal arts education. But his heart is right, his instincts are sound, and his training is very practical."[1] Former civil rights activists such as Martin Luther King, Sr., black mayors, and religious leaders, realizing gradually that the Carter-Ford election would be close, stepped up their efforts. Many black leaders organized Operation Big Vote, a national effort to register black voters. In Buffalo, New York, black disc jockeys hosted dance parties to register young voters. Thousands of Baltimore Blacks were registered in shopping centers and at factory gates. In Chicago's South Side, hundreds of hungry Blacks registered in McDonalds' restaurants. Five thousand Houston Blacks registered while attending an event at the Astrodome.[2]

On television and radio commercials, Blacks were reminded repeatedly that their votes would be crucial in determining the outcome of the election. Black newspapers reminded Blacks that Richard Nixon had received 94 percent of the Republican vote, 66 percent of the votes from Independents, and 42 percent of all traditionally Democratic voters. In all, the Nixon-Agnew ticket received almost 70 percent of white America's vote.[3] In the aftermath of Watergate and Vietnam, with 15 percent black unemployment and welfare cutbacks, Blacks could no longer tolerate another Republican administration in Washington. "Black Democratic leaders turned right around and sold Carter to their followers with the zeal of late converts," *The New Republic* observed one year later. "Here," they said, "is not just your ordinary, run-of-the-mill Democratic liberal; here is a man who grew up poor amidst poverty, who was raised side-by-side with blacks, who understands black culture and aspirations." The descendant of slaveholders was carefully packaged for black voter consumption—and 91 percent of all black voters bought the merchandise.[4]

Black voters also provided the margin of victory in at least 11 important congressional races. In Louisiana, Democrats Richard Tonry and Jerry Huckaby were narrowly elected to Congress over conservative Republicans, largely with black support. South Carolina Blacks provided the winning margin for Congressmen Kenneth Holland and John Jenrette. In the Senate, black votes amounted to more than the candidate's margin of victory in three races in Ohio, Tennessee, and Michigan. In Missouri, Blacks cast 119,956 votes for Democratic underdog Joseph Teasdale, providing him with a 12,209 vote margin over the incumbent Republican governor, Christopher Bond. Black support for all Democratic candidates seldom fell below 80 percent.[5]

A second reason for the importance of November 2 was the nearly unanimous vote of confidence the black public voiced in their elected federal officials. Four of the 17 members of the congressional black caucus received over 90 percent of the vote in their district races. Twelve of the black representatives garnered over 80 percent majorities. Only four congressmen, Ronald V. Dellums (Berkeley), Andrew Young, William Clay (St. Louis), and Harold Ford (Memphis), were seriously challenged, but none of their opponents received more than 39 percent of the district's vote. Black elected officials, black labor union officials, civil rights workers, and community leaders had registered 9.5 million Blacks, an increase of one million over 1972. Sixty-four percent of all registered Blacks went to the polls, compared to 58 percent only four years before.[6]

Perhaps most importantly, the alternative of black Republicanism, which had quietly gained respectability within black suburbs and within the black business community in recent years, suffered a major defeat. The percentage of Blacks who consistently identified themselves with the interests of the Republican party increased from a low 2 to 3 percent in 1968 to roughly 8–11 percent in 1972. Large numbers of black petty bourgeois who had been attracted to Nixon's version of "black capitalism" in the early 1970s and who had been turned off by the rhetoric of black revolutionaries in the 1960s pulled the voting booth levers for Jimmy Carter.[7]

Those few black Republican leaders who publicly assessed the 1976 campaign were disillusioned about their party's prospective chances to gain black supporters. Robert Keyes, a black organizer for President Ford's California campaign, complained in the *Sacramento Observer* that Ford "ran a traditional white-oriented campaign, with virtually no minority or female input." Republicans feared "that any overt actions or appeals by President Ford to the Blacks would stop the trend of Southern white rednecks and right-wingers who were allegedly coming on the Ford bandwagon."[8] William Walker, an influential black newspaper editor and Republican, suggested that the Republican party had ceased to be a viable political organization for Blacks. "Gerald Ford's defeat," he wrote, "can be directly attributed to not getting any support from Negroes."[9] The net effect of the election was the crippling of the black renaissance within Republican politics. The massive public mandate seemingly guaranteed black elected officials that they would face no real opposition from black Republican opponents in the future.

Dozens of articles appeared in numerous black newspapers and journals, predicting that the Carter administration would appoint many Blacks to positions of authority within the federal bureaucracy. Typical of most remarks were the comments of Eddie N. Williams, president of the Joint Center for Political Studies. Williams argued that since Blacks had "played a major role" in electing Carter, it was now reasonable to assume that the new president would swiftly "make Blacks full partners in the nation's policy-making franchise." "If Jimmy Carter wants to show black America that he is aware of the role they played in his election and of their high expectations," Williams suggested, "he could start by integrating" all influential positions within the governmental "apparatus."[10] Black politicians, journalists, and intellectuals were sure that Carter would gradually proceed with the desegregation of the slate. "Black Americans, like all other citizens, have a nonnegotiable right to participate in government at all levels," J.K. Obatala argued in *The Nation*. The new president had "a moral obligation to do whatever is necessary to protect everyone's right to earn a living.... The right to work is not politically negotiable." The Democratic party and Carter were expected to "develop people who can go out into the marketplace and fend for themselves."[11]

Few black intellectuals, politicians, and civil rights leaders fully realized that Carter would not, nor had any intention to, initiate a second New Deal for the ghetto or at least revive the concept of full employment within the Humphrey-Hawkins bill. Robert S. Browne, founder of *The Review of Black Political Economy,* warned that "the gravest danger in President-elect Carter's victory is that too much will be expected of the new administration, with the inevitable dissapointment which will set in when he fails to work miracles." Browne added that the Carter administration might impose "a flurry of new programs upon our existing economic structure, but with results far short of what is desired."[12] Carter appointed relatively few Blacks to major administrative positions and for several months remained silent about the creation of federal jobs for minorities. Yet black Democrats remained hopeful—Andrew Young was appointed ambassador to the United Nations. Throughout the winter and early months of spring they decided to wait for the president to act.

By May 1977, the Carter administration announced an end to "new programs" for social welfare and education in an attempt to balance the federal budget by 1981. With the approval of Arthur Burns, Federal Reserve Board chairman, Carter announced that his new priorities were to cut inflation and to stimulate the business sector. Bert Lance, head of the Office of Management and Budget, and chief economist Charles Schultze criticized liberal Democratic economic proposals which emphasized the creation of public jobs for the chronically unemployed. Although Carter had campaigned the previous autumn that he would cut the defense department budget by 5 to 7 billion dollars, defense spending increased to 111.8 billion dollars. In June and July many liberal Democrats raised sharp criticisms from the Left of the Carter presidency. Senator George McGovern declared that "the corporations have cried the wolf of 'business confidence' and the administration has run scared." *The New Republic,* which had announced itself to be "Cautiously For Carter" on election eve, criticized Carter's foreign policies and attacked his "moral" opposition to the use of Medicaid funds for abortions.[13] Liberal intellectuals like Arthur Schlesinger, Jr., Barry Commoner, and Michael Harrington joined the growing chorus of trade unionist and progressive opposition to Carter's entire domestic policies. Gradually, black leaders, like the Urban League's Vernon Jordan, voiced cautious criticism of Carter.

One year after Carter's electoral victory, the political and economic climate within the black community is the worst since the severe recession of the late 1950s. Official unemployment figures for Blacks range from 14.5 percent for men to 40.4 percent for teenagers. Unofficial unemployment figures of the Urban League are considerably higher—up to 25 percent for black men, 45 percent for youths. Thousands of Blacks in virtually every major industrial city in the Northeast are waiting in line for jobs. The so-called economic recovery of 1976–77 never reached the ghetto. Black middle-class voters who had anticipated a flood of social legislation similar to Lyndon Johnson's Great Society were disgusted with Carter's budget-balancing and the small number of federal appointments made available to them. In late summer, 15 black leaders summited at the Urban League headquarters in New York City to propose a counter political strategy to meet the steadily deteriorating conditions of the black urban poor and working-classes. Many of the black leaders who attended the conference—Parren Mitchell, Bayard Rustin, Benjamin Hooks, and Jesse Jackson—had been major supporters of Carter only months before. Declaring that they had been betrayed, Jackson charged Carter with "callous neglect." Gary, Indiana, mayor Richard Hatcher explained, "Now it's difficult for any black leader who pushed the election of Jimmy Carter to face the people he campaigned with."[14]

What went wrong? Neither Carter nor the Democratic party can be accused of "betraying" the interests of Blacks and the poor, since they never committed themselves to the transformation of America's political economy, which is essential in destroying the inequities which black leaders complain about so vociferously. While the black petty bourgeoisie and the leaders of black civil society almost unanimously believe that the Democratic party can solve the continuing problems of black America, the majority of Blacks either do not vote or do not support the Democratic party at all.[15] Black leaders failed to understand that "there is no bargaining leverage in a situation where a black vote for the Democratic party is *expected* and *delivered*," wrote political scientist Ronald Walters. "Further, and more importantly, there is no structure through which commitments may be obtained if leverage cannot be exercised...."[16] Black Democrats had sparked false expectations of prosperity within their own constituencies after Carter's election, and were now attempting to divorce themselves from their own campaign slogans and promises of 12 months before.

As black civil rights leaders' and politicians' criticisms of the Carter administration become increasingly bitter, it becomes necessary to separate the political rhetoric from political reality. A critique of black politics and the class formations which black people occupy relative to the entire American political economy explain the origins of the current black political crisis. The failure of black politicians and intellectuals to clearly discern their tenuous relationship with the capitalist state and the rapidly developing class differences between petty bourgeois Blacks and black working-class and poor people is at the heart of this crisis.

The principal contradiction within black society is between the politically advanced but economically oppressed black majority and the politically backward but economically privileged black elite. The black petty bourgeoisie, represented in business and financial institutions, in churches and colleges, in the media, and in fraternal organizations, express tendencies toward political accommodation and class collaboration within the state. The black elite influences the politics of millions of less affluent, less educated Blacks to vote for the Democratic party against their best, long-run interests.

The base of the conservativism within black electoral politics is the newly emerged black middle class. According to U.S. Bureau of the Census statistics, between 1969 and 1973 the income of black families in which both the husband and wife worked and the husband was under 35 years of age rose from 84 percent to 92 percent of the median white family income. In 1969, black families (using the above criteria) earned $8,423 per year, compared to $9,926 for whites. Four years later, these black families were earning $11,873, compared to $12,962 per year for whites. Outside the southern states, black and white family incomes in which both partners work and where the husband is under 35 years of age are roughly equal. In 1970 these black families earned a median income of $11,045 per year, slightly more than the median white family income of $10,578 per year. Even during the recession year 1973, black family incomes in the North and West amounted to $13,235 per year, compared to $13,332 for whites. Political economist Alfred E. Osborne suggests that it is no longer possible to employ the standard black/white income ratio in many comparison cases, because it fails to measure the important income distinctions within the black community.[17]

A review of census statistics reveals not a general elevation of black income levels during the 1970s, but a polarization of many Blacks at extremely low income levels and the development of an affluent upper income strata. In 1971, for example, the median family income for Blacks was only $6,440. Almost 40 percent of all black families earned less than $5,000 per year, yet 10.6 percent of all black families earned $15,000 or more per year. Black families in which both the husband and wife worked and the husband was under 35 years of age accounted for about 16 percent of all black husband/wife families and only 10 percent of all black families. These young affluent families, plus the well-established black doctors, lawyers, ministers, businessmen, educators, and others constitute at least 15 percent of the total black population.[18] This economically privileged group of Blacks have been the recipients of new business and professional positions due to affirmative action and political pressures from government and civil rights groups. Thousands of Blacks attend formerly segregated graduate and medical schools; thousands more were hired into middle management positions by corporations and large foundations. The pursuit of class collaborationist politics by this new petty bourgeois strata has, during the past decade, paid economic dividends.

The single most influential element within this new black petty bourgeoisie is the black entrepreneur. Although there are fewer than 230,000 black businesses in the United States, black businessmen have always wielded significantly more political power and economic influence than their numbers would indicate. Thousands of black grocery store owners, gasoline station proprietors, bankers, black insurance executives, and record company distributors have for generations advocated "a segregated economic system" controlled by black businessmen, "which exists alongside of or within the larger U.S. capitalist system." Historian Arthur Tolson observed recently that once Richard Nixon became president, many "black Americans clamored for a realistic application of black capitalism." Tolson noted that large numbers of Blacks "have been and are still trying to get into the mainstream of the ... capitalist system."[19] Several black intellectuals, notably Theodore Cross in *Black Capitalism,* preached that black Americans should buy stock in corporations, purchase property in ghetto areas, open black banks, and assume a more active role within the expansion of private enterprise in black communities. Simultaneously, black politicians like the former head of CORE and black power advocate, Floyd McKissick, argued that both private foundations and major corporations could play a vital role in the creation of a black business sector, inside the traditional capitalist system. McKissick, Roy Innis of the Congress of Racial Equality, and other black power leaders advocated that "existing white-controlled economic enterprises be transferred to black ownership," while maintaining the concept of private enterprise.[20]

Within the marginal confines of black business, black economic institutions have grown substantially since 1969. The number of all black firms rose from 163,073 in 1969 to 194,986 in 1972. Black-owned businesses recorded gross receipts amounting to $4.5 billion in 1969; three years later, total gross receipts were $7.2 billion. Overall, however, black gross receipts accounted for less than 0.29 percent of the national total.[21] During 1974, black businesses increased sales by a scant 1 percent over 1973, while the top *Fortune* 500 industrial corporations reported gains averaging 25 percent in the same period. Motown Industries ($45 million), Johnson Publishing Company ($34 million), and Johnson Products ($33 million), the three leading black-controlled corporations for 1974, generated $112 million in sales—in contrast to Exxon corporation, the leading white-controlled corporation, which earned $42 billion in sales during the same period.[22] Despite the minimal growth of black-owned businesses in relation to the total economy, the illusion of the viability of black capitalism is promoted through the media, cultural propaganda, and even by the small black enterpreneurs themselves.

Unlike the white petty bourgeoisie, the Negro middle class never maintained a substantial economic base. Because black capitalism has consistently failed to produce any surplus capital, black political, business, and civic leaders place great emphasis upon obtaining federal subsidies and private foundation grants as a means of providing the base for cultural and political activities. At virtually every black college, medical, and graduate school, the highest educational priority is placed on "grantsmanship," the writing of proposals for outside money. Black fraternities and sororities play an important economic as well as cultural role within the life of black communities by raising money for social activities. Fraternal organizations have rebounded from near obscurity during the 1960s to provide the political and economic leadership on many campuses and college communities. Almost the entire structure of black middle class civil society—the churches, cultural centers, colleges, and community welfare groups—have become partially or completely dependent upon the state or private foundations for fiscal support. Increasingly all of these groups have come to view "desegregation" as increased economic dependence upon the state and the creation of more job opportunities within the state and existing economic institutions.

The black petty bourgeoisie generally reject the cultural images of the traditional South and the blues for images which reject its upwardly mobile aspiration to merge within white civil society. The black petty bourgeois demand for a "respectable" black presence in the media is a logical outgrowth of their rejection of traditional black culture. In increasing numbers the black petty bourgeois is cast in situation comedies, or reads the six o'clock news, or is illustrated in commercials. The standard Negro middle-class magazine, *Ebony,* and dozens of conservative, black-owned and operated local news weeklies across the country set the assimilationist aesthetic standards for black America.[23]

The hegemonic political influence of the black petty bourgeois strata over black working-class and poor people is perhaps best translated in the continued control of the Democratic party over the black community. Roughly 80 percent of all Americans, black and white, who earn in excess of $10,000 or more per year vote in the presidential elections. Americans who have attended college or who have at least a college degree also participate in presidential elections at a rate of 80 percent. Only 47 percent of all Americans with an eighth-grade education or less voted in 1972, and only 37 percent of all people who earn under $3,000 yearly go to the polls.[24] Since the percentage of Blacks beneath the poverty level or who do not finish high school is greater than the percentage of whites in the same category, the black voter profile has a greater bias toward upper-income groups than does the white voter profile. One could argue that the typical northern black businessman, accountant or college professor has at least twice the voting power or influence as does a southern black welfare mother, since statistically the former would be far more likely to vote consistently. This means that the average black politician will be far more responsive to the interests of a group of black lawyers, ministers, or technicians than a group of unemployed workers or factory laborers, even though the latter would outnumber the former group by far within any black community. Black congressmen are more sensitive to the stated class interests of the black petty bourgeoisie; therefore, while they rhetorically criticize the Carter administration's lack of concern for the poor, they collaborate with the state for political concessions which generally affect a minority of affluent Blacks.

Despite the development of a black middle class strata, the realities of black life are more desperate than ever before in recent history. While the income ratio for black, two-parent working families closed steadily and even surpassed white, two-parent working families, the real gap between all Blacks and all whites has increased. In 1971, median white family income was $10,672 compared to $6,440 for Blacks, a gap of $4,232. By 1974 white families were earning a median income of $13,356; Blacks were making only $7,808, a gap of $5,548. The median black family continues to earn only 58 percent of the amount earned by a similar white family.[25] The rapid inflation rate has made the old theoretical concept of "poverty," as based on a level of income, obsolete.[26] When measured by all social and economic criteria, there are today more Blacks in poverty, permanently unemployed, or who are working part-time involuntarily than in any time in American history.[27]

Class exploitation is experienced particularly by black women. There has been a tremendous increase in the number of black households headed by females—from 18 percent in 1950 to almost 33 percent in 1975. Two-thirds of all black poor families are headed by women.[28] In May 1975, black women received an average weekly income that was 75 percent of what black men earned and only 58 percent of what white men received. The unemployment rate for black teenage women was almost 40 percent several years ago and has risen since then.[29] About 60 percent of all families receiving food stamps are headed by women, and 55 percent of the current food stamp recipients fall well below the official poverty level. Many black women who are eligible for food stamps do not participate in these programs.[30]

The polarization of the black class structure reveals the political behavior of the black elected officials. The majority of Blacks who have not benefited from increased salaries during the desegregation of certain businesses and state bureaucracies in the past ten years remain outside the state. They usually do not vote because of a realistic cynicism toward the existing political order; they do not identify with the existing black leadership; when they do vote, it is a case of "the lesser of two evils" rather than a principled commitment to the Democratic party's liberal wing. The petty bourgeoisie, conversely, defends the gains of the civil rights movement by conscientiously voting for proponents of their class interests. By supporting the reformers within the Democratic party, the black middle class increasingly identifies their own political interests within the state.

Part of the crisis in black politics involves the breakdown in black leadership. Traditionally, the black church hierarchy provided black communities with effective political leaders who were, at least theoretically, capable of challenging the white establishment without fear of economic sanctions. The civil rights movement elevated ministers like Andrew Young, Ralph Abernathy, Hosea Williams, Jesse Jackson, and

Martin Luther King, Jr., to national prominence. The state's response to spontaneous uprisings by blacks in the streets was the elevation of a segment of the more conservative civil rights leadership into state and corporate positions. Many of these black lawyers, educators, and businessmen saw the new openings within business and government as a path toward personal fiscal security and political advancement, as well as a method of "legitimizing" the gains of the desegregation movement. Many hundreds of black state legislators, sheriffs, county commissioners, and small-town mayors believed that through their elected positions they would be able to expand the movement through increased social services for Blacks. As popular struggles in the streets and at colleges and community centers gradually died down, black elected and appointed officials discovered that they occupied a managerial relationship within the state; they could pacify the black constituency through increased public services and create public jobs for Blacks, but they could not challenge the historical direction of the state. They could not, as it were, demand the economic reorganization of the base which rationalizes the state's existence. As growing numbers of dissatisfied Blacks at all income levels express disapproval of the Carter administration, the black "leaders" are discovering that they are unable to lead their "constituencies." Somewhat opportunistically, they are reduced to bitching about a system they cannot change (and are now an integral part of); they are forced to condemn Carter, the candidate they campaigned for with such moral fervor only months ago.

There were several social forces in the early 1960s which could have posed an alternative challenge to the increasingly conservative black Democratic and business leadership. Black southern farmers and rural landowners had for decades organized effective political institutions—from the Colored Farmers Alliance of the 1880s to militant black tenant farmer organizations which were oriented toward political confrontation with the state rather than class collaboration. Black ministers as a group have often been the most effective moral critics of the state and white civil society. But both groups, for different reasons, failed to develop as hegemonic political forces within black politics.

The expansion of capitalism into the South during the post–World War II period effectively destroyed the prospect of an agriculturally based, southern black middle class. Blacks who had for generations owned large homesteads were forced off the land by corporations and were forced to migrate north or to work in southern cities like Atlanta, Charlotte, Memphis, and Birmingham. Alabama provides an excellent example of the economic disfranchisement which occurred throughout the South. From 1954 to 1969 black farm owners declined in number from 18,408 to 7,226, a 60.7 percent decrease. From 1959 to 1969 the number of acres owned by black Alabamians declined by 50 percent, from 1,262,583 acres to 636,859 acres. In 1969 the average black-owned farm made gross profits of only $3,226. Only 5.8 percent of all acreage in the state was owned by Blacks.[31]

The sudden transformation of the southern economy from a predominantly agricultural economy in the 1940s to a capitalist base today had important political consequences. Land-owning Blacks provided the major force for the rural civil rights movement in the 1960s. Black farmers were active in voter registration campaigns, were more likely to run for public office than nonland-owning, rural Blacks, and consistently provided a solid electoral base for independent black political parties (such as the Lowndes County Freedom Organization and the Mississippi Freedom Democratic party). Blacks owned less than 6 million acres in 1974 and were losing land at an annual rate of 250,000 acres.[32] The destruction of a black agricultural base has, in turn, led to the demise of the political influence of rural, land-owning Blacks and the proletarianization of southern urban Blacks. It also helped to promote the hegemony of predominantly northern, urban, middle-class Blacks over the general black electorate.

Hundreds of black ministers were selected for leadership positions within white churches during the 1960s, as white religious liberals placated the black community through financial donations and moral support for civil rights legislation. Gradually, most of these ministers quietly resigned their roles as advocates for progressive change. Gilbert Caldwell, professor at New York Theological Seminary, observed that many of his black colleagues give "the impression that we are the 'exceptional men,' that we were chosen because we were 'different.' In the minds of some, we are the overt manifestation of the church's readiness to embrace all God's children."[33] The major white religious denominations have pulled small but influential numbers of black members and clergy during the past two decades, circumventing their own guilt on the political issue of desegregation.[34] As most of these churches invest tens of billions of dollars each year in major American corporations such as Exxon, Gulf Oil, General Motors, IBM, Union Carbide, and Coca Cola, the church leadership assumes a quasi-state character. Black church members, like their political counterparts within the federal, state, and local governments, are absorbed into the conservative structures which they had intended originally to reform from within.[35]

Black politics of the seventies has assumed the modes of dependency, which Frantz Fanon spells out clearly in his essay on "the Negro and Hegel." The state, which stood before Blacks as a liberator in the civil rights movement, subsequently imprisoned them through equal opportunity, affirmative action, expanded public services, and so forth.[36] Conventional black political logic assumes, as given, that: popular, mass struggles accomplish little; violence should be avoided at all costs; and real political power lies within the liberalization of state institutions in their relationship with black people. As William R. Morris, Housing Director for the NAACP, recently wrote, Blacks should look "to their government to make it possible for them to secure decent housing ... freedom from crime, and other debilitating influences of the slums." Black businessmen and petty bourgeois taxpayers had a right to expect government intervention into private enterprise to promote "a fair share of the economic benefits" for Negroes. For example, "blacks desirous of careers in the housing industry need government help to overcome racially exclusionary practices in professional and trade organizations in housing."[37] The federal government must expand social welfare services to increasingly large numbers of Blacks.

The problem with this argument is that it comes precisely at a period of government wage freezes, public service layoffs, and a decrease in state support for programs within civil society. The black petty bourgeoisie view the state as neutral or even progressive, rather than as an institution which blunts class contradictions and racial contradictions. The state undertaxes the rich and shifts the burden of taxation on the poor and working-classes. Sales taxes and property taxes are largely the burden of lower-class apartment dwellers, small homeowners, and the working-class, generally. The state does not tax the interest on municipal bonds and even provides generous tax subsidies for corporations.[38] For the majority of black people, the state exists as an institution of exploitation. Any economic or social benefits derived from the marginally progressive elements within the state, such as affirmative action programs, seldom affect the oppressed black majority. Liberal capitalist reform programs have been punitive toward the poor, or at best paternalistic.[39]

The political dependency of the black petty bourgeoisie is manifested in its relationship toward the Democratic party. After flirting with the National Black Political Assembly at the Gary Convention in 1972, Ronald Walters observed, "some of the major black politicians (a few of whom were intimately connected with developing NBPA strategy) conveniently 'cut-and-run'" from the prospect of an independent black political formation.[40] The Black Congressional Caucus, black business leaders, and most black intellectuals are privately convinced that the concept of an independent black political party is unrealistic. Congressman John Conyers argued recently that "the liberal left wing of the party, it must be conceded, is the only viable political instrument for progressive change currently on the scene."[41] Julian Bond, perhaps further to the Left than any other major black politician, states that the only means to improve black economic and social conditions is through "seeking out coalitions" and "by increasing voter registration." Although the "Democratic party is in great disarray," Blacks could not constitute an independent political force. "We are only 12–13 percent at best of the entire population of this country. That percentage has never been able to do anything for itself."[42]

Unfortunately, the new "accommodationists" have nowhere to turn. Their political dependency upon the Democratic party has tended to make white America shift the burden of black poverty and economic oppression squarely on the shoulders of Blacks themselves and then stand aside, when, in truth, the burden is caused by capitalism's inability to provide full employment, the basic essentials of education, social welfare, and economic improvement at every level of black society. The black elite are unable to support their patrons and continue the protest traditions of the movement simultaneously. As poet Mari Evans writes, they are unable to "speak the truth to the people."[43]

Only a black political party, based on the material conditions of the majority of Blacks, can transcend the political impasse of what constitutes a black Thermidor.[44] Only a mass political party, rooted in the continued realities of black poverty and unemployment, can address the contradictions inside the black community. As Robert Allen reflected several years ago, black people can neither "afford the social injustices of capitalism," nor tolerate "some half-hearted compromise which would make the black community in general, and its educated classes in particular, subservient to the expansionist needs of corporate capitalism." [45] The final solution to the present crisis between the state and black people is the building of a genuine, anticapitalist black political party, which rejects fundamental compromise and class collaboration with the Democratic party.

~

REAGANISM, RACISM, AND REACTION
Black Political Realignment in the 1980s

INTRODUCTION

Reaganism, racism and capitalist economic reaction provide the terrain for black struggle in the 1980s. Under the Reagan Administration, American capitalism is currently attempting to respond to a profound structural crisis within the system. Reagan's bestial affirmative action policies and cutbacks in health care, welfare, and social services are only secondary aspects of a more basic effort to accelerate the accumulation of capital by superexploiting the working class, blacks and latinos. In the face of capitalism's uneven lurch toward authoritarianism and fiscal austerity, black political opinion is divided. A significant sector of the black elite has been co-opted into politics of neoconservatism and "Black Reaganism." Other civil rights leaders, members of the Congressional Black Caucus and black trade unionists have moved cautiously to the left, advancing left Keynesian economic policies and a social democratic political agenda.

Pressures from black workers and the permanently unemployed, the immediate victims of Reaganomics, have forced the black elite's activists to initiate boycotts, protest marches and militant demonstrations against the racist right. More significantly, progressive black nationalists succeeded in 1980–81 in institutionalizing two major forums for black struggle—the National Black Independent Political Party and the Black United Front. As the crisis deepens within the economy, a general realignment within black politics will occur. The effort to overturn Reagan is producing the foundations to overturn the entire racist/capitalist state itself.

RESTRUCTURING U.S. CAPITALISM

By the summer of 1981, the essential features of Reaganism had become brutally clear. In the area of affirmative action, Reagan mounted "a callous, insensitive and misguided abandonment of traditional remedies for employment discrimination followed by every administration since Franklin D. Roosevelt," in the words of Representative Augustus Hawkins.[1] The Department of Labor, for example, weakened an executive order which forces corporate recipients of federal contracts to file affirmative action programs. Under new rules, the minimum level for submitting such plans was raised from $50,000 to $1 million contracts. Annual affirmative action plans will be scrapped and employers will be reviewed only once every five years.

The Department of Education pressured the Justice Department to delete anti–sex bias laws against female employees of educational institutions. The Office of Federal Contract Compliance Programs privately instructed its field staff "to cut back, enforcement activities." David Stockman's Office of Management and Budget advocated tightened rules under which blacks, latinos and women could claim back pay for previous discrimination, Under Reagan, the Civil Rights Divisions of the Justice Department filed only five civil lawsuits on discrimination issues in its first six months of their administration. After almost one year, Reagan's lawyers had filed fewer than a dozen objections under the Voting Rights Act. Melvin L. Bradley, the senior black official at the White House, defended his boss to the press, explaining that "when faced with a set of circumstances he will, in my opinion, do the right thing, no matter what his real appreciation for what the black experience is." More candidly, White House spokesperson David R. Gergen admitted, "I don't think he's a crusader for civil rights."[2]

The most widely publicized effects of Reagan's budget cuts involved welfare and human services programs. On October 1, 1981, over 400,000 families were removed from federal and state welfare rolls. New rules for Aid to Families with Dependent Children (AFDC) were punitive at best. The amount of assets a family could own and still receive public benefits was cut from $2,000 to $1,000; food stamps and housing subsidies were now included as personal income in determining welfare; undocumented workers and strikers were declared ineligible for AFDC.[3] On September 4, 1981, the Agriculture Department reduced the amount of food served to 26 million children in more than 94,000 schools throughout the country. Dietary allowances were distorted in order to reduce federal expenditures for school lunches. At one point, Reagan's nutrition experts had even classified catsup and pickle relish as vegetables.[4]

Within months, black national opposition to Reagan's social policies—the abandonment of affirmative action, civil rights legislation, etc.—was virtually unanimous.[5] Most blacks attacked Reagan's budget cuts and gross expenditures in military hardware as socially unproductive. But on fiscal policies, no real black consensus emerged as to the reasons for the emergence of Reaganomics at this time which could lead toward a general critique of modern American capitalism. Indeed, most black criticisms of Reaganomics were at best highly confused and lacked any basic comprehension of the capitalist prerogatives behind the current public policies of the Reagan Administration.

Testifying before Congress, Chicago Urban League director James Compton suggested that he "could support" Reagan's agenda if it created "more employment opportunities for minorities."[6] The board of directors of the NAACP proposed the adoption of an alternative federal budget which increased defense expenditures and resulted in a $55 billion deficit, but also raised the income tax exemption for a family of four to $ 10,000 annually, The general direction of the proposal was a fairly conservative form of Keynesianism, not unlike the austere 1981 budget of Carter.[7] Some black commentators suggested that blacks themselves were somehow to blame for the economic mess. "With the Reagan budget cuts in full swing some middle class blacks are beginning to feel the razor's edge inching closer and closer to their necks," columnist Joyce Daniels Phillips wrote in the *Jackson Advocate*. The solution was developing a new set of austere socioeconomic values: "cutting back on material possessions, monthly mortgage payments, exorbitant car notes, and numerous charge accounts."[8] A few black politicians, such as Representative Harold Washington, attacked Reagan's budget cuts and tax policy as "nothing more than a transfer of wealth back to the rich from the poor," but professed no radical alternative fiscal program.[9] Some blacks denounced Reaganomics by declaring that the President was racist—without a concomitant explanation suggesting why neither Nixon nor Carter, who were equally racist, had not advanced these specific fiscal policies. Still others asserted that Reaganomics was merely economic "evil," and that "Reagan is the antichrist."[10]

In order to transcend the mystification and metaphysics which passes for analysis, a critique of Reaganomics must begin with a simple question: who benefits from the policies, and who loses? Three brief illustrations should suffice—food stamps, public housing, and Medicaid. According to the Bureau of the Census, 5.9 million households received food stamps in 1979. The median annual income of these families was $5,300, and 77 percent had incomes below $10,000. About 2.1 million household recipients of food stamps were black, or 35 percent, and 600,000 households were latino. Sixty-three percent of food stamp recipients, or 3.7 million families, were white. Last year 2.5 million households lived in public housing. Half of these families lived below the official poverty line, and the median annual income for the households was $4,980. Fifty-nine percent, or 1.5 million households, were white; 1.0 million were black, and 200,000 were Hispanic. The Census data illustrate that 18.1 million individuals or 8 million households were enrolled in the Medicaid program in 1979. Thirty percent, or 2.4 million households, were black; 9 percent, or 700,000 were latino; 68 percent, or 5.4 million, were white. A third were over 65 years old, and 36 percent of the households were headed by a single female.

Reagan's budget cutbacks affect black people proportionately moreso than whites primarily because blacks are more viciously oppressed than other sectors of the working class. It is important to note, however, that a majority of the potential victims of Reagan's cuts are white—the elderly, the unemployed, women, and the poor. As racist as Reagan's social policies actually are, we must also recognize the class aspect of the assault, which is aimed principally at all lower income groups irrespective of race.[11]

Reaganomics should be understood, fundamentally, as a conservative political response to the organic crisis of capital accumulation. Since 1973, real wages for

American workers have dropped almost 13 percent. The official unemployment rate for black workers, a figure far below the actual jobless ratio, increased from 7 percent in 1970 to about 15 percent. But things have not been rosy on Wall Street, either. From 1975 to 1980 total U.S. corporate profits after taxes averaged $104.3 billion per year; from 1965 to 1970, the average was $100.9 billion. In other words, total corporate profits adjusted for inflation rose only 3 percent in one decade. During this period, by way of contrast, the gross national product, which is the capitalist economy's total output of commodities and services, increased 35 percent. The real value of corporate stocks on the Dow Jones Exchange has plummeted 40 percent since 1970.

Corporate projections for the 1980s in many industries are even more disastrous. The average return on equity for older industries (steel, auto, construction, etc.) was 14 percent in 1975, 8 percent last year, and is dropping sharply. Since 1973, 23 major tire plants were closed; 11 percent of U.S. steelmaking capacity was "phased out" between 1977-1980. About 400,000 U.S. workers lost their jobs in 1979 alone due to plant relocations or closings. Older industries hurt by increased petroleum prices in the wake of the 1973-1974 OPEC embargo privately admit that many firms will not be able to afford key oil resources for production in the late 1980s. *Business Week* recently projected that oil prices, currently about $34/barrel, will range conservatively between $77 to $177/barrel by 1990. The period of American capitalist hegemony over the world's human and material resources, from 1945 to 1973, has come to an unceremonious end. The fiscal crisis of the state and many industries now only generates permanent inflation, high unemployment, and social chaos.[12]

All businesses within a capitalist society must continue to expand, in other words, to accumulate and reinvest capital derived from the surplus value exploitation of workers. What is termed "Reaganomics" is actually a coherent political strategy "to conserve the economic power and privilege of the dominant capitalist class while revitalizing the economy" at the expense of blacks, latinos, the working class and the poor. Economist Thomas Weisskopf outlines this conservative agenda as follows:

Reindustrialization and growth are to be stimulated by a sharp rise in corporate profitability and in the economic rewards to top executives and managers. To re-inflate profits and stimulate growth on terms most favorable to the economic elite, it will clearly be necessary to cut back on the economic claims of almost everyone else. Thus the growth of workers' wages and the whole apparatus of the welfare state—social security, publicly supported medical care, unemployment compensation, aid to urban areas and small businesses, etc.—must be trimmed. Moreover, those types of government regulation that aim to serve social goals by imposing costs on business by restricting their decision-making freedom—e.g., legislation to protect the environment, consumers, workers, and minorities—must be curtailed.[13]

Given the intensity of the financial crisis, Reagan's programmatic thrust becomes clear: reduce the wages of workers, abandon environmental standards, reduce or eliminate the social wage (health care, unemployment compensation, etc.), destabilize trade unions and bust public employee unions, (e.g., the vigorous suppression of the air traffic controllers strike) increase the level of permanent unemployment, and reduce corporate taxes to zero.Reagan's ambition to restructure U.S. capitalism and to eliminate the social wage cannot be achieved without creating permanent divisions within these working class/national minority groups. The primary tactic used has been the careful manipulation of social and cultural issues which have a special appeal to white ethnics and lower income groups. This reactionary social agenda advocates: an end to any and all forms of abortion; a restoration of prayer in public institutions; the maintenance of local schools and opposition to federal court-ordered busing; the defeat of the Equal Rights Amendment, gay rights legislation and all forms of federal or state intervention in the private sector promoting affirmative action in hiring policies; the renaissance of patriotism, anti-communism and the "work ethic." An important part of this cultural counter-revolution is the Moral Majority and other rightwing political action committees and lobbying agencies which have evolved from the modern evangelical religious movement. The ideological apparatus of the racist/capitalist state creates "allies" within the very sector of the working class that it is committed to exploit and even to destroy.

THE INEVITABLE FAILURE OF REAGANOMICS

Ironically, there is absolutely no indication that Reagan's program, even if enacted in its totality, would cement the diverse class forces it purports to serve. On May 28, 1981, Reagan complained before a conference of state and local officials that financial markets were unjustifiably critical of his tax cut proposals. "I have never found Wall Street a source of good economic advice," he snapped. The finance community "looks through a very narrow glass" and insists on misunderstanding [his] administration's agenda. The response from Wall Street was blunt and swift. A first vice president of Bache Halsey Stuart Shields informed the *Times* that "Reagan's comments [were not] justified, since Wall Street's qualms are well taken." Even Reagan's own $20–50,000 income constituency worries that their President's policies will not be very effective. One recent Lou Harris poll reports that by a margin of 55 percent to 35 percent the middle class "believes that inflation and interest rates will still be in the double-digit range" in the end of 1982. Most investment analysts have projected the rate of inflation to average about 9 percent annually in the 1980s, about the same level that existed between 1975–1981.[14]

In a survey of corporate executives whose incomes averaged $90,000 per year, completed in mid-May 1981, by the accounting firm Ernst and Whinney, over half said "they did not expect their standard of living to improve in the next two years, and despaired of keeping up with inflation." Almost one-fourth of these executives stated that their "only strategy for combating higher prices was simply to monitor personal spending more closely."[15] Many mortgage owners are so hard-pressed for cash that they have stopped paying their notes. According to the Federal Home Loan Bank Board, holders of over $6 billion in mortgages are at least two months past due in payments—an unprecedented figure.[16] The total debt for residential mortgages now exceeds the one trillion dollar federal debt. Outstanding loans owed by consumers, $320 billion, exceeds the total amount of all corporate profits before taxes by almost $100 billion. The economic foundations of American capitalism have not been so fragile since the Great Depression.[17]The general attitude of most black, liberal and feminist critics of Reaganism either discounts a socialist economic alternative or projects a revised version of Keynes and the welfare state. These reformist proposals, advanced by groups such as the NAACP, National Organization for Women, and a majority of Democratic Party liberals and some moderates, include efforts to restrain wage growth (wage-price controls), allocating federal government contracts to corporations prepared to reorganize themselves, bailing out failing industries (such as Chrysler), maintaining vigorous federal social programs (e.g., consumer safety, environmental protection, affirmative action, civil rights) and reducing tax burdens for low-to-middle income groups. This Keynesian strategy would only work in a period of massive capitalist expansion. It would not provide sufficient funds to restore older industries without generating massive federal deficits, which would in turn keep interest rates above 20 percent and threaten the stability of most banks and the stock market.

In this crisis period of capital accumulation, only two long-term outcomes are possible: (1) the acceleration of the corporations' exploitation of blacks, the working class, and the poor, or (2) the nationalization of heavy industries, the means of transportation and financial establishments by the public, and a general socialist reconstruction in America. Either the interests of maximizing profits come before human needs, or the system is restructured to place people before profits.

The inevitable failure of Reaganomics is a self-fulfilling prophecy. Reagan's newest round of budget cuts promises to create legions of enemies, even among white, ethnic, working-class voters, a central part of his electoral constituency. The great danger in this impending failure is two-fold. First, the majority of civil rights, Chicano, feminist, et. al. leaders have not yet assessed the profound dimensions of the crisis of capital accumulation. Franklin Williams, the director of the Phelps-Stokes Fund, commented recently that "in response to the current national mood, liberals seem to have raised the white flag of surrender." Many Democratic lawmakers, feminists and civil rights supporters "seem tired, utterly befuddled and strangely quiet."[18] A stale rehash of the Great Society, or even a "moderate" version of Reaganomics, will neither inspire nor organize the forces for fundamental progressive change.

Second, the proponents of Reaganomics will only be able to institutionalize their racist/capitalist offensive by developing an elaborate system of authoritarian repression and social control over the working class. Reagan and the corporations are committed to the salvation of capitalism, and would not hesitate to scrap the liberal democratic apparatus if it got in the way of renewed capital accumulation. Massive political repression against the perceived or real enemies of corporate America—black and Chicano nationalists, Marxists, democratic socialists—would not end on the fringes of the left. It would perhaps include any and all militantly dissident voices—feminists, environmentalists, anti-nuclear power activists, trade unionists, civil rights leaders, welfare rights workers, social democrats within the Democratic Party. By the end of the 1980s, the fight for socialism will become a fight to preserve democracy.[19]

BLACK REAGANITES

The Reagan Presidency, the rise of white vigilante violence against blacks and the organic crisis within the capitalist political economy all combine to make the 1980s potentially both the most dangerous yet promising period for black politics in recent history. Many black commentators consoled themselves in the wake of the "Reagan mandate" with the thought that blacks must inevitably pull together to confront the common enemy. Reagan's black apologists were few in number during the 1980 Presidential campaign. But in December 1980, 125 black academicians and business leaders caucused in San Francisco at a conference held by the Institute for Contemporary Studies to discuss the directions for black conservatism. Organized by Hoover Institution economist Thomas Sowell, the conference featured Reagan advisors Edwin Meese and Milton Friedman as honored guests. This meeting marked a significant turning point for national black politics, for it dramatized and made public the severe contradictions on major political, economic and education issues which divided the members of the black elite. By the autumn of 1981, differences within the elite had become so intense that any possibility of building a consensus position on major public policy issues was lost. Dissension within the ranks was the order of the day, as black actors opportunistically seized the subordinated roles which were given to them. A new political current was born—black Reaganism.[20]

Black conservatives do not represent a monolithic political/social force, but rather have evolved from radically different sectors of black society. In brief, there are at least four overlapping categories of black Reaganites: (1) conservative black politicians; (2) black philosophical conservatives; (3) black corporate executives, business managers and Reagan administrative appointees; and (4) former Black Power activists and nationalists who have not fully embraced Reaganism but nevertheless have become so closely aligned with this rightist trend that they merit the obloquy "fellow travellers."

Some of the most prominent black Republicans of the past two decades have been W.O. Walker, publisher of the Cleveland *Call and Post* and head of the national "Blacks for Reagan-Bush" organization in 1980; former Massachusetts Senator Edward Brooke; James Cummings, leader of the National Black Republican Council; Art Fletcher, former executive director of the United Negro College Fund and Labor Department officer under Nixon; Samuel Pierce, Reagan's Secretary of Housing and Urban Development; and William T. Coleman, Ford's Secretary of Transportation.

These blacks were subordinates within the Rockefeller wing of the Republican Party during the 1960s and early 1970s. During the Nixon Administration they consistently supported affirmative action programs, civil rights legislation and federal assistance to black-owned businesses. Coleman had been part of the legal team which successfully challenged school segregation laws in the 1954 *Brown* decision. During his two terms in the Senate, Brooke had been among the most consistently liberal voices in Congress. Like other liberal Republicans, notably former New York Senator Jacob Javits and Illinois Senator Charles Percy, they strived to reconcile their belief in limited federal government and unfettered capitalism with the desegregation of white civil society and equal opportunity legislation to promote the development of a black petty capitalist class.[21] The philosophical conservatives properly belong to the rabid right wing of the Republican party, advocating Milton Friedman's version of *laissez faire* capitalism, states' rights, and a dogged hatred of left-of-center politics. This militantly rightist faction includes Walter Williams, Professor of Economics at George Mason University; J.A.Y. Parker, a former official of the anti-Communist Young Americans For Freedom and currently president of Lincoln Institute and Educational Foundation; and Wendell Willkie Gunn, Assistant Treasurer of Pepsi Corporation.

The titular leader of this tendency is Thomas Sowell. After serving in the Marines, Sowell attended Howard University. Considering himself a Marxist, Sowell eventually received graduate degrees at the University of Chicago and Columbia. As he moved up the academic ladder his ideological views grew increasingly conservative. By the late 1960s he had become a Goldwater Republican and a bitter opponent of the welfare state. He condemned the emergence of Black Studies and black campus activism. By the election of Carter, Sowell had come to repudiate most of the ideals of the Civil Rights Movement. He condemned affirmative action legislation as detrimental to blacks' interests. His prescription for the plight of poor education within the ghetto was the imposition of "strict discipline" and mandatory expulsion of "rowdies who disrupt education for the majority." Sowell attacked the NAACP/Civil Rights leadership as a "light-skinned elite" whose policies served to provide "access to whites" for themselves but not for the black poor. In a major advertisement paid for by Smith Kline Corporation in 1981, Sowell praised capitalism as the vehicle for blacks to gain acceptance and upward mobility. "The rich are a red herring used by politicians to distract our attention," he declared. "There aren't enough rich people to make any real economic difference, whether they pay high taxes or low taxes. The great majority of the government's money comes from the great majority of the people." Like Reagan, Sowell believes that inflation, not unemployment, is the real problem within America's political economy. "Balancing the budget is not enough," Sowell warns. "Whether we yearn for government giveaways as the answer to our problems, we have to realize that every giveaway is also a takeaway. Anything the country can't afford without the giveaway, it can't afford with it."[22] Potentially the most influential faction among black Reaganites are the coterie of Administration officials and middle level executives from major corporations. In the executive branch of government, the list includes Thelma Duggin, formerly the Republican Committee liaison to the National Black Voters Program in the 1980 election and currently serving as deputy to Presidential Advisor Elizabeth Dole; Melvin Bradley, Senior Policy Advisor to Reagan, responsible for developing "public policy recommendations in the areas of food and agriculture, minority business development, urban affairs, free enterprise zones, small business administration, and Black colleges and universities"; and Thaddeus Garret, Vice Presidential assistant in charge of domestic policy and programs.

Major black corporate supporters of Reagan's policies include Gloria E.A. Toote, a New York attorney and millionaire real estate developer; William Pickard, owner of a lucrative McDonald's franchise in Detroit; Arthur McZier, President,

National Business Services Enterprises, Inc.; Constance Newman, President, Newman and Associates; Abraham Venable, Vice Chairperson of the Business Policy Review Council and director of General Motor's Urban Affairs Division; Fred Blac, Business Policy Review Council Chairperson and corporate executive in General Electric; Cyrus Johnson of General Foods; Philip J. Davis of Norton Simon, Inc.; and John Millier of the United State Brewer's Association.

These black corporate executives and bureaucrats had no ideological commitment to civil rights, affirmative action, or to the defense of any traditional institutions within the black community. They favor Reaganomics because it will generate greater profits for their client industries and monopolies. These corporate black Reaganites are even more dangerous than Sowell, because their blatant and vigorous support for conservative public policies is rooted not in any ideological commitment, but, purely in their own vicious desire for money and their hunger for power.[23]

The "fellow travellers" of the black Reaganite accommodationists include a number of would-be black militants who are disenchanted with liberalism and protest politics. At the top of the list are Charles V. Hamilton, professor of government at Columbia, and black media commentator Tony Brown. Both Hamilton and Brown attended the San Francisco Conference of black conservatives. The co-author of *Black Power*, Hamilton has experienced a radical metamorphosis since his days as mentor to Stokely Carmichael (Kwame Toure). Since blacks are a "relatively powerless minority," he informed the *New York Times*, the rise of a new black conservative trend was essential. "Frankly," Hamilton admitted, "I'd be very worried if we didn't have them"[24] Brown criticized the NAAGP's "hostile behavior towards President Reagan" when he appeared as a guest at their annual convention in Denver in 1981. Brown thought that Reagan really wants "to economically emancipate black ghettos," and that the President's brutal budget cuts were tantamount to a request for Afro-Americans to "return to the fundamental nationalism of their past. Ironically," Brown explained, "Reagan's philosophy of a sound economic power base for black America is more compatible with past black leaders such as Marcus Garvey, Booker T. Washington, Elijah Muhammad and Frederick Douglass, than are the modern-day disciples of the Black establishment." This massive distortion of black history by Brown scarcely masked his overt appeasement toward the forces of racism and political reaction.[25] What all four tendencies discussed above have in common is a firm belief that racism, in the words of Reagan apologist Nathan Wright, Jr., no longer has "a damn thing" to do with black underdevelopment; that socialist, Marxist, Keynesian and/or liberal economic programs will not work; and that black advancement is best served by initiatives of American capitalism.

THE OLD GUARD CIVIL RIGHTS LEADERSHIP

Challenged effectively on the right, the Old Guard Civil Rights Leadership was forced to move reluctantly to the left. Jesse Jackson, Southern Christian Leadership Conference President Joseph E. Lowery and Coretta Scott King participated in demonstrations involving 9,000 people in Mobile, Alabama, on April 26, and 3,000 people in Montgomery, Alabama, on August 9, to protest Congressional moves to repeal the Voting Rights Act of 1965.[26] Georgia State Senator Julian Bond and the Institute for Southern Studies led a thorough investigation of the murders of the Communist Workers Party members in Greensboro, North Carolina, in 1979, charging the police with "gross negligence."[27] Benjamin Hooks, Executive Director of the NAACP, Vernon Jordan, former Urban League head, and Coretta Scott King were speakers at the massive Solidarity March in Washington, D.C., on September 19, 1981, attracting hundreds of thousands of trade unionists and political opponents of Reaganism.[28]

One of the most publicized efforts of the Old Guard was the boycott of Coca-Cola products. Jesse Jackson's PUSH organization published information on the nonexistent affirmative action record of Coca-Cola, pointing out that not a single one of Coke's 550 bottlers or its 4,000 fountain wholesalers was black. The corporate giant had on deposit only $254,000 in ten black banks. When Coke executives balked during negotiations, PUSH and others initiated a black nationwide boycott of the soft drink on July 11, 1981. Coca-Cola was removed from the shelves of four black-owned Seven Eleven franchises in Washington, D.C., and white-owned franchises in that city did the same. Gary mayor Richard Hatcher, Chairperson of the Black Mayors Conference, authorized a move to ban Coke machines from 194 black-controlled city halls. When more than one hundred stores in Chicago's metropolitan area joined the boycott, Coke president Donald R. Keough announced his readiness to give black entrepreneurs "a piece of the action." The agreement represented a "promise that the free enterprise system can do more to develop opportunity for all elements of society."[29]

Coke's "moral covenant" with PUSH included the following provisions: increase the number of black-owned distributors to 32 within 12 months, establish a venture capital fund of $1.8 million for black petty capitalists, elevate a black to Coca-Cola's Board of Directors, double the amount of advertising capital spent with black agencies, quadruple the amount of financial deposits within black banks, and hire 100 black blue-collar employees. The total package amounted to $34 million. Black newspapers widely publicized the boycott, calling it a "wonderful reunion fellowship" of Martin Luther King, Jr.'s old colleagues, including Mrs. King, Lowery, Hosea Williams, Andrew Young, Maynard Jackson and Jesse Jackson. William Raspberry, never at a loss for words, proclaimed the historical deal "as important to black America as the boycott of the Montgomery, Alabama bus company a quarter of the century ago."[30]

The reality behind the rhetoric is somewhat different. Coke's white investors were furious with what was described as "outright blackmail" and "a $30 million giveaway plan." On September 3, Coca-Cola President Keough informed the *Atlanta Constitution* that the corporation had neither bowed to "pressure" from black leaders, nor had given the boycott more than "two minutes' attention because we never considered it a real issue." By October 1981, Coke officials informed the media that any money lent to blacks for venture capital will be at high market rates. No forced changes in bottling franchise ownerships will occur. Black advertising was increased to only $2 million from the previous $1.2 million figure. No loans will be made to black-owned banks except at competitive rates. Even the one hundred additional jobs may not materialize, because Coke "might be replacing blacks with blacks," declared a company executive. The conspicuous failure of the Coca-Cola boycott symbolized more than ever before the utter bankruptcy of "Black Capitalism."[31]

The lack of any basic grassroots orientation or support of the Old Guard was illustrated at the 11th Annual Congressional Black Caucus weekend in Washington, D.C., on September 25-27, 1981. The self-described "Black leadership family" included over 1,000 black doctors, lawyers, politicians and bureaucrats. One participant suggested that the Black Struggle in the 1980s would be led by "cadres of Black professionals." Joe Madison, an NAACP official, stated that: the militancy of the old days "during the Montgomery bus boycott" were passé. "We've got to develop technical militants out of these middle-class affluent Blacks who have received training, acquired good educations and have worked themselves into the mainstream of economic life."[32] Neither the multitude of fashion shows nor the $150-a-plate awards banquet could provide the cultural cohesion necessary to forge new unity among this "Untalented Tenth." Frequently they quarreled among themselves on a variety of public issues. Representative Gus Savage correctly denounced Vernon Jordan, publisher John H. Johnson, NAACP President Margaret Bush Wilson and Rev. Leon Sullivan for sitting on corporate boards and sharing in the "ill-begotten super profits" from doing business in "fascist South Africa."[33] At state levels, black Democrats joined forces with white Republicans in reapportionment cases to increase the percentages of blacks and/or whites within their respective Congressional districts. The most vocal advocate of the growing legislative detente between these unlikely forces is Julian Bond, a democratic socialist and the most "progressive" black elected official in the South. The *Atlanta Constitution* charged that "the cynical coalition" of "ghetto Black politicians and country club Republicans" sought "to gut Atlanta for the sake of electing [Bond] to the Congress," while simultaneously extending GOP hegemony across the state.[34]

CONCLUSION

History illustrates that the petty bourgeoisie of an oppressed nation or nationality is incapable by itself of struggling to achieve political and economic equality under capitalism. In *Class Struggle in Africa,* Kwame Nkrumah asserted that during national liberation efforts the black elite responds in one of three ways. "Firstly, there are those who are heavily committed to colonialism and to capitalist economic and social development." The second category, the nationalists, "want to end colonial rule" but oppose "a transformation of society." The third group simply "sits on the fence," supporting the militant actions of black workers and the peasantry when it suits their own narrow interests.[35]

Politically, the black elite will go so far as to subvert its own institutions, betray its own representatives, and coalesce with the most vicious racists if conditions for progressive change seem temporarily remote. During the historical period dominated by Booker T. Washington, a deliberate policy of subordination occurred in many cities and states wherein black petty bourgeois politicians became junior partners within white political machines. In Cincinnati during the 1890s, black Republicans joined the Democratic organization which "permitted the black bourgeoisie some limited mobility into other sections of the city, as well as certain material benefits." The Pendergast Democratic machine in Kansas City, Missouri, won black Republican support "through granting of patronage and welfare benefits" in the early 1900s. The Democratic machine of Harry F. Byrd dominated the black Republican electorate in Virginia for four decades "via policy enactment and paternalistic overtures," despite his "minimal interest in black rights," advocacy of poll taxes and literacy tests, and opposition to the *Brown* decision of 1954.[36] The modern realignment in black politics is essentially a repetition of this classical pattern of petty bourgeois opportunism and accommodation.

The goals of the Civil Rights Movement, which promoted at least rhetorically the necessity of social democratic reforms (e.g., food, public health care, child care, job training, free education, etc.) have been abandoned by major sectors of the black elite. It becomes the task of black progressive nationalists and activists in this period to complete this interrupted "revolution" for civil rights and social equality within the framework of the existing system. The burden of our history is two-fold. We must advance reformist programs within communities which reinforce black-owned socioeconomic and cultural institutions, advocating the maintenance of needed social service programs that affect the black working class and the poor. But we must insist uncompromisingly that the social crises confronting black people reflect a more fundamental contradiction created in part by the crisis of capital accumulation. Self-determination for black America cannot be forged unless our politics, in theory and in practice, also oppose sexual exploitation, imperialism, and monopoly capitalism. The revolt for reforms within the capitalist state today transcends itself dialectically to become a revolution against the racist/capitalist system tomorrow.

This strategy, which essentially involves a gradualist "war of opinion" culminating in a "war of maneuver" against capitalism, has strengths and weaknesses. The National Black Independent Political Party emerged during this current period of political realignment on August 23, 1980, at the fourth convention of the National Black Political Assembly in New Orleans. Reading a substitute motion drafted by Ohio activist Ron Daniels, the Reverend Ben Chavis called for the creation of a new kind of mass-based party for Afro-Americans. The function of such a party, Chavis declared, "is to advance a politics of social transformation and self-determination for the Black Nation ... primarily devoted to infrastructural, institutional and organizational development within the Black Community, providing community services, engaging in community struggles, lobbying around private and public policy issues and electoral politics."[37] During the planning sessions for the Founding Convention of the NBIPP, held in Philadelphia on November 21–23, 1980, the Party defined itself as a "progressive mass party" which serves "the interests of the working class and the poor and actively opposes racism, sexism, capitalism and imperialism." The Party also "aimed at altering the balance of power to affect the quality of goods and services to the people," while contending "for power within the existing socioeconomic institutions of America."[38]

The recent First Party Congress of NBIPP, held in Chicago on August 21–24, 1981, concretized this reformist/revolutionary analysis in the successful ratification of a permanent platform, program and statement of principles. The document is perhaps the most visionary yet practical statement on black liberation ever drafted by a delegate assembly in black history. The obvious strength of the policy is that NBIPP's potential for growth is practically limitless, given the chaotic state of the black elite, if it succeeds in building community-oriented institutions (e.g., consumer and producer cooperatives, liberation academies, etc.). The long-term danger does exist that many within NBIPP will stop their political praxis at the stage of reformism within the existing system, without recognizing the inevitable necessity of dismantling the capitalist state and expropriating the ownership of the means of production from the white, largely male, capitalist class. This transformation will not be achieved without violence.

There is no black capitalist or black petty bourgeois road toward black self-determination and liberation. The organic crisis of capital accumulation combined with the emergence of Reaganism within public policy promises to heighten the contradictions within society in the 1980s. Elements of the black middle class and intelligentsia who choose to commit "class suicide" in the manner described by Amilcar Cabral, combined with black workers and the unemployed, can wage a successful war of position to overturn the black Reaganites and the Old Guard Negro elites. In the final analysis, however, the historic goals of black nationalism cannot and will not be achieved, unless a firm commitment to a socialist reconstruction in America is placed on the public agenda. The future of the Black Nation will be determined by our relative success or failure to transcend our own history, making visionary yet practical demands that cannot be resolved within the existing order.

~

THE UNFINISHED REVOLUTION

Three events in 1983 symbolised for many Americans the tremendous advances gained by blacks during the previous three decades. In April, black Democratic Congressman Harold Washington was narrowly elected mayor of Chicago, the country's most segregated city. With an unlikely coalition of blacks, Hispanics, liberal trade unionists, feminists and white leftists, Washington upset a reactionary political machine which had dominated blacks for a half century. On 27 August, about 300,000 Americans (about three fourths of whom were black) staged a successful demonstration in Washington DC under the slogan, 'Jobs, Peace and Freedom'. Although technically promoted as the 'Twentieth Anniversary' celebration of the historic march of 1963 led by Martin Luther King Jr, the political programme was significantly further left of the earlier mobilisation, linking the issues of full employment, the necessity for massive cuts in defence expenditure and an end to US intervention in Central America. Finally, the sudden emergence of civil rights leader Jesse Jackson as a possible candidate for the Democratic Party's presidential nomination threw political leaders of both parties into disarray. Political analysts noted that black voters now comprise over one fifth of the normal Democratic Party electorate and that any massive registration drive within black communities would probably determine the 1984 elections, just as blacks had been a decisive component of Jimmy Carter's victory in 1976.

The massive changes in American race relations and politics are striking in other respects. In Birmingham, Alabama, only 20 years ago, police chief 'Bull' Connor unleashed dogs and levied clubs and firehoses against passive black protestors. Today, the mayor of Birmingham is a black progressive, Richard Arrington. In September 1968, Andrew Young was arrested for blocking sanitation trucks during a strike of black garbage workers. Four years later, he was elected to Congress; today he is the mayor of Atlanta. Less than a decade ago, Howard Fuller was an avowed proponent of 'Marxism-Leninism-Mao Tse Tung' thought, a leader of the revolutionary Malcolm X College in North Carolina. Late last year, he became a cabinet member and top black administrator to the governor of Wisconsin. Marion Berry, currently mayor of Washington DC, first became involved in politics two decades ago as a militant leader of the Student Non-violent Coordinating Committee. The defiant youths of the Black Power generation have now reached middle age and many are ensconced in higher education, government and trade union leadership. One could say that the civil rights and Black Power movements have come of age.

Superficially, the sheer numbers of blacks moving into positions of power seem to validate the myth of American cultural pluralism and democracy. The number of black elected officials nationwide jumped from 103 in 1964 to 5,003 in 1980. The number of blacks in Congress increased from 5 in 1964 to 21 in 1983. While, on the economic front—for young black adults with college degrees—the traditional income gap between white and black had virtually disappeared by 1977. In the northern and far-western states, the incomes of black two-parent families in this educational category actually exceeded that of white families—$16,715 to $16,691—by 1976.

The essential problem with this Horatio Alger saga of success is that these examples are exceptions to the rule. While about 9.4 million white family heads earn at least $35,000 annually, only 375,000 black families earn that figure, out of a black population of 28 million. As of three years ago, 548,000 white males reported personal incomes in excess of $75,000. Only 4,000 black men and fewer than 500 black women earned this figure—mostly professional athletes, celebrities, physicians and a few token administrators. There is a tiny black elite, but it has not become anything approaching a powerful class.

The number of blacks being trained in the professions is still pitifully small. A profile of the 1981–82 recipients of doctorates in the US illustrates the problem. Only 1,133 of the 31,048 Americans receiving doctorates were black, about 3.6 percent of the total. The vast majority of them, 850 or 75 percent, were concentrated in two fields: education and social sciences. Only 29 of the 3,348 doctorates in the physical sciences went to Afro-Americans; in advanced mathematics, 6 out of 720; engineering, 20 of 2,644; and, in the growing field of computer sciences, only about one out of 220 doctorates.

As a rule, black people tend to work in industries that are contracting. Over a quarter of all black workers are employed in manufacturing—steel, autos, textiles, etc—and another 13 percent are in the public sector. Conversely, blacks are under-represented in those areas of the economy which will experience the most rapid growth over the coming years—high technology, energy, agribusiness.

Thus the present and future employment status for the vast majority of blacks, short of some democratic socialist reorganisation of the US economy, is grim indeed. In 1969, non-white unemployment in the US stood at 6.4 percent, compared to 3.1 percent for whites. By 1977, 13.1 percent of all black men and 14.8 percent of black women were unemployed. After several years of Reaganomics in the 1980s, the situation became critical. Black youth unemployment in some ghettoes exceeded 80 percent last summer and, during Reagan's first year in office, the real median income of black families declined by 5.2 percent. Even Reagan's 'tax cut', passed two years ago to stimulate consumer savings, actually perpetuated racial inequality. The average white household was scheduled to receive $1,019 in tax breaks in 1983 and $1,369 in 1984, whereas black households averaged $542 in 1983 and $632 in 1984.

This steady deterioration of blacks' economic basis within American society has produced devastating socio-economic consequences: an alarming increase in alcoholism, drug abuse, crime and juvenile delinquency. By the late 1970s, over 2 million Afro-Americans were arrested *every year*. About half of the 600,000 American men behind bars and the 1,300 awaiting execution on death row are black. Over 10,000 black men are murdered every year. Black male homicide rates are eight to nine times higher than for white males. The black family has been fundamentally transformed by this process of social chaos. In 1960, for example, 75 percent of all black children lived with both parents, today, about 55 percent of all black families have only one parent or guardian, and the older social institutions which provided stability and order within black neighbourhoods during the segregation era—churches, civic clubs, community associations—have been seriously weakened, if not destroyed.

As if these problems were not enough, the re-emergence of a particularly virulent form of racist violence has compounded the plight of black labour. Since the late 1970s, nearly 500 cases of Ku Klux Klan terror and murders have been documented. Five hundred additional incidents of racist violence have been recorded—not counting other forms of brutality, such as police violence. One dozen lynchings and/or racist murders were recorded in Mississippi alone during 1980. Civil rights leaders, black politicians and community organisers have been arrested and beaten, with little media publicity. My wife's brother, a black policeman in a rural Georgia town, was killed by a racist seven years ago; in December 1981, her cousin was lynched by vigilantes. Former National Urban League Director Vernon Jordan was nearly assassinated in Indiana several years ago—his assailant later acquitted by an all-white jury. Despite the existence of 'anti-Klan' statutes and other federal laws to reduce racist violence, Reagan's Attorney General, William French Smith, has refused to pursue nearly all of these cases. The US Justice Department has prosecuted barely two dozen of such cases in the past three years. The terror continues.

Thus the central dilemma of black politics today is that the Afro-American community is no longer monolithic economically, culturally, or politically. The vast majority of blacks are trapped within either the lowly paid blue collar workforce, or are in the growing 'underclass' of the poor. Their world is filled with crime, decaying housing, inadequate social services and a constant fear of unemployment. The small black elite usually lives outside the sprawling ghetto, in the residential neighbourhoods of upper-middle-class whites. While this section of the black population forms part of the basis for the small trend toward political conservatism within minority communities, the black majority is forced to turn toward more radical socio-economic and political solutions. The elite looks to the Democratic Party as part of the solution; the black majority increasingly views it as part of the problem.

It is only in this context that the debate around a black presidential candidacy in 1984 can be understood. Jesse Jackson, the most charismatic black leader on the current scene, is the personification of *both* class positions of the black community, a curious mixture of populist demagogue Huey Long, black nationalist Marcus Garvey and Martin Luther King. Like many black nationalists, Jackson charges that the Democratic Party has been 'taking the black vote for granted and the Republican Party (has been) writing us off. For Democrats, race is increasingly becoming a litmus test and the central threat to the viability of the Party'. Jackson observes that black

Democrats 'have won primaries in South Carolina, North Carolina, Mississippi' and other states, but 'significant numbers of white Democratic leaders and voters' are supporting white Republicans over blacks. This racist backlash is also occurring in a climate of severe economic chaos, with 'the rapidly deteriorating conditions within black and poor communities'.

Jackson's black nationalistic rhetoric culminates in a two-pronged 'assault' on the system. First, black consumers must be united to force corporate concessions to the fragile black entrepreneurial class. 'Corporate economic rape', to use Jackson's term, can be curtailed by forcing 'joint trade agreements' between civil rights agencies and big businesses. Typical of Jackson's efforts was the four-year 'covenant' signed between Operation PUSH and the Burger King Corporation, on 18 April 1983. The food chain (which is worth an estimated $450 million and owns 3,400 restaurants worldwide) promised to increase the number of black employees, upgrade existing minority-owned restaurants and increase significantly the number of black franchises. Using black nationalist bluster, these agreements are actually a 'Black Capitalist' strategy, designed to win the favour of the black elite.

The second and more 'leftist' aspect of Jackson's effort revolves round the concept of a black presidential strategy. Relying upon a bizarre series of mixed metaphors, Jackson asserts that a black candidate within the Democratic party primaries would be able to 'advance the issues of concern to Hispanics, women, the poor and whites who are interested in social justice ... as well as blacks, A black should run because bargainers without bases are beggars not brokers ... We cannot ride to freedom on Pharaoh's chariot ... All of Santa's other reindeer have had their chance to pull and lead the sleigh and present their gifts to the American people. Now it may be time for Rudolph, who has consistently pulled more weight, to have his turn ...'

The issue of a black campaign has split the black community primarily on class lines. The black poor and working class overwhelmingly endorse Jackson's call for a black revolt inside the Democratic Party. Visiting urban ghettos and rural black Southern towns throughout the summer, Jackson attracted thousands of enthusiastic blacks. Despite the presence of NAACP leader, Benjamin Hooks, Coretta Scott King and other black middle-class dignitaries, Jackson emerged as the 'star' of the 27 August march on Washington, as thousands cheered in unison, 'Run, Jesse, Run!' Some black entrepreneurs, who have directly profited from Jackson's corporate covenants, have backed the effort, as have the more liberal and socialist members of the Congressional Black Caucus.

Most black middle-class leaders, however, have expressed outrage, even outright contempt, for the black presidential boom. Bayard Rustin, a founder of the Congress of Racial Equality and the leading black apologist for the AFL-CIO bureaucracy, claims that 'an exclusively black candidacy not only would end in political failure and split the black electorate, it would do harm to the strategy of coalition politics and to the interests of the black community.' National Urban League President John F. Jacobs declares that 'a black presidential candidate would be a retreat to symbolism' amd would 'shatter black expectations'. Coleman Young denounced Jackson by name, stating: 'We cannot afford to support a black candidate who cannot win,'

Andrew Young has tried to distance himself from the controversy: 'I talk to Jesse all the time so it's hard for me not to support (him). But I think blacks ought to be in any campaign where the candidate is likely to be elected president.'

No matter what the outcome is of Jackson's effort, it has been the opening stage of a more fundamental shift in black political culture, and in the directions of the civil rights movement as a whole. Working-class and poor blacks are recognising in growing numbers that their 'race leaders' in the NAACP and Urban League do not speak for them. The black elite's tactic of coalescence with the centrist policies of the Democratic Party under Carter and, if elected, a Mondale or Glenn, would do nothing to alter the socio-economic crisis within their committees. By 1988 the renewed call for an independent black challenge will, of necessity, include a left social democratic programme—full employment, national health care, massive reductions in military expenditures, increases in public housing—to provide institutional and social support to the black ghetto. If such a black revolt is combined with a coalition of similarly disposed groups within Hispanic and white populations, and in concert with the more left-oriented feminist, peace and environmentalist groups, a major shift in the entire American political terrain may be possible. The next stage of the unfinished civil rights movement may place the question of a kind of uniquely American form of democratic socialism on the national agenda.

~

African Links

In late 1984, two separate events occurred on opposite sides of the globe which culminated in the most dramatic and unexpected social movement in recent US history. Last September, approximately 50,000 mineworkers went on strike inside South Africa. Mobilising millions of nonwhites, the United Democratic Front, a multiracial coalition of more than 600 groups, initiated a series of protest actions. Tensions peaked on 5–6 November, when one million workers staged a general strike. The apartheid regime responded in the only language it comprehends. Almost 200 people were murdered, several thousand were detained without charges, and roughly 6,000 labourers were dismissed from their jobs.

On 6 November in the US, Ronald Reagan was re-elected to a second term in office by an historic 'mandate'. As in the struggles inside South Africa, the dimension of race was crucial in the national political culture. Approximately 66 percent of all white voters endorsed Reagan, compared to barely 10 percent of the Black electorate. Reagan received key support from white Southerners (72 percent), 'born-again' white Christians (80 percent) and whites with annual incomes above $50,000 (68 percent).

One important factor contributing to Blacks' hostility towards the Reagan Administration was its record of close cooperation with apartheid. During his 1984 presidential campaign, civil rights leader Jesse Jackson repeatedly attacked the President's policy of 'constructive engagement' with Pretoria—the decisions to back IMF loans to South Africa, the US training of the South African Coast Guard, the sending of 2,500 electric shock batons to apartheid's police force, and the establishment of offices in Johannesburg designed to stimulate US investment in the country.

Jackson's emphasis on South Africa forced the Democratic Party's 1984 platform to include a call for the immediate release of African National Congress leader Nelson Mandela, and the freeing of 'all other political prisoners in South Africa.' This was the *first* time that any major US party has denounced apartheid unconditionally.

Given Reagan's fresh electoral victory, it seemed probable that the Administration would do absolutely nothing to pressure Pretoria over the next four years. Similarly on domestic issues, the Administration was likely to escalate its attacks on civil rights legislation, public housing, and social services essential to the Black community. Activists felt that some form of aggressive protest was necessary to restore the momentum from the Jackson campaign, as well as to provide active solidarity to the militants inside South Africa.

The prime architect of the Free South Africa Movement (FSAM) was Randall Robinson, executive director of Trans-africa, a lobbying agency based in Washington DC. Robinson and two other supporters of last year's Jackson campaign, Civil Rights Commissioner Mary Frances Berry and Black Congressman Walter Fauntroy, decided to hold a non-violent protest at the South African Embassy on 21 November. The choice of 'non-violent' tactics was inevitable: Fauntroy had been a close associate of Dr Martin Luther King Jr, and was the co-ordinator of the 1983 March on Washington. The three leaders obtained an interview with the South African ambassador and upon their arrival announced their intention not to leave the building. Embassy officials panicked and called police; the three were 'pleasantly surprised' when they were arrested for trespassing.

Within several days, other members of the Congressional Black Caucus held nonviolent demonstrations in front of the South African Embassy and were arrested. Rosa Parks, the initiator of the famous 1955 Montgomery, Alabama, bus boycott movement, and the Reverend Joseph Lowery, leader of the Southern Christian Leadership Conference, soon followed. In weeks, the FSAM began to acquire national dimensions. Virtually all of the leaders of Jackson's 'Rainbow Coalition', plus many other liberals who had supported either Walter Mondale or Gary Hart for the Democratic nomination, volunteered to be among those arrested.

Even groups which had vigorously opposed Jackson's candidacy found it difficult to disagree with the new movement. Initially a few Orthodox and Conservative Jewish groups refused to join the protests, primarily because of Israel's extensive economic and political links with the apartheid regime. But within two weeks, virtually all of the major Jewish organisations, including leaders of the American Jewish Congress and the Union of American Hebrew Congregations, had taken part in the demonstrations. Even 'celebrities' got involved: among those arrested were two children of the late Senator Robert F. Kennedy, tennis star Arthur Ashe, actor Harry Belafonte, and recording artist Stevie Wonder who chose to accept his Oscar award last week in the name of Nelson Mandela, and promptly got his music banned in South Africa. Most of the media coverage focused on the Washington DC and New York City demonstrations, but thousands of Blacks and progressive whites initiated actions in other cities as well. On 6 December, Fauntroy and Lowery led several hundred demonstrators in a 'pray-in' protest at the home of the honorary South African consul in Mobile, Alabama. The next day, in Berkeley, California, one thousand students staged an anti-apartheid rally, blockading the central administration building for three hours, resulting in 38 arrests. Simultaneously in Cleveland, Ohio, over 200 trade unionists, religious leaders and civil rights activists held a public demonstration. On 9 December, four hundred demonstrators in Seattle, Washington, picketed the home of the honorary consul, leading to 23 arrests.

Since virtually all of the protests involved civil disobedience, and occurred without physical confrontations with police, most of the religious community quickly lined up behind the FSAM at both local and national levels. Religious supporters included the United Church of Christ Board of World Ministries, the National Association of American Nuns, the American Muslim Mission, and the National Conference of Catholic Bishops. Conservative evangelicals were left in the cold. The Reverend Jerry Falwell fumed that 'if we aren't (in South Africa), the Soviets will take over.' But few leading clergy were listening.

As the protests increased, the Reagan Administration first tried to minimise their significance, announcing that they would have absolutely 'no impact' on Reagan's approach of constructive engagement' with South Africa. 'The real losers in this are the Black community,' blurted one White House official to the press. But sensing a sudden shift in public opinion, most members of Congress and local elected officials sided with the FSAM.

At local levels, FSAM supporters in 44 state legislatures introduced legislation demanding disinvestment of public funds from banks with ties to South Africa. The National Conference of Black Mayors, which includes over 300 cities, voiced support for public disinvestment. In a widely publicised visit to South Africa, Senator Edward Kennedy expressed sharp opposition to the Botha government's repression of trade unionists and leaders of the United Democratic Front. Although criticised in the US press for attempting to gain political leverage for his anticipated presidential campaign in 1988, Kennedy nevertheless was able to focus international attention on human rights violations in South Africa.

By mid-March, over 2,000 arrests had taken place, with the total number of protestors exceeding half a million nationwide. The media has tended to give low coverage to the demonstrations, however, and has focused attention on the issue of disinvestment. US investment inside South Africa, $15 billion in 1984, totals 20 percent of all foreign direct investment in South Africa. US corporations control 70 percent of the South African computer market, and an IBM computer helps run the stock exchange in Johannesburg. As of 1983, Mobil Oil had $426 million invested in South Africa, and a workforce of 3,577; General Motors, $243 million and 5,038 employees; Union Carbide, $54.5 million and 2,465 employees. American banks, led by Chase Manhattan, Bankers Trust, Chemical and Manufacturers Hanover, had outstanding loans in South Africa totalling nearly $4 billion in 1984.

The press has seized any Black figure it can find in recent weeks who advances the thesis that US investment, under 'liberal guidelines,' may actually promote a peaceful, democratic transition inside South Africa. The Reverend Leon Sullivan of Philadelphia, for example, has authored the 'Sullivan Principles' which advocate continued US corporate expansion in South Africa with provisions for desegregated workplace facilities, mandatory equal pay for jobs, and the training of non-whites in administrative and supervisory positions. In early February, Chief Gatsha Buthelezi, leader of South Africa's six million Zulus, met with President Reagan and strongly supported the Administration's opposition to economic sanctions.

The difficulties of these postures of accommodation by both Sullivan and Buthelezi are relatively simple to illustrate. First, as Free South Africa Movement leaders have noted, only 66,000 members of South Africa's six million labour force are employed by US firms which have signed the 'Sullivan Principles'. But even according to Sullivan's own annual reports, progress along such lines is at best marginal. In the 1983 report, it was noted that white employees filled 94 percent of all new managerial posts, and that non-white workers had 'lost ground steadily in clerical-administrative programs over the last three years.'

Secondly, a vital if problematic link, there is the negative impact of US corporate investment inside South Africa upon the American working class. The chief economic characteristic of apartheid is that rigid racial stratification of the labour force lowers the wage rate.

How does this investment affect American workers? Researchers for the Washington Office on Africa and the Civil Rights Department of the United Steel-workers of America recently prepared a brief study on this issue. Between 1974 and 1982 domestic steel production declined by 50 percent. In 1983, the seven largest steel producers reported losses of $2.7 billion that year alone. Major industrial towns dependent upon steel productivity to generate jobs have had staggeringly high rates of joblessness. Simultaneously, the US steel industry has siphoned off domestic profits and reinvested them in Third World nations where authoritarian regimes guarantee a low wage and non-unionised labour force. Imports from foreign nations producing steel now exceed one fifth of the domestic market. And since 1975, US imports of apartheid's steel have increased by 5,000 percent.

South African steel is largely produced by a state-owned firm, the Iron and Steel Corporation (ISCOR). All of the major US companies which have experienced difficulties producing steel at home—ARMCO, Allegheny Ludlum, US Steel, Phelps Dodge, and others—have invested millions into apartheid's industries. Recently, Chicago's Southworks steel plant, owned by US Steel, laid off several thousand workers, on the rationale that US workers weren't sufficiently productive and that the plant wasn't making profits. Then local steel workers learned that the steel beams used to build a new state office building in Chicago had been imported from South Africa—despite the fact that Southworks produces the identical steel beams. Even more outrageous was the fact that Continental Illinois Bank has loaned money to ISCOR, which had produced these beams. In short, Chicago labourers were giving their hard-earned wages to a local bank, which in turn financed a competitor which was stealing their jobs!

For these economic reasons, the conservative AFL-CIO has broken with tradition by vigorously supporting the FSAM. Thomas R. Donahue, secretary-treasurer of the AFL-CIO, Charles A. Perlik, president of the Newspaper Guild, Leon Lynch, vice president of the United Steelworkers, and Joslyn Williams, president of the Washington DC Central Labor Council, were among those arrested in Washington DC.

Workers in San Francisco made perhaps the most militant contribution to the FSAM. On 26 November last year, longshoremen in that city refused to unload cargo which had originated in South Africa. After nearly a two week stalemate, a court injunction forced them to unload the cargo. Longshoreman Leo Robinson explained to the press that workers comprehended the connections between trade union struggles in South Africa and in the US. 'The shipping interests,' he said, force us 'to unload cargo such as steel and auto glass, made by slave labour at non-union wages. It has meant that we unload steel from South Africa, which means that steel workers here lose their jobs.' Robinson added, 'Our conscience makes us rise above such laws. It's a matter of conscience, with us, and of thinking about our brothers and sisters in apartheid-run South Africa.'

One must not minimise the fragility of such a united front which has attempted to link international and domestic agendas. Moderate elements within the FSAM have become increasingly uncomfortable with the spontaneous, mass dimensions of the mobilisation. Some problems can be traced to Robinson's selections on the FSAM Steering Committee. Some Committee members chosen—notably NAACP leader Benjamin Hooks—have little knowledge of the anti-apartheid movement or the issues at stake. Others who were left off the Committee, such as Black militant Jean Sindab of the Washington Office on Africa, might have strengthened the activist tendencies of the protests. Some Marxists and Black nationalists question the value of peaceful, almost passive protests, noting that lists of each day's demonstrators are regularly provided to the Washington DC police. Arrests are made with the agreement that the acts of civil disobedience are purely symbolic, and that all criminal charges are to be dropped by authorities.

Probably the major weakness of such a social movement is found in its historical and theoretical orientation. Although many Black Americans in earlier generations retained a strong sense of cultural and social identity with Africa, during most of the twentieth century such expressions of solidarity were muted. The principal political contradiction confronting Afro-Americans was produced by the rise of racial segregation. Blacks were denied the right to vote, were refused employment or service in public establishments, and were forcibly removed from white neighbourhoods. Over five thousand Black Americans were lynched between 1882 and 1927, and many publicly burned. The new racial codes segregated all sports facilities, restaurants, buses and trains. Birmingham, Alabama, even outlawed Blacks and whites from playing checkers or dominoes together.

Facing the reaction against racial equality, most Black American leaders now advocated a political philosophy of civil rights and integration. Blacks were 'fully American', and as such, should be extended basic civil liberties and rights shared by whites. Any connection with Africa was deliberately ignored or forgotten. Gradually, by the 1950s, most Black Americans knew little about Africa's history or its people.

Yet the links between Africa and Afro-Americans did not disappear entirely during these years. W E B Du Bois, noted civil rights leader, sponsored an important series of political conferences which brought together West Indians, Black Americans and Africans between 1900 and 1945. In increasing numbers, African intellectuals came to the US and took part in desegregation campaigns. Nhamdi Azikiwe of Nigeria and Kwame Nkrumah of Ghana both attended all-Black Lincoln University in Pennsylvania. Their respective rise to power in the 1950s was covered extensively in Black American newspapers, and the achievement of African independence captured the imaginations of US Blacks.

After African independence, connections across the Atlantic deepened in both symbolic and concrete ways. In downtown Dar-es-Salaam and in Nairobi, major streets were named in honour of Du Bois, the 'father of Pan-Africanism'. In South Africa, young Black leaders such as the late Steve Biko developed their 'Black Consciousness' movement against apartheid by drawing upon the rhetoric and tactics of the 'Black Power' movement of the 1960s. Black American students and tourists in increasing numbers began to make pilgrimages to their 'homeland'; US Black cultural fashions and hairstyles began consciously to imitate African patterns.

Ironically, it was only with the achievement of desegregation and the granting of democratic political rights in the 1960s that Black Americans could fully revive their political and cultural relations with Africa. Black mayors and elected officials began to use their offices to develop closer economic and civic ties with their African counterparts. Black members of Congress lobbied for increased US aid to support Africa's development, and pressured administrations to halt economic and political support for apartheid.

Yet this renewed interest in Africa obscured the fundamental differences between national liberation struggles and racial reforms within a bourgeois democracy. There was, and still exists, a tendency to view the events in South Africa through the prism of the civil rights and Southern desegregation experience: thus many protestors today carry signs stating that 'the Ku Klux Klan is in power' in South Africa. Tactics developed to fit a particular conjuncture of political and social forces in the early 1960s are therefore revived in an uncritical fashion, without efforts to encourage political education among the masses of protestors on the political economy of apartheid. Pragmatically, the campaign has succeeded in mobilising an eclectic array of constituencies around an important public policy issue, but it is exceedingly problematic whether this unity, lacking deep roots, can be maintained beyond the next 12 months.

There are, fortunately, some signs that the FSAM has gained results. Manufacturers Hanover Bank recently announced its refusal to grant any loans to the South African government or to sell its Kruggerrand gold coins unless it initiates steps to 'generate improved circumstances for the whole population' of South Africa. A total of 40 American universities have disinvested over $175 million in stocks linked to South Africa. This Thursday, 4 April, hundreds of thousands of US students plan to stage simultaneous protests against apartheid. And on 20 April, thousands of Americans will protest in Washington DC, calling for the destruction of the South African regime, as well as opposition to US intervention in Central America.

President Reagan may have received a sweeping electoral victory last year, yet it is clear that the progressive spectrum of American politics has taken away his 'mandate'. The issue of apartheid has reinforced democratic social protest in both domestic and international arenas—and promises to remain a major concern of US political life.

~

BLACK POLITICS IN CRISIS

For a quarter of a century, "black politics" has meant Democratic politics, and the black electorate has been the most progressive electoral bloc. But times are changing, not least because many black politicians have asked what, precisely, blacks have gained from their faithful allegiance to the Democratic Party.

The number of black Democrats in Congress has risen from five in 1964 to twenty-two in 1987, but black legislators as a group have little power. The Congressional Black Caucus was founded in 1971, but white Democratic leaders all but ignore it on most public-policy issues. The only black elected to the Senate during this period was Edward Brooke of Massachusetts, a liberal Republican. Few black Democrats have achieved statewide office, and those who seek such positions are often discouraged by their party's hierarchy. Black votes amount to 20 percent of the national Democratic bloc in Presidential elections, yet blacks are still treated as second-class citizens in the Democratic Party.

The early 1980s were a time of political upsurge in the black community—the 1983 March on Washington, the first mayoral campaign of Harold Washington in Chicago, the 1984 Presidential bid by Jesse Jackson—an upsurge that was part of a massive social reaction to the Reagan agenda and the triumph of the Right in national politics.

No one doubts that the black community is in the midst of a major social, economic, and political crisis. *Ebony* magazine recently called it "perhaps the biggest crisis blacks have faced since slavery time," one characterized by "a series of economic upheavals, exacerbated by an epidemic of hard drugs and structural faults in the American economy, [which] have undermined the social infrastructure of black America."

The statistics speak for themselves. More than 40 percent of all black families are headed by women, and more than half of all black children live in poverty. The poverty rate is 67 percent for all black female-headed households. The official unemployment rate of blacks has generally exceeded 14 percent in the 1980s, and more than a fourth of all black adults are permanently outside the labor force. Social welfare programs, public housing, and education have been gutted. And this misery is directly related to the Hobbesian social policy of the Reagan Administration.

The political response—especially the Jackson candidacy—was really a social-protest movement manifested inside the electoral arena. And its essential contradiction was its necessary link to the Democratic Party. Most white Democratic leaders concur with central tenets of Reaganism: major reductions in social-welfare programs, huge increases in military expenditures, an aggressively anticommunist foreign policy, and so on. Jesse Jackson's Rainbow Coalition won no major concessions in the Democratic Party platform in 1984, but in post-election analyses party regulars were quick to blame him for their failure to attract white middle-class voters.

The recognition by many blacks of their status as second-class Democrats, as well as Jackson's inability to solidify the Rainbow Coalition at local levels and the stampede to the right by white Democratic leaders, have led, in some quarters, to a renaissance of black Republicanism. This conservative current is still weak but is beginning to gather strength.

In 1986, blacks ran as Republican candidates for Congress in Arkansas, Massachusetts, Michigan, Georgia, Illinois, Ohio, and Maryland. In Maryland, attorney George Haley (brother of Alex Haley, the author of *Roots*) was an unsuccessful Senate candidate in the Republican primary. In Atlantic City, New Jersey, James Usry, the black Republican mayor, was re-elected in a nonpartisan race. The black electorate will often vote for moderate Republicans, black or white, if they are perceived as friendly to blacks' traditional political interests and if they are running against Democrats who have little or no credibility among minorities.

The best such example came in New Jersey in 1985, when 60 percent of the black vote was cast for Republican Governor Thomas Kean. His pragmatic advice to blacks was that they should break their fifty-year allegiance to the Democrats. When he delivered that message to the San Francisco convention of the National Urban League last summer, he received a standing ovation.

"You have one party that the black community has given 85 to 90 percent of their votes to," he said, "and how much black leadership do you see in that party? I can tell you what's going on in my state. I don't see any black county chairmen, I don't see black state chairmen for that 90 percent. I don't see as many black legislators or mayors outside the black community. I don't see any gains."

Although Kean's analysis begs many questions and obscures the distinction between the respective social-class bases and programmatic orientations of the two major parties, his general point is correct. Blacks as a social group have not received political benefits from the Democratic leadership commensurate with their high levels of electoral support since 1940. Ambitious black politicians now recognize that they can go only so far in the Democratic Party's hierarchy, and no farther.

This was the political reality behind the well-publicized switch to the Republican Party made by Michigan politician William Lucas in May 1985. Lucas's background—former New York City police officer, FBI agent, and sheriff—appealed to the law-and-order constituency, and his fiscal conservatism and anti-abortion stance won the praises of right-wing populists and mainstream Republicans even when he served as Wayne County executive in Detroit. And as a black politician, Lucas was astute enough never to isolate himself from Detroit's black middle class. When he ran for governor in the 1986 Republican primary, thousands of black Democrats crossed over to vote for him, and he won the nomination.

Facing conservative Democratic incumbent Governor James J. Blanchard in the general election, Lucas had a more difficult time. Despite great dissatisfaction with Blanchard's tenure, a substantial majority of blacks supported a white "lesser evil" over a black rightist who campaigned with the endorsement of evangelist Pat Robertson. Lucas received only 31 percent of the vote but helped to reinforce the Republicans' public commitment to black candidates.

The Right's domination of the politics of white America has directly contributed to the. growth of ideological and cultural conservatism among blacks: "Black Reaganism." Some black conservatives have operated from within the Administration—Bush aide Thaddeus Garret, Reagan assistant Melvin Bradley, Thelma Duggin, formerly the Republican National Committee's liaison to the National Black Voters Program, to name a few.

The group's prime theoreticians have been economists, however: Thomas Sowell, Walter Williams, and Glenn Loury. Almost without exception, black Reaganites reject the traditional civil-rights agenda of affirmative action, government-sponsored social-welfare programs, and coalitions with liberal constituencies. Williams has condemned what he calls the "use of racial quotas for the purposes of redressing historical grievances" and urges the creation of a sub-minimum wage to promote black employment. Sowell, a former Marxist, best articulated the black conservative approach in late 1980 when he said, "Camelot seems unlikely to return and we cannot bet the future of twenty million blacks on its return. We have to recognize that many [liberal] methods were failing before they even lost public support."

Robert Woodson, president of the National Center for Neighborhood Enterprise, is another rising star of the black Right. Unlike Sowell and Williams, who often isolate themselves by their extreme laissez-faire rhetoric, Woodson maintains considerable credibility among black business and political leaders. In a recent interview, Woodson offered a thoughtful, if erroneous, critique of the strategic shortcomings of civil-rights organizations.

"Most groups in this society," Woodson said, "didn't start off trying to achieve political equity. They went into business. Blacks, unfortunately, have focused almost exclusively on civil rights for the past twenty years or so, as if applying civil-rights solutions would somehow translate into economic equity. It does not."

Woodson's basic argument—that "political power does not translate into economic power"—is an oversimplification. It is true that specific social classes with political leverage may not wield similar authority in the marketplace, and vice versa. But it is pure fantasy to suggest that social classes or even ethnic groups that achieve a level of political empowerment do not at least indirectly increase their capacity to realize their objective interests in the economic realm.

Moreover, Woodson hastily attempts to rewrite black political history as he juxtaposes the struggle for civil rights with black economic development. The first March on Washington, organized by trade unionist A. Philip Randolph in 1941, culminated in Executive Order 8802, which desegregated defense factories. The second March on Washington, twenty-two years later, called for a comprehensive jobs program. Affirmative action, a central tenet of the civil-rights agenda, has created hundreds of thousands of job opportunities for minorities and women. Despite the actual record, though, Woodson insists that civil-rights leaders have ignored economic issues, "If you have economic power," he repeats, "you vote every day with your money. If you have political power, you vote only once every two years."

To Woodson's right stands Harvard professor Glenn Loury, perhaps the most prominent black conservative since Reagan's reelection. Loury's argument, as presented recently in *The Christian Century,* is this: "It is time for the Negro middle class to rise up from its stool of indifference, to retreat from its flight into unreality and to bring its full resources—its heart, its mind, and its checkbook—to the aid of the less fortunate brother.... Our work today is not to change the minds of white people, but to involve ourselves in the lives of black people."

For many blacks, this notion has seductive appeal. No matter their political ideology, they often reiterate the ideals of black self-sufficiency, collective aid, and racial solidarity. The political history of this rhetoric can be traced in part from the ideas of black nationalism as expressed by Martin Delany, Marcus Garvey, and Malcolm X. However, when this language of self-assertion is combined with a political alliance with conservative Republicans and a blind faith in the power of American capitalism, it becomes the anachronistic program of Booker T. Washington.

Washington's political and educational achievements, including the establishment of Tuskegee Institute and the National Negro Business League, cannot be minimized. But his strategy of alliances with conservative white capitalists and Republicans was fundamentally flawed. Washington retreated from the political arena, tacitly accepted disfranchisement of black folk, and acknowledged the unequal status quo. Black families would simply have to learn to survive on their own, without government support. Washington never understood that the road of accommodation and black self-help, without a concomitant movement for equal rights and a struggle for social justice, led to a dead end.

When Loury and other black conservatives today declare that "our work is not to change the minds of whites," they contribute directly to the destruction of civil-rights and affirmative-action programs. Ultimately, they accelerate the economic and social crisis that affects black people as a whole.

Black self-help has never, by itself, been a substitute for an aggressive civil-rights movement which seeks to uproot racism. The plight of black communities worsens every time housing, health-care, and jobs programs are reduced or eliminated by the Reaganites of both political parties. When black women and men are forced into jobs at sub-minimum wage rates, how can they sustain healthy families? When welfare and education benefits are reduced to provide more funds for the Pentagon budget, how are the basic interests of the black community served? How can a poor black family pull itself up by its own bootstraps, when it has no boots?

Only a few black politicians realize that the Afro-American community's difficulties cannot be resolved by jumping from one capitalist party to another. The real problem is the inability of blacks and other liberal constituencies to construct an alternative political vehicle to advance their public-policy interests. As California Democratic Representative Ronald V. Dellums puts it, "Maybe we've arrived at a point where this system does not serve us well. I don't see anything sacrosanct about the two-party system."

A desperate people will turn to almost anything that promises some relief from oppression. A national environment of apathy toward the Afro-American condition translates into an insular political mentality among blacks themselves: "If our leaders are ineffective, if our organizations lack vision, and if the political system has turned against us, who will champion our interests?"

This reasoning has led many blacks to one of two strategies. The first is the black Reaganism of Sowell, Loury, and company, an updated version of Booker T. Washington's accommodationism. The second, potentially far more dangerous, is an unprecedented alliance with extreme ultra-rightists while continuing to pay lip service to the black community's traditional interests.

Consider the careers of James Bevel and Ralph David Abernathy. In the 1960s, Bevel was an important figure in the desegregation campaigns. With Marion Barry, James Lawson, and John Lewis, Bevel led the successful sit-in movement in Nashville. Bevel was a key strategist and stalwart for Martin Luther King Jr. in the difficult Birmingham desegregation campaign of 1963. Bevel was in Memphis with King five years later when he was assassinated. Abernathy was, of course, second only to King as a pivotal leader of the Southern struggle from Montgomery to Memphis.

Deprived of King's guidance, however, both men foundered, personally and politically. Abernathy was unable to keep up the momentum of the Southern Christian Leadership Conference (SCLC). Within a few years, he was overshadowed in the civil-rights field by his charismatic junior lieutenant, Jesse Jackson. Both Bevel and Abernathy ran unsuccessful races for Congress. As King's other protégés continued to make headlines—most prominently, Andrew Young—the flow of public events bypassed both these veterans, neither of whom exercised any clout within the Carter Administration.

In the 1980 election, Abernathy took a decisive step away from King's political legacy by endorsing Ronald Reagan for President. He justified this unexpected action by accusing the Carter Administration of a variety of sins. Coretta Scott King promptly attributed Abernathy's endorsement to sinister forces. Less charitably, some black journalists bitterly ridiculed Abernathy as a modern-day Judas or Uncle Tom.

Such criticism obscured the reality of a new conservative trend within sections of the black middle class. At least 12 percent of all blacks voted for Reagan in 1980. Two prominent black newspapers, Atlanta's *Daily World* and Cleveland's *Call and Post*, also backed the conservative Republican. Art Fletcher, the former executive director of the United Negro College Fund joined Reagan's campaign staff. His candidacy was also supported by Nathan Wright, the convenor of the famous 1968 Black Power Conference in Philadelphia, and by Georgia State Representative Hosea Williams, a past leader of the Student Nonviolent Coordinating Committee and organizer of the Poor People's Campaign of the late 1960s.

Abernathy and Bevel drifted even further to the right after 1980. Bevel became a Republican Party leader in Chicago's black community and soon earned a reputation as a right-wing extremist. By 1985, both former leaders had been drawn into the political orbit of CAUSA, an anticommunist front established by the Reverend Sun Myung Moon. Last April, Abernathy joined black radical-turned-reactionary Eldridge Cleaver at a CAUSA conference in Los Angeles. In May, Bevel and Abernathy were the key participants in a two-day "Freedom Rally and Convention" sponsored by CAUSA and held in the impoverished Lawndale section of Chicago's west side. CAUSA was created six years ago by supporters of the Unification Church, in an effort to forge conservative links to educators, clergy, and local elected officials.

The sad conversion of Abernathy and Bevel to CAUSA's agenda highlights the expanding role of the Unification Church within the black community. For more than a decade, Moon and his followers have pursued policies totally at odds with black interests. The church has donated hundreds of thousands of dollars to right-wing groups such as the National Conservative Political Action Committee, which opposes affirmative-action legislation and civil rights.

Moon's early public statements on race relations appear to have more in common with segregationst Lester Maddox than with Martin Luther King. In 1974, for instance, Moon stated his ideas on racial characteristics: "Orientals can contribute in the spiritual aspect, white people can contribute in the analytical, scientific aspect, while black people can contribute in the physical area." The actual number of black converts to the Moonies remains small. Yet CAUSA recently reprinted an early speech by King critical of communism, which provides a suitable ideological cover for their growing activities with blacks. Abernathy and Bevel, perhaps unwittingly, have become key pawns in this strategy. The right-wing sect of Lyndon LaRouche has also initiated a campaign to recruit black supporters. Like the Unification Church, the LaRouchites work primarily through fronts, the Schiller Institute and the National Democratic Policy Committee. Again, the LaRouchites have been linked to a number of racist and extremist groups, including the Liberty Lobby, the Ku Klux Klan, and neo-Nazis, Currently, they vigorously oppose sanctions against South African apartheid.

But this cult has also taken advantage of the current dissension and political malaise within the black electorate to gain adherents. In early 1985, the LaRouchites opportunistically sponsored a "Martin Luther King Jr. Day Rally" in Washington, D.C. As hundreds of unsuspecting blacks gathered, LaRouchites gave speeches in favor of Star Wars. In last year's municipal elections in several cities, black candidates who had little or no prior knowledge of the group were recruited to run for public office.

The most prominent black leader close to LaRouche is Roy Innis, who heads the remnants of the Congress of Racial Equality (CORE). Innis denies membership in the cult, but he recently acknowledged "an ongoing collaboration." In 1986, Innis ran an unsuccessful campaign in the Democratic primary against black progressive Representative Major Owens of Brooklyn. Innis was supported by the National Rifle Association and endorsed by Bernhard Goetz, the controversial "subway vigilante." Since the mid-1970s, Innis has championed the cause of Jonas Savimbi, the terrorist and leader of the Angolan rebel group UNITA, who is also supported by South Africa.

What Abernathy, Bevel, and Innis share is a near-total lack of accountability to any significant working-class constituency inside the black community. Opportunism is nothing new in black politics; these former civil-rights leaders have simply found it convenient to advance conservative dogma in a conservative climate; What is more significant is the failure of most progressive-to-liberal black leaders and organizations to expose and criticize their behavior and their alliances with ultra-rightists. Most blacks continue to take for granted a unity of political purpose and collective vision which no longer exists among black activists. As Major Owens finally recognized, CORE has "become a vehicle for the opposition, and Innis is an agent of the opposition.... We've been silent for too long in the name of black unity."

For forty years, the political mainstream of blacks has been consistently and sharply to the left of white America. The black electorate has traditionally supported a progressive policy agenda that most European labor-party activists might recognize instantly as their own: increased unemployment programs, expanded public housing, national healthcare plans, major reductions in military spending, criticism of U.S. intervention in Central America. Despite all of its internal weaknesses, the black freedom movement has represented in practice the strongest and most articulate force for what in Europe might be termed leftist social democracy.

Because of this country's failure to develop a strong socialist or progressive third party, blacks had no choice but to bring their agenda into the Democratic Party by World War II. Gradually, alliances for civil-rights legislation were formed with organized labor. At the zenith of the Second Reconstruction, in 1964 and 1965, the liberal coalition secured passage of the Civil Rights Act and the Voting Rights Act, as well as the War on Poverty. Shifts in demography and political culture, as well as the impact of Black Power and the debate over the war in Vietnam, slowly destroyed this coalition. Twenty years later, the AFL-CIO commanded less than 20 percent of the American working class, and more than half of all white trade unionists voted for Reagan in 1984. Since 1968, Democratic Presidential candidates have never won more than 46 percent of the white vote; in 1984, Walter Mondale's share was only 34 percent. Thus the black social-democratic constituency is in crisis partly because it has no effective allies.

The clearest evidence that blacks and white middle-class Americans live in separate political worlds is provided by the 1986 elections. Between 86 and 89 percent of the black electorate supported Democratic Congressional candidates. According to a recent *New York Times*/CBS poll, the only other significant constituencies favoring Democratic House candidates nationwide were Hispanics (75 percent), Jewish voters (70 percent), and members of union households and government employees (63 percent each). Non-Jewish whites voted for the Republican candidates by roughly 53 to 47 percent.

In at least five states, blacks provided the margin of victory for Democratic Senatorial candidates. For example, Republican Senator Jeremiah Denton of Alabama was firmly ahead of conservative Democrat Richard C. Shelby among whites, by a 61 to 39 percent margin. But Alabama blacks comprised 21 percent of the state's voters. Despite Shelby's right-wing views on most issues, he was considered more acceptable than the dangerous Denton. With 88 percent of the black vote, Shelby narrowly upset Denton by 6,823 votes. And in Louisiana, Democrat John B. Breaux defeated

Republican Henson Moore for the Senate by winning 85 percent of the black vote. Moore gained 60 percent of the white vote, but it wasn't enough.

The racial bifurcation in electoral behavior is also reflected in an October 1986 opinion survey conducted by the Joint Center for Political Studies and the Gallup Poll. The vast majority of blacks still define themselves as either "strong Democrats" (49 percent) or "weak Democrats" (29 percent). Eighty percent of blacks polled said they will probably vote for the Democratic nominee in the 1988 Presidential election. Only 7 percent of all blacks identify themselves as Republicans.

More importantly, most blacks polled consistently favor activist-oriented and liberal solutions to public-policy issues. When asked whether the Federal Government should secure a job and a good standard of living for each American citizen, 65 percent of the blacks said it should, compared to only 24 percent of whites. More than half (56 percent) of all blacks cited unemployment as one of the most important issues on the nation's agenda; only 29 percent of the whites agreed. Eighty percent of all blacks concurred that "the Federal Government should make every possible effort to improve the social and economic position of blacks" while only 27 percent of the whites agreed. White respondents were, by contrast, much more favorable to laissez-faire solutions to economic and social problems than blacks, and strongly opposed to extensive state intervention in the private sector.

The collapse of white centrist liberalism and the concurrent Reaganization of both major parties have isolated and frustrated black leaders and their community. In this environment, a political realignment within that community was inevitable. Black neoconservative theorists like Sowell and Williams were, at best, on the periphery of political respectability among blacks only a decade ago. Today, as the striking isolation of most black middle-class leaders from the main currents of white power and privilege has become abundantly clear, the voices of black neo-conservatism are gaining credibility and a modest base. Like European leftists whose faith in socialism has deteriorated, a growing number of black leaders are backing away from their assumptions based on social democracy in favor of the capitalist virtues of individualism and self-reliance.

Even Jesse Jackson has recently given verbal support to Tuskegee-like responses to racism. "Black Americans must begin to accept a larger share of responsibility for their lives," he said, "for too many years we have been crying that racism and oppression have to be fought on every front.... I don't believe that we will produce strong soldiers by moaning about what the enemy has done to us." This is essentially the language and logic of accommodation. It says to the Right: "We have no ability to regain the public-policy high ground against you. We must ultimately be responsible for uplifting ourselves."

Yet another contributing factor to the internal crisis is the paradox of desegregation. Neither Martin Luther King Jr. nor his contemporaries within the leadership of the civil-rights movement anticipated the political and social problems that would be generated by their successes. During the Jim Crow era, the black middle class was small, but it was highly organized and organically connected with every element of black working-class life. Black doctors and dentists opened their offices in black neighborhoods because they had no choice; few or no whites would be their patients.

Black teachers were usually employed in all-black school systems. Black attorneys normally had black clients. Black entrepreneurs looked to black consumers for their sales. Racial segregation created barriers that were repressive on the one hand and an asset to black solidarity on the other.

This is not nostalgia for Jim Crow. The totalitarianism of rigid racial stratification and the denial of democratic rights and civil liberties were odious to every black American. The desegregation struggle was a populist movement that galvanized the near-unanimous energies and broad support of every segment of the national black community. The popularity of this mass movement was partially a function of the clarity of the issues. To oppose Jim Crow was to strike a blow against second-class schools, segregated neighborhoods, and inferior social services.

A vote for Lyndon Johnson in 1964, from a black perspective, was an endorsement of voting-rights legislation, expanded welfare programs, increased educational opportunities, and other liberal reforms of immediate and direct benefit. As the Great Society fell apart, however, the question of group interests became more complex. Affirmative action pitted traditional liberal allies against each other, as conservative Republicans began to make successful bids for disenchanted white workers and Dixiecrats. The white liberals who had campaigned for Eugene McCarthy and George McGovern gravitated to Gary Hart and his not-so-new ideas. Each segment of the liberal alliance went its own way, leaving blacks politically isolated.

Within the black community, class stratification increased dramatically between 1970 and 1985. As the numbers of college-educated blacks soared, a new social stratum began to break away from the working class and the poor—the black urban professionals, or "buppies." By racial tradition, they are Democrats. But in terms of their own historical experiences and class expectations, they are next of kin to the new white petit bourgeoisie, or "yuppies."

They are too young to have taken part in the sit-ins and massive desegregation campaigns of the 1960s and have no personal experience of civil disobedience. The buppies, unlike the older black middle class, do not live or work in all-black environments. They have few direct or intimate ties with cultural and social institutions inside the black community. The paradox of desegregation, in short, is the creation of a class of black parvenus who are at odds with the very concept of black solidarity around progressive economic and social policies. In this sense, Loury and Williams are buppie theorists: uncritical advocates of capitalism and consumerism, opponents of fundamental social change. The confused and contradictory social strata they represent provide the fertile terrain for Black Reaganism.

The crisis of black politics can only be resolved through the development of multiclass, multiracial, progressive political structures—agencies of social change that bring together all elements of the black community. The Rainbow Coalition has the potential for uniting the educated and relatively affluent black middle class with the vast majority of blacks who remain unemployed, impoverished, or within the working class. The Coalition also may reach out to the traditional labor movement, to feminists, peace activists, and segments of the old liberal alliance that hold the greatest promise for a new progressive coalition in the 1990s.

In the long run, though, success for such a coalition depends on a radical realignment of the Democratic Party—and probably a decisive split between the party's liberal and conservative wings, Until that occurs, we can expect the continued defection of some black politicians and intellectuals to the Right and a deepening of the crisis inside the black electorate as a whole. Unless the black freedom movement quickly regains its capacity to take the offensive against the Right, the entire American Left may be isolated in the political wilderness for a generation.

SECTION III

On Black Protest and Politics: The 1990s to the Present

BLACK POLITICS AND THE
CHALLENGES FOR THE LEFT

In the 1980s, there were two fundamental responses by African-Americans to the economic and social crisis generated by Reaganism. The first was represented at the local level by the mayoral campaigns of Harold Washington in Chicago and Mel King in Boston, and at the national level by the Rainbow presidential campaigns of Jesse Jackson in 1984 and 1988. These electoral campaigns were the products of democratic social protest movements, the consequence of thousands of protests against plant closings, cutbacks in housing, health care, and jobs, racial discrimination in the courts, and political process at the local level. The Jackson campaigns were a revolt against both Reaganism in the Republican Party and the capitulation of the Democratic Party to the repressive policies of the Reagan administration. In capitalist societies with parliamentary governments, the Rainbow campaign would have been expressed as a multiracial, left social democratic party, a political formation calling for the state to eliminate racial discrimination and disparities of income between people of color and whites and to expand federal expenditures for human needs, employment, and education. Jackson's discourse was grounded in a tradition of resistance and the previous struggles against Jim Crow, a heritage which defined politics not simply as an electoral phenomena, but as the struggle for power on a variety of fronts. In effect, the Rainbow campaign called for a progressive social contract, a positive relationship between the people and the state which would guarantee full employment, universal health care, and housing; safeguard civil rights, and create the material and social conditions for a more democratic and egalitarian order.

The black petty bourgeoisie supported Jackson's effort along with the African-American working class and the unemployed, but for different reasons. The poor and working class had been hit with a severe deterioration of wages, the expansion of drug traffic in their neighborhoods, and the collapse in public transportation systems, health care, and social infrastructure. Voting for Jackson was a protest against Reaganism, racism, and the political domination of the two-party system. The black middle strata mobilized for different reasons. In the period 1979–87, African-American managers and professionals actually had larger income increases

81

than whites with identical educational backgrounds and vocations. (Conversely, the rate of income growth for blacks in all other vocational categories was much lower than that of whites.) Much of the gain to this new professional/managerial stratum had come from affirmative action policies of the federal government. More than half of all black college graduates have jobs tied directly to public-sector spending. Reaganism represented a very real threat to the fragile gains of the middle class elite. The Democratic Party's failure to vigorously contest cutbacks in economic set-asides for nonwhite entrepreneurs, the non-enforcement of affirmative action and equal opportunity legislation, and the destruction of the Civil Rights commission also alienated and outraged most middle class blacks. They saw Jackson as a symbolic advocate of their own interests.

In the quarter century since the passage of the historic Voting Rights Act of 1965, the number of black elected officials has soared from 100 to 6,700. The overwhelming majority of these are elected from majority black constituencies. The principal reason for this is that most whites simply will not vote for a black candidate, regardless of his/her political program, party affiliation, or personality. This means that in virtually all cases, African-Americans never consider running for statewide offices or in Congressional or mayoral races in which whites constitute more than 60 percent of the electorates. Consequently, since middle class black politicians look to black workers and the unemployed for votes, they are usually forced to articulate a social democratic–style agenda to win popular support. Their own immediate class interests are not fully served because the weight of the black petty bourgeoisie is very small compared to that of other classes within the black community.

The second response to the economic and social crisis is a form of electoral accommodationism. "Accommodation" is historically a gradualistic response within African-American politics, which seeks reforms by cooperation with the white corporate establishment, collaboration with the more conservative elements of the major parties, and an advocacy of private self-help and the development of a minority entrepreneurial strata. Booker T. Washington was the architect of accommodation during the era of Jim Crow, the first prominent advocate of "black capitalism." Nearly a century later, in a period of expanding racial segregation and manifestations of racist violence, in a political context of pessimism and defeat for the black left, and in the social chaos spawned by drugs and the decay of social institutions, the political space for a new type of accommodationism has developed. The new accommodationists seek to articulate the interests of sections of the white middle class and corporate interests, rather than the black community. The accommodationist reformers still use the discourse of the civil rights movement, but lack any political commitment to civil disobedience or disruptive activities to achieve more equal rights and economic justice for the black working class. Unlike Booker T. Washington, this new leadership of the black middle class does not have to embrace legal racial segregation to win white support, but it does have to espouse a compromising approach to black political and economic development and to do nothing to challenge the brutal class oppression and social deterioration in the urban ghetto. This neo-accommodationist approach can be described as "post black politics."

　　The November 1989 elections of David Dinkins as New York City's mayor and Douglas Wilder as governor of Virginia symbolize this second approach, despite the fact that both victories have been widely applauded as triumphs over American racism. To be sure, Dinkins is a progressive Democrat on many issues, and no doubt he is preferable to both former mayor Ed Koch and the Republican candidate in the general election, Rudolph Giuliani. The more moderate Wilder was clearly superior to the anti-reproductive rights, conservative demagogue he opposed in Virginia's gubernatorial election. However, neither election represented a fundamental advance for the masses of black working class and poor people, nor advanced a progressive or left social-democratic strategy which might push the boundaries of bourgeois politics to the left.

　　Both candidates, and especially Wilder, ran essentially mainstream-oriented campaigns, rather than constructing broad-based coalitions of black, Latino, and white workers, liberals, and leftists, on the model of Harold Washington's campaign. Both had recognized years ago that their own electoral constituencies of African-Americans were too small to provide the necessary core for successful bids to high office. Over a decade, they cultivated political records which would place them well within the moderate mainstreams of their respective political cultures in order to appeal to white liberal-to-centrist constituencies.

　　This was especially the case with Wilder. After the mid-1970s he effectively remade himself in the image of the classical Southern patriarch—conservative, pro-corporate, anti-crime, and abundantly safe. He couldn't cross the color line personally, but he would do so in terms of his political image. So Wilder sought to become a Southern version of Los Angeles mayor Thomas Bradley, a moderately conservative politician who was "post black"—beyond identification with race. Wilder reversed his opposition to the death penalty. He backed away from his earlier advocacy of granting the District of Columbia full statehood rights, which in effect would place two African-Americans into the U.S. Senate. Moving away from liberal Keynesianism in economic policy, Wilder opposed any changes in Virginia's rigid "right to work" laws, which prohibit compulsory membership in unions within individual businesses.

　　After four terms in Virginia's Senate, Wilder was successfully elected Lieutenant Governor, the state's second highest office, in 1985. Almost immediately speculation began concerning his chances for governor, since Virginia prohibits incumbent governors from seeking reelection. One of Wilder's chief difficulties was maintaining his natural base among the African-American electorate, which had strongly supported the insurgent presidential campaigns of Jesse Jackson in both 1984 and 1988, while reassuring white voters that he was just as conservative and pro-business as any Southern white politician. Wilder placed one foot in each of two dramatically divergent political cultures, recognizing that both were necessary for him to achieve his goal. He praised Jackson personally, but took pains to distinguish the charismatic campaigner's liberal-left agenda from his own. He defused the critics by suggesting, somewhat falsely, that Jackson's electoral mobilization represented symbolism without substance. "Jesse runs to inspire," Wilder observed, "I run to win."[1]

　　The political terrain of New York permitted Dinkins to assume a more liberal ideological posture than Wilder's. Nevertheless, he made several strategic political compromises to secure the support of the white upper middle class, and especially Jewish voters who had supported neoconservative mayor Ed Koch in the Democratic primaries. Dinkins distanced himself from Jackson politically, and reminded white voters that he had denounced black nationalist leader Louis Farrakhan. Dinkins's lieutenants shunned efforts by Brooklyn's Arab-American Democratic Club to hold a fund-raising event, for fear of alienating the Jewish electorate. Campaign manager Bill Lynch told Arab-American leaders "not to seek to be visibly associated with the candidate," but Dinkins staffers added that they would still accept their financial contributions. In effect, New York City's Arab-American community of 100,000 was disavowed by a "liberal" who had worked closely with them in the past.[2] After his election, Dinkins and his associates refused to honor promises of appointments to several black progressives and nationalists who had been pivotal in mobilizing African-American voters.

Rather than denying the reality of race, Wilder and Dinkins sought to "transcend" the color line, offering generous platitudes of how racism had supposedly declined in significance during the 1980s. The problem with this perspective is that all the evidence suggests that white voters still remain highly race conscious, far more so than African-Americans or Latinos. Since black democrats can never hope to escape the burden of racial prejudice entirely, they must address the issue squarely and without rhetorical subterfuge. The strategy of declaring victory against racial prejudice may produce some short-term victories, but it will only reinforce white supremacy within the electoral process in the long run.

A second, and paradoxical, problem challenges black political activists, community leaders, and civil rights advocates. They must now ask themselves, "What has the African-American electorate actually won?" Once safely in office, will Doug Wilder's administration actually produce more government jobs for Virginia's blacks, or a more aggressive affirmative action policy than that of the previous white Democratic governor? Will Wilder's conservative support for right to work laws advance the interests of African-American blue collar, semiskilled, and unemployed workers? How will a Wilder administration provide better health services, public welfare, and quality education to the most dispossessed classes when he campaigned specifically on a "no tax increase" platform?[3] Can Dinkins really empower the African-American and Hispanic neighborhoods at the expense of the corporations, real estate developers, and banks? How can Dinkins's economic and social policies really be significantly to the left of those of former mayor Ed Koch, when before the election, the black Democrat named Koch's former deputy mayor Nathan Leventhal to lead his transition team? With the exception of Dinkin's educational policy group, most of the transition planning team were clearly more conservative than the new mayor's electoral constituency.

The Dinkins-Wilder victories represent unique problems for both Jesse Jackson and more generally for the American left. Jackson's strategy in 1984 was essentially to build a broad-based coalition of forces representing roughly 80 percent of black America, combined with small fractions of the Latino, progressive white, and labor constituencies. Jackson stood for a liberal/black revolt against the failure of the Democratic Party to mount a strong opposition to the social devastation of Reaganism.

The 1988 Jackson campaign was different in many ways from the 1984 experience. First, it was much more an electoral effort than a social protest movement in electoral form. In 1984, the vast majority of black elected officials had opposed Jackson, or only belatedly embraced the Rainbow; in 1988, they were generally out front, and used their influence to steer the movement toward the safe boundaries of acceptable bourgeois politics.

Consequently, the black nationalists, Marxists, gay and lesbian activists, left environmentalists, and others exercised less leverage in setting the Rainbow's agenda than they had previously. There was also a subtle change in Jackson, particularly in the wake of his stunning defeat of Dukakis in the March 1988 Michigan caucuses. The best evidence indicates that Jackson actually believed that he could be the Democratic Party's nominee, or failing this, that he might achieve the Vice Presidential nomination. Even people on the left argued that Jackson might pull off the electoral upset. Ron Daniels, the head of the Rainbow, was transferred to the electoral campaign. The Rainbow itself as a national independent political force was not developed, and today it remains a political shell rather than a viable formation.

When the inevitable occurred, and Dukakis got the nomination and shifted to the right, Jackson and the Rainbow were not prepared to advance a coherent program of critical support for the Democratic nominee, while developing their own apparatus to the left of the party. After the election, Ron Brown's promotion as head of the Democratic National Committee and the year-long speculation about Jackson's potential challenge to Marion Barry in Washington's mayoral race indicate that even the more progressive elements of the black leadership placed their individual upward mobility ahead of the empowerment of the Black masses as a whole.

Both the Democratic Socialists of America and the Communist Party, in different ways, have pursued a strategy of moving American politics to the left by working with Democratic Party liberals. The hope has been to polarize the Democrats in such a manner that either the conservatives (e.g., Sam Nunn, Charles Robb, Lloyd Bentsen) purge the left, or the liberals force out the right. We have to recognize that neither of these options exhaust the possibilities. Most of us have not anticipated an ideological shift among many African-American or Latino politicians, using racial solidarity rhetoric to ensure minority voter loyalty, but gradually embracing more moderate to conservative public policy positions, especially on economic issues. The real model for this nationally isn't Wilder, but Philadelphia Representative William Gray, who has been groomed for the Vice Presidency for six years.

But the left must establish an independent identity, organizationally and programmatically. An inside-outside strategy which supports progressive Democrats must also be prepared to run candidates for public office against both Democrats and Republicans, especially in municipal and congressional races. The left must establish a network bringing together progressive local constituencies around projects which define politics as a struggle for empowerment, not just in electoral terms. It must recruit the thousands of young people who were politically developed through the anti-apartheid mobilizations of the mid-1980s and involved in the Jackson campaign. At a minimum, such a network would require a statement of principles for operational unity, a national publication, and the local autonomy necessary for groups to engage in independent nonelectoral, community-based struggles.

Along with the development of institutions, the left and the black movement must reassess the potential weaknesses and strengths of mounting yet another national presidential campaign behind Jackson. We need to be clear that Jackson will never be awarded the Democratic Party's presidential nomination, even if he wins every primary and caucus. The rules will be changed to deny him victory—or even more drastic measures will be taken. Moreover, the Democratic Party will never be transformed into a left social democratic, much less socialist, formation. There is too much history, ideological baggage, and domination by sectors of the ruling class for progressives to achieve a transformation from within. More than channelling our meager resources into a costly, labor-intensive national campaign, we desperately need to reinforce our organizational capacity for nonelectoral as well as electoral struggles at grassroots levels. Socialism and black liberation cannot be achieved merely by electing a socialist president. It requires the careful and difficult construction of a thousand black, Latino, and progressive formations and local movements in cities, towns, and rural areas.

A socialist labor party in the traditional sense would be premature, at least at this point, but an effective network or loose progressive confederation could accomplish much. But we cannot build consensus for social justice and fundamental, structural changes within the political economy simply by continuing to tail liberals, even those like Jackson. We must demand a greater political price from such politicians for our critical support; and if it is not forthcoming, we must be prepared to employ our resources elsewhere. The selection of the "lesser evil" election after election is in the long run self-defeating. We should engage in a "war of position," the building of the political culture and structures of radical democracy, not advocating traditional Keynesian liberalism. There will never be a distant "war of maneuver" against capital so long as American Marxists act like liberals, because liberals will inevitably act like Republicans in order to get elected. A radical, democratic vision of social change, socialism-from-below, but in a popular discourse which the majority of blacks, Latinos, feminists, and the American working people readily understand, must inform our political practice and strategic decisions for the 1990s.

~

Eurocentrism vs. Afrocentrism
The Impasse of Racial Politics

Since the Black Power movement of more than two decades ago, the dialogue between white and black intellectuals and activists on theories of social change has been at best fragmentary, and at times, nonexistent. The racial bifurcation of protest movements in the sixties and seventies created a bitter political impasse. The result: a chasm of silence.

As blacks shifted their concerns from the civil rights movement to questions of empowerment within the African-American community, whites who had previously been an integral part of the desegregation struggles gravitated to the anti-Vietnam War mobilizations or to the nascent feminist movement. Animosities simmered between traditional allies (such as black Americans and the Jewish community) over a range of domestic and international issues. As the seventies progressed, blacks came to believe that efforts to empower their community conflicted with the interests of many white liberal and labor constituencies. As neoliberal intellectuals and Democratic party politicians disavowed progressive policies, African-Americans felt increasingly isolated.

Tensions deepened after Ronald Reagan's victories in 1980 and 1984. The Reagan administration was at odds with virtually every major public policy position favored by the vast majority of blacks. While massive reductions in health care, public housing, federal jobs programs, and affirmative action enforcement certainly hurt whites, they devastated African-American and Hispanic neighborhoods. Millions of black families never recovered from the 1982 recession, when blacks' median income compared to that of whites plummeted. Inspired by the President's hostile attitude toward minorities, racist groups became active. This intensified the sense of isolation among blacks. They watched a Republican administration invade Grenada, pursue "constructive engagement" with apartheid South Africa, and carry out policies of urban destruction that promoted widespread poverty, drug dependency, and black-on-black violence. They looked to the Democratic party for progressive leadership—and found an aging liberal shell with an increasingly Reaganized content. With the exception of Jesse Jackson and few other left-liberals, Democrats had ceased to function as an opposition party. Desperation and anger among blacks rose.

Historically, black nationalist ideologies and protest movements gain strength at the conjuncture of these factors: the rejection of racial equality and black empowerment by both major political parties; racial hostility in the criminal justice system; economic expansion in which blacks' gains lag behind those of the white middle-class majority; an increase in racial vigilantism and overt discrimination against people of color; and, finally, the failure of established, middle-class, black leaders to articulate the grievances of African-Americans who are impatient with the pace of change.

Black nationalism—which includes a belief in the cultural integrity and heritage of people of African descent, criticism of black-white alliances, an emphasis on all-black economic, educational, and political institution-building, and the advocacy of value systems drawn solely from the African/African-American historical experience—arose in the 1850s, a period of crisis characterized by the factors mentioned above. New leaders, such as Martin Delany, Henry Highland Garnet, and Mary Ann Shadd Cary, challenged the integrationist and liberal political assumptions of abolitionist Frederick Douglass. In the 1920s, the same factors produced the black nationalist movement of Marcus Garvey. Garveyism rejected white-black alliances, favored limited emigration of African-Americans back to Africa, and opposed the desegregationist agenda of W.E.B. Du Bois and the NAACP.

History repeats itself once again in the late 1980s and early 1990s. As white capitalist America congratulates itself on the collapse of communism and distorts the failed legacy of Stalinism to undermine the promise of democratic socialism, scholars of color increasingly look away from the models of Soviet communism *and* Western capitalism. Historical conditions and a sense of racial crisis have convinced them that any hope of salvation for the black masses must be found in the reconstruction of an African consciousness around which a separatist political agenda is developed. European and American social systems are fatally flawed, the argument goes, because of "Eurocentrism"—a perception of a world in which white values dominate nonwhite people.

Molefi Kete Asante, director of the most important African-American studies department in the United States, located at Temple University, is today the most articulate advocate of "Afrocentrism." An impressive scholar, Asante has mastered the history of African and black American social protest and culture. Consequently his critique of western discourse and the biased empirical foundations of Eurocentric scholarship is highly persuasive. His suggestions for addressing the intellectual and political dilemmas of black scholarship and activism, however, lend themselves to a black nationalist orientation which could aggravate the alienation of black working-class people.

In Asante's *The Afrocentric Idea,* all social and political theories drawn from a Eurocentric context are dismissed as irrelevant for people of African descent. "Marxism is not helpful in developing Afrocentric consciousness that excludes the historical and cultural perspectives of Africa," Asante argues. "Because it emerged from the Western consciousness, Marxism is mechanistic in its approach to social understanding and development, and it has often adopted forms of social Darwinism when explaining cultural and social phenomena." Much of what Asante asserts is certainly true. Both European social democracy and Stalinism were inclined toward economic determinism, failing to take into account the independent and dynamic role of social factors such as race, gender, and ethnicity in the evolution of social formations. But if Marxism is taken not as a religion with an economistic catechism, but rather as a method of social analysis recognizing that values, culture, and ideology are of central importance to the development of both social classes and communities, such criticisms no longer appear valid. *The Afrocentric Idea* argues that "Afrocentrism"—an identification with the creative culture, values, and rhetoric of people of African descent—is the philosophical foundation for all important advances in the struggles of black people. Looking backward, Asante reconstructs black political history within this analytic framework. Examining the abolitionist controversies between the integrationist Frederick Douglass and the militant black nationalism of Henry Highland Garnet, Asante insists that there was a "fundamental cleavage in the black antislavery movement." Blacks who opposed Garnet's call for insurrection against slavery had "capitulated to a Eurocentric view of the struggle for black liberty. Fear of offending white political and social interests grasped the minds" of some black activists "in a political vise, tightened by the overwhelming cultural and image context of white Americans." This nationalist/integrationist dichotomy explains much about black politics, past and present, but it doesn't explain everything. It assumes that class divisions within the African-American community are either secondary or nonexistent; it suggests that blacks who are critical of racial separatism are simply "Eurocentric."

When the bulk of historical evidence doesn't confirm the Afrocentric model, Asante then selects details that do support the thesis. For example, he dedicates his book to Du Bois and attempts to project this monumental black socialist in seminationalist terms. Du Bois's famous quote of 1900 is praised as prophetic and Afrocentric: "The problem of the twentieth century is the problem of the color line." Du Bois's influential thesis of "double consciousness," advanced in his 1903 book, *The Souls of Black Folk*, stated:

"One ever feels twoness—an American, a Negro; two thoughts, two unreconciled striving; two warring ideals in one dark body, whose dogged strength alone keeps it from being torn asunder. The history of the American Negro is the history of this strife ... to attain self-conscious manhood, to merge his double self into a better and truer self."

For Asante, this passage indicates that Du Bois was responding to the issue of "white domination"; the concept of double consciousness describes how "the African looked at himself through someone else's eyes."

This interpretation is only partially correct. Actually Du Bois insisted that black Americans were African peoples—and "American"—committed to full participation within the institutions of a democratic society. Du Bois explains: "He would not Africanize America, for America has too much to teach the world and Africa. He would not bleach his Negro soul in a flood of white Americanism, for he knows that Negro blood has a message for the world. He simply wishes to make it possible for a man to be both a Negro and an American … " From a Du Boisian analysis, both "Eurocentrism" and "Afrocentrism" are incomplete paradigms for the construction of social theory and political engagement.

The problems confronting African-Americans are enormous, and our allies in the struggle seemingly are few. But we cannot find the analytical tools for the construction of theoretical and programmatic models for social transformation by resorting to an approach that separates us from constituencies that have also experienced the weight of oppression. In the American Southwest, Mexican-Americans have been the victims of racial discrimination, economic exploitation, and educational underdevelopment for generations. Native Americans know the meaning of political genocide; white working-class people in the gutted industrial towns of Flint, Michigan, and Youngstown, Ohio, recognize the realities of hunger, unemployment, and poverty. Oppression may be manifested in a racial discourse, but it is fundamentally linked to the inequality of America's class structure and the domination of capital over working people.

Historical evidence indicates that white Americans of all social classes only rarely see beyond racial blinders to recognize the human needs that bind them to the demands of people of color. Asante's search for a philosophy grounded in his own culture is therefore a logical consequence of the realities of Eurocentric domination, of the left and right. The challenge for democratic socialists is to create a movement that truly values the unique cultural heritage, values, and political traditions of people of color. We must challenge racism in every form. When the left demonstrates the capacity for a humanistic and culturally pluralistic politics in the tradition of Du Bois, it may attract people of color as equal partners in struggles for democratic change.

~

A New Black Politics

We have reached the end of a long, historical phase of the black political experience in America. Well-worn political assumptions no longer are effective or meaningful. Even Jesse Jackson's unprecedented electoral mobilizations of 1984 and 1988 seem slightly anachronistic when compared to the elections of Douglas Wilder as governor of Virginia and David Dinkins as mayor of New York City. There is an awareness that the system of institutional racism has changed in the past two decades, but civil-rights leaders have failed to alter their general strategy or tactics.

The black movement's disarray and apparent fragmentation stem from the convergence of three great crises which it has failed to address comprehensively—the crisis of ideology, the crisis of politics, and the crisis of consciousness or historical imagination.

These three great crises have not been addressed by black politicians, civil-rights officials, and other leaders of black society because this elite is a prisoner of its own historical successes. Its finest triumph, the dismantling of the system of legal segregation and the selective integration of minorities into the political mainstream of American society, has proved to be its last hurrah on the national stage.

In the aftermath of his great civil-rights achievements, and in the midst of his opposition to the Vietnam war, Martin Luther King Jr. tried to challenge his followers to move beyond their traditional civil-rights agenda.

"Where do we go from here?" King asked. None of his lieutenants, not even Jesse Jackson, was willing to go where he was prepared to take the movement. A quarter of a century later, we must answer King's question with new strategies and programs. But we cannot use old theoretical tools to build a new movement.

The first and most important measure we must take to restructure and resurrect a viable black protest movement is to forge a new synthesis of an old feud.

The organizational structures of black protest movements from abolitionism to the present have been based on two fundamental racial ideologies that guided nearly *all* strategies and tactics: integration and black nationalism.

Racial integrationists, beginning with Frederick Douglass and culminating with King, have consistently advocated the elimination of all restrictions that kept blacks from participating fully in the mainstream of society. They perceived racial designations of any type as a stigma and hoped for the ultimate elimination of the ghetto. Their primary strategic weapons were legal challenges in the courts and activism in the political system to elect politicians favorable to liberal goals. Integrationists consequently emphasized the construction of multiclass political coalitions and, after the New Deal, promoted a strategic long-term alliance with the Democratic Party. Culturally, they wanted to believe in the myth of the melting pot. They perceived themselves first as Americans and only secondarily as members of a discriminated-against racial minority.

There were important differences of opinion within the ranks, but they all could agree that a color-blind society was their immediate goal.

Confronting the integrationists were their ideological rivals, the black nationalists, who bitterly rejected integration as a political and cultural hoax designed to deepen the levels of exploitation and economic oppression. They were suspicious of alliances with whites and preferred the development of political linkages to nationalists in Africa and the Caribbean. They advocated black community-controlled schools and viewed busing for school integration as a liberal racist plot to fragment their neighborhoods.

The black nationalists' most important difference with the integrationists was over economics. The nationalists were unpersuaded that desegregation of the business establishment and trade-union movement would actually translate into black economic empowerment. Instead, they favored the use of legal segregation as a catalyst for the mobilization of land, labor, and capital. Black-owned insurance companies would sell policies to blacks; black-owned farms would provide fresh produce to black-owned inner-city grocery stores for black consumers. The insight that segregation could provide the basis for the growth of a black entrepreneurial elite was the heart of Booker T. Washington's strategy of early Twentieth Century black capitalism and Marcus Garvey's Universal Negro Improvement Association. Today, it is the central economic plank of the nationalist platform of Louis Farrakhan.

Despite their differences, a subterranean unity existed between both ideological paradigms. Both essentially followed a race-based strategy for societal change. The integrationists used race as a means of organizing liberal constituencies toward the goal of abolishing race; the nationalists used race as a technique for building group solidarity. Both sides, for different reasons, minimized the growing class divisions among blacks.

Only one major figure in black political history, W.E.B. Du Bois, tried to bridge the chasm of racial ideologies. His approach was a search for synthesis; he sensed correctly that a dialectical approach for black activism must include two components: the nationalists' reaffirmation of black identity, culture, and values, and the integrationists' demand for full rights within a democratic political system. But Du Bois's approach was never accepted or fully understood.

Now, however, we must refocus. Instead of emphasizing electoral politics above all other activities or pursuing purely separatist objectives, we must turn to the practical problems experienced by the majority of African-American people in the central cities.

The basic question for the early Twenty-first Century must be: What constitutes an economically productive, socially pluralistic, and democratic urban community?

I am not suggesting a hasty updating of Saul Alinsky's community-organizing strategy. The current socioeconomic crisis experienced by millions of Hispanics, African-Americans, and working-class whites in our cities no longer takes shape in the context of old-style Jim Crow segregation. Nor do the basic conflicts occur primarily in the workplace, although struggles against job discrimination remain important. The greatest manifestations of oppression now occur in what can be termed the living place, or the urban, postindustrial community.

Struggles over housing, health care, day care, schools, jobs, and public transportation all revolve around this question of the future of the postindustrial city. The urban and working poor are second-class citizens, denied access to a quality of life which a minority of white, affluent Americans take for granted. Both political parties ignore their demands, and their material conditions continue to deteriorate.

According to the Economic Policy Institute, the share of the nation's wealth owned by the highest one-tenth of all households increased from 67.5 percent in 1979 to 73.1 percent in 1988. The percentage of all after-tax income earned by the richest one-tenth of all American families increased from 29.5 percent in 1980 to almost 35 percent today. Conversely, the Business-Higher Education Forum reported in June that the median wealth of black households is only 9 percent of that of white households. Even with the increase in the minimum wage legislated earlier this year, the inflation-adjusted buying power for those earning minimum wage has declined by one-fourth since 1981. In the absence of significant change, the deterioration of black communities and family life will continue.

A new community-based agenda will require detailed social-science research on the particular problems of dozens of cities, particularly the medium-sized ones—those that used to be manufacturing and industrial towns with significant minority populations.

Advances in progressive urban planning and policy must be based on empirical research, not rhetoric. One outstanding model for future work comes from the Center for Applied Public Affairs Studies at the State University of New York at Buffalo. Directed by Henry Louis Taylor Jr., its recent comprehensive study of the changing socioeconomic status of Buffalo's African-American community provides the foundation for a series of innovative economic, social, and educational proposals for progressive activity.

This refocus on practical problems is, once again, the first and foremost measure we must take.

Second, we must discard the idea that electoral activity is the only form of politics, or even that it is the most important arena for political conflict. And we must discard the theory that the Democratic Party can be "humanized," or "reformed from within," or transformed into a labor party.

The leftist version of the Democratic Party's realignment finds its origins in both Stalinism and unorthodox Trotskyism. The strategy was echoed by the late Michael Harrington, Bayard Rustin, and many leftists who worked hard for Jesse Jackson in 1984 and 1988.

But it won't work.

Understanding the collapse of the old liberal coalition of minorities, organized labor, and the Democratic Party is critically important to understanding the new political environment—the period since the demise of "black power." Race was transformed into more complex structures of domination, and the influence or leverage on public policy of such integrationists as the NAACP was greatly reduced.

As the majority of America's white electorate shifted from the cities to the suburbs, becoming better educated and reflecting entrepreneurial values, the social base for New Deal liberalism declined. The AFL-CIO's influence on national Democratic Party politics fell sharply. Traditionally liberal constituencies divided with blacks over a broad range of issues—Jewish-Americans, for example, over affirmative action, Israeli connections with South Africa, and Jesse Jackson. As the white electorate became more conservative and elitist, candidates for public office increasingly reflected these trends. The relative political and social weight of both national parties declined, as candidates became more independent of partisan affiliations.

Over time, a rough division of labor developed between the Republicans and the Democrats. The Republicans projected themselves as the party of "national management," capable of running the Executive Branch and making decisions in foreign policy. White upper-middle-class Americans consistently favor Republicans to reduce taxes on income and capital gains, expand opportunities for capital, and push back demands by minorities, workers, and the poor for redistribution of income.

The Democrats are now perceived as the party of "parochial interests," the politicians who are best at defending the local interests of various constituencies. Because Democrats still control most state legislatures, they have managed to gerrymander many Congressional districts to maximize their ability to compete elector-ally. Then, with the advantages of incumbency, most Democrats are able to win handily. The re-election rate in the House of Representatives was 98 percent in 1986 and 1988.

In effect, we have been experiencing a coalition government of "national unity," a marriage operating more from consensus than from competition. Both national parties now have a vested interest in maintaining this electoral partnership, which is the principal reason the Democrats have ceased to function as a loyal opposition in anything but name.

Many Democrats recognize that they could probably win the Presidency by the route advocated by Jesse Jackson—expanding the electoral base to include millions of nonvoting blacks, Hispanics, poor, and working-class voters, and advancing an American version of leftist social democracy, attacking the power of corporations. This would force the Democrats into a truly antagonistic relationship with the Republican Party and with virtually all elites in corporate America.

It would also require the organizational restructuring of the party, an idea that party bureaucrats everywhere find abominable. Democratic Party leaders would rather lose a Presidential election, and cooperate with George Bush and Robert Dole in coordinating national policies, than permit the ranks of the poor and powerless, minorities and liberal feminists, to assume authority within their party.

The ideological transformation of the party system is largely responsible for the small but growing cohort of "post-black politicians"—elected officials, recruited largely from the professional classes, who are racially and ethnically "black" but who favor programs with little kinship to the traditional agendas of the civil-rights movement. One prominent example is Virginia Governor Douglas Wilder, who is already being touted as a possible candidate for Vice President in 1992 or 1996. Yet another likely post-black candidate is Philadelphia Congressman William Gray.

Post-black political candidates generally favor the death penalty, oppose new taxes, and support corporate interests. They are presented to working-class and poor blacks as their symbolic victories, direct proof that racism has declined in significance. Their election can be viewed as a psychological triumph for African-Americans, but they represent no qualitative resolution to the crises of black poverty, educational inequality, crime, and unemployment.

Conversely, another group of black politicians has also emerged lately, largely based in the ghetto. They opportunistically manipulate racial symbols and language to enlist constituencies among the poorest blacks. These charlatans rely on the old nationalist rhetoric of racial solidarity, but lack any progressive content because they are detached from any social protest movement for empowerment or resistance. A few examples are Washington Mayor Marion Barry, Chicago Congressman Gus Savage, and Atlantic City Mayor James Usry.

In the past decade, many of Barry's chief advisers have been indicted, convicted, imprisoned, or forced to resign because of various improprieties. Barry himself is on trial for use of crack cocaine. Yet for months, he held the city hostage to his own blind ambition, rallying his supporters by emotional appeals to racial unity. His public antics have reversed and set back the progressive campaign for District of Columbia statehood for the next twenty years.

Long known as the least effective member of the Congressional Black Caucus, Savage used anti-Semitic smears against a black challenger in the recent primary, deriding his opponent for accepting campaign contributions from Jews.

Particularly shameful was the rhetoric of Usry, the Republican incumbent who had been endorsed by New Jersey Governor Thomas H. Kean in 1986. Challenged by city councilman Jim Whelan, a white Democrat with significant support among blacks, Usry resorted to crude racial slogans to polarize Atlantic City's electorate. His campaign literature exhorted African-Americans to vote for him because of "the color of my skin" and because the Lord wanted him to "make life better for you—my people." Usry won the endorsement of the Nation of Islam's local representative and the backing of activist Dick Gregory, who asserted that whites had "rigged" voting machines to steal the election.

The opportunism and poverty of so many black elected officials are rooted in the bankruptcy of black political ideas and electoral organization. Most poor and working-class blacks sense this, which explains the recent popularity of those who advocate extreme, militant solutions.

In Milwaukee last February, alderman Michael McGee threatened to create an armed militia of street-gang members, trained for urban race war, unless the city government funneled $100 million for job programs into the ghetto. McGee was widely denounced as "irresponsible" by more moderate blacks. Yet even the head of the local NAACP chapter, Felmer Cheney, admitted, "McGee is probably as frustrated as everybody else. Where in hell do we go?" The black middle-class leaders' inability to address this issue indicates the limitations of their theoretical and programmatic perspective.

The only viable alternative generated within black politics since the end of the civil-rights movement has been Jesse Jackson's Rainbow Coalition. But after two notable Presidential campaigns, the idealism that inspired thousands of progressives has disintegrated. In 1984, Jackson entered the fray without any serious hope of winning the Presidential nomination. His campaign was essentially a social-protest movement that used the Democratic primaries to increase black voter turnout and reinforce the liberal-left wing of the Democratic Party. By 1988, Jackson had shifted closer to the center, permitting black officials who had campaigned vigorously against him in 1984 to dominate municipal and statewide mobilizations.

But the Rainbow Coalition failed to develop a coherent national apparatus, with a national newspaper, regional political organizers, and trained cadre on campuses and in communities. Local activists drawn into the Jackson campaigns weren't encouraged to develop autonomous coalitions independent of the national electoral effort. Jackson's frenetic, larger-than-life personality and his chaotic organizational style, consisting largely of a coterie of loyalists who rarely disagree with the boss, work against genuinely democratic decision-making. Leftists who were members of the national leadership of the Rainbow recognized these problems but were reluctant to voice even mild criticisms of Jackson, who offered them a path out of their own sectarian political ghetto.

Part of the problem was the bitterly ironic relationship that developed unexpectedly between Jackson and such newly prominent post-black politicians as Wilder. Jackson's Rainbow had been responsible for elevating black politics to the national arena, illustrating that a black candidate could compete successfully, winning Presidential caucuses and primary elections in states without sizable minority groups. It was Jackson, not David Dinkins, who proved that a black candidate for high office could win a plurality of votes against more conservative white candidates in New York City.

Jackson's candidacy forced the Democratic Party to liberalize its posture toward women—witness the Vice Presidential nomination of Geraldine Ferraro in 1984—and toward blacks—witness the 1989 selection of Ronald Brown as head of the Democratic National Committee. His campaigns opened the political space for local African-American officials to seek statewide and mayoral positions, although their challenges were ideologically to Jackson's right.

Wilder's success in Virginia was based on a Rainbow-style approach, controlling nearly all black votes plus about one-third of the state's white electorate. But his political program was substantially more conservative than Jackson's. Once elected, Wilder lost little time endorsing centrist policy positions and repudiating liberal activism. Andrew Young's gubernatorial campaign in Georgia, in which he has endorsed the death penalty, faithfully follows Wilder's model, not Jackson's. Jackson's continuing flirtation with Presidential politics, and his refusal to run against Marion Barry in the District of Columbia's mayoral race, is attributable, at least in part, to his legitimate fear that Wilder or Gray is being groomed to eclipse him on the national stage.

Complicating matters is Jackson's tense and ambiguous relationship with Louis Farrakhan. Jackson has known Farrakhan intimately for more than a quarter of a century; Chicago was the political base for both men. In 1984, especially in the early days of the primary season, Jackson relied heavily on the Nation of Islam for security. People in Jackson's inner circle state candidly that he is intensely afraid of alienating Farrakhan personally or his black-nationalist constituency. Farrakhan has developed an extremely loyal cadre which expounds a conservative version of racial separatism and entrepreneurialism. Jackson fears a split with the nationalists that would repeat the hostilities that separated Martin Luther King from Malcolm X a generation ago.

Personally repelled by the crude anti-Semitism and authoritarian elements of the Nation of Islam's ideology, Jackson still believes he cannot denounce them for fear of turning this militant movement against him. In the absence of principled or decisive action condemning Farrakhan's anti-Semitism and sexist and chauvinist statements, the impression lingers that Jackson tolerates bigotry.

Thus a stalemate exists in black politics: Rainbow activism has reached a dead end, while post-black, centrist politicians are beginning to take the decisive initiatives. The failure here is not simply tactical but strategic. Jackson's political perspective is still frozen in the lessons of the civil-rights era. His basic instincts are to pressure the Democratic Party to the left, not to map a strategy for effective counter-hegemonic power.

But the grand realignment of the Democratic Party is a grand illusion. It is in the interests of both parties in our national-unity government to maintain the electoral status quo regardless of the destructive social and economic consequences for millions of Americans. We should not play cards with a stacked deck; rather, we should change the rules of the game.

Black and left activists must revive the traditions and tactics of non-electoral political protest; they must develop new institutions of creative resistance.

Freedom schools, for example. Open, multiracial academies, held during late afternoons and on weekends for secondary-school and college students, could offer a public protest curriculum. Learning how to organize street demonstrations, selective buying campaigns, and civil disobedience, reading about the personalities and history of American protest—such activities would help revive the radical consciousness of this generation.

Changing the rules requires innovations in the electoral process itself. The traditional plurality system in American elections gives the victory to the candidate with the most votes. This system is not only easily usurped by corporate interests, but also, by its nature, manipulates public preferences in time-worn outcomes. In multicandidate, citywide elections, in which minority constituencies represent one-third of the total vote or less, it becomes virtually impossible to elect candidates who represent their interests. Two results are predictable: Either the turnout rate of blacks gradually declines in national elections, which has occurred for the past fifteen years, or candidates emerge who are more conservative and thus politically palatable to the white upper middle class and corporate interests.

A better idea would be to restructure voting procedures to permit minority interests to be expressed democratically. Civil-rights attorneys in several states have pushed for changes in local elections that give each voter several votes in each multi-candidate race. The votes could be clustered behind one candidate or shared in blocs with coalition partners. The result would be to give minorities a much greater chance of being represented even in citywide races, yet the system would not discriminate against white majorities.

The best research in this area is being done by Lani Guinier of the University of Pennsylvania Law School. Her soon-to-be-published manuscript, "Black Electoral Success Theory and the Triumph of Tokenism," provides a blueprint for innovative challenges to the concept of democratic representation.

Instead of worrying about whether Jackson will contest the Democratic Party's Presidential nomination in 1992, progressives should refocus electoral efforts on other priorities. More resources should be devoted to increasing the size of the electorate. The National Voter Registration Act, passed last February by the House of Representatives, should be a major legislative priority for civil-rights groups. The bill calls for automatic updating of voting rolls with information provided by drivers' license and renewal applications and reports of address changes given to motor-vehicle departments. Since nonvoters are disproportionately nonwhite, poor, unemployed, and/or working-class women, any significant increase in turnout should shift the electoral results leftward.

We must rethink our current organizational forms and our approach to building coalitions. Has the NAACP, created during the nadir of Jim Crow segregation, outlived its political utility? To raise the question, and to answer it affirmatively, by no means denigrates the organization's outstanding contributions to the freedom struggle. Both reform-minded integrationists and separatist-oriented nationalists presume a form of race-based politics that does not recognize the subtle ways in which political, economic, and social institutions are assuming a nonracialist form, but nevertheless perpetuate the prerogatives of domination.

The passage of the Civil Rights Act of 1964 marked not the end of institutional racism but its transformation. The new, mutant version of inequality began to employ a race-neutral discourse while maintaining the objective of minority domination. It soon became difficult for civil-rights veterans to distinguish allies from antagonists, since nearly all adhered to the language of equality. Integrationists sensed that the rules of the game had changed but did little to modify their tactics. The habits and reflexes of five consecutive generations socialized by traditional segregation were too deeply ingrained to be questioned.

Black legal scholar Kimberle Crenshaw accurately characterizes the political environment since the demise of Black Power as the "post-reform period." Among the new elements of social inequality are such economic factors as the steady erosion of jobs, falling real incomes, and the swollen ranks of the poor, unemployed, and homeless in the ghetto. Thousands of African-American young people who are seeking work are unable to find it at an income level that could support a family. For the first time in recent history, a majority of young black women and men have never had or expect to have meaningful, rewarding employment any time in their lives.

A second element of the new political economy of domination is the set of intractable social problems proliferating inside urban black neighborhoods: high infant mortality rates and declining health standards, the growing numbers of juvenile pregnancies and female single-parent households, the increase in crime, street-gang activity, and use of hard drugs. These social problems are invoked by conservative intellectuals and politicians to undermine blacks' traditional demands for equality. Thomas Sowell, Charles Murray, Glen Loury simplistically attribute them, *ad nauseam,* to the welfare system, the black family, sexual promiscuity, and/or the lack of a work ethic among blacks.

The social crisis of the inner city is far more likely caused by the deindustrialization of urban areas, the flight of capital to the suburbs and overseas, and the absence of a comprehensive Federal policy for families and neighborhood development which could include expansion of public transportation systems, free child care, well-staffed public health clinics, adequate and affordable housing, and job-training programs.

The cruelest example of urban underdevelopment may be the Government's attitude toward public education and child development. A rapidly emerging educational underclass is unable to compete successfully for the new jobs requiring computer-related skills. This generates a tremendous amount of bitterness and frustration among young people.

Yet another by-product of urban decay and disruption is fear. Most middle- and upper-class whites employed in the financial and commercial districts of major cities flee to the suburbs after dark, seeking the safety of elaborate burglar-alarm systems and private security guards. Black and Hispanic working-class families living next door to crack houses aren't as fortunate. Blacks have long been the chief victims of violent crime. A typical white male's statistical chance of becoming a murder victim is one in 186; a black man's odds are one in twenty-nine. Black women are nearly twice as likely to be rape victims than are white women. Fear means that elderly black people and young single mothers with children are reluctant to leave their homes at night to attend civic meetings. Fear paralyzes a segment of the black middle class living in the suburbs, which wants to engage in socially constructive projects inside the ghetto but also wants to avoid crime.

These new forms of domination are not exclusively applied to blacks—they are used to hold down other minorities as well. The changing forms thus require activists to shift ground, from a racial to a truly multi-ethnic focus.

The development of constructive relations between African-Americans and Hispanics, Native Americans, Asian/Pacific Americans, and other ethnic minorities is foremost. Neither the traditional civil-rights groups nor the Congressional Black Caucus has continuing dialogues with parallel groups among Puerto Ricans or Mexican-Americans. Black-Hispanic political relations in many cities have become more fractious than fraternal. Cooperation between Hispanic and black caucuses in most state legislatures and city councils is, at best, inconsistent. African-Americans make few gestures to learn Spanish or to appreciate the unique perspectives and problems articulated by progressive Latino groups. Even Jackson's notable overtures to the Latino community didn't go far beyond the expression of political platitudes, without subsequent programmatic cooperation among these urban ethnic constituencies after the Democratic primaries ended.

African-Americans have to recognize demographic trends and the new multi-ethnic realities. Until the middle of the Twentieth Century, "race relations" in America meant black-white relations. This is no longer true. Today, one in four Americans is nonwhite. Three decades from now, the nonwhite population will have doubled, to 115 million, while the white population will remain the same. But Hispanics, not African-Americans, will make up the dominant group.

Any progressive urban policy agenda must emphasize the many economic, educational, and social problems shared by blacks and Hispanics. Despite the perception among some blacks that the majority of Hispanics are middle class or relatively privileged, statistics show a different reality. In 1988, the Census Bureau reported a poverty rate for whites of 10.1 percent; for Hispanics and blacks, the rates were 26.8 percent and 31.6, respectively.

In recent months, Asian-black tensions have erupted in many urban areas. The well-publicized economic boycott by black activists of Korean merchants in Brooklyn's Flatbush neighborhood is projected superficially as a manifestation of "black racism." But, as ethnic studies scholar Ronald Takaki observes, the "harmful myth of Asian superiority" is used to divide people of color with common interests.

Like African-Americans, Asian-Americans have experienced racial discrimination and vigilante violence. The tragic 1982 case of Chinese-American Vincent Chin, who was killed by Detroit auto workers who thought he was Japanese, is only one example of a disturbing trend. Many Asians are working-class or poor. One-fourth of New York's Chinatown population in 1980 was below the poverty level. And middle-income Asians frequently confront the same problems faced by middle-class blacks. Asian professionals complain about the "glass ceiling" inside corporations and academic institutions, limiting their upward mobility. The "affluent, hardworking" Korean shopkeepers, according to Takaki, have household incomes of between $17,000 and $35,000 annually, hardly ranking them with the idle rich. The reality behind the image of Asian-American affluence is that there is economic and social common ground with other people of color, and the foundations for coalitions exist.

We must refocus our tactical approach toward the majority of white Americans as well. Liberalism and appeals to moral suasion are no longer effective. The recent electoral behavior of the white middle and upper classes is largely dictated by perceptions of narrow, material self-interest. Whites will have to be shown in concrete terms that they have a direct stake in the consequences of the urban crisis. Investments in economic development, public transportation, public housing, and health care which benefit people of color are absolutely necessary for the productivity of society as a whole.

In *The Burden of Support*, sociologist David Hayes-Bautista notes that more than one-half of all children in California will be Hispanic by the year 2030, but whites will total about 60 percent of the elderly. A similar situation will exist across the United States within forty years: the existence of a retired leisure class over age sixty-five which will be largely white, subsidized by the growing wage deductions paid by an increasingly nonwhite labor force. It's easy to envision a political revolt against Social Security and other Federal programs for the elderly by racial and ethnic minorities.

Finally, we must rethink the concept of blackness itself, as a political category and as it relates to the construction of coalitions.

In the Caribbean, radical scholar-activist Walter Rodney used the term "black power" to connote a strategic alliance among people who were racially and ethnically designated as black, East Indian, and Chinese to struggle against neocolonial rule. In the United Kingdom in the 1970s, the antiracist mobilization of Asians, Africans, West Indians, and even radical whites was fought under the rubric of "black power."

We must recognize that black oppression is not biologically or genetically derived; it is driven by the systematic exploitation of black people in the economic system, and through their political and social domination within society. Perhaps the term "people of color" could be the basis of a new strategic unity of Chicanos, Puerto Ricans, African-Americans, West Indians, Native Americans, Asian/Pacific Americans, the unemployed and poor of any race who experience second-class citizenship because of corporate greed and a nonresponsive Government.

Black politics must go beyond the notion of a Rainbow Coalition—essentially an electoral mobilization with sporadic and uneven connections between multiracial and multiclass constituencies—to a more advanced level of organization based on the struggles to improve the quality of urban life and labor and build a truly democratic, pluralistic society for the majority of Americans.

~

Black America in Search of Itself

Conspiracy theories always tell you something, if not historical truth. They abound at present in the black community. Many believe that AIDS, which has struck disproportionateloy among people of color, is some kind of white supremacist medical conspiracy. Many African-Americans remember the perverse medical experiment conducted by the Federal Government in Tuskegee, Alabama; for forty years beginning in the 1930s, 399 black men suffering from advanced cases of syphilis went untreated in this program.

Three years ago, an aide to then-Mayor Eugene Sawyer of Chicago had to leave office after declaring that "Jewish doctors were infecting black babies with AIDS."

In September 1990, *Essence,* a popular black women's magazine, featured an essay headed AIDS: Is IT GENOCIDE?

When a *New York Times*/CBS News poll in August asked African-American and white residents of New York City whether AIDS "was deliberately created in a laboratory in order to infect black people," the differences in racial perceptions were striking. Only 1 percent of all whites polled thought this statement was true, and another 4 percent thought it could possibly be true. Ten percent of all blacks accepted the statement as valid, with another 19 percent agreeing it could be possible.

When blacks were queried about the reasons for the accessibility of crack cocaine and other illegal drugs within the African-American community, the results were similar. One-fourth of all blacks questioned agreed that the Federal Government "deliberately makes sure that drugs are easily available in poor black neighborhoods." An additional 35 percent agreed that this assertion was "possibly true."

When millions of people are absolutely convinced that they are being systematically destroyed, whether by an onslaught of drugs, criminal violence, or medical mayhem, any nascent racial polemicist can gather a constituency around himself and acquire a degree of legitimacy. Blacks ask themselves: Why is it so much easier to obtain crack cocaine and heroin in our neighborhoods than it is to buy fresh milk, eggs, and bread? Why are so many white educators so hostile toward the introduction of African-American studies and multicultural requirements within the core curricula of public schools and colleges?

Leonard Jeffries Jr., chair of the African-American Studies Department at New York's City College, started a firestorm in July, at the Empire State Black Arts and Cultural Festival in Albany, by delivering a public address that included several blatantly anti-Semitic remarks.

Jeffries, whose speech was broadcast over an Albany cable-TV station, asserted that blacks were the victims of "a conspiracy planned and plotted and programmed out of Hollywood" by "people called Greenberg and Weisberg and Trigliani." He claimed that "Russian Jewry had a particular control" over the film industry and that "their financial partners, the Mafia, put together a financial system of destruction of black people." He criticized those who opposed the inclusion of African and African-American history and culture in the state's high school curricula. He particularly condemned Assistant Secretary Diane Ravitch of the Department of Education, a Bush appointee, as "a Texas Jew" and "a sophisticated, debonair racist."

The response from the white political establishment, the media, and educational officials was swift. Many Democratic and Republican politicians, including New York Governor Mario Cuomo, denounced Jeffries. Democratic Senator Daniel Patrick Moynihan deplored the speech, noting that "conspiracy theories about 'rich Jews' are nothing new. What is new is for such things to be said by a professor at City College."

Moynihan insisted that Jeffries "ought to resign" and that if he was not removed, then the trustees of City College should resign. Harold Jacobs, a member of the City University board of trustees, declared that if Jeffries was "teaching bigotry in his classes, instead of African-American studies, that's consumer fraud being paid for by the state." The college's alumni association also demanded that Jeffries be fired as department head. Jewish leaders were particularly outraged. Michael Riff, local leader of the Anti-Defamation League of B'nai B'rith, said the controversial speech had "the tinge of classical anti-Semitism: to create a web of conspiracy by suggestion, innuendo, and half-truths."

The Jeffries controversy generated more heat than light, because no dialogue exists between Jeffries's critics and defenders over the real issues that divide them. Neoconservative writer Julius Lester, who is both black and Jewish, reviewed a videotape of the speech and found that the media "misrepresented some [of Jeffries's] statements." The speech certainly made anti-Semitic assertions, but most of Jeffries's remarks had nothing to do with Jews or black-Jewish relations.

Many black scholars suspect the condemnation of Jeffries is actually a smokescreen for a more general assault on multicultural perspectives in education. Jeffries served as principal consultant to a statewide curriculum-review committee for public schools in New York, which recently mandated a multicultural requirement. Even James De Jongh, chair of City College's faculty senate, admits that those who opposed the adoption of multiculturalism "are finding it easier to attack Jeffries on an obscure speech than to confront the curriculum."

Most black educators and leaders disagree with the expressions of anti-Semitism in Jeffries's public address, but they quietly question what the dispute is really about. It is difficult to take sympathetically the appeals of Moynihan, who a quarter of a century ago authored the notorious "black matriarchy" thesis, asserting that the black family is dysfunctional because it lacks patriarchal character. Blacks suspect that calls for firing the tenured professor, which in any case would be extremely difficult to accomplish legally, have little to do with anti-Semitism as such, and more with white hostility to affirmative action and the educational and political agenda of the black freedom struggle.

This perception hardened into certainty when another City College professor, Michael Levin, was vindicated by a Federal court. Levin had made public statements declaring that African-Americans overall are "significantly less intelligent" than whites, and college administrators had established a committee in 1990 to investigate allegedly racist statements in his classroom lectures. The ruling said the administrators were in error in ordering this investigation, and also erred in failing to discipline protesters who disrupted Levin's classes.

Levin's statement following this decision targeted Jeffries as well as all other African-Americans who favor greater ethnic diversity within education. "This whole subject of black studies," Levin said, "is a made-up subject that shouldn't be at any college anywhere." Jeffries and others teaching it only offer students "introductory resentment, intermediate resentment, and advanced resentment."

Many Jewish and white leaders were virtually silent about the Levin case and his legal victory, a fact not lost on black activists and scholars who reject both anti-Semitism and black chauvinism.

The absence of media focus on Levin also seemed to reinforce the conspiracy thesis of Jeffries and other African-American nationalists. In this context, it is not difficult for some to ignore the objectionable and even odious elements of Jeffries's address and to insist that the attack against the black educator was racially and politically motivated.

Conversely, many Jewish leaders are upset over the apparent silence of blacks over the anti-Semitic smears of Jeffries. The Anti-Defamation League has recorded a 50 percent increase in anti-Jewish harassment and violence on university campuses since the mid-1980s. Jewish stereotypes seem to be making a comeback in Hollywood: Witness the Jewish-American princesses in *White Palace,* or the untrustworthy Jewish characters in *Bonfire of the Vanities, Class Action,* and *Regarding Henry.* "Kill-the-Jew" computer games are now being sold in Europe. From the perspective of many Jews, the Jeffries incident is the most threatening of a series of events—including Jesse Jackson's "Hymie" smear of 1984 and the rising popularity of Black Muslim Louis Farrakhan among young inner-city African-Americans. If mainstream black leaders fail to condemn vigorously a demagogue such as Jeffries, some reasoned, it must be because they quietly embrace anti-Semitism themselves.

Simmering racial grievances finally boiled over into violence this summer in Brooklyn's Crown Heights neighborhood, where Hasidic Jews and blacks dwell in uneasy coexistence. On an evening in August, Yosef Lifsh, a Hasidic Jew, lost control of his automobile and smashed into several black children on the sidewalk, killing one seven-year-old boy. Witnesses reported to police that Lifsh had run a red light and was speeding; others spread the rumor that he had been drinking, and that ambulance attendants assisted him before they saw to the black children. Outraged, hundreds of young black people took to the streets, hurling rocks and bottles at police and Jewish residents. Apparently in retaliation, a group of twenty or so young blacks surrounded and killed a visiting Hasidic scholar from Australia, reportedly chanting, "Kill the Jew!"

To most blacks, both deaths were criminal homicides. To New York's Jewish community and most whites, the deaths were entirely different—the first a regrettable accident, the second a deliberate murder provoked by vicious black anti-Semitism. Many black activists were troubled when attorney Barry Slotnick, who had represented subway murderer Bernhard Goetz, stepped forward as a spokesman for Lifsh. When Brooklyn District Attorney Charles Hynes announced that no charges of criminally negligent homicide would be filed against Lifsh, the grief and resentment of thousands of blacks turned into deep outrage.

Instead of trying to understand the origins of black anger and violence in poverty and a sense of powerlessness, many whites leaped to the conclusion that anti-Semitism and violent sentiments have acquired a mass base of support among blacks.

Few white commentators were more vehement on this baseless theme than *New York Times* columnist (and former editor) A.M. Rosenthal. Blaming the recent upsurge of racial violence on "the black political marauders who goad mobs into the streets against Jews," Rosenthal asserted that their "strategy is to blow up all political and emotional bridges between blacks and nonblacks." Rosenthal linked the Crown Heights incident with the earlier Jeffries controversy, which he characterized as "weirdo speeches of a Jew-hairing professor on the public payroll and by bigotry's apologists, supporters, and conveyor belts in the black press and radio." Rosenthal offered his own self-fulfilling prophecy and warning to New York Mayor David Dinkins and other black elected officials, wondering aloud whether "any black will be chosen mayor for a long time" because "so many nonblacks have been antagonized."

Nowhere in Rosenthal's diatribe did he recognize that many black politicians, and especially Dinkins, have taken a principled, public stance against anti-Semitism throughout their careers. To blame them for the actions of a small minority is, in effect, a concession to the worst form of racist bigotry. Nowhere in this none-too-subtle linkage of Dinkins with Jeffries did Rosenthal acknowledge that Jewish political behavior in recent years has grown more conservative ideologically—and has specifically opposed blacks' interests on such issues as affirmative action.

The sources of genuine tension between Jews and African-Americans cannot be so simplistically attributed to the actions of anti-Semites within the black community. From the vantage point of blacks, bridges with the liberal Jewish political establishment were torched by other, far more significant events—the gradual shift in political sympathies from Israel to the Palestinians among America's black leadership and activists, the geographical flight of many Jews from the problems of the inner city to the affluent suburbs, the general Jewish hostility toward the Rainbow Coalition and Jesse Jackson.

Rosenthal's feeble appeals to interracial dialogue were disingenuous precisely because he and others like him in the white media and political institutions refuse to face the legitimate differences which have separated African-American and Jewish interests in the old civil-rights coalition of a generation ago. This failure is particularly difficult for blacks such as myself, who still feel a special sympathy and political kinship with the historical struggles of Jewish people and a keen opposition to all forms of anti-Semitism.

Why is this happening? Why these disturbing and disruptive social trends *now?* What is their long-term significance for black politics and culture?

Deeply embedded within the fabric of black American culture is the messianic myth of Moses and the ordeal of the ancient Hebrews. Gleaned from the Old Testament and reshaped to fit the contours of America's plantations and slave society, it became a beacon of hope and faith for successive generations of African-Americans yearning to be free.

The sons and daughters of slaves saw themselves as the children of bondage, oppressed by a wicked and unjust power. But a gifted, charismatic figure would arise from their ranks, a figure who would embrace both the spiritual strivings and secular ambitions of his people. This black messiah would lead his flock across the barren wilderness to the blessed banks of the River Jordan and into the golden horizon of the Promised Land.

A century ago. the messiah's mantle rested on the shoulders of Frederick Douglass, the great abolitionist orator. A generation ago, the weight of moral leadership was borne by Martin Luther King Jr. King recognized that his powerful presence in the lives of African-Americans was not due solely to his sonorous rhetoric, but rather to his kinship to the messianic cultural tradition of salvation and liberation.

"The Bible tells the thrilling story of how Moses stood in Pharaoh's court centuries ago and cried, 'Let my people go,'" King once declared. In identical fashion, he thought, the Southern desegregation movement demonstrated that "oppressed people cannot remain oppressed forever. The yearning for freedom eventually manifests itself." If the Hebrews found the courage to follow their convictions. African-Americans could do no less.

But nearly a quarter-century after the assassination of the civil-rights movement's messiah, and after a decade of pain imposed by the Reagan-Bush conservative reaction, African-American political culture has taken a new and very disturbing direction.

The desegregation struggle had been informed by a political ideology of what I call "liberal integrationism." Its central tenets were: the eradication of all legal barriers to blacks' gaining full access to civil society, economic exchange, and political institutions; an increase in the numbers of African-Americans representing their race in both real and symbolic positions of authority within the state: a strategic alliance with liberal whites, especially the national leaders of the Democratic Party, after the Great Depression.

Several generations of African-American leaders were nurtured in this secular creed and unthinkingly accepted its implications. Blacks as a group could be guaranteed continued upward mobility within the system if the rules of the game were liberalized, as larger numbers of African-American elites were elevated into the Federal judiciary, legislatures, and corporate board rooms.

Brown v. Board of Education, the 1954 Supreme Court decision outlawing segregated schools, had created the legal framework for a democratic, "color-blind" society within the structures of liberal capitalism. This liberal faith in the system was employed to justify all the sacrifices and hardships by the children of bondage. In destroying legal Jim Crow segregation, African-Americans had escaped the clutches of a dictatorial Pharaoh; their experiences since the 1960s seemed to represent a sojourn in the wilderness. But all along this bitter path, the image of a promised land of racial equality and economic democracy seemed to loom just ahead.

Then the myth veered off course. The messianic figure of the former slaves was murdered several days into the difficult journey through the wilderness. None of his closest comrades and lieutenants seemed able to bear the dual burden of political emancipator and moral guide. The creed of liberal integrationism and color-blind institutions, once affirmed with Talmudic certainty, began to be perceived as strangely anachronistic and even counterproductive.

The new generation of the oppressed, born and raised not under the old Jim Crow order but in the sterility of a political wilderness, inevitably challenged the faith of their fathers and mothers. Speaking for this lost generation, Anthony Parker, writing recently in *Sojourners,* questions the future identity of African-Americans as a people.

"Unlike the generation of blacks who reached maturity before and during the early 1970s," Parker writes, "my generation has no memory of credible black leaders, such as Malcolm X or Martin Luther King Jr. But the practice of integration created the illusion of equality with the wider culture, effectively wresting control of the black freedom movement by holding it hostage to Federal good will and weakening or destroying those institutions that influenced blacks' world view."

One major factor in the demise of black consciousness and identity was the materialism and greed inherent in the existing American political economy and secular society. By asking to be integrated into the existing structures of society, rather than demanding the basic transformation of the system, blacks became hostage to their own ideological demands.

"Inoculated with secular values emphasizing the individual instead of the community," Parker observes, "young blacks rarely recognize each other as brothers and sisters, or as comrades in the struggle. We're now competitors, relating to each other out of fear and mistrust."

Other black intellectuals have also sensed that African-Americans have reached a secular epiphany, a moment of self-realization and uncertainty, when the old beliefs can no longer be sustained, but the new insights into social reality cannot be fully comprehended. One of black America's most perceptive critics, Professor Cornel West of Princeton's Afro-American Studies Department, describes the contemporary spiritual crisis as a "profound sense of psychological depression, personal worthlessness, and social despair ... widespread in black America." West recognizes that "black people have always been in America's wilderness in search of a promised land. Yet many black folk now reside in a jungle with a cutthroat morality devoid of any faith in deliverance or hope for freedom."

On a national level, the mantle of leadership apparently passed to Jesse Jackson. Despite Jackson's incredible and largely unanticipated electoral success in the 1984 and 1988 Democratic Presidential primaries, however, the promise of his Rainbow

Coalition was never fulfilled. From its inception, the idea of the Rainbow brought together two contradictory currents—liberals who sought to make the Democrats a "social-democratic-style" party and leftists who wanted to launch a progressive third party from the bankrupt ruins of the New Deal and the Great Society.

In the wake of George Bush's election, Jackson tactically shifted to the right, siding with the liberals. He demanded and obtained the authority for his national board to veto all important political and legislative initiatives by local Rainbow chapters. In effect, the democratic grassroots leadership responsible for much of Jackson's electoral success was muzzled from above. Efforts to build a more structured membership organization with a formal dues system and a regular newspaper were silenced.

The results were inevitable. In 1989–1990, the Rainbow Coalition's political-action committee raised $549,973; in the first six months of 1991, the PAC raised only $33,657. Jackson's refusal to run for mayor of Washington, D.C., reinforced perceptions that the "country preacher" has no stomach for the nitty-gritty work of actual governing.

Valuable statewide leaders of the Rainbow defected in droves. In Louisiana, progressives bolted when Jackson ordered all local initiatives to be approved by his handpicked lieutenant. Dissidents promptly created an independent group. In Vermont, New Jersey, and Pennsylvania, core Jackson activists are building their own local alliances. Elsewhere, there is a bitter sense of frustration and betrayal. As Kevin Gray, the 1988 campaign coordinator for Jackson in South Carolina, declared, "The movement is not supposed to be a continual photo opportunity for Jesse Jackson for President, but that's what it's been."

Unlike King, Jackson never succeeded in balancing his own personal ambitions with the broader goals of the democratic protest movement that thrust him into public prominence. But the real dilemma confronting Jackson and other African-American leaders is the limitations of their own political ideology, which is liberal integrationism.

Despite his rhetorical posturing, Jackson never believed that the American political system could be transformed from without, via the challenge of a third party or even a quasi-independent movement like the Rainbow Coalition. He retains a deep faith that the Democratic Party can be transformed from within into an effective vehicle for the aspirations of the poor, the working class, women, racial minorities, and others experiencing discrimination and social injustices.

But what is strikingly clear after the crushing of Jimmy Carter, Walter Mondale, and Michael Dukakis in successive Presidential elections, and the ideological capitulation of mainstream Democratic Party politics to many of the central tenets of Reaganism, is that American liberalism is bankrupt. The belief in an internal, progressive realignment of the Democrats is belief in a hopeless illusion never to be achieved or realized so long as the party has some utility to corporate capitalism. It is the activists themselves who become transformed.

The crisis within black political culture is also intensified by the fraying of the bonds among virtually all African-Americans. Once, segregation led to a sense of shared suffering and group identity. An artificial yet powerful wall of race had been built around our community, giving us simultaneously a sense of oppression and a collective will to resist.

On Sunday mornings in the churches of my childhood, I can distinctly recall the people who came together for the ritual of spirit and unbowed faith—the school teacher and his family in the pew ahead, the automobile mechanics and sanitation workers beside me, the doctors and dentists in the pews behind. A wide range of vocations was represented, because segregation forced every class to cooperate with each other. A black lawyer looked to the black community for his or her clients. A black entrepreneur, anxiously opening a new business, had to depend on the faithful patronage of black consumers from her or his neighborhood, civic club, fraternity, school.

Now, in the post-civil-rights era of the 1980s and 1990s, even the definition of the term "black community" is up for debate. The net result of affirmative action and civil-rights initiatives was to expand the potential base of the African-American middle class, which was located primarily outside the neighborhood confines of the old ghetto. By 1989, one out of seven African-American families had incomes exceeding $50,000 annually, compared to less than $22,000 for the average black household. Black college-educated married couples currently earn 93 percent of the family income of comparable white couples.

But the general experience of the black working-class, low-income people, and families on welfare—the overwhelming majority of African-Americans—is one of steady deterioration. According to *African Americans in the 1990s,* a recent report by the Population Reference Bureau, the average annual income of African-Americans is only 56 percent that of white income, significantly less than the 63 percent ratio in 1975. Black female-headed households average less than $9,600 annually.

Stark differences in patterns of home ownership, income, and education indicate that there are "two separate worlds inhabited by poor and middle-class black children," the report says. This strongly implies that "the African-American population will become more polarized as these children mature."

Many white liberals take such statistics to mean that the source of material and social inequities which separate the races—institutional racism—no longer exists or at least, in the words of influential black sociologist William Julius Wilson, has "declined in significance." A shift in liberal governmental policy from race-based remedies to economistic, class-based programs is therefore required. From the vantage point of liberal Democrats, this would solve the perception problem among millions of white males that the party's social agenda is being held hostage to the interests of blacks. Class-based programs would eliminate the argument of "reverse discrimination," because all benefits would, theoretically, be distributed in a color-blind manner.

Stuart Eizenstat, domestic policy adviser in the Carter Administration, defends this thesis. So does Richard Cohen, liberal columnist for *The Washington Post.* "If economic need, not race," Cohen writes, "became the basis for what we now call affirmative action, most Americans would not object. Whites, too, could be helped. . . . After all, poor is poor, although a disproportionate number of them are black."

When minority community leaders read such statements, most cannot help but feel a sense of outrage and repudiation. The overwhelming majority of Federal programs *were* based on income, not race. Poor whites shared substantial benefits from the initiatives of the Great Society.

Currently, more than one-third of all students enrolled in the Upward Bound program, designed to prepare low-income students for college, are white. One-third of the children who attend the preschool Head Start program are white. The majority of people living in public housing, or who receive public assistance, are white.

The basis of affirmative action is the recognition that, within this society, there is systemic discrimination grounded in race and gender. Despite the passage of the Civil Rights Act of 1964 outlawing discrimination in public accommodations, race is a powerful factor in determining the actual conditions of life for any person of color, regardless of income and education. My children stand a much greater likelihood of being harassed or arrested by the police, for example, than the children of my white colleagues at the university, solely because they are black.

Through practical experience, African-Americans of every social class recognize this reality. To argue that a shift in affirmative-action policies from race to class will benefit them seems, at best, a gross distortion. At worst, it is taken as yet one more piece of evidence that liberal integrationism has failed as a political strategy. Black intellectuals and politicians increasingly are convinced that white liberals have turned their backs against us; both parties have repudiated our very presence at any serious debate on public policy.

Many millions of African-Americans believe that most whites live a racial double life, that whites follow a hypocritical racial etiquette in the presence of blacks which disappears whenever they are among themselves. This is the basic premise of the recent film *True Identity,* which features a black man who dons white makeup. He discovers that whites interact very differently with each other than they do with minorities.

Abundant evidence supports this thesis. Earlier this year, a study of the American Bar Association published in *Harvard Law Review* indicated that car dealers charge African-Americans and women higher prices than white males. Male and female researchers, black and white, presented themselves as middle-class car shoppers at ninety car dealerships in the Chicago metropolitan area. They used identical negotiation styles and bartered for identical automobiles. The car dealers' offers to the consumers followed a pattern of gender and racial inequity. The final offer to white males averaged $11,352; to white women, $11,504; to black men, $11,783; to black women, $12,237.

Affirmative action is a particular sticking point in the 1990s. In the workplace, most white males behave publicly in a race-neutral manner. Virtually no one openly calls African-American employees or supervisors "niggers." But millions of whites harbor deep resentment against black and Latino co-workers, who they believe have been unfairly advanced and receive excessively high wages because of affirmative-action and equal-opportunity programs.

In one recent survey of several thousand white male corporate employees, only 10 percent expressed the opinion that "women were getting too much help" through affirmative action. But 50 percent stated that blacks and Hispanics unfairly gained "too much" of an advantage by affirmative action. Conversely, 55 percent of all Latino and black employees polled stated that "too little was being done for them" through corporate affirmative-action efforts.

Many whites perceive the presence of people of color in their workplace as a "zero-sum game"; the additional appointment of any single black person means that the potential job pool for whites has decreased. Instead of fighting to increase the size of the economic pie, many whites now want to take away the small slice served up to Latinos and blacks through affirmative-action initiatives.

Such programs forced police departments to hire and promote thousands of minorities and women, partially in an attempt to respond to the changing urban demographics of race. But many whites have never reconciled themselves to these policy changes, which they perceive as an erosion of "standards" and "professionalism." This anger and alienation is projected on black and Latino citizens, who are generally assumed to be guilty in any confrontation.

For example, a public commission reviewing the Los Angeles Police Department reported several months ago that it found more than 700 racist, homophobic, and sexist remarks made by officers on the department's car-communications system over the previous eighteen months. Typical of the statements: "Sounds like monkey-slapping time" and "I would love to drive down Slauson [a street in a black neighborhood] with a flamethrower. We would have a barbecue."

But the best evidence of the pervasiveness of white privilege is found in daily life. When inner-city blacks and Latinos return from work in the downtown district, they watch the striking changes in the allocation of commuter buses and trains, which shuttle upper-class whites in comfort to their suburban enclaves. They feel their worthlessness in white eyes as they wait for graffiti-scarred, filthy trains in urine-stenched stations. They feel the anger held in check, seeing crack-cocaine merchants operate on their street corners as police cars casually drive by, doing nothing.

Everything in daily life tells them that, to those with power and wealth within the system, African-American life, property, beliefs, and aspirations mean nothing.

In the ruins of ideology, bereft of messianic leadership, the African-American community reaches a moment of painful introspection. When hope of the New Jerusalem and the possibility of political liberation dies, part of the spirit dies as well.

Locked in an urban abyss of poverty, drugs, and black-against-black violence, the working class and dispossessed increasingly retreat into themselves, psychologically and culturally. If the creed of liberal integrationism no longer makes sense, and if our leaders have failed to deliver us from the wilderness, then we must turn within our own group, reviving the images and symbols for survival. The temptation is to seek refuge in the narrow alleys of racial chauvinism and political parochialism.

Black America still sees itself as the essential litmus test on the viability and reality of American democracy. Indeed, the African-American striving for freedom and human rights embodies this country's best examples of sacrifice and struggle for the realization of democracy's highest ideals.

A century ago, black scholar W.E.B. Du Bois suggested that the "concrete test of the underlying principles of the great republic is the Negro Problem." Yet this historic burden of race cannot be comprehended solely in legislative initiative or in the struggles for voting rights. This sojourn through the wilderness is a quest for full self-consciousness, a "spiritual striving of the freedmen's sons" which represents a "travail of souls whose burden is almost beyond the measure of their strength, but who bear it in the name of a historic race, in the name of this land of their fathers' fathers, and in the name of human opportunity."

It is precisely here, at the juncture of faith and political ambition, of spirit and struggle, that the black freedom movement must revive itself, casting aside the parochial chains of chauvinism and isolation. We can find value in our culture and heritage without needing negative stereotypes and myths of other ethnic groups. We can express ourselves ethnically without resorting to the false discourse and rationales of race.

In the process we will discover that the proverbial promised land of full equality and economic equity can be achieved, but only in concert with other groups of the oppressed—especially Hispanics, Native Americans, Arab-Americans, Asian/Pacific-Americans, and the unemployed and economically and socially disadvantaged of all ethnic backgrounds.

Ethnic pride and group awareness constitute a beginning stage, not an end unto itself, for a richer understanding of the essential diversity and pluralism that constitute our America. That awareness of diversity must point toward the restructuring of the elaborate systems of ownership and power that perpetuate the unequal status of these ethnic groups and oppressed social classes. This leap of awareness depends on our willingness to define our political, educational, and social goals in a way that is truly majoritarian, that speaks for the commonwealth of the whole society, that realizes a new level of struggle for the black freedom movement.

~

African-American Empowerment in the Face of Racism

The Political Aftermath of the Battle of Los Angeles

INTRODUCTION

The racial violence which erupted across Los Angeles this year represented the most profound urban unrest in the United States since the turbulent sixties. Yet the fires which torched thousands of buildings had not even cooled before white politicians and the media attempted to attribute the rebellion to various sociological problems within the African-American community. Vice President Dan Quayle pointed to the factors of sexual permissiveness, welfare, and the breakdown of the nuclear family as contributing to the racial unrest among African Americans. Others in the media criticized African-American political leaders, especially Congresswoman Maxine Waters, for characterizing the "riot" as a "rebellion," and for failing to uphold law-and-order in the ghetto. Lost in all the accusations was any serious effort to comprehend the social significance of this cathartic event.

There are at least three pivotal questions which should provide the background to an understanding of the racial "Battle of Los Angeles." We must first identify the root causes for the racial uprising. The disgraceful verdict of the Rodney King trial, which vindicated the brutal actions of four white police officers, was only the immediate catalyst for the social explosion. Second, how did the uprising affect sectors of the African-American community specifically, and various racial and ethnic groups generally? What was the special significance of the Rodney King trial, for example, to upper-middle-class African Americans who lived miles away from southcentral Los Angeles? What is the importance of the assaults aimed at Asian-American-owned property by young African Americans? How did white Americans perceive this unanticipated revolt?

113

Thirdly, and most significantly, is the burning issue of violence in a racist society. We can't begin to analyze Los Angeles without exploring the essential nexus between coercion or violence and the historical and contemporary status of African Americans as an oppressed people. Racism is, in essence, institutionalized violence aimed against African-American people—in economics, education, employment, political affairs, and all aspects of daily life. When African Americans resort to violence against that system of social control, are they simply "rioting," or do their collective actions have a more profound meaning? And given the history of racist coercion, what are the future prospects for more serious African-American acts of violence against the system in the near future?

THE RACE/CLASS FAULT LINE: WHITE REACTION

For generations, California has been known for its San Andreas fault, the geological fracture beneath the earth's crust. The periodic eruptions along the fault line have been responsible for massive destruction and hundreds of deaths.

Yet, far more devastating than the San Andreas fault is America's "race/class fault line," the jagged division of color and income, education and privilege which slashes across the soul of this nation. In California, the race/class fault line rudely separates the posh affluence of Hollywood and Beverly Hills from the crime, fear, and hunger of southcentral L.A. That same race and class division runs down Detroit's Eight Mile Road, separating the poor, unemployed, and homeless from comfortable, suburban white enclaves. It sets apart Harlem and Bed-Stuy from the multimillion-dollar estates in Connecticut's posh suburbs. The Los Angeles race uprising can be understood only from the vantage point of the race/class fault line, because the violence unleashed by Rodney King's court case was just a tremor along that division.

On different sides of the race/class fault, each group tends to perceive issues in radically different ways. The vast majority of all Americans—African-American, Latino, Asian-American and white—believed that the innocent verdict in the King case was wrong. But according to one recent poll in *USA Today,* 81 percent of all African Americans stated that the criminal justice system was clearly "biased against Black people." Sixty percent of all African Americans agreed that there was "very much" police brutality against people of color, and another 33 percent believed that such violence was "considerable." Conversely, only 36 percent of all whites who responded believed that the justice system was racially biased. Only 17 percent of whites were convinced that there was "excessive police brutality" against minorities.

The white public's racist attitudes were reinforced by the rhetoric and contempt for African Americans displayed by the nation's white elected officials. For example, in a shameful display of political cowardice, President George Bush's initial instinct was to attribute blame for the Los Angeles race revolt on the liberal "Great Society" programs of Lyndon Johnson, a quarter century ago. But when pressed for specific programs which had contributed to the racial crisis of today, White House press secretary Marlin Fitzwater could only mumble, "I don't have a list with me."

Did Bush mean the 1964 Civil Rights Act, which had outlawed racial discrimination in public accommodations? Was the President blaming the National Housing Act of 1968, which established the National Housing Partnership to promote the construction of houses for low-to-middle-income people? Or maybe the reason people rioted was due to the 1965 Voting Rights Act, which had established the principle of "one person, one vote" a century after the abolition of slavery. Bush's pathetic effort to rewrite racial history, to blame the victim, was yet another example of his "Willie Horton" racial politics. The current agony of our inner cities is a direct and deliberate consequence of Reagan-Bush policies, and no amount of historical distortion can erase that fact.

On the white side of the race/class fault line, the response of most middle and upper-class white Americans to the Los Angeles unrest was profoundly mixed. Opinion polls showed a new appreciation of the ghetto's socioeconomic problems and greater sympathy for the racism experienced by African Americans within the legal system.

But middle-class whites in southern California also took immediate steps to protect themselves, fearing that the police would be unable to check the unrest. In the first eleven days of May, California residents purchased 20,578 guns, a 50 percent increase over last year's rate. Frightened corporate executives and professionals who had never owned firearms now stood in line, demanding shotguns and semiautomatic weapons. The National Rifle Association, with 2.8 million members, added one thousand new members each day in the month after the racial explosion. Newspapers even reported instances where suburban whites fled in panic when confronted by anyone with a Black face—delivery boys, mail carriers, and sanitation workers. Motivated by racism, guilt, anger, and fear, many whites tried to isolate themselves from the social chaos. In downtown L.A., at the peak of the unrest, dozens of whites drove the wrong way down one way streets, speeding through red lights. Barricades were erected in Westwood, and a swank shopping mall in Beverly Hills was closed.

THE RACE/CLASS FAULT LINE: AFRICAN-AMERICAN REVOLT

But the same race/class fault line which trembled and shook across impoverished southcentral Los Angels also runs directly beneath the affluent white suburbs as well. This time, African-American and Latino young rebels weren't content to destroy the symbols of ghetto economic exploitation. Violence and arson unexpectedly struck against white-owned property across Los Angeles County. The Bloods and Crips street gangs established a fragile peace pact, announcing to the media that the current street violence was "a slave rebellion, like other slave rebellions in Black history." One local Samoan rap group declared that the rebellion was "great," but that the violence against property should have been directed not against the Korean stores, but at "the rich people in Beverly Hills."

Much of the violence was indeed directed against the Asian-American community. Over 1,800 Korean-owned stores were destroyed or vandalized, with property damage estimated at $300 million. Yet as deplorable as this violence was, it represented a dual tragedy for both Asian Americans and African Americans. Young African Americans need to understand that it is not the Korean-American small merchant who denies capital for investment in the African-American community, or controls the banks and financial institutions. It is not the Korean-American community which commits police brutality against Latino and African-American citizens, or controls governmental policies, or dominates the political parties. Aggression against people of color is misplaced and misdirected. This doesn't negate the legitimate grievances or differences of opinion which separate Korean Americans from Latinos and African Americans. But it makes a unified response to race and class oppression virtually impossible.

The unanticipated eruption of rage stripped away the facade of African-American progress in the central cities, boiling with the problems of poverty, drugs, gang violence, unemployment, poor schools, and deteriorating public housing. The white media tried desperately to turn attention away from these issues, in part by arguing that the Los Angeles uprising was merely a "riot" which was opposed by most African Americans. This ignores the historical evidence about the dynamics of all civil unrest. After the Watts racial rebellion of 1965, for example, sociologists later determined that only about 15 percent of all African-American ghetto residents had actually participated in the arson and violence. However, between one-third to one-half of all residents later expressed support for those who had destroyed white-owned property and attacked symbols of white authority. About two-thirds later agreed that "the targets of the rebellion got what they deserved." So although the majority of African Americans in southcentral L.A. didn't take to the streets, that doesn't mean that they aren't alienated and outraged by race and class oppression.

A critical distinction must be made, therefore, between the concept of a "riot," versus other forms of collective resistance: "insurrections," "revolts," "rebellions," and "strikes." The term "riot" connotes widespread criminal behavior disconnected from political objectives. An individualistic desire to loot and burn can be interpreted as just antisocial behavior, linked to Daniel Patrick Moynihan's "Black Matriarchy Thesis" and the absence of strong parental role models, at least according to Quayle. But any analysis based on what young African Americans are actually saying and feeling in the streets should lead to an opposite conclusion. Los Angeles was an "insurrection" or a "rebellion," precisely because people acted collectively rather than as individuals. There was a clearly political motivation for hurling rocks at police squad cars, which symbolized the vehicles of an oppressive, occupying army in the African-American community. No one, except perhaps the Israelis, would denigrate the "Intifada" as just a "riot" against political authorities in the occupied West Bank. Similarly, African Americans engaged in violence against white-owned property are motivated by the same political alienation which we see in the faces of young, militant Palestinians.

For the African-American middle-class professionals, many of whom had come to believe the mythology about racial progress under the Reagan-Bush era, the King verdict was like a "firebell in the night." They were jolted into the realization that they, like Rodney King, could be halted by the police, brutalized, kicked, and possibly killed—and that their assailants in police uniforms would probably walk away free. They were awakened by the haunting fear that their college-bound sons and brothers could be stopped for minor traffic violations, and later be found dead or dying in the city streets. This is what Representative Floyd Flake of Brooklyn meant when he explained why the hopes of millions of African Americans in the inherent fairness of the legal system were shattered: "When Rodney King was on the ground getting beat, we were all on the ground getting beat."

But if we listen carefully to young African Americans in the streets, this genera- tion is telling us more than just its dissatisfaction with the King verdict. The violence was not directly generated by reactions to courtroom decisions. What our young people painfully realize is that the entire "system"—the government and its politi- cians, the courts and the police, the corporations and the media—has written them off. They recognize that Bush had virtually no coherent policies addressing urban problems, until he was confronted by massive street violence. They feel instinctively that American businesses have no intention of hiring them at real "living wages," that the courts refuse to treat them as human beings, and that the politicians take their votes and ignore their needs. By taking to the streets, they are crying out to society: "We will be heard! We will not be ignored, and we will not go away quietly. And if the system, and society, refuses to listen to us, we intend to burn it to the ground."

RACE AND VIOLENCE: PAST, PRESENT, AND FUTURE

White America wonders whether the Los Angeles "riot" represents just the beginning of a new wave of social unrest and violence throughout urban America. But the young people who challenged police cars and public authorities in the streets earlier this year weren't responsible for introducing the question of violence into the context of American race relations. The essential definition of "racism" throughout American history has been the systematic discrimination and exploitation of a people defined as a subordinate and inferior "racial group." And the force which perpetuated inequality of material conditions between African Americans and whites, the absence of full voting and legal rights, the substandard pay at places of employment, was violence. During the period of slavery, from 1619 until 1865, few whites ever questioned whether African Americans were not inherently inferior to whites. Slaves were the constant victims of all types of violence, from the forced separation of families to systematic rape and whippings.

Violence against African Americans was endemic to the Jim Crow segregated South. Between 1884–1917, more than 3,600 African Americans were lynched across the South. The terror was a deliberate part of a social order designed to maintain the permanent inferiority of African Americans. The violence also preserved whites as a group with a privileged status, giving them access to higher wages, better schools and homes than any African Americans could ever hope to attain.

When World War I broke out, African Americans overwhelmingly supported the popular effort to defeat Germany. They purchased over $250 million in war bonds, hoping that their patriotism would help shield them from racist violence and permit them to secure greater democratic rights. Yet immediately following the conflict, in the "Red Summer of 1919," over 70 African Americans were lynched and eleven were burned alive—some still in uniform.

When African Americans mobilized in nonviolent demonstrations to overthrow the Jim Crow system a generation ago, they were again confronted by white violence. African-American churches and homes were bombed, civil rights leaders and community organizers by the thousands were beaten and arrested, and dozens of key leaders were assassinated, most prominently Dr. Martin Luther King, Jr., and Medgar Evers.

The eruption of inner-city violence of the 1960s was the fist significant demonstration of illegal force by thousands of African Americans, aimed against the symbols of white civil authority and private property. The urban "riots" of 1964–1972 led to 250 deaths, 10,000 serious injuries, and 60,000 arrests. In Detroit's 1967 civil unrest, 43 residents were killed, about 2,000 were injured, and over 2,700 white-owned businesses were torched and vandalized, with half completely gutted by fire. Although the media described these acts of collective violence as "riots," this obscures both the political element which motivated thousands of young African Americans into the streets, as well as the degree of concurrence for these actions by African Americans who stood along the sidelines. People committed arson, theft, and assaults not because they were "lawbreakers" or "criminals," but acted in the belief that the established civil authorities and the standard rules of society were structured in a way to preserve white power and domination over African-American lives. Thus African Americans acted in violence against a system and its symbols which, in turn, represented violence and inequalities in their daily lives.

Violence by whites against African Americans also continues to permeate African-American life, although it manifests itself no longer in the traditional forms of lynching or terrorism against African-American leaders. High rates of unemployment, the closure of businesses in African-American areas, the proliferation of drugs, and the failure by government to provide decent housing and health care for the poor are perceived as forms of institutional "violence."

Although virtually all civil rights leaders and African-American elected officials are firmly committed to legal forms of protest and oppose violent acts of disruption against civil authority or vandalism of property, the Los Angeles uprising may easily trigger a series of massive urban conflagrations over the next decade. For the young men who have been socialized in a world of urban street gangs, drugs, and Black-on-Black murder feel within them a nearly ungovernable rage against all forms of power and privilege. That rage may express itself in collective acts of violence and selective terror similar to those identified with the Irish Republican Army in the United Kingdom, or by several radical Palestinian groups. If people feel that all avenues of realistic, effective change within the established order are blocked, they may move to a new level of violence which could be targeted at officials, prominent executives. and the police. The next stage of racial violence could become more sophisticated and terrifying for the authorities.

If violence descends into terror, the historical figure which might provide the greatest insights for this generation of young African Americans may not be Malcolm

X, but George Jackson. Sentenced at the age of 18 to a term of "one year to life" for the theft of 70 dollars, Jackson spent his entire adult life in a California prison. Yet such was his radical influence within the Black Liberation Movement that he was appointed national "Field Marshal" of the Black Panther Party while imprisoned. Before his execution in San Quentin prison in August 1971, Jackson authored two texts on the uses of "revolutionary violence," *Soledad Brother* and *Blood in My Eye*. For Jackson, the struggle against racism and class exploitation had to transcend the nonviolent policies of Martin Luther King, Jr., and the civil rights movement.

"Any claims that nonviolent, purely nonviolent political agitation has served to force back the legions of capitalist expansion are false," Jackson wrote in *Soledad Brother*. "There is no case of successful liberation without violence. How could you neutralize an army without violence?" Jackson believed that only through armed struggle could African Americans finally achieve full human rights and self-determination. And if the government attempted to eliminate prominent African-American leaders and street organizers, the only appropriate response was political assassinations, bombings, and other methods of violence. "If terror is going to be a choice of weapons," Jackson warned, "there must be funerals on both sides."

The "Battle of Los Angeles" raises the fundamental question of whether white, mainstream America will accept the missions of inner-city African Americans and Latinos on the basis of full human equality, unless thousands of office buildings, businesses, and police stations are assaulted and burned to the ground. If George Jackson is right, then retaliatory violence by African Americans and the widespread use of terror may be necessary. There will indeed be "funerals on both sides," so long as the legitimate grievances of African Americans go unanswered. But ultimately, the choice of "violence vs. nonviolence" is not ours, but white America's. Those who make peaceful change and democratic advancement impossible make violent revolution inevitable.

AFTER THE MARCH

"There is a great divide, but the real evil in America is not white flesh or black flesh. The real evil in America is the idea that undergirds the setup of the western world, and that idea is called white supremacy." So declared Louis Farrakhan on 16 October in his two-hour keynote speech before hundreds of thousands of black men from across America who had gathered in front of the Capitol for the "Million Man March".

The demonstration was the culmination of a year-long mobilisation, led by Farrakhan, leader of the Nation of Islam, and former National Association for the Advancement of Colored People (NAACP) secretary, Benjamin Chavis, and endorsed by more than 200 national black organisations. Although the march's official position was at first to exclude women—Farrakhan's advice to women was to stay at home, pray and watch the children—several women's organisations also endorsed the event, including the National Council of Negro Women and the National Black Women's Political Congress.

Farrakhan's call included a demand for "atonement"—that African-Americans should recognise "wrongs done and make amends", and apologise for all offences "against the Creator". The march agenda spoke relatively little about contemporary public policy issues, such as affirmative action, immigration and welfare reform. Instead, it emphasised the need for blacks to assume "personal responsibility" for their own circumstances, and challenged African-American males to provide leadership for their families and communities.

Farrakhan's controversial history, including public statements describing Jews as "bloodsuckers" and Judaism as "a gutter religion", at first led most US politicians and the media to dismiss or condemn plans for the mobilisation. Many prominent black feminists, including Angela Davis, publicly condemned the march's position that women could not participate. Many black gay men were turned off by Farrakhan's homophobia, such as in his 1993 statement; "We must change homosexual behaviour and get rid of the circumstances that bring it about". Many black progressives criticised the march for not attacking the Republicans' "Contract With America".

Yet it is to Farrakhan's credit that he recognised the deep emotional and cultural crisis at the heart of the African-American community. Those who participated in the gathering all described a deep sense of fellowship. Men wept openly, embracing each other, committing themselves to new levels of personal and civic engagement. Many explained that they had not come to Washington in support of Farrakhan's political agenda. Rather, they were there to express a deep desire for the black community to come together, in a process of healing.

In one opinion poll, 85 percent of all African-Americans expressed support. Thousands of people returned to their homes with a new dedication to participate in black organisations. For example, although the National Urban League and its affiliates refused to endorse the march, many blacks returning from it contacted this moderate civil rights body to volunteer their services.

Even so, one must keep in mind that the majority can be wrong. In 1991, the majority of African-Americans favoured the appointment of Clarence Thomas to the US Supreme Court. Thomas's subsequent conservative tenure has represented a disaster for black people. Mass popularity is no guarantee that the masses are pointed in the right direction.

So what explains the cathartic outpouring of emotion and enthusiasm that characterised the day in Washington? One fundamental factor is the destruction or elimination of an entire generation of progressive African-American leaders since the civil rights movement. Beginning with the assassinations of Malcolm X and Martin Luther King, the American government has aggressively attempted to isolate or imprison black leaders on the left. The Black Panther Party was specifically targeted and wrecked by the FBI and local police. Since then, hundreds of progressive black elected officials have been indicted and imprisoned.

Jesse Jackson's Rainbow Coalition seemed to represent a breakthrough by blacks to mainstream electoral politics. In 1988, Jackson received more than seven million votes for the presidency. But the defeat of his left social democratic programme and the decline of the Coalition left a deep vacuum in US politics.

Another lost opportunity was represented by Benjamin Chavis's short and controversial leadership of the NAACP, the nation's largest civil rights organisation in 1993–94. Chavis's programme represented a fundamental challenge to the reformist, inclusionist strategy of traditional civil rights leaders and most black elected officials. He expanded the NAACP membership to reach out to alienated urban youth and the most oppressed sectors of the black community. He initiated a constructive dialogue among a broad spectrum of leaders and constituencies, seeking the grounds for practical cooperation, and advocating what was in effect a left social democratic agenda: expansion of government investment in the inner cities, full employment, a universal health care system, construction of low-to-middle-income housing, and vigorous enforcement of affirmative action and civil rights legislation.

When Chavis was attacked for engaging in a dialogue with Farrakhan, he carefully distinguished his own politics from those of Farrakhan's Nation of Islam. In the *New York Times* in July 1994, he reiterated his support of the "long and honourable alliance" between African-Americans and Jews, emphasising that "neither I nor the NAACP have ever embraced anti-Semitic beliefs, nor would we countenance them." But, he explained, it was wrong to claim that a dialogue with Farrakhan implied an acceptance of his philosophy. Within days, however, charges that Chavis had misappropriated NAACP funds to cover up allegations of sexual harassment eroded the moral and political base of his leadership. Funds dried up, as funders demanded his expulsion. A compliant board, some of whom had benefited from the internal corruption and patronage within the NAACP hierarchy, summarily fired him.

Depite his sacking, Chavis still commanded substantial influence among key sectors of the black middle class, churches and many NAACP branches. By recruiting him as "national chairperson" for the Million Man March, Farrakhan and the Nation of Islam were able to reach new constituencies where previously they held only marginal influence. Chavis, in turn, was prepared to jettison much of his previous left-of-centre politics for a black nationalist programme centred on patriarchy, "atonement" and self-help conservative economics."

At an ideological level, the march represented a kind of pragmatic united front, anchored in cultural nationalism and the racial politics of the aspiring black middle class. Neither Farrakhan nor Chavis has significant influence within black labour unions or the Coalition of Black Trade Unionists. Their core programme was designed to appeal in the broadest possible terms to racial solidarity, while saying next to nothing about the growing class stratification within the black communities.

Perhaps the primary reason the march acquired such widespread support was the general recognition that blacks are faced with an unprecedented crisis within the US political and economic system. Politically, both major parties have largely repudiated the legacy of civil rights reforms and the social welfare expenditures of the "Great Society". While politicians have campaigned aggressively against affirmative action, minority economic programmes and majority-black legislative districts, blacks have been caught in a cycle of unemployment, growing social inequality and imprisonment Indeed, the single most important material reality of American society in the 1990s is the vast polarisation of classes, the unprecedented rise in personal incomes and profits among a small minority of American households, and the expansion of social misery, falling incomes and inequality for the majority of the population of the country.

As of 1993, the top 1 percent of all income earners in the US had a greater combined net wealth than the bottom 95 percent. According to a survey of the 85 largest metropolitan areas in the US, between 1973 and 1989, average incomes fell by 16 percent. In the New York borough of Manhattan, the poorest one-fifth of the population in 1990 earned an annual average income of $5,237. The richest one-fifth earned $110,199.

The same profile of inequality exists in every American city. In Los Angeles, the median annual incomes of the poorest and the wealthiest fifth in 1990 were $6,821 and $123,098 respectively. In Chicago, the figures were $4,743 and $86,632; in Detroit $3,109 and $63,625. Millions have been pushed into unemployment and poverty, while for America's privileged and powerful elite, things have never been better.

The conservative political agenda, from Reaganism to Newt Gingrich's "Contract With America", rests fundamentally on this core reality of escalating inequality. The ruling elites have to hide these statistics, or at least blame the hardships of white working-class people on the behaviour of blacks, Latinos and other people of colour. "Race" is deliberately manipulated to obscure class inequality.

The primary response by elected officials and the corporate elite has been the massive expansion of public and private security forces, and the incarceration of literally millions of black, Hispanic and poor people. Between 1980 and 1990, the number of police in the US doubled. And in addition to the 554,000 officers employed by local and state police forces, there are now 1.5 million private security officers. Much of the new suburban housing being built today in "planned communities" is surrounded by walls, wired for electronic surveillance, and guarded by private security personnel.

It was in this context in 1994 that the US Congress passed President Clinton's $30-billion Omnibus Crime Bill. As author Phil Gasper has observed, the Crime Bill's provisions included: "$10.8 billion in federal matching funds to local governments to hire 100,000 new police officers over the next five years, $10 billion for the construction of new federal prisons, an expansion of the number of federal crimes to which the death penalty applies from two to 58 (the bill also eliminated an existing statute that prohibited the execution of mentally incapacitated defendants), a so-called "three strikes" proposal which mandates life sentences for anyone convicted of three 'violent' felonies" and so on. Even more striking has been the massive expansion of the US prison system. In 15 years, the prison population tripled, from 500,000 in 1980 to 1,500,000 in 1995. In California alone, between 1977 and 1992, the prison population soared from less than 20,000 to over 110,000.

The racial oppression that defines US society is most dramatically apparent in the criminal justice system and the prisons. Today, about half the inmates in prison and jails, more than 750,000 people, are African-Americans. One quarter of all African-American males in their twenties are today either in prison, on probation or parole, or awaiting trial. A recent study in the District of Columbia estimated that 70 percent of black men would be arrested before the age of 35, and that 85 percent would be arrested at some point in their lives.

These statistical profiles of racial oppression should not obscure the class dimensions of who is arrested and imprisoned in the US. In 1989, more than 14 million Americans were arrested; about two percent of the total male labour force in the US today is in prison. According to a 1991 survey, about one-third of all prisoners were unemployed at the time of their arrests, while two-thirds of all prisoners have less than a high school level education and few marketable skills. The prisons of the US are vast warehouses for the poor and unemployed, for low wage workers and the poorly educated, and most especially, for Latino and African-American males. White-collar criminals, who embezzle hundreds of millions of dollars, are rarely given prison sentences. The wealthy and powerful almost never go to prison for the crimes they commit. But for the most oppressed, prison is frequently an improvement in life circumstances: free health care, three meals a day, shelter and some modest training programmes. Today, there are hundreds of thousands more black men in prison than are enrolled in colleges or universities. Statistically, a young black man has a greater likelihood of being arrested than obtaining a job that adequately supports him and his family. It is this tough reality that gives Farrakhan such legitimacy among millions of African-Americans.

Yet this is why the march's emphasis solely on the plight of black males is so short-sighted. No one doubts the physical and psychological agony of African-American men. But the burden of unemployment, inferior education and nonexistent health care weighs equally upon black women. And in many other respects, African-American women must bear an overwhelming burden alone: raising their children, working at two or more jobs to survive, and struggling in human terms often without the personal intimacy or sharing of a partner. To construct a politics grounded in patriarchy, however "benevolent", is to denigrate the real struggles, responsibilities and interests of our sisters.

The racial essentialism of the "Million Man March" obscures the growing reality of class polarisation among blacks. One example of the political and class divisions just beneath the surface within the African-American community is provided by the phenomenon of General Colin Powell, the former chairman of the Joint Chiefs of Staff. In a *USA Today*/CNN/Gallup poll this month, far more whites than blacks supported Powell for the presidency. In head-to-head competition against Clinton, Powell as the Republican candidate would win a majority of whites' votes, by 54 to 37 percent. But African-Americans overwhelmingly endorsed Clinton over the black challenger, by 68 to 25 percent. Among African-Americans, Powell's support is weakest among the most oppressed, those with low incomes, lacking a college education, who live in the south. Powell's greatest support among blacks comes from those with college degrees, whose incomes are $30,000 and above, and who believe the O J Simpson verdict was wrong. The black middle class, the chief beneficiaries of affirmative action and minority economic set-asides, are searching for an acceptable political alternative to advance their own class interests. In this sense, Colin Powell and Louis Farrakhan represent two sides of the same political coin. Middle-class Republicanism and conservative black nationalism have similar social and economic philosophies: self-help, less reliance on government, entrepreneurial capitalism, hostility to trade unionism and the left.

The great unknown in the aftermath of the "Million Man March" is the political future of Jesse Jackson. For months, Jackson refused to endorse the march, on the grounds that it lacked a strong public policy agenda, and, to some extent, because it focused too narrowly on black policy issues. Jackson changed his mind, and his speech at Washington resounded with much greater clarity and vision than anything Farrakhan represented.

Jackson declared: "We come here today because there is a structural malfunction in America. Why do we march? Because the media stereotypes us. We are projected as less intelligent than we are, less hard-working than we work … Why do we march? Because we are trapped with second-class schools and first-class jails. What is the crisis? Wealth going upward: jobs going outward. Middle class coming downward: the poor expanding rapidly." Following the march, Farrakhan committed the Nation of Islam to conduct a massive voter registration campaign, bringing millions of new black voters to the polls in 1996. This represents a challenge to the remnants of the Rainbow Coalition and the traditional civil rights establishment. Does Jackson embrace Farrakhan's leadership, or does he attempt to regain the political initiative?

Can Jackson revitalise multi-cultural, multi-racial, left-of-centre politics, speaking beyond black and white? If he fails, black America may increasingly turn within itself, moving away from the possibility of multi-racial democratic reform.

Before Benjamin Chavis's expulsion as NAACP leader, he urged the black freedom movement to eschew the politics of racial chauvinism and social isolation from progressive constituencies. Chavis wrote: "Let us not be distracted from our central task: building a nation where we are not separate and unequal, where no group is relegated to poverty, and where race or creed does not determine one's destiny." Although Chavis has become Farrakhan's lieutenant, his previous observation remains the central challenge for both black and progressive US politics. A strategy that addresses poverty and imprisonment should understand the burden of race, but must also speak a language of class. A social vision that transcends the narrow confines of black nationalist separatism remains vital to the reconstruction of American democracy.

~

FACING THE DEMON HEAD ON
Race and the Prison Industrial Complex

We know through painful experience that freedom is never voluntarily given by the oppressor; it must be demanded by the oppressed.
  —Martin Luther King, Jr., "Letter from Birmingham Jail," April 16, 1963

I

When I was a child, the only two prisons I had ever heard about were Alcatraz and Sing Sing. Alcatraz was the formidable, stone citadel, perched on a small island in the middle of the San Francisco Bay. I saw *The Birdman of Alcatraz* starring Burt Lancaster, and the film left a deep impression about prison life. I suppose my knowledge of Sing Sing was acquired in a similar fashion. My images of crime and punishment were derived from Edward G. Robinson, or perhaps some obscure character actors who were usually cast as hoodlums. Somehow, though, I knew that the phrase to "send him up the river" meant a one-way trip along the Hudson River to the infamous Sing Sing Prison.

Nothing I have seen or experienced prepared me for the reality of Sing Sing. The prison itself seems literally carved out of the side of a massive cliff that hovers just above the Hudson River. Parking is usually difficult to find near the prison, so you have to walk a good distance before you come to the outer gate, the first of a series of razor-sharp barriers. The main entrance looks remarkably small, compared to the vast size of the prison. Entering the front door, you find yourself in a relatively small room, with several guards and a walk-through metal detector. Your clothing and other personal items are carefully checked. Permission to go inside the prison is severely restricted, and you must be approved through a review process well before your visit.

On the other side of the entrance area, shielded by rows of steel bars, is a hallway that is lined with wooden benches on either side. It is here that inmates wait before being summoned to their hearings to determine whether they have merited early release. During my first time visiting Sing Sing, there were about a half dozen young males, all African Americans and mostly in their twenties, who were sitting nervously on the benches. Most would be forced to wait for hours in order to have fifteen minutes before the parole board. In fifteen short minutes, they would learn whether they would be released, or ordered to serve another term of years behind bars. You could see clearly the hopeful anxiety in each man's face, trying to anticipate the queries of their inquisitors. The right answer at the right moment could bring their suffering to an end.

The prisoners also know that the parole board's decisions are directly influenced by authorities in political power. Under former Governor Mario Cuomo, for instance, approximately 54 percent of violent offenders received parole on their first appearance before a parole board. Since 1995 under Governor George Pataki, only one-third of violent offenders were granted parole after their first review. As Robert Gangi, the director of the Correctional Association of New York, observed, "Given the practice of the parole board, there are more and more long-termers that no matter how well they behave, no matter how many programs they complete, the parole board is not going to let them out."

As you walk through the prison, you go down a series of hallways, separated by small containments that have two sets of steel bars on either side, and secured by a prison guard. Only one set of doors opens at a time. The guard must lock and secure the first door before you're permitted to walk through the second door. Because the prison was constructed on a side of a cliff; there are also a series of steps that must be climbed to go from one area to another.

At the end of one hallway is the infamous, seventy-year-old structure, Cell Block B. The guards informed me, with considerable pride, that Cell Block B was one of the largest enclosed incarceration areas of its kind in the world. One must first walk through a series of double barred steel doors separated by a small interlocking security chamber. Once passing through the second door, one enters a vast open space, surrounded by massive concrete walls and ceiling. In the center of this chamber, filling up nearly the entire space, is a solid iron cage, five stories high. Every story or tier contains 68 separate prison cells, front and back, for a total of 136 cells on each level. Each tier is separated by small-railed catwalks and narrow stairwells.

Each cell is a tiny confined space, with barely enough room for a prisoner's toilet, sink, and bed. Prisoners are not allowed to place any clothing or items covering the front of their cells, except when using their toilets. In effect, personal privacy is nonexistent. The massive metal structure is like a huge iron and steel echo chamber, where every sound from tier to tier resonates and can be easily heard. The whole oppressive environment—the pungent smells of sweat and human waste, the absence of fresh air, the lack of privacy, the close quarters of men who have been condemned to live much of their natural lives in tiny steel cages—is so horrific that I find it even now impossible to express in words its awesome reality. Perhaps the only word for it is evil.

Ted Conover, the author of *Newjack: Guarding Sing Sing,* who worked for nine months as a correctional officer at the prison, had a similar experience when he spent his first day on the job in Cell Block B. Conover was immediately overwhelmed by the constant level of noise, the demands of his supervisors, and the general chaos. "Being a new face," Conover noted, "was like being a substitute teacher. They test you. They defy you. And your job is to get them to comply." Conover questioned the ability of anyone to withstand the psychological stresses and physical levels of brutality that permeated the entire character of life in Sing Sing. "Every day is terrifying," Conover observed. "From the first minute, you're presented with challenges no one prepared you for. It's like working in an explosives factory. You think you're going to get killed. But you have to put it out of your mind."

Violence against prisoners is a daily occurrence. Conover described the process of carrying out a "shakedown" of solitary confinement cells. The guards go from cell to cell, demanding that each individual prisoner strip, turn around, raise his arms, and permit himself to be body searched. For prisoners who refused to be humiliated by this demeaning procedure, a group of guards pushed their way into their cells and forcibly carried out body searches. It was months after Conover was working in Sing Sing, however, that he realized that prisoners who resisted being physically searched were trying to hold on to some element of self-respect, to refuse to participate in their own violation. "If enough people did that together," Conover recognized, "the correctional system would come tumbling down."

In this man-made hell-on-earth, something within the human spirit nevertheless flourishes. About two decades ago, the prisoners of Cell Block B somehow managed to overwhelm their guards, protesting their inhumane conditions. For several days seventeen correctional officers were held as hostages. But in the end, the prisoners recognized that escape was impossible, and that this act of resistance was more symbolic than anything else. To demand to be treated as a human being in an inhumane environment is to be a revolutionary.

Seven years ago I received an invitation to visit Sing Sing from the Reverend George William ("Bill") Webber, who in 1982 had started the master's degree program at New York Theological Seminary (NYTS). When Bill began visiting Sing Sing on a regular basis, he observed that there were a small but highly motivated number of prisoners who had finished their bachelor's degrees and wanted to take more advanced courses. NYTS began to offer a graduate program designed for long-term prisoners at the facility. As the NYTS program developed, inmates at various correctional facilities throughout New York State were selected for admission and then transferred to Sing Sing. About fourteen to sixteen men were selected every year, with a waiting list of one or more years.

I was escorted to the rear quarters of the prison, which consist of religious quarters and chapels of different denominations. At the bottom of a stairwell was the entrance to a classroom. The students were already waiting there and were eager to introduce themselves. There was Louis, a twenty-nine-year-old man of Puerto Rican descent, who had already spent twelve years of his brief life inside penal institutions; Kevin, a middle-aged African-American man, articulate and serious, who had been in Sing Sing for nineteen years, and who was now actively involved in AIDS awareness and antiviolence programs within the inmate population; "Doc," a thirteen-year prisoner who planned to be a counselor; Paul, a seventeen-year inmate interested in working with teenagers and young adults after his release; and Felipe, a prisoner for nineteen years, who was preparing himself for the ministry.

The NYTS program is basically designed to prepare these men for community service. There is a rigorous academic program, where lectures and classroom discussions are held three hours a day, five days a week. Forty-two credit hours must be taken to complete the degree. Inmates are also required to perform an additional fifteen credit hours of field service within the prison, which can range from working in the AIDS ward to tutoring other prisoners. Since the program was established, more than 200 men have graduated with master's degrees. Only 5 percent of those inmates who have completed the program and were released were subsequently returned to prison.

The NYTS program is exceptional, in part, because so few educational programs of its type exist in U.S. prisons. In 1995, only one-third of all U.S. prisons provided college course work, and fewer than one in four prisoners were enrolled in some kind of educational or tutorial program behind bars. There are only about 11,000 paid teachers who are currently employed by penal institutions, or about one teacher per ninety-three prisoners.

One can only imagine the personal courage and determination of these men, most of whom entered prison without a high-school diploma or GED. From the first day of their sentences inside Sing Sing, they experienced what the NYTS 1994 program graduates accurately described as "social death": "We are told what we can eat, when we can eat it, and how we must eat it. We are told what type of clothing we can wear, when to wear it, and where we can wear it; when we can sleep and when we cannot sleep; where we can walk and where we cannot walk; when we can show affection to our families and when we cannot show affection; where we can sit and where we cannot sit; where we can stand and where we cannot stand." Despite the hostility of many prison guards, most of whom come from the same oppressed classes of those whom they are employed to guard, the men involved in the program withstand the daily abuse and harassment. In their own words, "We see ourselves as agents of change."

II

For a variety of reasons, rates of violent crime, including murder, rape, and robbery, increased dramatically in the 1960s and 1970s. Much of this increase occurred in urban areas. By the late 1970s, nearly one-half of all Americans were afraid to walk within a mile of their homes at night, and 90 percent responded in surveys that the U.S. criminal-justice system was not dealing harshly enough with criminals. Politicians like Richard M. Nixon, George Wallace, and Ronald Reagan began to campaign successfully on the theme of law and order. The death penalty, which was briefly outlawed by the Supreme Court, was reinstated. Local, state, and federal expenditures for law enforcement rose sharply. Behind much of anticrime rhetoric was a not-too-subtle racial dimension, the projection of crude stereotypes about the link between criminality and black people. Rarely did these politicians observe that minority and poor people, not the white middle class, were statistically much more likely to experience violent crimes of all kinds. The argument was made that law-enforcement officers should be given much greater latitude in suppressing crime, that sentences should be lengthened and made mandatory, and that prisons should be designed not for the purpose of rehabilitation, but punishment.

Consequently, there was a rapid expansion in the personnel of the criminal justice system, as well as the construction of new prisons. What occurred in New York State, for example, was typical of what happened nationally. From 1817 to 1981, New York had opened thirty-three state prisons. From 1982 to 1999, another thirty-eight state prisons were constructed. The state's prison population at the time of the Attica prison revolt in September 1971 was about 12,500. By 1999, there were more than 71,000 prisoners in New York State correctional facilities.

In 1974, the number of Americans incarcerated in all state prisons stood at 187,500. By 1991, the number had reached 711,700. Nearly two-thirds of all state prisoners in 1991 had less than a high-school education. One-third of all prisoners were unemployed at the time of their arrests. Incarceration rates by the end of the 1980s had soared to unprecedented rates, especially for black Americans. As of December 1989, the total U.S. prison population, including federal institutions, exceeded 1 million for the first time in history, an incarceration rate of the general population of 1 out of every 250 citizens. For African Americans, the rate was over 700 per 100,000, or about seven times higher than for whites. About one-half of all prisoners were black. Twenty-three percent of all black males in their twenties were either in prison, on parole, on probation, or awaiting trial. The rate of incarceration of black Americans in 1989 had even surpassed that experienced by blacks who still lived under the apartheid regime of South Africa.

By the early 1990s, rates for all types of violent crime began to plummet. But the laws sending offenders to prison were made even more severe. Children were increasingly viewed in courts as adults and subjected to harsher penalties. Laws like California's "three strikes and you're out" eliminated the possibility of parole for repeat offenders. The vast majority of these new prisoners were nonviolent offenders, and many of these were convicted of drug offenses that carried long prison terms. In New York, African Americans and Latinos make up 25 percent of the total population, but by 1999 they represented 83 percent of all state prisoners and 94 percent of all individuals convicted on drug offenses. The pattern of racial bias in these statistics is confirmed by the research of the U.S. Commission on Civil Rights, which found that while African Americans today constitute only 14 percent of all drug users nationally, they account for 35 percent of all drug arrests, 55 percent of all drug convictions, and 75 percent of all prison admissions for drug offenses. Currently, the racial proportions of those under some type of correctional supervision, including parole and probation, are one in fifteen for young white males, one in ten for young Latino males, and one in three for young African-American males, Statistically today, more than eight out of every ten African-American males will be arrested at some point in their lifetime.

Structural racism is so difficult to dismantle in our nation today, in part, because political leaders in both major parties have deliberately redirected billions of our tax dollars away from investments in public education into the construction of what many scholars now describe as a prison industrial complex. This is the terrible connection between education and incarceration.

A 1998 study produced by the Correctional Association of New York and the Washington, D.C.–based Justice Policy Institute illustrated that in New York State hundreds of millions of dollars have been reallocated from the budgets of public universities to prison construction. The report stated: "Since fiscal year 1988, New York's public universities have seen their operating budgets plummet by 29 percent while funding for prisons has increased by 76 percent. In actual dollars, there has nearly been an equal trade-off, with the Department of Correctional Services receiving a $761 million increase during that time while state funding for New York's city and state university systems has declined by $615 million." By 1998, New York State was spending nearly twice what it had allocated to run its prison system a decade ago. To pay for that massive expansion, tuitions and fees for students at the State University of New York (SUNY) and the City University of New York (CUNY) had to be dramatically hiked.

For black and Latino young adults, these shifts have made it much more difficult to attend college than in the past, but much easier to go to prison. The New York State study found: "There are more blacks (34,809) and Hispanics (22,421) locked up in prison than there are attending the State University of New York, where there are 27,925 black and Hispanic students. Since 1989, there have been more blacks entering the prison system for drug offenses each year than there were graduating from SUNY with undergraduate, masters, and doctoral degrees—combined."

The devastating pattern of schools versus prisons in New York exists throughout our country. In California, thousands of black and Latino young adults were denied access to state universities because of the passage of Proposition 209, which destroyed affirmative action. Thousands more have been driven out by the steadily growing cost of tuition and cutbacks in student loans. Meanwhile, hundreds of millions of dollars have been siphoned away from the state's education budget and spent on building prisons.

In 1977, California had 19,600 inmates in its state prison system. By 2000, the number of that state's prisoners exceeded 163,000. In the past two decades of the twentieth century, California has constructed one new state university, but twenty-one new prisons. California's prison system "holds more inmates in its jails and prisons than do France, Great Britain, Germany, Japan, Singapore, and the Netherlands combined." And future trends are worse. The California Department of Corrections estimated in 2000 that it would need to spend $6.1 billion over the coming decade just to maintain the present prison population. There are more employees at work in the American prison industry than in any Fortune 500 corporation, with the one exception of General Motors.

Instead of funding more teachers, we are hiring extra prison guards. Instead of building new classrooms, we are constructing new jails. Instead of books, we now have bars everywhere.

III

The latest innovation in American corrections is termed "special housing units" (SHUs), but which prisoners also generally refer to as The Box. SHUs are uniquely designed solitary confinement cells in which prisoners are locked down for twenty-three hours a day for months or even years at a time. SHU cell blocks are electronically monitored, prefabricated structures of concrete and steel, about 14 feet long and 8½ feet wide, amounting to 120 square feet of space. The two inmates who are confined in each cell, however, actually have only about 60 square feet of usable space, or 30 square feet per person. All meals are served to prisoners through a thin slot cut into the steel door. The toilet unit, sink, and shower are all located in the cell. Prisoners are permitted one hour "exercise time" each day in a small concrete balcony, surrounded by heavy security wire, directly connected with their SHU cells. Educational and rehabilitation programs for SHU prisoners are prohibited.

As of 1998, New York State had confined 5,700 state prisoners in SHUs, about 8 percent of its total inmate population. Currently under construction in Upstate New York is a new 750-cell maximum-security SHU facility that will cost state taxpayers $180 million. Although Amnesty International and human-rights groups in the United States have widely condemned SHUs, claiming that such forms of imprisonment constitute the definition of torture under international law, other states have followed New York's example. As of 1998, California had constructed 2,942 SHU beds, followed by Mississippi (1,756), Arizona (1,728), Virginia (1,267), Texas (1,229), Louisiana (1,048), and Florida (1,000). Solitary confinement, which historically had been defined even by corrections officials as an extreme disciplinary measure, is becoming increasingly the norm.

The introduction of SHUs reflects a general mood in the country that the growing penal population is essentially beyond redemption. If convicted felons cease to be viewed as human beings, why should they be treated with any humanity? This punitive spirit was behind the Republican-controlled Congress and President Clinton's decision in 1995 to eliminate inmate eligibility for federal Pell Grant awards for higher education. As of 1994, 23,000 prisoners throughout the United States had received Pell Grants, averaging about $1,500 per award. The total amount of educational support granted prisoners, $35 million, represented only 0.6 percent of all Pell Grant funding nationally. Many studies have found that prisoners who participate in higher education programs, and especially those who complete college degrees, have significantly lower rates of recidivism. For all prison inmates, for example, recidivism averages between 50 percent and 70 percent. Federal parolees have a recidivism rate of 40 percent. Prisoners with a college education have recidivism rates of only 5 to 10 percent. Given the high success ratio of prisoners who complete advanced degree work and the relatively low cost of public investment, such educational programs should make sense. But following the federal government's lead, many states have also ended their tuition benefits programs for state prisoners.

The economic consequences of the vast expansion of our prison industrial complex are profound. According to criminal-justice scholar David Barlow at the

University of Wisconsin at Milwaukee, between 1980 and 2000 the combined expenditures of federal, state, and local governments on police have increased about 400 percent. Corrections expenditures for building new prisons, upgrading existing facilities, hiring more guards, and related costs increased approximately 1,000 percent. Although it currently costs about $70,000 to construct a typical prison cell, and about $25,000 annually to supervise and maintain each prisoner, the United States is still building hundreds of new prison beds every week.

The driving ideological and cultural force that rationalizes and justifies mass incarceration is the white American public's stereotypical perceptions about race and crime. As Andrew Hacker perceptively noted in 1995, "Quite clearly, 'black crime' does not make people think about tax evasion or embezzling from brokerage firms. Rather, the offenses generally associated with blacks are those ... involving violence." A number of researchers have found that racial stereotypes of African Americans—as "violent," "aggressive," "hostile," and "short-tempered"—greatly influence whites' judgments about crime. Generally, most whites are inclined to give black and Latino defendants more severe judgments of guilt and lengthier prison sentences than whites who commit identical crimes. Racial bias has been well established, especially in capital cases, where killers of white victims are much more likely to receive the death penalty than those who murder African Americans.

The greatest victims of these racialized processes of unequal justice, of course, are African-American and Latino young people. In April 2000, utilizing national and state data compiled by the FBI, the Justice Department and six leading foundations issued a comprehensive study that documented vast racial disparities at every level of the juvenile justice process. African Americans under age eighteen constitute 15 percent of their national age group, yet they currently represent 26 percent of all those who are arrested. After entering the criminal-justice system, white and black juveniles with the same records are treated in radically different ways. According to the Justice Department's study, among white youth offenders, 66 percent are referred to juvenile courts, while only 31 percent of the African-American youth are taken there. Blacks make up 44 percent of those detained in juvenile jails, 46 percent of all those tried in adult criminal courts, as well as 58 percent of all juveniles who are warehoused in adult prison. In practical terms, this means that young African Americans who are arrested and charged with a crime are more than six times more likely to be assigned to prison than white youth offenders.

For those young people who have never been to prison before, African Americans are nine times more likely than whites to be sentenced to juvenile prisons. For youths charged with drug offenses, blacks *are* forty-eight times more likely than whites to be sentenced to juvenile prison. White youths charged with violent offenses are incarcerated on average for 193 days after trial; by contrast, African-American youths are held 254 days, and Latino youths are incarcerated 305 days.

Even outside of the prison walls, the black community's parameters are largely defined by the agents of state and private power. There are now approximately 600,000 police officers and 1.5 million private security guards in the United States. Increasingly, however, black and poor communities are being "policed" by special paramilitary units, often called SWAT (Special Weapons and Tactics) teams. Researcher Christian Parenti cited studies indicating that "the nation has more than 30,000 such heavily armed, military trained police units." SWAT-team mobilizations, or "call outs," increased 400 percent between 1980 and 1995, with a 34 percent increase in the incidents of deadly force recorded by SWAT teams from 1995 to 1998.

What are the practical political consequences for regulating black and brown bodies through the coercive institutional space of our correctional facilities? Perhaps the greatest impact is on the process of black voting. According to the statistical data of the Sentencing Project, a nonprofit research center in Washington, D.C., forty-eight states and the District of Columbia bar prisoners who have been convicted of a felony from voting. Thirty-two states bar ex-felons who are currently on parole from voting. Twenty-eight states even prohibit adults from voting if they are felony probationers. There are eight states that deny voting rights to former prisoners who had been serving time for felonies, even after they have completed their sentences: Alabama, Florida, Iowa, Kentucky, Mississippi, Nevada, Virginia, and Wyoming. In Arizona, ex-felons are disfranchised for life if they are convicted of a second felony. Delaware disfranchises some ex-felons for five years after they finish their sentences, and Maryland bars them from voting for an additional three years.

The net result to democracy is devastating. The Sentencing Project released these statistics in 2002:

- An estimated 3.9 million Americans, or one in fifty adults, have currently or permanently lost their voting rights as a result of a felony conviction.
- 1.4 million African-American men, or 13 percent of black men, are disfranchised, a rate seven times the national average.
- More than 2 million white Americans (Hispanic and non-Hispanic) are disfranchised.
- Over half a million women have lost their right to vote.
- In seven states that deny the vote to ex-offenders, one in four black men is *permanently* disfranchised.
- Given current rates of incarceration, three in ten of the next generation of black men can expect to be disfranchised at some point in their lifetime. In states that disfranchise ex-offenders, as many as 40 percent of black men may permanently lose their right to vote.
- 1.4 million disfranchised persons are ex-offenders who have completed their sentences. The state of Florida had at least 200,000 ex-felons who were unable to vote in the 2000 presidential elections.

The Sentencing Project adds that "the scale of felony voting disenfranchisement is far greater than in any other nation and has serious implications for democratic processes and racial inclusion." In effect, the Voting Rights Act of 1965, which guaranteed millions of African Americans the right to the electoral franchise, is being gradually repealed by state restrictions on voting for ex-felons. A people who are imprisoned in disproportionately higher numbers, and then systematically denied the right to vote, can in no way claim to live under a democracy.

The consequence of such widespread disfranchisement is what can be called "civil death." The individual who has been convicted of a felony, serves time, and successfully completes parole nevertheless continues to be penalized at every turn. He/she is penalized in the labor force, being denied certain jobs because of a criminal record. He/she has little direct access or influence on the decision-making processes of the political system. He/she may be employed and pay taxes, assuming all of the normal responsibilities of other citizens, yet may be temporarily or permanently barred from the one activity that defines citizenship itself—voting. Individuals who are penalized in this way have little incentive to participate in the normal public activities defining civic life because they exercise no voice in public decision making. Ex-prisoners on parole are also frequently discouraged from participation in public demonstrations or political meetings because of parole restrictions. For many ex-prisoners, there is a retreat from individual political activity; a sense of alienation and frustration easily leads to apathy. Those who experience civic death largely cease to view themselves as "civic actors," as people who possess the independent capacity to make important changes within society and within governmental policies.

Criminal-justice scholars have described prison as a metaphor for the most oppressive and socially destructive conditions of structural racism in America. As Alvin J. Bronstein observed in the *Prisoners' Rights Source-book* (1981), edited by Ira Robbins:

> In a very real sense, the prison is the outside world, squeezed into a very small space. The total and largely self-contained society that is prison contains all of the evils of that outside world, only much more concentrated.... Hence, militancy is especially great in prison, not because of a few agitators, but because the repression—whether justified or not—is harsh and undiluted. Because prison is one of the most severe sanctions in our society, the subjects of that sanction include the most alienated and the most aggressive members of society. And since the sense of injustice is most developed where the penalties are the greatest, the resentment and bitterness ... [are] deep and pervasive.

Many women and men who do manage to survive incarceration often acquire critical insights about the nature of the legal process and the criminal justice system that could provide important and powerful lessons for young people in racialized minority communities. Like Frederick Douglass and Fannie Lou Hamer before them, they frequently do not have formal educational credentials or middle-class privileges. Yet from theorizing about their practical day-to-day experiences within the prison system, they come to a richer understanding of how that system actually works and how to develop innovative and creative ways to subvert it. As Bronstein noted, "It is no coincidence that many of the classics of black literature, such as those by Malcolm X, Eldridge Cleaver, Bobby Seale, and George Jackson, are prison memoirs, in whole or in part." Paradoxically, such strong personalities, who were able to survive the system, found ways to learn its lessons and to become empowered in the process. An essential step in transforming this system is in "reproducing" leaders like Malcolm X. The site of the most extreme oppression could have the greatest potential for creating the most effective leadership.

IV

It is absolutely clear that a new leviathan of racial inequality has been constructed across our country. It lacks the brutal simplicity of the old Jim Crow system, with its omnipresent "white" and "colored" signs. Yet it is in many respects potentially far more brutalizing, because it presents itself to the world as a correctional system that is theoretically fair and essentially color-blind. The Black Freedom Movement of the 1960s was successful largely because it convinced a majority of white middle-class Americans that racial segregation was economically inefficient and that politically it could neither be sustained nor justified. The movement utilized the power of creative disruption, making it impossible for the old system of white prejudice, power, and privilege to function in the same old ways it had for nearly a century. How can Americans who still believe in racial equality and social justice stand silently while millions of our fellow citizens are being destroyed all around us?

It is abundantly clear that the political demand for mass incarceration and the draconian termination of voting rights to ex-felons will only contribute toward a more dangerous society. No walls can be constructed high enough, and no electronic surveillance cameras and alarms sophisticated enough, to protect white middle- and upper-class American families from the consequences of these policies. Keep in mind that approximately 600,000 people are released from prison every year; that about one-sixth of all reentering ex-prisoners, 100,000 people, are being released without any form of community correctional supervision; that about 75 percent of reentering prisoners have substance abuse histories; and that an estimated 16 percent suffer from mental illness. Nearly two-thirds of this reentering prison population will be arrested again within three years. The madness of our penal policies and of the criminal-justice system places the entire society at risk. Dismantling the prison industrial complex represents the great moral assignment and political challenge of our time.

During my last visit to Sing Sing, I noticed something new. The prison's correctional officials had erected a large, bright yellow sign over the door at the prison's public entrance. The colorful sign reads: "Through these doors pass some of the finest corrections professionals in the world."

I stood frozen for a second, immediately recalling the chillingly brutal sign posted above the entrance gate at Auschwitz and other concentration camps: *Arbeit Macht Frei* ("Work Makes Us Free"). I later asked Bill Webber and a few prisoners what they thought about the new sign. Bill thought a moment, then said simply, "demonic." One of the M.A. students, a thirty-five-year-old Latino named Tony, agreed with Bill's blunt assessment. But Tony added, "Let us face the demon head on." With more than 2 million Americans who are now incarcerated, it is time to face the demon head on.

SECTION IV

On the Southern Question

~

TUSKEGEE AND THE POLITICS OF
ILLUSION IN THE NEW SOUTH

INTRODUCTION

There are two statues in Macon County, Alabama: the first is an old Confederate War Monument, situated on the town square in central Tuskegee, surrounded by the major commercial district of the county. The second, at a distance of less than two miles from the center of town, is located on the campus of Tuskegee Institute, in the shadow of the new college chapel. Beneath several impressive, spreading ferns stands the statue of Booker T. Washington, the famous black educator, lifting the veil of ignorance from the face of a black slave. It is of this famous yet ambiguous statue that Ralph Ellison wrote poignantly that it was impossible to tell whether the veil was being lifted or being lowered.[1]

Both statues represent two historical, opposing social forces which have dominated the cultural terrain and general civil societal formations of central and southern Alabama for four generations—the defeated, white racists who reconquered the governments of state and local communities after the Compromise of 1877, and the aspiring black intelligentsia, whose political horizons were first sketched by the "wizard of Tuskegee," Booker T. Washington. Both sculptured symbols represent a profound interdependency. The Negro academic strata Washington created and inspired could not exist without key compromises in politics to the white establishment. Yet, the white dominated economic base would collapse without the continued economic support of the black petty bourgeoisie. Both statues represent, as it were, two central elements of the bitter drama which is Southern history and politics. Neither could have existed in the twentieth century without the other; therein lies the central burden of Southern politics.

The possible outline for transcending the tragedy of Tuskegee's political past was offered in Charles V. Hamilton and Stokely Carmichael's best seller, *Black Power*. Devoting an entire chapter to Tuskegee, Alabama, the authors claimed correctly that the city and county were "undoubtedly one of the most significant areas in the history of the black man in this country."[2] Ten years ago, blacks within the county had refused to use their newly won electoral majority to create the politics of Black Power, preferring instead to employ the "politics of deference" and bi-racial government to achieve their limited goals. However, Hamilton and Carmichael's interpretations do not adequately explain what happened after 1967: with the election of a majority-black county and city government, a prominent, aggressive black mayor and the retreat of many whites from the vicinity, serious political and economic contradictions still threaten the existence of Macon County. To understand why "black politics" failed within this Black Belt, Southern county, it is essential that the entire historical traditions and class structure of black and white Tuskegee be critically reexamined. By unearthing the past, we can more clearly discern the historical terrain upon which future Black Belt political struggles will be fought.

ORIGIN OF ACCOMMODATION

The politics of accommodation, or "deference," underscores the entire historical experience of Macon County and Tuskegee since the Civil War. The lack of honesty and representation with black-controlled municipal government today is a culmination of the turbulent political legacy of the postbellum South. Since the establishment of Tuskegee as a center for cotton speculators, planters and struggling black artisans, political *mauvaise voi* and segregation between the races have been the cornerstones of the society and its political economy. The founding of Tuskegee Institute and the Veterans Administration Hospital, the creation of the Tuskegee Civic Association and the local chapter of the N.A.A.C.P., and the violent desegregation of the town's public school system were events which were played out upon these deeply rooted, historical conditions.

It was not "Black Power" which aided in the creation of Tuskegee Institute in 1881, as Carmichael and Hamilton claimed, but rather an accommodation of selfish interests on both sides of the color line.[3] During the election of 1880, Colonel Wilbur F. Foster, a crusty, Confederate war veteran, was a Democratic candidate for the Alabama legislature, representing Macon County. Foster and his close white political associate, Arthur L. Brooks, also a candidate for the state legislature, needed substantial votes from the black community to carry their districts. Both white politicians went to Lewis Adams, a former slave who had learned the art of tinsmithing and shoemaking, to see if he could use his influence in favor of their candidacies. According to local legend, Adams and other black Republicans agreed to support the Bourbon Democratic ticket on the promise that the politicians would secure passage of a bill establishing a black normal college near Tuskegee.

In the important election of 1880, Democrats finally achieved total control over the Black Belt, receiving almost twice as many black votes for governor as they had received in 1874. Foster and Brooks won by handsome margins, thanks to black Tuskegee's support. In gratitude, by early 1881 the House by a margin of 48 to 20 and the Senate by 21 to 7 approved the creation of a black institution, which became Tuskegee Institute.

What Lewis Adams and other black Republicans and independents who voted for Brooks, Foster and the entire Democratic ticket could not observe, however, were the whites' selfish, private interests in establishing a black college. Arthur Brooks was then publisher of the *Tuskegee Macon Mail* and a former county superintendent of schools. Brooks used his position as newspaper publisher and as the county's most influential lawyer to get white businessmen to see the advantages of a local black school. Some black families had fled the county in the late seventies, when white racism was especially harsh. Formerly one of the wealthiest small towns in the state and a center for cotton marketing, Tuskegee's population was declining and white merchants were suffering through a major recession. The white students who went to the Alabama Conference Female College and to Park High School did not generate enough capital. White merchants, former slaveowners and educators alike concluded that an all-black industrial and normal college within Macon County would put money in their pockets. The quality of black education itself was, at best, a "separate and unequal" consideration.

A second reason for the consummation of the deal between Foster, Brooks and the black community was political. By agreeing to support the candidates of the Democratic Party, blacks were casting their ballots for economic conservatism and "white supremacy." Despite the important gain of Tuskegee Institute, the black community effectively disbanded their political organizations to accommodate themselves to the political hegemony of paternal racists like Foster and Brooks. Within a decade, blacks in Tuskegee and throughout Black Belt Alabama would become increasingly disenfranchised, lynched without trial and brutally assaulted, largely because they lacked an effective political organization.

The historical importance of this political compromise which created Tuskegee Institute, and in turn a large black academic, petty bourgeoisie, cannot be overestimated. The Bourbon Democrats were the major architects of Jim Crow legislation and racist, Southern Progressivism through the early 1900s. Without strong black support in Macon County and elsewhere, Alabama white Populists would have won an overwhelming victory during the critical gubernatorial contest of 1892. Black votes favoring the "white supremacy" party were 3 to 1 over the Populist ticket. As in the recent election of 1976, the black vote throughout the cotton belt/plantation South gave white Democratic candidates a narrow margin of victory.[5] These Democratic candidates whom Tuskegee blacks voted for were ultimately the very same political elite who drafted the Alabama state constitution of 1901 which virtually eliminated all black electoral political participation until the late fifties.

The political isolation of Macon County whites from electoral politics was a gradual phenomena, beginning markedly in 1948. After the Second World War, white Democrats within Black Belt counties became increasingly alienated from national Democratic politics, due to their growing alliance with Northern black voters. Harry Truman was not even on the ballot in Alabama in 1948. Black Belt Democrats abandoned their party in droves to cast their ballots for Strom Thurmond. Democratic voting percentages in nearby Dallas County declined from 45 percent in 1952 to 11 percent in 1964, and from 58 percent to 8 percent during the same period in Wilcox

County. In 1968 and 1972 Macon County whites cast their votes overwhelmingly for George Wallace, American Independent Party candidates, and Richard M. Nixon, respectively. By 1976 local whites refused to follow their governor, Wallace, back into the Democratic Party by supporting Jimmy Carter. This fierce, white political movement on the right within the Black Belt has not been translated into many municipal positions or county offices for local whites, because blacks still vote in sufficiently large numbers to defeat many of them. Nevertheless, at the statewide level, ultra-conservative, white politicians control most major contests. Without the black vote, Ford carried Alabama's electorate by a margin of 56 percent to 44 percent. Within Macon County, Ford carried the white vote by a margin of about three to one.[6]

As whites retreated from electoral forms of government they re-established themselves within the confines of a separate sub-society. Significant numbers of white merchants, businessmen and land owners continued to own valuable property in town but moved to new homes in Auburn or built new homes in Franklin or Notasulga, two small communities in Northern Macon County. Those remaining whites who continued to live in Tuskegee gradually accepted the integration of the downtown shopping area and restaurants as inevitable, but in certain ways they have retreated from other social contacts with blacks. Macon County Academy was established a decade ago to accommodate the white children of Tuskegee, because white parents refused to accept the desegregation of the public schools. No black people nor news reporters are encouraged to visit the segregated school grounds, and the Academy has no black children in attendance. White churches in Tuskegee are still strictly segregated. Many whites have even gradually stopped reading the *Tuskegee News* because of its wide coverage of black events, and recently initiated an alternative newspaper, located in Notasulga. Whites still own almost all the major businesses and both banks in the downtown area. Young black children and most Tuskegee students know little of the traumatic selective buying campaign during the late fifties. In short, whites still dominate the basic means of production and commercial exchange within the county and have moved prudently from open challenges in municipal political society to a subtle, segregated civil society which serves as the central organizational vehicle for the white community. The interests of local white voters have shifted away from community political questions, which they can no longer control, to state and national political forms, which they still control successfully. *De jure* segregation has ended, but *de facto* segregation and an ongoing culture of white racism remain unchallenged.

Just as important as the political metamorphosis was the drastic transformation of the rural economic structure. Tuskegee is representative of a more profound, region-wide transition from a cotton-producing economy to an agribusiness and light industrial economic base. Large numbers of rural blacks who worked as farm laborers lost their jobs with the introduction of modern agricultural equipment and labor saving machinery. In 1940, 6,162 were employed in agriculture in Macon County, but by 1960 only 1,729 people were working. Ten years later only 299 farm employees remained.[7] The number of farm proprietors in Macon County declined from 1,635 in 1959 to 1,181 in 1969. Three hundred eighty-eight farmers were forced to work a minimum of 100 days annually to supplement their incomes. Almost half of all farmers found employment off their land at least a portion of the year. However, the real value of farm products sold during the period increased by 147.2 percent from 1959 to 1974, at a rate almost twice the national average. This economic paradox indicates a general consolidation of small, private, black-ownd farms under the control of agribusiness and the erosion of a rural black working class.[8]

The city of Tuskegee and the surrounding suburbs experienced a population and economic boom at the expense of the countryside and neighboring rural communities. The number of manufacturing employees in Macon County increased from 252 to 925 between 1940 and 1970, and the capital value of industries rose to over $5.4 million by 1972. The demographic statistics of Macon County and Tuskegee illustrate a general population decline throughout the rural areas and an increase within the city of Tuskegee:[9]

	1920	1970
Macon County		
Total Population	23,561	24,840
Little Texas-Society		
Hill District	2,920	1,724
Notasulga District	3,148	2,862
Tuskegee and Suburbs	6,425	15,934

The major increase in urbanization occurred during the turbulent decade of the sixties. Large numbers of rural black families, dispossessed from their farms, travelled into town in search of regular employment. With the staff expansion of both the Institute and the Veteran's Administration Hospital, many black farmers sold their property and purchased or rented homes near or in Tuskegee. The migration into the town more than balanced an out-migration of many whites who left the area after desegregation.

Macon County Population[10]

	Total Census Pop.	Urban Pop.	Rural Pop.	Percent Urban Pop.
1960	26,717	3,561	23,156	13.3
1970	24,841	11,209	13,471	44.4

The white citizens of Tuskegee are mostly the descendants of the affluent class of Bourbon planters, bankers and cotton buyers who made their wealth off the systematic exploitation of black slaves. It was this comfortable class of white citizens who, in 1895, organized a lynch mob and chased a black man, Thomas A. Harris, out of the city for establishing a law practice.[11] It was the children of the Bourbon elite who in 1957 encouraged the state legislature to gerrymander all but ten black voters outside the municipal boundaries to preserve the hegemony of white elected officials.[12] And after all the bloody struggles toward integration, their worldview has changed remarkably little. The grey statue of the stern, Confederate warrior, rifle in hand, symbolically facing north, represents the last generation of a dying, segregationist culture.

BLACK PETTY BOURGEOIS POLITICS, SOUTHERN STYLE

Tuskegee's present black petty bourgeoisie is still essentially an academic elite. Tuskegee Institute employs over 350 full-time professors, several hundred administrators, staff personnel and other technical workers.[13] The Veterans Administration Hospital, founded immediately after World War I amid a political struggle of major proportions involving the federal government, local whites and Tuskegee's black educators, for salaries of doctors, interns, nurses, staff and administrators. This professional strata of predominantly middle-class, upwardly mobile blacks constitute perhaps three thousand people out of the county's total population of about 26,000. Yet, it is this black elite that directs the total political and cultural life of the black community. Within this strata were the members of the Tuskegee Men's Club, which in 1941 became the Tuskegee Civic Association. From its demands for integration and civil rights came the selective buying campaign of 1957–1960. The black middle class donated thousands of dollars to support the legal battle against the gerrymandering of the city, leading to the famous *Gomillion vs. Lightfoot* Supreme Court decision of 1960. This group inspired thousands of Tuskegee students to join the N.A.A.C.P. and sent representatives to the marches in Selma, Jackson and Washington, D.C. But history's victories impose a special burden upon any group, and especially upon the black petty bourgeoisie. By 1972, after the election of Johnny Ford, a native black Tuskegeean, there seemed to be no more political worlds to conquer. White Macon County residents had retreated into their private, segregated world, and no longer deprived blacks of their Constitutional rights. For the majority of blacks within this academic elite, the goal of "Black faces in high places" connoted an end to concerted political struggles.[14]

The central illusion which plagued black middle-class Tuskegeeans was the continued belief that fundamental political power could be found within electoral politics. The struggle for Black Power, as it was initially understood by even the most militant students and members of S.N.C.C., was the struggle to achieve "majority rule": total black representation on the City Council, a black mayor and a black state representative. Even among the more conservative members of the Macon County Democratic Club, a black organization which in the sixties vehemently opposed Black Power and the "majority rule" concept, civil rights connoted equal representation within electoral political forms and an end to official discriminatory practices. This illusion finds its origins in the black political ideology of black Reconstruction and the period of the Foster, Brooks and Adams compromise which established Tuskegee Institute. Bourbon Democrats controlled the government and the court system of Tuskegee, but they also controlled the basic means of production as well as many cultural institutions. What blacks failed to comprehend during their lengthy political struggle of civil rights was that the electoral domination of the white merchant class represented their general hegemony over the entire structure of the total society. The ideology of white racism as it was manifested within civil society was by far the most important superstructural element of white rule within Macon County. Elected political positions did not create the political economy of racism; rather, the reverse is true.[15]

Since black politicians and the middle class had defined freedom as the integration of state institutions, blacks anxiously expanded governmental services once in office. A bureaucratization of the Movement occurred: Johnny Ford and other lesser-known participants in the civil rights activities either won election or appointment to city or county offices. Through his support for President Richard Nixon, Johnny Ford was able to obtain a $5.3 million federal grant for a new sewage system. The size of the municipal police force expanded to 34, an amazingly high number of policemen for a town of less than 12,000. The police budget rose accordingly to $400,000 annually. The Mayor's salary was increased to $15,000 per year, a higher amount than a salary of most mayors of cities twice the size of Tuskegee. In April 1969, a Model Cities Program was launched. Model Cities initiated an Economic Development Office which attempted to attract outside investment into the town and increase local employment opportunities. Its Summer Youth Employment project provided scores of jobs for black youths between the ages of 16 and 22 years of age. Through Model Cities and the Community Development Corporation, Tuskegee and Macon County benefited from ongoing federal appropriations during the eight years of the Nixon-Ford administration, a period when most black communities were losing such programs.[16]

As Tuskegee's economic climate seemed to prosper into the early seventies, the enthusiasm of the Movement and its altruism declined. Few students took an active interest in local politics after 1972. Campus fraternity and sorority life became more popular as a new generation of black undergraduates came to campus, students who had taken no part in the desegregation campaigns of the fifties and Black Power demonstrations and take-overs of the sixties. The black academic petty bourgeoisie became directionless; having achieved all its major goals in the last decade, its desire for renewed political involvement evaporated once more. Nevertheless, among elements of the small working class within the poorer east end communities of Black Tuskegee and even among elements of the black middle class, a sense of unrest and malaise persisted. Something was wrong within Tuskegee's society, but what was it? No one was quite sure. A number of black professionals were disturbed when one disgruntled black Tuskegean, a resident of 41 years, wrote to the *Montgomery Advertiser-Alabama Journal* on January 30, 1977, that "All of the money coming into this town from the government for help has gone in the pockets of the elected few." The vision of a black government in Tuskegee had turned into a political nightmare. "We put Black[s] in office downtown," the man observed, "and look what they have done."[17]

The rapid expansion of bureaucratic forms within local government and the increase of expenditures by the federal, state and city agencies created major social dilemmas by the middle and late seventies. Rising black sociopolitical expectations, particularly among the members of the black petty bourgeoisie, could not be maintained except through deficit spending on the part of the city government. Local bureaucrats understood that only through the expansion of the city's tax base, that is, through the introduction of heavy industry and finance capital, could the local governmental services and new agencies be maintained. The major issue of the 1976 mayoral campaign was the question of municipal solvency. Running against two blacks in his bid for reelection, Ford insisted that the city government could continue to provide the needed community services which had begun in the late sixties and early seventies without a major revision in the local tax structure. The government of Tuskegee, Ford's supporters argued, was in the black, literally and figuratively: the politics of Black Power had triumphed in Macon County.

During the summer months, the mayoral campaign became as bitter as Ford's initial campaign in 1972. Spending thousands of dollars more than both of his opponents combined, Ford repeatedly used the two local newspapers and the radio stations to promote himself. At one point, Ford delivered a prayer over the radio in a paid advertisement, asking black Tuskegeeans to vote for him. In response, opponent Willie Whitehead asserted that Ford's high personal salary was indicative of the city's general mismanagement and "lack of conservatism." "This government should have more to show for the millions of dollars given it by the federal government," Whitehead argued. "This should be evidenced by having paved streets, sidewalks and the elimination of blight from the communities." Tony Haygood, the 24 year old son of one of the city's most influential black ministers, directly charged the Ford administration with complete incompetency. "City services have suffered not because the city did not have the money, but because money was improperly spent and wasted."[18]

By the week before the election, many residents called the election a stand-off. Some of Ford's supporters, worried about the election's outcome, then resorted to a Watergate-style campaign. In the newspapers and on the radio, Ford advocates charged that the Haygoods were attempting to "re-enslave" local citizens by initiating "one family control in Tuskegee and Macon County."[19] Black oil refiner and Republican Charles Wallace and other local black businessmen pooled several thousand dollars to fund a public fish fry for the incumbent.

On a hot Sunday afternoon, August 8, over three thousand Tuskegee residents drove or rode buses, free of charge, to the mammoth feast given by Ford and his petty bourgeois supporters.[20] Not unlike the days of the Bourbon Democrats, when plantation owners gave a free chicken away to each black male supporter, black voters marched off to the polls two days later and gave Johnny Ford a commanding victory of 58 percent of the total vote. Observers noted privately that Ford's black supporters spent more money for his fish fry feast that Sunday afternoon than did both Whitehead and Haygood in their entire campaigns.[21]

Three short and safe weeks after Ford's reelection, the Tuskegee City Council was forced to borrow $150,000 from a white-owned bank. Mrs. Mildred Moore, the city clerk-treasurer, told the *Tuskegee News* that the city had only $16,000 in remaining funds, and that it could not borrow money from its utilities department. The mayor was not immediately available for comment. During the campaign, the mayor had mentioned that "we may borrow in order to get through this 1976 program year." Nevertheless, the economic health of Tuskegee was excellent, Ford reiterated. Tuskegee "is richer than it has ever been because we have cut our debt ... down to $30,000."[22]

The residents of Tuskegee received another shock several weeks before Christmas, when the mayor and the newly elected council moved to enact two new taxes: a one-cent sales tax and an occupational tax, depositing 1 percent of any employee's salary earned within the city limits into the town treasury. The one-cent sales tax made Tuskegee's tax rate seven cents on the dollar. Both taxes were scheduled to take effect on January 1, 1977. Overnight, popular support for the mayor, particularly among the poor and students, completely evaporated.[23] Students were angered that the occupational tax would be levied against their federally sponsored grants. Lower-income people claimed an inability to pay the occupational tax. At one fiery town meetng on February 8, one irate citizen called the Ford-sponsored taxes "unchristianlike." Student government leaders challenged the political decisions of the bureaucrats and elected officials at city hall as other students had done a decade before—except that this time it was black against black.[24]

Ford initially refused to tolerate even mild criticisms of the new taxes. When J.J. Johnson, *News* staff writer, urged in a signed editorial a repeal of the occupational tax and reviewed Ford's less than candid role as a candidate in misleading his supporters, Ford responded with an amazingly vitriolic statement. "I consider this a personal attack upon my character," the mayor wrote the *News,* "and will consider any future such assertions by you as libelous and subject to legal action." Threatened by a massive public rejection of his fiscal programs, Ford found it necessary to repeat that despite the city's "cash flow problem," Tuskegee "still is not broke." "I will not be intimidated by you," the mayor declared angrily.[25]

The severe criticism from all levels of Tuskegee society and Representative Thomas Reed's opposition doomed the 1 percent occupational tax within two months. On March 8, the town council's five members and the mayor unanimously voted to kill the tax, and asked local employers to return all fees deducted from employees' paychecks since January 1. *News* editor Stan Voit observed that the "unworkable, unpopular" tax was supported by "few people outside of the Mayor and Council...."[26]

The occupational tax confrontation was the first major political battle that Ford had lost in five years as mayor of Tuskegee. But few of Ford's pet bourgeois opponents had observed that a black-controlled government had generally failed to solve the pressing economic and political problems which confronted the community, exactly as the white-controlled government had failed in previous administrations. Blacks running for elective offices placated the community with fish fries, full promises and fat salaries for themselves, but had failed to discern the long-term problems of the county and city. Politics was in its nature the problem facing the black community, but electoral politics did not provide any lasting solutions.

More significantly, most black Democrats and elected officials had ignored the central political problem of the seventies in the South—the subordination of the municipal and county governments to the initiatives of the state government. Macon County whites no longer control Tuskegee's government, but the victory of integrationist politics at the local level forced white Democratic politicians to move the decision-making or prerogative powers from the county courthouse level to the capital at Montgomery. At the state level, Dudley Perry, the former campaign manager for Wallace in the North Carolina Democratic Primary in 1976, represents Macon County's 83 percent black majority in the State Senate. Institutions in politics and education in Macon County have become vitally dependent upon state loans and subsidies. One example of a state power was illustrated last August when the State Senate recessed for the year without appropriating $1.2 million for Tuskegee Institute. The college administration was caught completely unprepared for this crisis—President Luther Foster was en route to Taiwan on a tour. The administration decided to defer 10 percent of all faculty salaries over the amount of nine thousand dollars until the state agreed to give Tuskegee its traditional grant. Ironically, it was Perry and not Reed or Ford who engineered the bill through the Senate in February 1977. The appropriation would probably not have passed without the expressed approval of Wallace, who for reasons of his own has usually supported Tuskegee Institute.[27]

Without an independent political party and devoid of the critical political perspective, the black petty bourgeoisie of Tuskegee finds itself in a position of municipal power which means increasingly very little. Macon County blacks are represented in Congress, for example, by Representative Bill Nichols, a conservative, white Democrat of the "States-Rights" variety who has changed his position not one inch from the era of sit-ins and freedom rides. Every black elected official in Macon County argues that a compromise of interests with the white-controlled state legislature is essential for the economic development of the Tuskegee black community. Out of selfish political interests, the Wallace-Democratic Party and Macon County black Democrats have moved into a political alliance of sorts. In January 1977, on the anniversary of the birth of Dr. Martin Luther King, Jr., Wallace was the featured speaker at the Alabama Conference of Black Mayors, hosted by Johnny Ford. This political detente between former segregationists and the leaders of the Movement for civil rights is a logical, and unfortunately, a necessary consummation of class interests, working to the detriment of the real interests of the black community.[28]

SOUTHERN BLACK ENTREPRENEURS

The business community of Tuskegee has been dominated traditionally by white merchants, bankers and entrepreneurs. Although a small number of black artisans like Lewis Adams were allowed to practice their trades, black business was never a vital factor in the economic base of the city. The Movement and the impetus toward desegregation created a limited number of economic opportunities for Afro-Americans within Macon County, and the foundations for a growing black entrepreneurial/petty bourgeoisie were created, about a decade ago. The handful of black small businessmen in Tuskegee had fewer illusions than their counterparts on the campus about the importance of gaining a certain number of black elected officials in restructuring the local social and economic order. Culturally, unlike the integrationist-minded campus elite, the black entrepreneurs did not identify desegregation per se as being vital to their interests; after all, it was segregation itself which limited white competition within the Negro community and allowed the black merchant to control his own neighborhood. Nevertheless, black entrepreneurs were experiencing their own set of problems for which traditional economic theories could not account.

The academic black elite began to shop regularly in Auburn and Montgomery after the major stores and shopping centers were desegregated a decade ago. This took a certain amount of business away from aspiring black capitalists who, sometimes after graduating from Tuskegee Institute, attempted without success to put some principles of the master into practice within Macon County. Black groceries, usually the "mom-and-pop" variety, were unable to receive credit from white Tuskegee banks. Some black merchants were forced to allow their customers certain conveniences which white merchants would often refuse, such as extended credit and check cashing facilities. The number of black business ventures which had failed mounted in the mid-seventies. The high tax rate of the county did not attract many prospective middle-level businesses, and created in effect a market where the only attractive resource was cheap, black labor power.[29]

Black entrepreneurs understood that the depleted local economy and the strained political climate were ultimately bad for business, but have not as yet come up with a viable solution to restructure the economic and social forms within society to their advantage. In the tradition of Booker T. Washington, some black businessmen looked to what might be termed an "African solution" to the problems of Tuskegee. A small group of black entrepreneurs in the lumber processing and home building trades were accompanied by attorney Fred Grey, the defender of Rosa Parks, in investigating the possibility of creating an Afro-American business concession within the interior of Liberia. Travelling to Liberia five years ago, the small group of Tuskegeeans met with African government officials and discussed the details concerning the cutting and processing of African timber for distribution and sale in the United States. For a variety of economic reasons, the black businessmen decided against the African project. Remarkably, a similar solution to Tuskegee's dependency upon white capitalism was first suggested by Emmett J. Scott, the private secretary of Booker T. Washington, six decades ago.

In 1914 Scott became a member of the Board of Directors of the African Union Company of Brooklyn, New York, an organization of black businessmen and professionals who sought to develop private enterprise in colonial Africa. Scott was involved in the Company's scheme of transporting mahogany timber from the Gold Coast for sale in the United States under the direction of black Americans. Joseph Jones, the secretary and general sales manager of the Company, wrote numerous letters to Scott informing him of the organization's purchases of mahogany logs, timber-cutting procedures and projected plans for allowing Africans themselves to hold stock.[30] Films of the Tuskegee campus and of Washington's economic achievements were shown at Company meetings in the Gold Coast.[31] Both Scott and the black businessmen of Tuskegee today were unsuccessful in turning African timber into American capital.

Tuskegee's black entrepreneurs have attempted to initiate other money-making institutions. A large number of black appointed and elected officials, including state Representative Thomas Reed, believed that a dog track would provide the boost the region needed. As owner of several fried chicken fast food shops in downtown Tuskegee and at the Institute, Reed championed the concept among other black small businessmen. Reed pushed a bill through the lower house establishing a dog track in Macon County in early 1975, but state senator Perry blocked the proposal in the Senate. According to the State Attorney General's Office and F.B.I. records, Reed and a close associate of Mayor Ford, Ron Williams, attempted to persuade Perry to support the bill. Supposedly, Perry was offered as much as $50,000 annually to sit as a dog racing commission attorney, if he in turn worked for the bill's passage in the Senate. Reed was accused subsequently of bribery in the incident, but many black Macon County residents were convinced that the charges were groundless. After two well-publicized mistrials, Reed was finally convicted in Montgomery County Circuit Court in July 1977, "of attempting to bribe" and fined $500, but was not found guilty of bribery. Attorney General Bill Baxley subsequently cited Reed's conviction "as being an abridgement of 'moral turpitude.'" However, Reed was allowed to complete his term of office. The proposed dog track scheme once supported by the major elements of Tuskegee's political and business elite within the black community now appears dead.[32]

Another less controversial economic proposal which would expand the black economic base of the region is the construction of an oil refinery. Mayor Ford brought Charles Wallace, a black businessman, to Tuskegee to establish a proposed $300 million refinery in northern Macon County. Through extensive Small Business Administration loans and conservative political contacts, Wallace has become one of the wealthiest black businessmen in the country. Wallace's fortune was made initially as a fuel oil delivery company owner, supplying major government facilities in the New York and New Jersey area. The entrance of Charles Wallace into the political economy of Macon County has already had a deep effect upon electoral politics: certainly without Wallace's generous assistance, Ford might not have won reelection. Wallace also was a central element in the developing economic detente between black integrationist leaders of the previous decade and the George Wallace–segregationists who control the state bureaucracy in Montgomery. Wallace admitted recently that both "Southern militant blacks" and Governor George Wallace were strong supporters of his refinery project. "They were all fighting each other in the fifties but they all joined together for the ground breaking of my new refinery at Tuskegee," he states. Wallace's projected refinery is still mostly on the drawing boards, however, and has not yet helped the struggling economic picture for black Tuskegee.[33]

The local government and public school system have been plagued recently by charges of mismanagement and outright corruption. In November 1977, the F.B.I. charged Ezra Echols, Jr., the accountant of the Tuskegee Housing Authority, with embezzlement of over $250,000. A Montgomery grand jury charged that Echols had written unauthorized checks to himself, deposited Housing Authority money into his personal account, and diverted the rental receipts. A "mysterious fire in early 1975 destroyed some key records just prior to a scheduled audit," reported the *News,* but sufficient evidence remained to charge Echols with 39 separate counts of embezzlements.[34] During the same month, the *News* disclosed that a special appropriation of $250,000 from the state of the Macon County Board of Education was "apparently spent for purposes other than those the money was intended for."[35] Sheriff Lucius Amerson was indicted three times on different charges in 1977 alone. One grand jury charged Amerson with embezzlement "in connection with the sale of stock in a proposed motel venture five years before. Some charges against the black sheriff were dismissed by State Attorney General Baxley, but a trial on other charges remained possible.[36] Burglaries and other petty crimes increased with urbanization, and most town residents blamed "inadequate police protection and patrolling" of local communities. In October 1977, Tuskegee police staged a "sick-in," demanding a pay increase of 25 percent, which further alienated black taxpayers from the all-black police force and local government.[37]

The past history of struggle against racism and political injustice has been all but forgotten. Only traces of the rural blues culture exist, as disco music and popular forms of urban culture projected on television and local black-oriented radio stations assumed primary popular influence. In a large public rally in the center of town, Mayor Ford and representatives of Motown records and Governor Wallace proclaimed June 25, 1977, to be "Commodores day," named for a nationally known black musical group from Tuskegee Institute. The old town square was renamed "Commodores Square," as a portion of Martin Luther King highway was renamed for the black recording artists.[38] Several Tuskegee fraternities decided to refurbish the square and the crumbling Confederate War monument. After quietly receiving permission from the local chapter of the Daughters of the Confederacy, the black undergraduates eagerly placed neat rows of flowers at the base of the statue. The majority of Tuskegee Institute students had absolutely no knowledge or interest in the bitter desegregation efforts, mob scenes and nonviolent campaigns which had occurred at the very site which they dedicated for a disco band. For these and other reasons, native black Tuskegeeans wondered aloud whether the Movement had succeeded or failed. "What has happened to us as a community?" Guy Trammell, the youth specialist of the Tuskegee Housing Authority wrote in an open letter to the *News.* "What has happened to that community involvement" and spirit of change that "once characterized Tuskegee?"[39]

In truth, only the facade of change existed at Tuskegee. The marches, the murder of civil rights workers, and the celebrated elections of numerous black political figures had changed precious little. The pattern of accommodation, the ingrained assumptions of powerlessness on the part of the Negro petty bourgeoisie, had defined political progress in such narrow terms as to make it worthless. Both the black elite and the Bourbon aristocracy had erected their politics upon a mountain of lies and corruption, deceiving themselves and each other, generation upon generation. At the height of the Movement in 1966, Tuskegee Institute professor Arnold S. Kaufman observed that "Tuskegee has been living a lie" for almost one hundred years; "a lie made all the more dangerous by the apparent control that Negroes have secured over the political agencies of the community."[40] Even with the complete desegregation of civil society Carmichael and Hamilton observed in *Black Power,* "the black people of Tuskegee are perpetuating a deferential society."[41] The politics of accommodation became the politics of illusion and self-deception.

But the history of this Black Belt community has not yet ended; indeed, it may have only just begun. "Tuskegee, Alabama, could be the model of Black Power," Carmichael and Hamilton insisted. "It could be the place where black people have amassed political power and used that power effectively." A new history, a new culture rooted in the rich traditions of the blues culture of rural blacks in the ethical precepts of the Civil Rights Movement could become "a phenomenon we have not experienced to date in (U.S.) society."[42] With Fanon, we can assert: *"Je crois en toi, Homme."*[43] Within the ashes of Martin Luther King's dream may yet a new black society emerge.

~

The Land Question in
Historical Perspective

The Economics of Poverty in the
Blackbelt South, 1865–1920

I

A central chapter in the history of black America involves the evolution of black agriculture and land tenure in the Blackbelt South. After the Civil War, four million black people, about half of whom lived on the cotton-producing plantations of Georgia, Alabama, and Mississippi, owned almost nothing except their own clothes, some agricultural tools, farm animals, and their own labor power. Their immediate prospects for economic survival during this period of heightened racial tensions, black code legislation, and Ku Klux Klan terrorism seemed bleak. By 1910, a generation after Appomattox, blacks had seemingly succeeded in achieving a minor economic miracle in the Deep South. The number of black owned-operated farms that year was 212,972, almost double that of only twenty years before. A small, yet growing black petty bourgeoisie controlled important trades inside major cities. With the financial support of black-owned banks, black farmers were purchasing land on credit, speculating on the cotton market, and successfully competing with most small white farmers and tenants. After World War I, the number of black owner-operators of farms gradually declined; a black exodus grew to major proportions as black families abandoned agriculture. The story of tremendous black land acquisitions prior to 1910 and the immediate causes for Blackbelt land losses after World War I are largely obscured from the pages of black history.[1]

The historiographical emphasis placed upon black migrations from the Deep South and upon the ghetto experiences of subsequent generations neglects the fact that the vast majority of these people were farmers until the Great Depression of the 1930s. Most black people chose freely to live and work in the South after slavery. From the end of the Civil War through the 1870s, there was an increase in black migration into such urban centers as Mobile, Macon, and Selma, Alabama. It is probable that "the city was a much safer place for the independent-minded freeman than many of the more remote rural areas where it was relatively easy for hostile whites to take the law into their own hands with little chance of exposure or prosecution."[2] The majority of black men, women, and children who left their homes chose to move into the Blackbelt rather than into southern cities, the Upper South, or the northern states. Many Blackbelt counties in Georgia and Alabama experienced a black population increase of up to 25 percent within ten years. Historian Peter Kolchin wrote that "hundreds of blacks left the mountain and Piedmont counties of northern and central Alabama and relocated in the heart of the cotton country."[3] Simultaneously, many whites left the Blackbelt for the Piedmont counties north of Atlanta and Huntsville. The reason for the sudden relocation of blacks toward the old cotton plantation region was primarily economic; almost all black men "expected the plantations of their ex-masters to be divided among them."[4] In many areas, whites feared the "widespread rumor of a Negro insurrection due to the idea" that the plantations were "going to be distributed among them."[5]

Unfortunately, the basic pattern of southern land tenure changed very little after 1865. With the defeat of the southern armies and the emancipation of almost four million former slaves, the prospects for fundamental economic change seemed to be realistic. Historian Peter Camejo noted that "the land of the richest 70,000 slaveholders and public lands in the hands of the ex-Confederate states totaled 394 million acres. To give one million black families 40 acres each only amounted to 40 million acres."[6] In 1869, there were 6,496,421 acres of public domain in Alabama, and 4,718,517 acres in Mississippi.[7] The class and caste structure which had been constructed upon the foundations of black slavery did not relinquish its hegemony over the remainder of society. W.E.B. Du Bois wrote: "The great black belt plantations ... had hardly been disturbed by war. The barons ruling there, who dictated the policy of the state, were to the last degree reactionary."[8] The occupying Union army did little to rearrange economic relations between masters and their former slaves, and southern whites of every *class* did everything in their power to resurrect the *ancien regime*. "Alarmed by the sharp rise in the number of independent black farmers," many white planters refused to sell property to blacks.[9] Blacks were able to buy several thousand acres of land confiscated by the federal government in Alabama, Mississippi, and other southern states, but much of this property was not as fertile as the Blackbelt.[10] During Reconstruction (1867–1877), the Republican justices of the peace and courts often sided with black farmers in legal disputes over property or wages. Generally, black people's demands for land always exceeded its availability.[11]

The plantation system was severely shaken by the war and Reconstruction, but it was hardly destroyed. Between 1850 and 1880, there was a significant increase in the number of farms in the Deep South and a decrease in the average amount of acres per farming unit. In Mississippi, the number of farms increased from 33,960 to 101,772, and the average acreage declined from 308.9 acres to 155.8 acres. Alabama farms increased from 41,964 to 135,864, and average acreage declined from 289.2 acres to 138.8 acres. Georgia recorded the greatest change: an increase from 51,759 farms in 1850 to 138,626 in 1880, and a reduction in acreage from 440.9 to only 187.9.[12] Most of these new farms were purchased by poor whites or yeomen farmers, many of whom lived in the Piedmont or extreme southern Appalachians. Through skill and determination, however, hundreds of thousands of black men did purchase what land was available to them. According to the statistics of the Georgia comptroller general, the 83,318 black men who were registered to vote in 1874 owned 338,769 acres of land valued at $1.2 million. Their taxable property was worth $6.2 million, and virtually all had been slaves only a single decade before. Still, the majority of black farmers, financially unable or not allowed to purchase land, stuck to sharecropping as the best of possible alternatives.[13] As historian C. Vann Woodward reflected, "The lives of the overwhelming majority of Negroes were still circumscribed by the farm and plantation. The same was true of the white people, but the Negroes, with few exceptions, were farmers without land."[14]

Despite the presence of thousands of new farms, the planter class still controlled a huge percentage of the land in the South. In most counties, the wealthiest 5 percent of all landowners controlled 40 percent of the property or more. The upper tenth of all farmers owned from one-half to two-thirds of all land in every county. Most planters had four to six tenant families working their property. The dramatic changes in property relations had occurred without challenging the hegemony of the wealthy, Bourbon planter elite. For the newly freed blacks, this meant that the social and political, as well as economic institutions of southern life would continue to be dominated by their former slavemasters.[15]

The new economic relationship that replaced slavery in the Blackbelt was termed sharecropping. Under a typical sharecropping agreement, the black farmer rented several acres of land and paid the planter a portion of his cotton crop, usually about one-half. Surprisingly, both the landlords and the laborers preferred sharecropping to wage labor. The planters initially desired a system where blacks labored for a period of twelve months for a predetermined wage, but the acute shortage of currency after the war made this impractical. Many black people considered sharecropping to be a partnership between themselves and their former master. Blacks were free to grow their own food without the landlord's constant interference, and they were able to determine the length of each individual workday for themselves. In most Blackbelt counties, the sharecropper occupied a higher social status than the wage laborer. The planters gradually accepted sharecropping, and despite the degree of independence it afforded blacks, the system was superior to slavery as a means of extracting surplus value from black labor. The planter forced the cropper to buy his own farming implements, seed, and household goods on credit at outrageous prices. The planter weighed and marketed his cotton after the growing season and kept all records. Eventually, most white planters realized that the long-term effects of sharecropping reinforced their hegemony over black labor in a more subtle yet permanent manner.[16]

Throughout the period, the major crop black farmers grew was cotton. King Cotton had breathed life into the nearly moribund body of slavery at the beginning of the nineteenth century. The crop was the economic staple for the frontier southern states of Mississippi, Louisiana, Arkansas, and Alabama. The pattern of black antebellum life evolved around the annual cycle of cotton production. "The picking season must have struck the slaves as a mixed affair," historian Eugene D. Genovese wrote, "It meant hard and distasteful work and sometimes punishment for failure to meet quotas . . ."[17] DuBois observed that the liberated slaves and their former masters returned to cotton as their major, and too often, sole means of survival. "By 1870, DuBois noted, "the cotton crop of Georgia had surpassed the largest crop raised under slavery."[18] Few farmers were overly concerned with the disastrous aspects and long-range problems involved with monocrop agriculture. Historians Gilbert C. Fite and Ladd Haystead wrote in their review of southern agriculture, that "nobody worried about building a better diet. It was easier to grow only a cash crop, cotton, and then buy from the North much of the sketchy foods which were necessary."[19] The entire Blackbelt continued to depend upon cotton even after sharp decreases in its market price after the 1870s. So permanently scarred was the Blackbelt by its backward mode of agricultural production that life and labor patterns well into the 1900s seemed timeless. As late as 1944, sociologist Gunnar Myrdal in his epic study, *An American Dilemma,* could write that "in the main, cotton is cultivated by a primitive labor-consuming agriculture which has not changed much since slavery."[20]

Black sharecroppers and owner-operators of small farms had little knowledge of the scientific farming techniques essential for the rapidly depleted soil of their region. The production of cotton year after year robbed the earth of important minerals. As early as the 1850s, many southern farmers realized that commercial fertilizers were essential for restoring the soil, but few acted upon this knowledge. Tidewater planters in Virginia and Maryland frequently used guano and marl.[21] Guano sold for $40 a ton and 450 to 900 pounds were needed to restore a single acre. Agricultural journals of the antebellum era commented frequently that Mississippi farmers refused to use either guano or marl, and planters in Alabama and Georgia applied it incorrectly by not using enough to make a real difference. Some Blackbelt planters used cottonseed to fertilize their corn crops, but relied on barnyard manure for their cotton fields.[22] Manure fertilizing demands meticulous storage as well as care in application. About 400 tons were needed to restore one exhausted acre, Genovese reported, and manure cost $2 per ton in 1850.[23] After emancipation, black owner-operators had no extensive experience in applying guano and marl and very few could even afford it.

Crop rotation on a planned basis would have aided black farmers in producing larger yields. But general scientific methods of planting and rotation, commonly practiced in the North, were used infrequently in the Blackbelt. Few small farmers realized that closely spaced cotton plants, which appeared to maximize the yield per acre, actually reduced the amount of cotton. High-density planting adversely affects the size of cotton bolls, plant height, and stem diameter. Without uniform plant distribution and careful hoeing, techniques about which the former slaves knew little, the total cotton yield became smaller and smaller with each consecutive growing season.[24] Farmers had known that annual crop rotation helped to restore their soil, but the overwhelming majority did not rotate with legumes (plants that would have returned needed nitrogen to the soil). Most alternated cotton with corn, a system that retarded soil depletion and erosion but did absolutely nothing to prevent it.[25]

Across the board, blacks who rented, sharecropped, or owned property planted a greater percentage of cotton than did white farmers. White owner-operators on the average planted 44.8 percent of their acreage in cotton; black renters planted more than 60 percent of their land in cotton. The average white planted three or four crops, in addition to cotton, and devoted an average of 10.1 percent of his tilled acreage to crops other than cotton and corn combined. Black farmers seldom planted anything except cotton and corn. On the average, only 3.7 percent of black farmlands were planted in some other crop. The soil on black-owned farms therefore declined in productivity and value at a much faster rate than normal.[26] The domination of cotton led to a real decline in food production throughout the South. The per capita production of corn in 1870 fell to less than one-half the level of 1850, and remained there for several decades. The per capita production of swine dropped from 2.11 in 1850 to .73 in 1890; per capita production of sheep fell from .47 to .22. The decline in agriculture and livestock productivity was offset by the overproduction of cotton.[27]

Black farmers were caught within a poverty cycle which was almost impossible to transcend. In 1880, for example, the number of acres of cropland per worker on an average farm was 12.4 for white-owned farms and 7.5 for black-owned farms. Black sharecroppers averaged 8 acres per farmworker, while owner-operated black farms tended to be somewhat smaller, 6.6 acres per worker. Economists Roger Ransom and Richard Sutch, in their extensive study of southern agriculture, *One Kind of Freedom*, assert that the inequality of acreage per farmworker had numerous economic consequences for blacks. Black farmers were forced to cultivate crops on a significantly larger portion of their property every year than were whites. The ratio of uncultivated acres per cultivated acre on black small family farms was only .63 acres, but 2.72 acres on white owner-operated farms. The ratio of uncultivated acres per cultivated acre for black sharecroppers was only .34 acres. Ransom and Sutch estimate that more than one-third of all white owner-operators of small farms regularly purchased fertilizer, but only one-fifth of all black farmers could afford to do this. Without sufficient capital to pay for commercial fertilizers, black farmers relied upon their animals' manure to fertilize their crops. However, the average black farmer owned 1.3 work animals and only 5.2 swine, compared to 1.9 work animals and 9.9 swine owned by white farmers. This shortage of animals meant an insufficient supply of barnyard manure, which lowered agricultural yields, promoted soil erosion, and depleted the soil of nitrogen. Since sharecroppers traditionally gave half of their annual crop to their landlords, it becomes clear that the exploitation of slavery continued to be present within the new form of economic relations. "Emancipation removed the legal distinction between the South's two races, but it left them in grossly unequal economic positions," Ransom and Sutch noted, "Black farmers had less capital, smaller farms," and were "more susceptible to exploitation."[28]

The entire cotton-producing South was extremely rural and existed, in effect, as a domestic colony for the remainder of the nation. In 1880, there were only three cities in the Blackbelt that had a population in excess of fifteen thousand people and five banks—Montgomery, Atlanta, and Memphis. Jackson, the capital city of Mississippi, was a sleepy, conservative hamlet of barely five thousand people. Athens, the former capital of Georgia, was a more prosperous village of 6,100, possessing two banks, twenty general stores, and the state's university. Other than that, the Blackbelt was overwhelmingly agricultural, its towns sparsely populated and culturally backward. Town merchants came to dominate both the flow of trade and the relative accessibility of credit, due to the general lack of banking facilities. Several important towns, such as Tuskegee with a population of almost 2,500 in 1880, had no bank at all. Tuskegee's merchant class operated the town's sixteen general stores and was responsible for supplying credit to all farmers and planters, giving them canned goods, fine cloth, flour, sugar, seed, and farm equipment in the winter and early spring of each year in return for a promised share of the farmers' fall profits. This pattern of a merchant-dominated economy occurred in county after county. In Selma, Alabama's third largest city, there were only two banks but twenty general stores, all in the active business of making short-term loans to cotton planters and sharecroppers. Cotton-producing communities such as Demopolis, Alabama, Albany, Georgia, and Greenville, Mississippi, each having only one bank, required the lending services and continued support of their merchant classes.[29]

County merchants were charged anywhere from 3 to 15 percent interest by wholesale merchants and suppliers for their goods. The local merchants not only passed these expenses along to rural customers, but made a prosperous living by extending credit for periods of less than one year at extraordinary high rates. An average Georgia merchant in 1889 would have charged 66 cents for one bushel of corn purchased in cash, but would charge 87 cents for the same corn if purchased on credit. The average cash price for a pound of bacon in Georgia that same year, $7.91, was much lower than the credit price of $10.38. During the 1880s, the average interest rates charged by Georgia merchants for one pound of bacon and one bushel of corn paid four months after initial purchase were 88.9 percent and 92.8 percent, respectively. In several years, the interest rate for the purchase of corn exceeded 120 percent for a four month period. Part of the reason for these exorbitant rates was that the majority of communities in the Blackbelt contained only one or two stores within a radius of ten or fifteen miles. Sometimes an affluent merchant would purchase property and become a landlord or manager of sharecroppers; occasionally, the planters themselves went into the grocery store business. Generally, a single owner of a store or group of stores developed a small but tight monopoly for himself at the expense of poor farmers and tenants in the county.[30]

Black sharecroppers and small planters alike depended upon the rural merchants in the country stores throughout the region to extend them adequate credit for each growing season. During dry seasons or in the winter, farmers often borrowed on their next year's crops, purchasing items that they could not pay for without credit. These county merchants who were often in debt to their regional suppliers and investors were in a position to demand that only crops producing a sure profit could be planted. In practical terms, the merchants insisted that cotton be grown at the expense of any other staple, since cotton had always brought a handsome profit on the market. As a result, many black farmers who might have planted corn or other vegetables for their families were forced to grow cotton and purchase some of their food at the country store. These farming practices further depleted the soil and led to annual reductions in yields. Most important, the overproduction of cotton caused by merchants' demands depressed the market price of cotton. From 1865 until 1898, the price of cotton declined steadily: from 29 cents per pound in 1868, to 11 cents per pound in 1890, to about 5 cents in 1898. It cost roughly 7 cents per pound just to grow cotton, excluding any profit.[31]

Cotton's monopoly across the Blackbelt made millions of dollars for white planters, affluent merchants, businessmen, and cotton market speculators. As long as the world demand for cotton was high, the impetus for establishing alternative staples in agriculture was low. Cotton's monopoly also degraded black and white labor, depleted the soil, and concentrated the bulk of the best farmland in the hands of a racist, class-conscious aristocracy. "For the South as a whole, cotton specialization was not more profitable than diversified economy with a balance between agriculture and industry," Ransom and Sutch asserted. "The curse of King Cotton was the lack of prosperity he imposed upon the South."[32]

II

The development of a number of small, black-owned banks and lending institutions helped to transform the poverty of black life in the South. During the 1880s, a small number of determined black ministers, entrepreneurs, and educators pooled their resources to begin savings banks for blacks in several southern cities. The Reverend W.R. Pettiford, pastor of the Sixteenth Street Colored Baptist Church, started the Alabama Penny Savings Bank in Birmingham and gradually opened branch offices in Montgomery, Anniston, and Selma. Booker T. Washington, principal of Tuskegee Institute, initiated a savings department at the college which functioned as a local bank. In the first decade of the twentieth century, dozens of black banks were established which loaned thousands of dollars to poor black farming families, desperately attempting to compete within a demanding marketplace. By 1911, there were seven black-owned banks in Alabama and two in Georgia. Mississippi boasted eleven such banks located in Jackson (two), Vicksburg (two), Yazoo City, Columbus, Greenville, Mound Bayou, Indianola, Natchez, and Shaw. These black-owned banks and forty-two others throughout the country did an annual business of 520 million in 1910.[33]

The rise of literacy tremendously aided prospects for black rural development. Immediately after slavery ended, 90 percent of all black people over twenty years of age were unable to read and write. As planters maintained all records and county merchants kept credit records, it was likely that many if not all blacks were cheated on a regular basis. The creation of primary and secondary schools and agricultural colleges gradually lowered illiteracy rates, especially among the younger blacks, By 1890, about one-half of all blacks between the ages of ten and nineteen were literate. As illiteracy diminished below 50 percent after 1900, a greater number of black people were able to compete for jobs requiring a minimal education. Black people across the Blackbelt were aware that literacy and an aptitude in basic mathematics would make them more self-sufficient and ultimately more in command of their own lives.[34]

The development of a strong black land base became an ideological imperative of black thought by the 1890s. Throughout the Blackbelt, black farmers organized small agricultural fairs, exhibiting and selling swine, cows, sheep, and other livestock, vegetables, and cotton. The Agricultural and Mechanical College for Negroes was established in Normal, Alabama, in 1875, where many black students learned the essentials of crop rotation, proper fertilization techniques, and other skills necessary for progressive farming. With the financial support of northern philanthropic agencies and churches, dozens of black agricultural and teachers' training colleges were established. The largest and most influential institutions included the Georgia State Industrial College in Savannah, Knox Academy in Selma, Tuskegee Institute, Haines Normal and Industrial Institute in Augusta, Utica Normal and Industrial School in Utica, Mississippi, and the State Normal School in Montgomery. W.H. Holtzclaw, the principal of Utica Institute, established a company which purchased plantations for resale to black sharecroppers. Most of these schools held yearly farmers' conferences, and many offered monthly training institutes on advanced agricultural techniques. Within a single generation, thousands of young black men were trained to become more competent in the agricultural sciences than any white plantation owner had ever been. It was, of course, only a beginning. However, proper eduation and a gradually improving economic climate enabled young black graduates from these small institutions to compete with white owner-operators on a more equal basis.[35]

Booker T. Washington was perhaps the most influential advocate of Blackbelt agricultural development. Better known as the architect of the "Atlanta Compromise" of 1895 which acquiesced to the emergence of segregation and white racism, Washington was actually a complex and ambitious man. Always the pragmatist, he sensed the shift in the political winds and responded accordingly, issuing ambiguous statements which appeased white racists while guaranteeing a continued flow of funds into his college and other black educational institutions. From the founding of Tuskegee Institute in 1881, Washington was a strong advocate of scientific farming and increased black land tenure. Students at Tuskegee cultivated sweet potatoes, corn, peas, okra, and vegetables of all kinds for consumption and sale from the Institute's farm.[36] Through Washington's subtle political initiatives and compromises, hundreds of black farmers became successful in their efforts to buy land. In 1900, 157 black farmers in Macon County owned land; by 1910, the number increased to 507. Tuskegee graduates established "social settlements" in a sharecropping area of Lowndes County, Alabama, purchasing old plantation property and reselling it to eager black farmers.[37] Washington remained convinced that a rural black petty bourgeois elite of farmers, small bankers, and merchants could form the basis for a black economy inside American capitalism. In a lecture titled "How To Build a Race," given at the Institute's chapel on a Sunday night in October, 1898, Washington described in detail the problem of black agricultural underdevelopment and possible solutions:

> We are living in a country where, if we are going to succeed at all, we are going to do so by what we raise out of the soil. Without this no people can succeed. No race which fails to put brains into agriculture can succeed; and if you want to realize the

truth of this statement, go with me this month into the back districts of Georgia, Mississippi and Alabama and you will find these people almost in a starving condition, slowly starving to death and yet they are surrounded by a rich country. Are you going to stand still and see these people starve? Are you not willing to make any sacrifice in order to prepare yourselves to help these people? I believe you will learn all you can about agriculture and about the use of improved machinery.

Washington warned his students that agricultural development was "our only (hope for) salvation as a race."[38]

A substantial petty bourgeoisie slowly began to take shape—black undertakers, grocery store owners, tailors, insurance men, and bankers. In Atlanta a number of the city's most prosperous contractors and builders were black entrepreneurs; in Charleston, blacks controlled the city's barbering and butchering trades. According to the statistics of the National Negro Business League, between 1900 and 1914 the number of black-owned drug stores increased from 250 to 695; black undertaking firms grew from 450 to 1,000; the number of black retail merchants increased from 10,000 to 25,000.

Individual examples of black economic self-sufficiency and success existed in every major southern city and in many rural counties. R.R Church of Memphis quietly accumulated real estate in that city and by the early 1900s was worth approximately one million dollars. Charles Banks, a leading citizen of the all-black community of Mound Bayou, established a cottonseed oil mill, a loan and investment company, and a bank. Many of these black entrepreneurs shared Washington's philosophy of racial pride and his faith in the capitalist system.[39]

As economic conditions improved in the early 1900s, the prospects for Booker T. Washington's vision of a self-sufficient black economy seemed increasingly realistic. Despite a general decline in cotton prices, there was an increase in southern industrial output. The number of cotton mills increased from 161 in 1880 to 400 in 1900, the greatest increase coming during the 1890–1900 period. Capital investments in cotton mills soared from $17.4 million to $124.6 million between 1880 and 1900. During the same twenty years, the number of cottonseed oil mills increased from 45 to 353.[40] By 1908, coal production in north-central Alabama had increased three times over the amount produced in 1890. Thousands of black sharecroppers abandoned the land temporarily or permanently to work in Birmingham's rich coal mines.[41] Increased industrialization of the South, combined with a rapid rise in cotton prices after 1898, made farming a profitable venture once more. Black farmers succeeded in buying millions of acres of land which had previously been unavailable to them. Between 1900 and 1910, Carolina blacks purchased more than one million acres of farmland. Thousands of sharecroppers and tenant farmers in Mississippi, Alabama, and Georgia were able to purchase their own farms and compete with poorer white farmers. As Washington predicted boldly in 1898, "the vast unoccupied lands in the South ... are simply waiting for those with capital, foresight and faith to step in and occupy."[42]

Virtually all economists agree with the observation of Richard T. Ely and George S. Wehwein that black land tenure "in the South reached its peak in 1910."[43] There were 2,143,176 black farmers in 1911, a few of whom were just as prosperous and efficient as the most wealthy white landlords. Deal Jackson of Albany, Georgia, a former slave, owned more than 2,000 acres of rich farmland and held "forty (black) families" as tenants "on his plantation." Georgia blacks owned property worth $34 million and possessed 1,639,919 acres of land.[44] The thirst for land was so great within the black rural South that some blacks migrated directly to communities where there was an immediate "history of lynchings and mob violence, so long as land could be purchased at low prices."[45] "For a decade, the cotton belt had enjoyed a happy conjunction of rising production and rising prices," historian George B. Tindall wrote in *The Emergence of the New South.* "On the eve of (World War I) cotton fetched thirteen cents a pound, and a bumper crop of more than sixteen million bales, the largest yet known, was being laid to ripen."[46] About two-thirds of this amount was exported to Europe.[47] In these flush times, black people acquired the largest amount of property they would ever own within the United States. In 1910, there were approximately 175,000 farms fully owned by blacks, 43,000 partially owned, and 670,000 sharecropped. There were also one thousand black managers and supervisors of farm property. Blacks operated 890,000 farms and had become the proud owners of more than 15 million acres of land. In the late summer of 1914, Washington's dream of a flourishing black economy in the South seemed to be on the verge of reality.[48]

III

The outbreak of World War I marked the beginning of the long and tragic decline of black agriculture and land tenure in the South. European nations which had been the largest consumers of cotton closed their doors to transatlantic commerce for about three months. All farmers were forced to sell their cotton to speculators at 5 to 8 cents per pound, well below current market value. Many struggling black farmers hauled their cotton into town and learned to their amazement that no one would buy it at any price. Southern politicians and regional capitalists realized that immediate steps had to be taken to help cotton producers, but most of the assistance went to white planters and merchants. Senator John H. Bankhead of Alabama proposed that his state extend $40 million worth of credit to farmers and store their cotton in state warehouses. Asa G. Candler, Atlanta millionaire and a director of the Coca-Cola company, offered low-interest loans to white planters and stored one-quarter of a million bales of cotton in his huge warehouses. Within two months, southern farmers lost about $500 million. The 1913 average farm price for cotton was not achieved until June 1916, when drastic cuts in the amount of cotton produced created an artificially high price.[49] The cotton disaster of 1914 ruined many thousands of black and white farmers, and affected southern agriculture for years to come. As bourgeois economist John Kenneth Galbraith observed, "Unlike most industry, agriculture is peculiarly incapable of dealing with the problems of expanding output and comparatively inelastic demand."[50]

Black farmers who borrowed money to purchase their land suddenly had no way to pay annual mortgage payments and notes of credit. Sharecroppers who owned no property were not as threatened with sudden economic collapse as were black small owner-operators. However, both groups had no experience in growing any money crop other than cotton, and many desperate county merchants refused to allow blacks additional credit to plant anything except cotton. In the summer of 1916, severe rainstorms destroyed much of that year's cotton crop throughout Alabama and Mississippi. Robert R. Moton, then principal of Tuskegee Institute, informed the U.S. Department of Agriculture and Alabama state officials in September of that year that many black farmers "have grown discontented because of the lack of the most ordinary necessities." He pleaded for seed and agricultural supplies "so that they could have something growing, (and so) that many of them would be contented and not be inclined to leave the farm."[51] Making matters worse, many black banks were forced out of business with the collapse of the cotton market. By 1918, only one black-owned-and-operated bank remained in Alabama, the savings office of Tuskegee Institute. Only two black banks existed in Mississippi, in Mound Bayou and Indianola. With the failure of these financial institutions, a significant source of credit disappeared.[52] Many thousands of farmers sold their land for only a fraction of its real value to pay off mounting debts. Black sharecroppers who might have planned to buy land and sell their own cotton crops on the open market were certainly discouraged from doing so. My great grandfather, Morris Marable, was an independent farmer in Randolph County, Alabama, who operated his own cotton gin and marketed four or five bales of his cotton crop each year. With the reduction of the price of cotton, he was forced out of the market. In several years, he abandoned agriculture entirely, like thousands of other black farmers and small entrepreneurs.

More destructive than the impact of the war upon cotton prices was the coming of the boll weevil. Entering from Mexico and Central America into southern Texas, it spread across the state within ten years, destroying thousands of acres of cotton. By 1908, it had crossed the Mississippi and was mining cotton fields along the rich, black delta country. The weevil, unlike other insects or worms, was especially difficult to detect until damage was already done. The adult female weevil lays her eggs in the fruit of the plant during the spring. When the eggs hatch in late summer, the young eat the cotton.

By 1916 every county in Alabama was infested with boll weevil and by 1920, every Georgia county reported insect damage. In each state in the Deep South, the boll weevil limited the number of acres planted as well as the normal yield of cotton lint in pounds per acre. In the four years preceding boll weevil infestation in Georgia, for example, an average of 4,953,000 acres of cotton were planted; four years after complete infestation, an average of 3,476,000 acres were planted with cotton, a reduction of almost 30 percent. The average yield of cotton lint per acre in Georgia was 230 pounds before infestation; after the insect's appearance, the average yield was reduced to 117 pounds, a decline of 49 percent.[53] Blackbelt farmers reduced the cotton acreage planted and because of the pests, they obtained approximately one-fifth to one-half less cotton lint per acre. Few sharecroppers and black owner-operators could afford expensive insecticides or poisons, and it was almost impossible to contain the spread of the insects. "Field after field of cotton was eaten away," Haystead and Fite wrote. Some farms were spontaneously "abandoned."[54]

Compounding the economic troubles of black farmers was a general worsening of race relations in the Blackbelt. Those blacks who continued to vote after 1900 found that virtually every major or minor white political tendency in the Deep South, whether Democratic, Populist, or Republican, had repudiated the principle of black suffrage. In northern Alabama, black Republicans published the *Huntsville Republican* and attempted to organize support for whites who sympathized with Negro rights. By 1902, the Republican Lily White faction succeeded in purging the integrated Black and Tan group from the state convention by placing armed guards at the doors to keep blacks out. Within the decade, Black and Tan Republicanism was dead in Mississippi and Alabama.[55] After World War I, Alabama blacks organized suffrage leagues and initiated court challenges to *de jure* segregation, but most cases failed at the local level. During the 1920s, neither the conservative or progressive factions of the Democratic party sought to expand the slender black electorate. The number of black voters in Alabama declined from a statewide total of 3,742 in 1908, to 1,500.[56] For practical purposes, the Fifteenth Amendment no longer existed in the Blackbelt. Georgia led the nation in lynching between 1885 and 1918 with 398. Mississippi was a close second with 381 and Alabama was fifth with 246. In 1915 there were 18 lynchings in Georgia alone, twice as many as in any other state. Approximately, both Mississippi and Alabama were tied for second place that year with 9 illegal hangings of black people.[57] Carter G. Woodson, reviewing the economic chaos which had befallen black farmers throughout the South, refused to attribute the exodus of blacks to the North to any but political reasons. "It is highly probable that the Negroes would not be leaving the South today," the Negro historian wrote in 1918, "if they were treated as men."[58]

Facing economic disaster, most white farmers had sufficient resources to change the production habits of a century. Thousands of white farmers began to purchase and raise cattle. In Mississippi the number of cattle and calves produced rose from 873,356 in 1900 to 1,250,479 in 1920. Georgia cattle production went from 899,491 in 1900 to 1,156,738 in 1920.[59] Farmers in the pine hills and wire grass country of southern Georgia and southeast Alabama discovered that their red soil was excellent for peanuts, and peanut production increased during the 1920s.[60] Whites borrowed heavily to maintain their land, and by crop diversification and decreased production of cotton, they were usually able to stay in business. Black farmers, several years behind in debts, could do little else except abandon their property and go into sharecropping, or leave their outstanding debts and flee to the North. Many chose the second option. From 1880 to 1910, only 79,400 blacks left the Blackbelt for the North; between 1910 and 1920, the figure leaped to 226,900, and from 1920 to 1930, about 444,400 black migrants fled the Deep South. Most if not all of these people were sharecroppers, small owner-operators, or workers in jobs connected with agriculture.[61]

There are many reasons which explain in part the demise of black land tenure in the Blackbelt South, and the destruction of an authentic, black landowning class. Several causes have been isolated—the emergence of white racism and Jim Crow legislation, the fall of cotton prices, the coming of the boll weevil, the lack of adequate credit at reasonable rates, the general erosion and depletion of the soil. All of these reasons and others stem from a larger and as yet unanswered dilemma—the existence and survival of black people within the context of the American capitalist system. In theory, capitalism is characterized by a degree of labor mobility and a free movement of capital from disadvantageous enterprises to more profitable sectors. However, under the economic conditions of the capitalist system prevalent in the post-bellum South, an elite group of white planters, bankers, investors, and merchants held a tight monopoly over the monetary supply, credit sources and rates, and the entire agricultural, production of the region. Millions of poor white and black farmers were forced to supply an international market with cotton at the expense of building a viable industrial base within the South. This economic monopoly gradually promoted the collapse of the black economic miracle which black educators and entrepreneurs such as Booker T. Washington dreamed of building. Given the structure of the domestic economy, it was inevitable that black farmers would be forced off the land and evicted from their homes to work at factory jobs in the cities of the New South and the urban ghettos of the North.

An economist Paul Sweezy observed critically in *The Theory of Capitalist Development*, "the very essence of monopoly is the existence of effective barriers to (the) free movement of capital."[62] Neither the white South's social institutions, corrupted from the bottom up by racist ideology and violence, nor its electoral political institutions, which actually represented roughly one-fifth of the entire adult population, could provide fundamental solutions to the region's regressive economic order. History illustrates clearly that the goal of black economic self-sufficiency within the framework of the existing capitalist system is a bitter illusion rather than a possibility; the collapse of black land tenure in the Blackbelt South was not a failure of black people, but a failure of the state and private enterprise to promote equality of economic opportunity for all members of the society.

~

The Tchula 7
Harvest of Hate in the Mississippi Delta

For millions of blacks living in the rural counties and small towns of the "New South," the terrors of Jim Crow and racial exploitation which sparked the civil rights movement of the 1950s still exist. Nowhere is this more vivid than in the sovereign state of Mississippi.

The roots of black poverty and political powerlessness in Mississippi are found in the economics of racism. In 1949, black farmers owned 80,842 commercial cotton-producing farms in Mississippi's black belt region, about 66 percent of all cotton farms in the state. During the 1950s and 1960s, "agribusiness"—corporations which went into agricultural production—aggressively pushed thousands of these small rural farmers out of business. By 1964, the number of black-owned cotton farms declined to 21,939 state-wide: Five years later, the figure dropped to only 1000. Since the civil rights movement, the number of black farm residences has fallen still further, both in Mississippi and across the country.

Part of the reason for this process is the extreme difficulty which black farmers have in obtaining capital. According to a 1982 Civil Rights Commission report, "Many insurance companies, which finance the bulk of farm loans, require loans to be at least $100,000. While commercial banks lend lesser amounts, they often require payment within five years, a term too short for the average black land-owner. Federal land banks tend to require amounts of collateral that are too great for blacks to qualify."

The Federal government has done little to reverse the decline in black farming. For example, the Farmers Home Administration (FmHA), which is the principal public lending agency for farmers, lent $6.3 billion in fiscal year 1980 and almost $7 billion in fiscal year 1981 to farmers nationwide. Loans to blacks were so few, however, that in March 1981, black Mississippi farmers helped stage a 21-day sit-in at one FmHA county office to protest discrimination. In Mississippi alone, the number of black FmHA committee members declined 53 percent from 1979 to 1980. Between 1980 and 1981, not surprisingly, the number of farm ownership loans to blacks in Mississippi also fell—from 101 to 30. Under intense criticism, the Carter administration authorized the FmHA in 1980 to initiate a project especially "geared to reach small farm enterprises with gross annual incomes as low a $3000" in Mississippi and six other Southern states. However, no loans were ever made under the project, and few black potential borrowers ever learned about the project's existence. Under Reagan the FmHA discontinued the program.

Economically, rigid racial segregation was always a curse and a blessing. The South's version of *apartheid* was never confined to social and civil separation of the races. It provoked the rise of white vigilante groups such as the Ku Klux Klan, and justified the lynching, castration and mutilation of literally thousands of blacks throughout the South. In Mississippi alone, between 1882 and 1927, 517 black men and women were lynched—the highest state total in the country.

DESEGREGATION—AND DISPOSSESSION

Despite these brutalities, however, segregation was also paradoxically a barrier which permitted the development of small black businesses. In 1887 for example, a former slave, Isaiah T. Montgomery, established an all-black town, Mound Bayou, Mississippi. In less than ten years, Mound Bayou had several banks and real estate-firms, a technical school, one newspaper, a sawmill *and* a power and light company—all owned and operated by blacks.

Desegregation in the 1960s and early 1970s was, of course, supported by the overwhelming majority of blacks as a necessary and progressive reform. But in the process, as white-owned banks, insurance companies, laundries, groceries and restaurants began to accommodate black customers, the market for black entrepreneurs was seriously eroded

Losing their land, many rural black merchants and potential businesspersons tried to establish themselves in Jackson, Greenville and smaller Mississippi cities. With rare exceptions, they were unable to compete with larger, white-owned firms and quickly went out of business. In Greenville for instance, a middle sized city with about 38,000 residents in 1977, 179 of the town's 247 black-owned firms do not possess a single paid employee. The five black-owned real estate firms in the city have average gross receipts of $5,000. The 68 black shops without employees collected an average gross of only $11,320 in 1977. This process of underdevelopment, therefore, afflicts urban blacks as well as farmers, and their collective economic plight has actually become worse with desegregation. The current economic conditions of rural Mississippi blacks are symbolized, again, by Mound Bayou By 1979 the all-black town was over $133,000 in debt. When the town lost a civil lawsuit judgment that year, which totalled an additional $59,000, bankruptcy seemed imminent. Banks froze the city's accounts, and the 19 acres of city property, including a park, the city's public swimming pool, and its only municipal building were sold at auction. Southern Bell cut off the city's telephones because of an unpaid $1,700 bill, and Mississippi Power and Light threatened to halt city services. In April 1982, a Memphis radio station helped to raise $120,000 to pay off some of Mound Bayou's bills. But without adequate state or federal assistance, the status of this town's 2,900 people seems bleak.

RACIST TERROR UPSURGE

The general economic decline for most Mississippi blacks since the 1960s has been accompanied by the resurrection of white racist terrorism and political violence. In May 1981, the *Jackson Advocate* reported that in Mississippi alone there have been 12 murders "in as many months which are suspected by blacks of being (racially motivated)." The tortured body of one unidentified black man was found floating down the river in Cleveland, Mississippi. The man's sex organs had been hacked off and the coroner later reported finding his penis in his stomach.

On January 11, 1981, the body of 45-year-old Lloyd Douglas Gray was found hanging from a tree in Tallahatchie County, Mississippi. Tallahatchie coroner A.W. Hulett pronounced Gray's death a suicide, and no autopsy was performed. A month later, the body of 32-year-old Roy Washington was found in Cypress Creek, in Holmes County, Mississippi. Washington had been "badly beaten in the head and face," his hands bound behind him, and then shot in the head at point-blank range. The corpse was weighed down with a car jack and wrapped by barbed wire. Scars around his neck indicated that he had also been lynched. Local white newspapers were silent on the murder. Holmes County police did not aggressively pursue leads in the case, and even followed a black reporter around while he conducted his own investigation. The majority of the other black men who have been found beaten or hanging in Mississippi have also been officially labeled suicides. Familiar with the pattern of racial violence, one black resident of Tallahatchie County declared, "if they say it was suicide, it was probably a lynching."

What kind of human beings can commit such hideous crimes? To understand contemporary Mississippi race relations, one must invariably return to the past. Consider William Alexander Percy's classic, *Lanterns on the Levee,* first published in 1941. Percy explains that the nightmare of white supremacy ushered into the public arena a series of "vain demagogues" who competed with each other in denouncing blacks' rights.

The most successful practitioner of race-baiting was Theodore G. Bilbo of Pearl River County. From 1907 until 1946, Bilbo was elected state senator, lieutenant governor, governor and US Senator. To describe Bilbo as an obscene racist would be too modest: he was also an outrageous anti-Semite. Before one congressional committee during World War II, he "defended himself against charges of racial and religious intolerance [by stating] that he was for 'every damn Jew from Jesus Christ on down.'" He campaigned vigorously for repeal of the Fifteenth Amendment to the Constitution, and voiced support for plans to transport all blacks "back to Africa."

But if the wealthy planters of the Mississippi River delta, the sons and grandsons of slaveholders, could agree with Bilbo in the necessity to disfranchise the Negro, they found Bilbo and his extremist colleagues repulsive. Percy explains that:

> [Bilbo] *was a pert little monster, glib and shameless, with that sort of cunning common to criminals which passes for intelligence. The people loved him. They loved him not because they were deceived in him, but because they understood him thoroughly;*

*they said of him proudly, 'He's. a slick little bastard.' 'He was one of them and he had
risen from obscurity to the fame of glittering infamy—it was as if they themselves had
crashed, the headlines.'*

And what of the white voters who repeatedly put Bilbo into public office? Percy
captured their mind and mood in his description of a typical white Mississippi crowd
during an electoral campaign:

> *I looked over the ill-dressed, surly audience, unintelligent and slinking. They were
> the sort of people that lynch Negroes, that mistake hoodlumism for wit, and cunning
> for intelligence, that attend revivals and fight and fornicate in the bushes afterwards.
> They were undiluted Anglo-Saxons. They were the sovereign voter. It was so horrible
> it seemed unreal.*

Unquestionably, the white population of Mississippi was the South's vanguard in the
"Massive Resistance" campaign to preserve white supremacy in the 1950s and 1960s.
Upon Bilbo's death in 1947, John C. Stennis, a racist politician by all accounts, was
elected to replace him in the Senate. He is still there today.

When Paul B. Johnson, Jr., was elected governor in 1963, he denounced integration in messianic terms: "Evil days are upon the land. We must fight fire with fire."
Yet Johnson had been defeated in a previous gubernatorial race in part for being "too
soft" on the "Negro Question"! This is a state where George Wallace polled 63% of
the presidential popular vote in 1968; where NAACP state chairperson Aaron Henry
was illegally banned from speaking at the University of Mississippi for years; where
lynchings are still not uncommon occurrences.

White Mississippi politicians frequently describe their state as the most "progressive" in the nation today as far as electing black officials. Superficially, this assertion
appears to be true. As of July 1977, Mississippi had 295 black elected officials, the
highest number in the US. But a detailed analysis of this figure, more than double the
total number of black officials in the entire country in 1965, reveals some incongruities.

Only four of Mississippi's 98 state representatives and state senators are black.
Virtually all of the other black officials are mayors or city councilpersons in small,
rural majority-black towns, law enforcement officers, or serve on municipal school
boards. None are Congressional representatives.

Furthermore, the black percentage of Mississippi's statewide population, at
35.9 percent in 1975, is significantly higher than in Illinois, Michigan, and Arkansas. Yet, proportionately, these states have elected a much larger number of black
officials—Illinois, 281; Michigan, 251; Arkansas, 218.

Moreover, many black elected officials in Mississippi took no leading roles
locally in the desegregation struggle of the 1960s. According to Charles Tisdale,
the editor of the *Jackson Advocate,* at least three-fourths of these 295 black "public
servants" are on the "payroll" of former segregationists, corporate interests, and local
white political machines. Independent black politicians who criticize the state's power
structure are few and far between.

THE CASE OF EDDIE CARTHAN

Eddie Carthan understands Mississippi—its heritage of segregation, racial brutalities, and economic exploitation of the black working class and rural poor. As a youngster he attended the "Freedom Schools" conducted by idealistic activists in the Student Nonviolent Coordinating Committee. He witnessed the political intimidation of black farmers who tried to register to vote. In his home town of Tchula, the population is 85 percent black. Thirty percent of the town's adults are unemployed; 66 percent are on welfare; 81 percent of all Tchula's housing units are classified as "deteriorating."

As the first black mayor of a Mississippi Delta town, elected on a reform platform in 1977, Carthan thought that "I could represent those who had come through slavery, knowing nothing about voting, about going to a motel, sitting in the front of a bus or eating in a restaurant." But Carthan's election was an intolerable threat to the racist power structure of Holmes County, and indirectly, of the entire state.

Carthan recognized that the county, which is statistically the tenth poorest in the US, could not develop without massive federal assistance. The mayor obtained CETA funds to weatherize and remodel Tchula's homes. A nutrition project was established to provide meals to senior citizens and the handicapped. A federal grant was solicited for the projected construction of a public library. A child care program was begun specifically for mothers who worked or who lived on AFDC payments. A public health clinic was started in Tchula, and plans were made for a cable TV system door-to-door mail service and the construction of public basketball and tennis courts. In less than three years, Carthan obtained $3 million in federal and private support for the town and created 80 new jobs.

But change in a repressive society does not come about without opposition. Upon Carthan's election, a political representative of the "four most powerful men in the state—more powerful even than the governor," offered the mayor a $10,000 bribe if he agreed to do things "the way they have always been done." When Carthan refused the bribe, the forces of reaction began to move.

Two "loyal" blacks on the town council sided with the lone white alderman, John Edgar Hayes, to undermine Carthan's progressive program. In 1979 they forced the black city clerk to resign, replacing her with a local white; forced the black water supervisor to resign, replacing him with the sister-in-law of the white county supervisor; and refused to pay costs for the city's telephone and light bill. Carthan's salary was lowered from $600 to $60 per month.

When local black supporters of Carthan protested, the aldermen voted to increase their property taxes. For two months, they refused to pay city employees. To intimidate Carthan, they locked city hall for eight weeks and placed white police chief Sharkey Ford at the front door. Shotgun in hand, Ford was ordered to "shoot anyone who tries to enter." Carthan's family began to receive threatening phone calls and racist letters.

The situation worsened in 1980. In April 1980, Ford finally resigned. Carthan appointed a black officer, Johnny Dale, as temporary police chief. At a special meeting of the city council, called specifically to hire a permanent police chief, Carthan's opponents left the session before a vote could occur. Walking to a local convenience store, they immediately phoned Jim Andrews, the white whom Carthan had defeated for mayor in the previous election. Andrews was told to "take over as police chief." Without taking an oath or being bonded, Andrews put on his "old uniform," picked up his service revolver, and took over the police department.

When Mayor Carthan learned about Andrews's actions, he located two regular police officers and several auxiliary policemen. Carthan and his police officers confronted Andrews at city hall. Andrews refused to leave, and pulled his gun when Carthan informed him that he would be arrested if he didn't leave. Andrews was finally disarmed nonviolently. Subsequently, both Carthan and Andrews filed charges against each other, but only Andrews's charges were acted upon. On April 12, 1981, Carthan and six co-defendants were convicted on charges of simple assault of a "law enforcement officer." The co-defendants received three year suspended sentences and fines. Eddie Carthan was ordered to spend three years in the Mississippi State Penitentiary.

But Carthan's legal troubles were not over. A local white businessman claimed that he had paid Carthan a bribe for signing papers for a bank loan, which federal authorities say was fraudulently obtained. Although the federal government's attorney conceded that Carthan's signature on the documents presented to the bank for a loan was "forged," the mayor was convicted. Carthan's bond was revoked on August 30, and he is in jail pending appeals as of this writing. But even with the destruction of Carthan's political influence, the Old Guard of white supremacy fears any open discussion of the cases. When the *Jackson Advocate* published information favorable to Carthan last December, the newspaper's office was fire-bombed. Organizing efforts still continue to free Carthan and the "Tchula Seven." On October 11, a national march will begin at Tchula, culminating in the state capitol on October 16. A broad coalition of civil rights activists, church leaders, legal aid agencies and civil liberties groups have endorsed the march.

Three decades ago, V.O. Key asserted that "the beginning and the end of Mississippi politics is the Negro." Despite desegregation and the election of black office-holders, this statement is still true today. The battle for civil rights, black economic development and simple justice has not ended in Mississippi: it has hardly begun.

SECTION V
On Black Leadership

~

A. Philip Randolph and the Foundations of Black American Socialism

The Negro intellectuals and radical theorists of the 1920s and 1930s did not, them-selves, fight for intellectual clarity. They were unable to create a new black revolution-ary synthesis of what was applicable from Garveyism ... and Marxism. Yet with such a theoretical synthesis, Negroes would not really have needed the Communist Party. They could have laid down the foundation for a new school of revolutionary ideas ...
—Harold Cruse, *The Crisis of the Negro Intellectual,* New York, 1967

Radicalism is a relative term and three decades hence may pronounce the radicals of today as the reactionaries of tomorrow.
—A. Philip Randolph, *Messenger,* March, 1919

Asa Philip Randolph was the most influential black trade unionist in U.S. history. Most social historians would argue that Randolph was, perhaps next to W.E.B. Du Bois, the most important Afro-American socialist of the twentieth century. His accomplish-ments in the fields of black union organizing, militant journalism and political protest were unequaled for decades. His controversial newspaper, the *Messenger,* was the first socialist journal to receive a widespread hearing among black working and middle-class people. In 1941 he led the first Negro March on Washington Movement to protest racial discrimination in federal hiring policies, establishing a precedent which was to be revived over two decades later at the high point of the Civil Rights Movement. Early in his productive career, Randolph had earned the hatred and fear of the capitalist elite and federal government officials. Not for nothing did President Woodrow Wilson refer to the black socialist leader as "the most dangerous Negro in America."

Later in life, Randolph's contributions to the Afro-American freedom struggle came under severe criticism from many quarters. Young black industrial workers in the late 1960s condemned Randolph and other trade union leaders for not representing their problems and vital interests. To the black activists in the League of Revolutionary Black Workers, he came to represent a modern Booker T. Washington without the Tuskegee educator's acumen for political compromise and power. In 1968 when blacks demanded greater decision-making authority in New York's Public School system and charged the United Federation of Teachers (U.F.T.) with racism, Randolph heartily defended the U.F.T. and its leader, Albert Shanker. In 1976 he lent his support to Daniel Patrick Moynihan, a conservative, racist Democrat, when the latter was running for the U.S. Senate in New York. Randolph's image as a radical socialist and militant trade unionist had been utterly erased. Upon his death in May 1979, Vice President Walter Mondale glorified the black leader, declaring that "America can speak out for human rights around the world, without hypocrisy, because of the faith A. Philip Randolph ... showed in our country."

Thus, we approach the great legacy of Randolph with some sadness and uncertainty. So many questions are left unanswered by the path of his brilliant and yet contradictory career. Some Marxists suggest that the "decisive break" in Randolph's career occurred in 1919, when he parted company with other black socialists like Grace Campbell, Cyril V. Briggs and Frank Crosswaith, who joined the fledgling Communist Party. "The issue was clear cut," argued Irwin Silber of the New York *Guardian,* "not support for socialism in general or in the abstract, but support for and defense of the Bolshevik revolution." Randolph's decision to choose "the path of social democracy" was "the decisive turning point in a political life devoted to preventing revolutionary forces from winning leadership of the black liberation struggle."[1] As we shall observe, this split was nowhere nearly as decisive as Silber or others suggest. Randolph's admiration and support for the Russian Revolution continued for many years. Throughout his early career, especially between the years 1919–22 and 1935–40, he welcomed the support of Marxist-Leninists, while reserving the right to differ with them politically. In general, there is actually much greater continuity within the political thought and practice between the younger and older Randolph than is usually thought.

This essay does not attempt to present Randolph's entire political life in any comprehensive manner. There are numerous books and articles which document his long and productive career, usually in a very positive light.[2] Instead, this essay will examine Randolph's early career as a militant journalist, Socialist Party candidate and trade unionist; from his arrival in New York in 1911 until the late 1920s. Many of Randolph's major accomplishments, such as the founding of the National Negro Congress during the Great Depression, his March on Washington Movement of 1941 and the civil disobedience campaign against military conscription in 1948 are either discussed briefly or not at all. This is because the fundamental outlines of Randolph's socialism and political activism were firmly established during this early period. The roots of his thought are developed during the chaotic experiences of World War I and its aftermath. Secondly, the foundations for subsequent black working class activism and modern black nationalism are established in the twenties. The competing political forces in Harlem of that period—Garveyism, left black nationalism, militant integrationism, Marxism-Leninism—are themes which constantly reoccur within the black movement today. The political decisions which Randolph made during the twenties, for better or worse, set much of the pattern for socialism and trade union work within the black commuity. The attempt here is to critique Randolph's emergent theory of social transformation during his formative decade of political activism and to develop an understanding for the consequences of his sometimes eclectic political practice. The legacy of Randolph's politics and trade unionism which is carried on by his protege Bayard Rustin will also be considered in this light.

BACKGROUND TO HARLEM RADICALISM

The historical period of World War I and the immediate postwar years brought substantial changes both to blacks in the U.S. in general and for blacks in industrial labor in particular. For the first time in history, a substantial number of Southern, rural blacks were moving to the industrial urban North. Against the paternalistic advice of Booker T. Washington, between 1900 and 1910, the percentage of blacks living in New York City increased by 51 per cent, while in Chicago and Philadelphia blacks increased by over 30 per cent. Almost one half million black men, women and children left the South before and during World War I. Simultaneously, writes Philip Foner, "the first black industrial working class in the United States came into existence." The number of blacks employed in U.S. industry between 1910 to 1920 rose from 551,825 to 901,181. By 1920 about one third of all Afro-American workers were employed in U.S. industry. However, only about 15 per cent of these workers held skilled or semiskilled jobs. The great majority of black workers earned a living in the very lowest paying and physically difficult jobs.[3]

As the political economy of black America took a decisive shift toward the industrial North, a number of competing political interests became involved in organizing, leading and interacting with the new black labor force. Broadly conceived, there were at least four potential political forces which presented alternative agendas to black industrial workers during this period. They consisted of (1) the old Booker T. Washington–capitalist alliance, which included conservative local black ministers, businessmen and journalists who preached cooperation with the capitalist class; (2) the American Federation of Labor, which in theory called for black support, but in practice upheld a strict Jim Crow bar; (3) the Marxist trade unionists in the Workers Party, later the Communist Party and many members of the Socialist Party, which advocated black-white labor unity; (4) independent all-black labor organizations, which operated outside the "House of Labor," including black nationalist groups influenced by Marcus Garvey. Randolph was simply one of a number of voices, competing for the allegiance and leadership of the new black working class.

The very success of Booker T. Washington in attracting white capital to his many enterprises, from the National Negro Business League to Tuskegee Institute, spelled ultimate disaster to the new black working class in the North. Washington's Northern constituency, the aggressive but fragile black entrepreneurial elite, firmly supported the idea of a capitalist-Negro alliance against white labor. Washington had argued that blacks should appeal to white employers to hire black workers, since they were "not inclined to trade unionism" and not in favor of strikes. Tuskegee scientist and inventor George Washington Carver was an intimate friend of auto industrialist Henry Ford. Thus, major black newspapers such as the Chicago *Defender* supported Washington's strategy of alliance with the capitalist class. Many prominent black ministers, Republican politicians and businessmen counseled black workers to reject unionism. Despite this influence, the overwhelming majority of new immigrants from the rural South quickly saw through this strategy for what it was, a "dead end" Jim Crow policy which only perpetuated the lower level economic status for the black working class.

On paper, the American Federation of Labor (A.F.L.) sought to recruit the budding black proletariat to its cause; in actual practice it was scarcely less reactionary than the Ku Klux Klan. Between 1919 to 1927 the number of black locals in the A.F.L. dropped from 161 to 21. Many unions had a long established policy of Jim Crow. Sometimes blacks were admitted to separate lodges, and then forced under the authority of a white local. The new president of the A.F.L., the United Mine Workers (U.M.W.) former secretary-treasurer William Green, was no friend of black workers. Green had tolerated Ku Klux Klan influence within the U.M.W., and had never taken a strong stand against racial segregation. Green's concern for black labor was only stimulated in the 1920s when it appeared that many Afro-American workers were moving toward Marxism and/or independent trade union activism.[4]

The only white groups which defended black worker's rights during this period were on the left. Growing out of the militant tradition of the Industrial Workers of the World (I.W.W.), thousands of socialist organizers of both races campaigned for worker unity against the issue of white racism. When the "Wobblies" split over the question of the Soviet revolution, many joined the Communist Party (C.P.), such as William Z. Foster. In 1920 Foster brought together a biracial coalition of Marxists and reformist trade union activists to create the Trade Union Educational League. The T.U.E.L. advocated the building of a worker and farmers' political party, greater racial egalitarianism inside the A.F.L. and the creation of militant unions for noncraft workers. C.P. leader Earl Browder edited the T.U.E.L.'s publication, the *Labor Herald*. In 1925 the C.P. was also active in the formation of the American Negro Labor Congress, an all-black labor group which advocated the building of "inter-racial labor committees" to promote the introduction of black workers into previously segregated crafts. As the Communists grew more influential in organizing black workers, the fears of A.F.L. leaders mounted.[5]

Related to these developments in the labor left was the rapid growth of independent black workers' organizations. As thousands of black laborers came to the North, the base for all-black, militant activism in labor increased dramatically. In 1915 a national organization of black railroad workers was created, the Railway Men's Benevolent Association. Within five years it had 15,000 members. In 1917 the Colored Employees of America was founded, one of the first of many groups which attempted to organize all black laborers. Two years later the National Brotherhood

Workers of America was established, a coalition of black workers from almost every occupation, including blacksmiths, electricians, dock workers, porters, riveters and waiters. Until its demise in 1921, it represented a potential alternative to the racist policies of the A.F.L. To the left of these organizations, black radicals and Marxists urged the development of independent socialist strategies for black labor.[6] Randolph's entire life must be viewed against this initial period of his activism, a time of tremendous growth and opportunities for black labor in the industrial North.

Randolph's personal background conformed in most respects with that of other first-generation black immigrants from the South. Born in Crescent City, Florida, on April 15, 1889, Randolph grew up in Jacksonville during the "nadir period" of black-white anti-racial relations. Inspired by the Du Bois's *Souls of Black Folk* as a teenager, young Asa decided to leave the South and settle in New York City. Arriving in Harlem in the spring of 1911, Randolph first desired to make his career as an actor. Failing at this, he drifted from one job to another. It is at this point, however, that Randolph's development became exceptional. From 1912–1917 he attended courses at the City College of New York. One leftist philosophy professor, J. Salwyn Shapiro, acquainted Randolph with Marx's writings and other socialist literature. His discovery of socialism was so "exciting," he later reflected, that he studied "Marx as children read *Alice in Wonderland*."[7] He formed a group of radical "free thinkers," called the Independent Political Council, and began to follow closely the activities of the Industrial Workers of the World. He began to identify himself with Harlem's premier black socialist and "leading street-corner orator," Hubert Harrison. He joined the Socialist Party in the end of 1916, and began to lecture on black history and political economy at the Socialist Party's Rand School. By the beginning of World War I, Randolph and his new black friend, Chandler Owen, a fellow socialist, had become "the most notorious street-corner radicals in Harlem, exceeding even Harrison in the boldness of their assault upon political and racial conditions in the country."[8]

Randolph and Owen became involved in a series of efforts to organize black workers in their community. After several weeks' work they had succeeded in gaining the support of 600 black elevator operators in the city to start the United Brotherhood of Elevator and Switchboard Operators. The new union's demands included a minimum wage of $13 and an eight-hour day. Receiving a federal charter from the A.F.L., the short-lived organization tried, and failed, to organize a strike to force recognition. Randolph and Owen were also actively involved in the Headwaiters and Sidewaiters Society as editors of the union's journal, the *Hotel Messenger*. After a dispute with the Society's president, William White, the young Socialists were fired. Within two months, they organized their own monthly magazine, the *Messenger*, with the critical financial support provided by Randolph's wife, Lucille, who earned a living as a popular and successful Harlem hairdresser. Over the next months, the new publication acquired the enthusiastic support of older radicals like Harrison and younger militants like Jamaican socialist W.A. Domingo.[9] Between 1917 until 1928, the journal received the support of a wide variety of Harlem radicals and liberal black intellectuals of various shades: William Pickens, a field secretary of the N.A.A.C.P.; Robert W. Bagnall, N.A.A.C.P. director of branches; Wallace Thurman, Harlem

Renaissance author; esssayist George S. Schuyler, a socialist who evolved into a right-wing Goldwater Republican. The theoretical basis for Randolph's socialism in his early years, between 1914 and 1920, was an uneven combination of traditional religious reformism, economic determinism, a fervent internationalism, and Karl Marx. His father, the Reverend James Randolph, was a pastor in the African Methodist Episcopal Church. Upon his move to Harlem, the first organization he joined was the Epworth League, a social club whose principle activity was Bible study and prayer. Later friends recalled that "Randolph was the outstanding" participant in all "Epworth forums." Throughout Randolph's youth, his father regarded him "as a fine prospect for the A.M.E. ministry."[10] Randolph rejected the orthodoxy of the cloth, but not the meaning of black spirituality in his politics. The language of the Old Testament would inform many of his speeches, as he deliberately used religious principles of brotherhood and humanism in organizing black workers. Even at the high point of their radicalism, Randolph and Owen spoke at black churches and worked closely with progressive clergy. "There are some Negro ministers," the *Messenger* declared in March 1920, "who have vision, intelligence and courage. There [are] some upon whose souls the Republican Party has no mortgage."[11] Randolph continued to believe that the black church was "the most powerful and cohesive institution in Negro life." Like his friend Norman Thomas, Randolph's socialism was never rooted in an atheistic outlook on life.[12]

Like many other socialists of the day, especially those influenced by the intellectual debates between Eduard Bernstein and Karl Kautsky of the German Social Democratic Party, Randolph believed that socialism was a series of economic reforms taking place between management and labor. Through the vehicle of the trade union, the working class seized an increasingly greater share of the decision-making power within the workplace. The expression of working-class politics was, of course, the Socialist Party. The revolution against capital would be a revolt of the majority against the selfish interests of a tiny, isolated elite. Randolph's definition of socialism placed deterministic limitations on all of his subsequent life's work. If the Socialist Party was, as Randolph believed, the highest expression of working class consciousness, and if blacks were overwhelmingly working class, then no other political formation could address blacks' interests as well as the party. Race and ethnicity played no role in the "scientific evolution" of class contradictions; class was an economic category without cultural or social limits. Randolph increasingly viewed any form of black nationalism as a major obstacle between white and black workers in the struggle toward socialist democracy.

The outbreak of World War I deepened Randolph's commitment to militant pacifism and "revolutionary socialism." Like Debs, Randolph and Owen opposed World War I on the principle that "wars of contending national groups of capitalists are not the concern of the workers." The *Messenger's* first issues denounced the "capitalist origins" of the conflict in a fiery essay, "Who Shall Pay for the War?" The editors told black men that they should not serve when drafted, and charged that the Wilson Administration was "making the world safe for democracy a sham, a mockery, a rape on decency and a travesty on common justice."[13] In 1918 Randolph and Owen participated in a Socialist Party antiwar speaking tour. On August 4, 1918, the two were arrested by federal agents after a mass rally in Cleveland, charged with violating the Espionage act, and held in $1,000 bail. Defended by Socialist Party lawyer Seymour Stedman, the judge warned Randolph and Owen to "return to their parents' homes" and register for the draft. Despite the warning, the young men continued their lecture tour, visiting Chicago, Milwaukee, Washington, D.C., and Boston, where black radical Monroe Trotter joined their mass antiwar rally. In mid-August, Postmaster General Albert Burleson denied second-class mailing privileges to the *Messenger*. Within days, Owen was drafted and sent to a Jim Crow army base in the South. Only the armistice prevented Randolph from the November draft.[14]

Similarly, the Bolshevik Revolution inspired Harlem's radicals, seemingly vindicating their faith in revolutionary socialism. "Lenin and Trotsky ... are sagacious, statesmanlike and courageous leaders," the *Messenger* proclaimed in January, 1918. "They are calling upon the people of every country to follow the lead of Russia; to throw off their exploiting rulers, to administer public utilities for the public welfare, to disgorge the exploiters and the profiteers."[15] For several years to come, Randolph argued that the Communist revolution meant the "triumph of democracy in Russia." He praised the Soviet Army's defeat of the White Russians in 1920, stating that the capitalist opponents of socialism "had not reckoned with the indomitable courage and the cold resolution born of the unconquerable love for liberty."[16] Randolph boldly predicted that Bela Kun's Hungarian Communists would eventually defeat the Social Democrats and send the aristocracy "to that oblivion and obscurity to which they ought never to emerge;"[17] he also believed that British capitalism was at the brink of "an impending financial revolution."[18] Domestically, Randolph participated eagerly in the Socialist Party's activities. In 1917, the *Messenger* campaigned for Morris Hillquit, the Socialist Party's candidate for mayor. In 1920 Randolph ran as the Party's candidate for state comptroller and polled 202,361 votes, only 1,000 less than Socialist presidential candidate Eugene V. Debs in the state. In 1921 he ran another unsuccessful campaign for secretary of state. Despite these limited failures, Randolph's belief in a democratic socialist revolution remained uncompromised—up to a point.[19]

Randolph's decisive break from Du Bois—the major black leader of the N.A.A.C.P. and Randolph's intellectual mentor—did not occur until 1918, when the editor of the *Crisis* urged black Americans to support the war effort.[20] Up to this point, the *Messenger* had praised Du Bois' "full merit and worth" as a race leader and opponent of "disenfranchisement," condemning only his attitude on labor. "One has not seen where the doctor ever recognized the necessity of the Negro as a scab," Owen wrote, "allaying thereby the ill feeling against him by the working white man."[21] Du Bois' advocacy of the war crystallized Randolph and Owen's opposition to his entire political line—from the "Talented Tenth" theory to his worth as a critic of segregation. By July, 1918, Randolph condemned almost every major essay or book that Du Bois had ever written: his landmark sociological survey, *The Philadelphia Negro,* was criticized as "a heavily padded work, filled with superfluous matter"; *The Souls of Black Folk* was dismissed as "a mass of labored alliterations...." Du Bois was a "political opportunist," simply representing "a good transition from Booker Washington's compromise methods to the era of the new Negro."[22]

Never one to avoid a fight, Du Bois defended his anti-Socialist Party, antitrade unionist, anti-Bolshevik and pro-war positions head on. As early as January 1912, when he was a member of the Socialist Party, Du Bois complained about racism within the organization. He left the party to endorse the election of Woodrow Wilson later that year.[23] His opposition to trade unionism was well established and was reinforced by his essay, "The Black Man and the Unions," published in March, 1918.[24] Du Bois' position on the war evolved from a remarkable May 1915 essay, "The African Roots of the War," which examined the colonial and racist origins of the conflict. From the destruction of the German empire, Du Bois may have reasoned, the possibility for greater African self-determination may be a result.[25] As a result, he took the position that black Americans would receive a "reward" for their loyalty to the United States' war effort against Germany.[26] On the matter of Russian radicalism Du Bois was profoundly skeptical. After the "February Revolution" in early 1917, Du Bois suggested to his *Crisis* readers that the event "makes us wonder whether the German menace is to be followed by a Russian menace or not.[27] Although he criticized Alexander Kerensky's "blood and iron methods" in governing Russia, he said nothing about the Bolsheviks rise to power.[28] When radical Harlem Renaissance writer Claude McKay questioned why Du Bois "seemed to neglect or sneer at the Russian Revolution," he replied curtly that he had "heard things which [were] frighten[ing]" about the upheaval. I am "not prepared to dogmatize with Marx or Lenin."[29]

For the New Negro generation, these opinions relegated "the Doctor" to the status of "the old, me-too-Boss, hat-in-hand Negro generally represented by Robert Russa Moton of Tuskegee."[30] Hubert Harrison exonerated the *Crisis* editor in his journal, *The Voice*. Randolph declared that Du Bois was "comparatively ignorant of the world problems of sociological and economic significance," and that his publication was filled with "errors and misstatements."[31] In 1920, the *Messenger* charged that the *Crisis* had an editorial policy of "viciousness, petty meanness" and "suppression [of] facts pertaining to the N.A.A.C.P." It attacked Du Bois' associates, especially field secretary William Pickens, as advocates of "sheer claptrap."[32] It proclaimed that its God was "the toiling masses of the world," and laughed at Du Bois' provincial liberalism and staid social conformity. By the end of Wilson's administration, the Justice Department reported that the *Messenger* was "by long odds the most dangerous of all the Negro publications." Throughout Harlem, Randolph and Owen became known as "Lenin and Trotsky," the most revolutionary black Bolsheviks on the scene. Their political break from Du Bois seemed complete.[33]

FROM CLASS STRUGGLE TO CLASS COMPROMISE

Having declared war against Du Bois and the N.A.A.C.P. leadership, Randolph and Owen sought the support of other black activists within Harlem. By their own admission, Du Bois remained "the most distinguished Negro in the United States today."[34] Marcus Garvey seemed a likely addition to their struggle against the *Crisis*'s editor. Born in Jamaica, Garvey had established his Universal Negro Improvement

Association in 1914. Inspired by the racial "self-help" slogans of Booker T. Washington, the young black nationalist eventually settled in New York City in 1916. Randolph claimed the distinction of having been the first prominent black radical to invite Garvey to make an address in Harlem. He recalled years later that "when he finished speaking … I could tell from watching him then that he was one of the greatest propagandists of his time."[35] Garvey was attracted to Harrison, who by June 1917 had left the Socialist Party to form his own left black nationalist movement, the AfroAmerican Liberty League. Although Garvey was one of the main speakers at the League's first rally on June 12, 1917, he quickly established his own separate U.N.I.A. offices near the *Messenger* on 135th Street. Randolph and Garvey worked together in the International League of Darker Peoples, an organization which demanded that the African territories and colonized nations be represented at the Versailles peace conference.[36] Some Garveyites began to assist Randolph's efforts. Domingo, who was editor of Garvey's *Negro World,* actively worked as a contributing editor on the *Messenger.* Randolph certainly welcomed Garvey's public attacks on Du Bois as an "anti-bellum Negro."[37]

The first major disagreement between the black nationalists and Randolph probably occurred over the creation of the Liberty Party, an all-black political coalition of former Socialists, Republicans and Democrats, in late 1920. The state slogan of the party was "Race First"; it advocated running a black presidential candidate and independent candidates at local levels. Randolph went to great lengths to condemn the notion on all conceivable grounds. First, the Negro party was criticized because he had no prospects for support from white workers. "A party that has no hope of becoming a majority has no justification for independent action; for it can never hope to be of positive benefit to its supporters." Secondly, the party had no economic platform. Thirdly, the proposition of a Negro President was "tragically inane, senselesss, foolish, absurd and preposterous. It is inconceivable that alleged intelligent, young colored men could take such obvious, stupendous political folly seriously." Last, the Liberty Party consisted of "opportunists, discredited political failures who are now trying to capitalize race prejudice of the Negro." The basis for this vituperative attack rested with Randolph's basic proposition that it was in the interests of "Negro workers to join and vote for the Socialist Party."[38] Although it is not clear, it is probable that Harrison's Liberty League supported the new party. Another more menacing factor, of course, was Garvey, who had long been a proponent of an all black political party.[39] J.W.H. Easton, the U.N.I.A. leader for U.S. blacks, was the party's nominee for President.[40] The idea of a separate, race-conscious, political organization, rather than the Liberty Party per se, was the real issue. Randolph and Owen had begun to view militant black nationalism as being even more dangerous than the threat presented by Du Bois and his *Crisis.*

The *Messenger* began to challenge the Garvey Movement for hegemony within Harlem's black working class population. In December 1920, Randolph issued an editorial, "The Garvey Movement: A Promise or a Menace," which took the position that "the class-struggle nature of the Negro problem" was missing from the U.N.I.A.'s work. Revolutionary black nationalism "invites an unspeakably violent revulsion of hostile opposition from whites against blacks." In Randolph's view, any all-black organization could "only misdirect the political power of the Negro. All party platforms are chiefly concerned with economic questions" and not with race. Therefore, the *Messenger* concluded, Garvey's entire program "deserves the condemnation and repudiation of all Negroes."[41] Relations with Garveyites swiftly worsened. Randolph insisted that Garvey's advocacy of an independent Africa for the Africans was unrealistic, because the Africans do not possess "the ability . . . to assume the responsibilities and duties of a sovereign nation."[42] By mid-1922 the *Messenger's* editorials literally shouted its total opposition to Garvey. "Here's notice that the *Messenger* is firing the opening gun in a campaign to drive Garvey and Garveyism in all its sinister viciousness from the American soil."[43]

Nowhere in the black press of the time was the anti-Garvey campaign expressed so bluntly and with such anti–West Indian sentiments as in the *Messenger*. The most comprehensive statement on this theme was Randolph's essay, "The Only Way To Redeem Africa," published in two parts in the January and February 1923 issues. Every significant aspect of Garvey's program was denounced as either "foolish," "vicious," "without brains" or "sheer folly." The U.N.I.A.'s Black Star steamship line had "no hope" in succeeding; its proposal for a Booker T. Washington University will have "neither students nor teachers" since the former "will not trust it to give out knowledge" and the latter will not "trust it to give out pay." Garvey's wildest claim, that the U.N.I.A. had 4.5 million dues-paying members, proved that he was "a consummate liar or a notorious crook." Randolph failed to explain the reasons for Garvey's massive popularity among black workers in Harlem, and ignored the hard evidence of the U.N.I.A.'s progressive positions on African and international affairs. Nevertheless, he concluded that "the Garvey Movement is a social-racial disease germ to the Negro which must be destroyed in order that he may proceed to build up a powerful organization to protect his interests."[44]

As the Bolshevik Revolution forced the creation of a Third International, Randolph felt himself pulled gradually toward the right. For the first time in several years he was no longer "the first voice of radical, revolutionary, economic and political action among Negroes in America."[45] Revolutionary black activists outside both the U.N.I.A. and the *Messenger* faction were making political waves across Harlem. In the fall of 1917 Cyril V. Briggs founded the African Blood Brotherhood (A.B.B.), a leftist and black nationalist group. A native of the Dutch West Indies and a former editorial writer for the New York *Amsterdam News,* Briggs began to edit his own militantly nationalist journal, the *Crusader.* The members of the A.B.B., which included Lovett Fort-Whiteman, Richard B. Moore, and Otto Huiswood, quickly were recruited into the newly formed Workers, or Communist Party. Harrison did not "go over to the Communists," according to Harold Cruse, but he did "assist them" in certain situations.[46] By 1922, the Communists had begun "to assail Garvey's program as reactionary, escapist and utopian" while simultaneously trying "to influence, collaborate with, or undermine his movement."[47] As Marxist-Leninists, the A.B.B. also attacked Randolph's firm ties with the Socialist Party, his reformist and quasi-religious theories for social transformation, his bitter hostility toward black nationalism and growing tendency toward political and economic conservatism.[48]

The *Messenger* turned on its former leftist friends almost as viciously as it had turned against Garvey. Declaring all black Communists "a menace to the workers, themselves and the race," Randolph judged their policies "utterly senseless, unsound, unscientific, dangerous and ridiculous." Black Marxist "extremists" were hopelessly out of touch with the mentality of Negro laborers, since the latter had not "even grasped the fundamentals and necessity of simple trade and industrial unionism!" As further proof that "Communism can be of no earthly benefit to either white or Negro workers," Randolph pointed out that the Soviet Union's New Economic Policy of "State Capitalism" had replaced the radical socialist economics of the War Communist years. Soviet Communists [recognize] its impracticability at the present stage of economic development of Russia." In short, he wrote, the black Communists' "statements have revealed that they are utterly devoid of any respect for fact, truth, or honesty."[49]

With some desperation, the *Messenger* turned to the N.A.A.C.P. in its campaign against Garvey. There was no indication that Du Bois had changed on any of the major points that had separated him from Randolph during the war. If anything, Du Bois' opposition to "State Socialism," the "class struggle," and his advocacy of black "capital accumulation to effectively fight racism" placed him to the economic right of many Garveyites, and perhaps even Garvey himself at this time.[50] What had separated Randolph and Du Bois was now disintegrated by the very success of Garvey and his gospel of militant black nationalism. There was a remarkable degree of concurrence between the *Crisis* and the *Messenger*, from a principled opposition to all forms of racial separatism to a distrust of Garvey's business methods and even honesty. Both were also concerned about growing danger, as Du Bois put it, of "Communists boring into Negro labor."[51]

Working closely with the N.A.A.C.P.'s assistant secretary, Walter White, Randolph coordinated an elaborate campaign against Garvey, which included the distribution of anti-Garvey handbills throughout Harlem. In January 1923, Randolph, Owen, Pickens and several other black leaders drafted a memorandum to Attorney General Harry M. Daugherty asking for the conviction of Marcus Garvey on charges of mail fraud, various criminal activities and "racial bigotry." Garvey was eventually convicted of mail fraud, and was sent to a federal penitentiary in Atlanta in February 1925. By the late 1920s the U.N.I.A. had virtually collapsed, partially due to Randolph's anti-Garvey activities. The irony of this entire episode was that Randolph, a would-be leader of the black working class, had participated in the destruction of the largest black worker and peasants organization in U.S. history.

Compared to Garvey, Randolph's efforts to organize black workers met with little real success. Randolph and Owen created the Friends of Negro Freedom in 1920, a biracial group which promoted black entrance into trade unions and held lectures on economic and political issues. Friends of Negro Freedom included the participation of Domingo, Baltimore *Afro-American* newspaper editor Carl Murphy and black intellectual Archibald Grimke. In 1923 Randolph attempted unsuccessfully to establish a United Negro Trades organization to bring black workers into independent trade unions. Finally, in August 1925, a few Pullman porters asked Randolph to help them establish the Brotherhood of Sleeping Car Porters. Despite the fact that several black Pullman employees had been more instrumental in organizing rank-and-file support for the Brotherhood, such as W. H. Des Verney and Ashley Totten, Randoph was named the group's president. The initial prospects for this union's success looked just as dim as all the other groups that Randolph had led. The eleven thousand black porters working on Pullman cars faced the united opposition of the federal government, the Pullman Company and its black conservative allies.

Given Randolph's early inability to build a successful and popular mass organization of black workers, it is not surprising that he began to reassess his overall theoretical outlook and political practice. Gradually socialism was given less emphasis in his writings. By 1923 the *Messenger* had succeeded in attracting several black businessmen and merchants to advertise in its pages. Colleges and Negro industrial schools followed suit. Articles by Emmett J. Scott, the former secretary of Booker T. Washington, and even Robert Russa Moton of Tuskegee began appearing in the journal.[52] Quietly editorial policies began to change. In January 1925, Randolph declared that "Negro businessmen are rapidly rising to the high mark of responsibility." Many black entrepreneurs were "splendid, courteous" and a *"delight* to deal with."[53] Randolph's blanket condemnation of the A.F.L. and his critical description of Gompers—a "conservative, reactionary and chief strikebreaker"—mellowed into fawning and even syncophantic praise. The A.F.L. was no longer "a machine for the propagation of race prejudice," but by 1925, it was a progressive and democratic force. Randolph banned any articles critical of William Green, newly elected A.F.L. leader.[54]

The editors endorsed Hampton and Tuskegee Institutes' five million dollar fund drive by defending Washington's classical position of industrial education against Du Bois' Talented Tenth ideal. "Dr. Du Bois has probably been responsible for a great deal of misunderstanding about industrial education in America," they argued. "We need more brick masons, carpenters, plasterers, plumbers, than we do physicians; more cooks than lawyers; more tailors and dressmakers than pupils."[55] Given that there were approximately 40,000 black secondary and elementary teachers, 3,200 black physicians and only 900 black lawyers in the United States at this time, it is utterly remarkable that Randolph's statement could be taken seriously. The percentage of black children between the ages of 5 to 20 who were enrolled in school was about 50 percent; 25 percent of all adult blacks in the South were illiterate.[56] These remarks indicate that Randolph had moved toward a defense of private property and acknowledged the legitimacy of capitalism for blacks—a posture which he would never relinquish.

After several years as an independent, all-black union, Randolph persuaded the Brotherhood to apply for an international charter from the A.F.L. in 1928. Green was reassured by Randolph that the union would present no special problems to the A.F.L. The A.F.L. rejected the application for equal membership, and instead proposed a "compromise" of "federal union" status inside the organization. Despite criticism from leftists, black workers and some journalists, Randolph agreed to these terms. Both parties got something in the deal: Green and the A.F.L. acquired a major black union, silencing their Marxist and black critics like Du Bois; Randolph received the promise of assistance from organized white labor in his growing struggle with the Pullman Company.

With characteristic enthusiasm, Randolph devoted his total energies toward building the Brotherhood. Appeals to porters to join the union were acquired on "a racialistic and religious basis." Randolph recognized that socialist dogma would not find a receptive audience among most black workers, and used Biblical passages and paraphrases through his writings. "Ye shall know the truth, and the truth shall set you free" was the standard slogan on most Brotherhood stationery. In language reminiscent of some Garveyites, the Brotherhood's literature declared its faith in God and the Negro Race: "Fight on brave souls! Long live the Brotherhood! Stand upon thy feet and the God of Truth and Justice and Victory will speak unto thee!"[57] Randolph's efforts to organize the porters received a boost in 1926, when the Garland Fund, administered by the American Civil Liberties Union, donated $10,000 to the Brotherhood. The money allowed Randolph to hire Frank W. Crosswaith, a West Indian Socialist and graduate of the Party's Rand School in New York City, as a professional organizer and executive secretary of the Brotherhood.[58] Randolph was also encouraged by the wealth of intelligent and creative leaders among the ranks of the porters: Morris "Dad" Moore and C.L. Dellums of Oakland; T.T. Patterson of New York City; Des Verney and Totten. Chief among them was Milton Webster. Two years Randolph's senior, Webster had been fired by Pullman because of his militancy. In the twenties he became a bailiff and was one of Chicago's influential black Republican leaders. Webster was appointed assistant general organizer of the Brotherhood and chief organizer for the Chicago area. Next only to Randolph, the aggressive yet politically conservative Webster soon became the major spokesperson for many of the porters.[59]

Randolph's leadership was soon put to the test against the Pullman Company. On October 15, 1926, he informed the Board of Mediation, established by the Railway Labor Act of that same year, that a dispute existed between the Brotherhood and Pullman. The Board assigned a conservative Democrat and former governor of Kentucky, Edward P. Morrow, to investigate the case. Covertly working with Pullman executives, Morrow concluded with the company that the Brotherhood should not be recognized as the official bargaining agent of the porters. In August 1927, the Board declared that the parties could not reach an agreement and it recommended voluntary arbitration. Pullman refused to discuss the issue any further, and was blunt in its reasons for rejecting Randolph and his union.[60] Randolph had no other alternative at this point but to announce that he would call a strike to force Pullman Company into collective bargaining. The tentative date for the strike was June 8, 1928, at noon.[61]

Across the country, porters were excited at the prospect for a final confrontation between themselves and the Pullman Company. Despite red-baiting against Randolph's militant past, random firings and veiled threats, the porters almost unanimously backed the Brotherhood leadership. The strike vote, which was approved by a margin of 6,053 to 17, astonished even Randolph. Some porters made plans for a long seige, even blocking the use of strikebreakers. Ashley Totten and his associates in Kansas City began collecting "sawed-off shotguns, railroad iron taps, boxes of matches, knives and billy clubs" and storing them in a local black-owned building. Facing the prospect of an extensive and probably violent strike which would disrupt Pullman railroad service nationwide, Randolph began to have doubts. Could an all-black workers strike succeed without some measure of white trade union and working class support? On June 8, three hours before the scheduled strike, Green sent Randolph a telegram stating that "conditions were not favorable" for a strike. He suggested that the Brotherhood engage in "a campaign of education and public enlightenment regarding the justice of your cause." Randolph quickly ordered the strike off.[62]

It is difficult to determine whether the strike would have been successful. Throughout the remainder of his life, Randolph insisted that the possibilities were nil. The historical evidence points in the opposite direction. William H. Harris' research on Brotherhooid correspondence suggests that Webster had a great deal of difficulty in convincing his local members not to strike by themselves. "Aside from disruption of peak travel, what could be more damaging to interstate commerce than to tie up the rails during the time when both national political parties were holding conventons in such remote cities as Houston and Kansas City?" Harris asked. "Even the Pullman Company recognized this as a potential danger."[63] The union was "in shambles after the abortive strike." The *Messenger* was forced to halt publication; porters lost confidence in the Brotherhood and stopped paying their regular dues. Black newspapers like the New York *Argus* attacked the leadership of "A. Philip Randolph."[64] The Communists accused him of betraying Negro workers in the interest of labor fakers."[65] The American Negro Labor Congress charged that Randolph had "forsaken the policy of militant struggle in the interest of the workers for the policy of class collaboration with the bosses and bluffing with the strike." Within four years the brotherhoods membership declined from almost 7,000 to only 771 in 1932.[66]

It was only in April 1937 that the Pullman Company agreed to bargain seriously with the Brotherhood. On August 25 of that same year Pullman agreed to reduce the porters' monthly work load from 400 to 240 hours, and provide a substantial pay increase. But many of his critics, black and white, suggested that these and other accomplishments would have been achieved much sooner if A. Philip Randolph had a little less faith in the system and a little more confidence in the militancy of the black working class.

BEYOND CIVIL RIGHTS AND TRADE UNIONISM

In the Great Depression, Randolph again exhibited real courage and some of his former political independence. Contrary to Du Bois, Randolph charged that "the New Deal is no remedy" to black peoples' problems. It did not "change the profit system," nor "place human rights above property rights." Assisted by Alain Locke, Ralph

Bunche and other left-oriented black intellectuals, Randolph initiated the National Negro Congress in February, 1936. Hundreds of black trade unionists, radical civic reformers and communists participated in a black united front in blunt opposition both to Roosevelt's "welfare capitalism" and to the do-nothing acquiescence of the N.A.A.C.P. Despite the breakup of the Congress in the early 1940s over the issue of "Communist control," the organization represented one of the most advanced coalitions of black activists ever assembled.[67]

With the onset of World War II in Europe, the Roosevelt administration began a policy of expanding production in defense industries. Thousands of new jobs were created in industrial, clerical and technical fields related to wartime production prior to the U.S.'s direct involvement in the war. Generally, black workers were largely kept out of these positions because of a tacit policy of Jim Crow followed by white labor, big business and the federal government. Although Congress had forbidden racial discrimination in the appropriation of funds for defense training, the law was essentially a dead letter. With Randolph's resignation from the National Negro Congress in 1940, he turned his energies toward the issue of black employment in defense industries with federal contracts. Working again with Walter White, who by this time was Secretary and dictatorial leader of the N.A.A.C.P., Randolph sought to influence Roosevelt to initiate action against white racism.

By January 1941, Randolph was prepared to take what was, for that time, radical action. Randolph urged blacks to organize a militant march in Washington D.C. on July 1, to protest the discrimination against black workers. The idea of a "March on Washington Movement" seized the imagination of the black working class, the unemployed and even the petty bourgeoisie. The Brotherhood of Sleeping Car Porters was the central force behind the campaign. Hundreds of March on Washington Movement meetings were held in black churches, union halls and community centers. With the able assistance of Crosswaith and Howard University history professor Rayford Logan, Randolph succeeded in committing over 100,000 black people to the march. Foner observes that the "March on Washington Movement represented the first occasion in American history when a black labor organization assumed leadership of the struggle of the Negro masses on a national scale and became the spokesman for all black Americans, conservative and radical alike." Neither Garvey, Washington nor Du Bois had ever succeeded in forging a popular coalition of the black business and professional elites, the working class and rural blacks toward a single, progressive cause.

The driving force behind the 1941 March on Washington was black nationalism. Taking another page from Garvey's book, Randolph insisted that only blacks participate in the march. It was important for blacks to show white America that they were able to build an effective, militant, national organization without white assistance. C.L. Dellums explained that the Brotherhood informed its "white friends over the country why this had to be a Negro march. It had to be for the inspiration of Negroes yet unborn." White progressives and trade unionists were asked to offer "moral support, to stand on the sidelines and cheer us on."[68] The demand for an end to discrimination in defense plants appealed to the typical black industrial worker who, like porters in the twenties, was on the verge of militant class consciousness. But its expression among blacks was nationalism, a force involving religious, cultural and ethnic qualities which Randolph was forced to deal with in a concrete manner. Randolph's biographer emphasizes that "a certain strain of black nationalism ... ran through his social and religious heritage." Not surprisingly, "when the chips were down," Randolph had to return to his own origins to find the means to understand his own constituency and to articulate their aspirations. His biographer writes, "It is a wonder that black nationalism did not become the central activating force and principle of Randolph's political life."[69]

The Roosevelt administration began to take the black march seriously only in May, 1941. Roosevelt used his considerable powers of political influence to force the organizers to stop the march. As black workers in Harlem, Washington, D.C., Chicago and every major city prepared for the confrontation, Roosevelt finally agreed to sign an executive order prohibiting the "discrimination in the employment of workers in defense industries because of race, creed, color or national origin." The Democratic administration promised to create the Fair Employment Practices Committee (F.E.P.C.), a commission which would supervise the compliance of federal contractors to the executive order. Although this was not everything that the March on Washington Movement had asked for, Randolph and other leaders agreed to call off the demonstration on June 24.[70]

Historians August Meier and Elliott Rudwick point to the March on Washington Movement as the real foundation for the Civil Rights Movement of the 1950s and 1960s. "Though its career was brief the former organization prefigured things to come in three ways," they note. It was first "an avowedly all-Negro movement;" second, it involved the direct "action of the black masses;" third, "it concerned itself with the economic problems of the urban slum-dwellers."[71] Two additional points can be made as well. The F.E.P.C. was the beginning of today's Federal Office of Contracts Compliance Programs, the Department of Labor's affirmative action watchdog. The principle of equal opportunity for black people in employment was, for the first time, considered a civil right. Randolph's ideology behind the march also "prefigures" the 1950s–1960s because of the impact of Mohandas K. Gandhi in his approach to social change. In an address before March on Washington associates given in Detroit in September 1942, Randolph called attention to "the strategy and maneuver of the people of India with mass civil disobediance and non-cooperation." Huge, nonviolent demonstrations "in theatres, hotels, restaurants, and amusement places" could be a potential means to gain full equality. Years before Martin Luther King, Jr., Randolph envisioned the basic principles of *satyagraha* applied to the fight against Jim Crow.

Yet for all his foresight and commitment to the ideals of black struggle, Randolph's subsequent political behavior did little to promote the creation of a permanent, black protest organization. The March on Washington Movement's last major conference was in October 1946, and it lapsed completely the next year. Randolph's ongoing fights with A.F.L. officials still produced meager results. As in the past, Randolph's failure to carry out the threat of militant action compromised the pursuit of his long-range goals. Even at the peak of his influence, during the March on Washington Movement of 1940–41, Randolph failed to establish a mass-based, permanent force which promoted his rhetorical commitment to democratic socialism and black economic equality. Again and again, especially later in his career, he failed to trust the deep militancy of the black working class masses, relying instead upon tactical agreements with white presidents, corporate executives and labor bureaucrats. Curiously like Booker T. Washington, Randolph always preferred class compromise to class struggle.

With the end of World War II and the beginning of the Cold War, Randolph's creative contributions to the struggle for black freedom had largely ended. Like other labor leaders and socialists such as Norman Thomas, Randolph capitulated to the posture of extreme anti-Communism. Randolph and Thomas travelled to the Far East lecturing against the evils of radical trade unionism, for instance, under what later was revealed to be money from the C.I.A. He became an acknowledged "elder statesman" during the Civil Rights Movement of the 1950s. Making his peace with those black leaders he had formerly opposed in the N.A.A.C.P. and Urban League, Randolph had little to offer in the way of guidance or political theory to the newest generation of black radicals, the rebels of S.N.C.C., C.O.R.E. and S.C.L.C. Ironically, it was during this period that Du Bois, now in his eighties, moved toward a more thoroughly radical condemnation of the U.S.'s political economy than Randolph ever had. The old so-called "political opportunist" had become the active proponent for world peace and international liberation, while his "Young Turk" critic had become a defender of the conservative status quo.

Since the 1960s, Randolph's role in the A.F.L.-C.I.O. hierarchy has been filled by his trusted assistant Bayard Rustin. Like his mentor, Rustin is a socialist and pacifist with a long history of principled and at times even courageous struggle. As a participant in the Congress of Racial Equality's "Journey of Reconciliation" campaign of 1947, he tested local Jim Crow laws by sitting in white sections on interstate buses in the South. With other early "freedom riders" he received a thirty-day jail term on a North Carolina chain gang. Rustin was one of the major organizers of the 1963 March on Washington, and inspired a generation of younger black activists like S.N.C.C.'s Stokely Carmichael and Phil Hutchings. But as he became head of the A. Philip Randolph Institute, founded by George Meany and the A.F.L.-C.I.O. in 1965, he acquired the language and outlook of white labor's elites. Rustin bitterly denounced Malcom X as a "racist,"[72] and condemned the Black Power movement as "anti-white" and "inconsistent." Rustin and Randolph defended the Vietnam War and criticized King for linking domestic civil rights with the U.S. involvement in Southeast Asia.

In the 1970s Rustin's position within the black movement has drifted increasingly toward the right. At the September 1972 convention of the International Association of Machinists, he attacked black rank-and-file activists and defended the A.F.L.-C.I.O.'s shabby record on integration. The next year he was critical of the creation of the Coalition of Black Trade Unionists, arguing that the Randolph Institute should be viewed as the "catalyst" for black advancement in union leadership positions. On the international front at the time of Randolph's death, Rustin was a participant in a "Freedom House" delegation to Zimbabwe declaring that the white minority regime's fraudulent elections were democratic. Cruse analyzed him best in 1968, observing that "Rustin's problem is that in thirty years he has learned nothing new. He has done nothing new. He has done nothing creative in radical theory in American terms . . ."[73] Put another way, Rustin is a victim of what Marx postulated in "The Eighteenth Brumaire of Louis Bonaparte;" that "all great personages occur, as it were, twice—the first time as tragedy, the second as farce." Randolph's life is tragic, because of his greatness and yet untapped potential. Rustin's is a caricature, in another historical period, of that lost greatness.

Despite the remarkable changes and shifting images we may have of Randolph, certain fundamentals for future black workers' organization and political activism become imminently clear. Throughout his career, Randolph consistently perceived the problem of union organizing from a "top-down" rather than grassroots, mass-based approach. Although he was not a porter he asked for, and received, the presidency of the Brotherhood in 1925; he left the National Negro Congress' presidency after he realized that he could no longer exercise decisive authority over the leftists within the coalition. Another characteristic was his preference for compromise. Ending the 1941 March on Washington was the most outstanding instance but not the only one. Another compromise of a kind occurred in December 1965, after the establishment of the Randolph Institute. After years of criticizing the racial policies of the A.F.L.-C.I.O., Randolph reversed himself at the San Francisco national convention by announcing that racism had virtually disappeared from organized labor.

Another central feature of Randolph was his dire inability to appreciate the relationship between black nationalism, black culture and the struggle for socialism. Randolph and Owen's editorials in the *Messenger* declared that "unions are not based upon race lines, but upon class lines," and that "the history of the labor movement in America proves that the employing class recognize no race lines." This crude and historically false oversimplification led Randolph into pragmatic alliances with the white Marxists, with the A.F.L. after 1923, and later with the Kennedy and Johnson administrations. His successes in establishing the Brotherhood's rights to higher wages and shorter working hours were achieved at the expense of building any autonomous, all-black protest movement which was critical of both racism and capitalism. The *Messenger*'s vicious attacks against Garvey did not stop hundreds of thousands of rural and urban black workers from defending black nationalism. Randolph was ill equipped to understand the rank-and-file revolt of black industrial workers in the past two decades who were influenced by Malcolm X, Frantz Fanon and their Black Power disciples.

Cruse's comments on the entire generation of Harlem radicals, both in politics and the arts, are an appropriate critique of Randolph as well. Because "the Negro intellectuals of the Harlem Renaissance could not see the implications of cultural revolution as a political demand," Cruse notes, "they failed to grasp the radical potential of their own movement." Like Renaissance poets and novelists, Randolph was hesitant to place black culture, ethnicity and nationalism on the same agenda with other social and political concerns. "Having no cultural philosophy of their own, they remained under the tutelage of irrelevant white radical ideas."[74] This same assessment is also made by Du Bois in a speech, *The Field and Function of the Negro College,* presented at Fisk Universtiy in 1933. Du Bois criticized the literary Renaissance as "literature written for the benefit of white readers, and starting primarily from the white point of view. It never had a real Negro constituency and it did not grow out of the inmost heart and frank experience of Negroes ..."[75] Similarly, Randolph's economic determinism, his political pattern of compromise and reconciliation, his narrow definitions of class and culture proved harmful throughout his entire career. When he did turn to the black workers with an avowedly nationalistic style and program for political confrontation of the segregationist status quo, the first Negro March on Washington, he was dramatically successful. When he overcame his Socialist Party training and used some of the language of the black church and Southern black political protest traditions to appeal to his Brotherhood's rank-and-file, he had a potentially revolutionary force. Yet his ambiguous hostility toward the Negro's nationalism negated the full potential of his efforts.

Randolph's contribution to the ongoing struggle for black self-determination was unique and profoundly important. His activities in creating the Brotherhood of Sleeping Car Porters, the National Negro Congress and the March on Washington Movement of 1940–41 were necessary preconditions to the black activism of the 1950s and 1960s. For all its faults, as Cruse suggests in *The Crisis of the Negro Intellectual,* "not a single Negro publication in existence today matches the depth of the old *Messenger.*" Randolph was the first truly great leader of the black urban working class. But unlike Du Bois, he was unable to reevaluate himself and his movement dialectically; ultimately he became a prisoner of his own limited vision for black America.

In the next stage of history, black working people and activists must transcend Randolph's contradictions. If they succeed, as they must, they will begin to realize the full meaning of socialism as it applies to all aspects of black social existence. In doing so, they will carry out the legacy of Randolph, that he was unable to achieve for himself and his own generation.

~

KING'S AMBIGUOUS LEGACY

Martin Luther King was the most influential black minister in 20th-century American life. Most studies on the civil rights movement concentrate on King's role as a political figure, as the leader of the Southern Christian Leadership Conference (SCLC), and the relationships between various ideological tendencies within the desegregation campaign. Very few historians, however, have explored the movement's impact as a political factor in the evolution of black religion and in the political activities of black clergy. In the decades immediately preceding 1954, the black clergy as a group experienced a decline in political influence and social status relative to other middle-class blacks. The civil rights movement provided an historic opportunity for activist preachers to direct their working-class congregations in the practical struggle to overturn Jim Crow laws, improve housing conditions and to exercise the right to vote. King and other black ministers succeeded in their efforts to achieve democratic reforms within the system, but could not alleviate the roots of white racism or economic oppression within the ghetto.

As Black Power and the Vietnam War destroyed the fragile consensus within the civil rights leadership, King was forced to advance a more progressive human rights agenda which was clearly opposed to US foreign and domestic interests. But the black clergy, which still occupies an important position within black society, have been generally unwilling or unable to follow King's example.

The *Brown* decision of the Supreme Court in May 1954, outlawing "separate-but-equal" schools, presented new challenges to black ministers. To the surprise and chagrin of many Negro clergy, a key element in the forces of "massive resistance" to desegregation was led by white ministers. Dr. John H. Buchanan, Birmingham, Alabama's leading white clergyman, declared in 1956 that "the good Lord set up customs and practices of segregation." The American Council of Christian Churches, with a total membership of one million, declared solemnly in 1958 that integration "does violence to the true gospel of Jesus Christ." The Alabama American Baptist Convention even proclaimed in October 1959 that integration was a communist plot. White Christian clergy and laypersons expressed few reservations about becoming involved in the fight to preserve white supremacy.

The Montgomery bus boycott, initiated on December 1, 1955, by Rosa Parks, was the beginning of the "Second Reconstruction," a massive ethical movement by blacks and their white liberal allies to destroy racial segregation. The idea for the nonviolent boycott had been that of E.D. Nixon, an experienced member of the 1941 March on Washington Movement (demanding increased black employment opportunities) and trade union activist in black socialist A. Philip Randolph's Brotherhood of Sleeping Car Porters. A chief administrator in the boycott itself was Bayard Rustin, a black Quaker and social democrat who had participated in the earliest "freedom rides," or Journey of Reconciliation in the late 1940s. Black ministers were a minority on the major black political organization of the city, the Montgomery Improvement Association, yet it was the black clergy which provided the moral, social and political context for the entire struggle: the Reverend L. Roy Bennett, Reverend Ralph David Abernathy, Reverend Martin Luther King, Jr., among others. King's address at Montgomery's Holt Street Church at the outset of the boycott established the popular framework for black resistance: "One of the great glories of democracy is the right to protest for right.... We are protesting for the birth of justice in the community. Our method will be that of persuasion, not coercion. Our actions must be guided by the deepest principles of our Christian faith. Love must be our regulating ideal. Once again we must hear the words of Jesus echoing across the centuries: 'Love your enemies, bless them that curse you, and pray for them that despitefully use you.' If we fail to do this our protest will end up as a meaningless drama on the stage of history, and its memory will be shrouded with the ugly garments of shame. In spite of the mistreatment that we have confronted, we must not become bitter and end up hating our white brothers. As Booker T. Washington said, 'Let no man pull you down so low as to make you hate him.'"

Martin Luther King's life and martyrdom, long etched in black history, and popularized within black and American culture, requires little rehearsal here. Several important social factors within King's legacy, however, and in the history of the black freedom movement, are usually grossly ignored. The emergence of King, Ralph Abernathy, and other black clergy in the forefront of the desegregation struggle was to an extent a progressive response to white clergy who had taken up the cause of white supremacy in Alabama and across the South generally. If Christ could be portrayed by white Baptists as a Ku Klux Klansman, then He could just as easily be enlisted in the ranks of bus boycotters and freedom riders by black Baptists. The civil rights movement occurred at a time when the social and political role of black preachers was steadily diminishing. By participating in their people's struggles, black ministers could once again set the political and moral climate for millions of blacks who over previous decades had become alienated or disillusioned with church inactivity on secular issues. As in the years of Reconstruction, from 1865–1877, the black church provided the necessary social space for political discussions, strategy sessions and effective protest. With the creation of the Southern Christian Leadership Conference (SCLC) in 1957, King and other black ministers forged an appropriate political vehicle for the battle to destroy Jim Crow.

SYMBOLIC ROLE SUPREME

King was the most prominent black minister of the civil rights movement—yet his rise to greatness should not obscure the fact that hundreds of other black preachers and laypersons were responsible for many of the real accomplishments of the movement. In Lynchburg, Virginia, the SCLC affiliate led by the Reverend Virgil Wood initiated numerous nonviolent direct-action campaigns. The Reverend Fred Shuttlesworth was responsible for much of the successes combating Bull Connor's racist police force and the white power structure in Birmingham. The Reverend James Lawson assisted King in the founding conference of the Student Nonviolent Coordinating Committee (SNCC) at Shaw University in Raleigh, North Carolina. Other influential black activist pastors included C.K. Steele of Tallahassee, Florida; C.T. Vivian, the central coordinator of SCLC; Bernard Lafayette of Selma, Alabama; Walter Fauntroy, director of the SCLC Washington, D.C., Bureau; Wyatt Tee Walker of Petersburg, Virginia; and a host of younger black divinity students and pastors like Jesse Jackson, Andrew Young and James Bevel. In Northern states, black ministers who had previously done little in the way of political or economic protest were stirred to act. In May 1960 in Philadelphia for instance, 400 black clergymen decided. to pressure white-owned corporations to hire black employees in "decent positions." Confronting the racist policies of one company, the ministers initiated a boycott of the firm's products, an act supported by virtually every black Masonic lodge, church organization and social club in Pennsylvania.

Yet it was King alone who captured the imagination of the black masses, while earning the respect of the media and white Establishment. In the early years of the sit-in movement, it was not unusual for teenage protesters to ask each other, "What do you suppose Martin Luther King would do in this situation?" King biographer William Robert Miller writes that by 1960 "King's symbolic role was supreme, his charismatic stature was universally recognized. In the flux of rapidly proliferating and chaotic events, he towered as a pillar of strength." For whites, confronted with the growing radicalism of SCLC and the Congress of Racial Equality (CORE), notes Miller, King made the "nonviolent direct-action movement respectable." Historian August Meier recognized in 1965 that "King's very tendencies toward compromise and caution, his willingness to negotiate and bargain with White House emissaries, his hesitancy to risk the precipitation of mass violence upon demonstrators, further endear him to whites. He appears to them as a 'respectable' and 'moderate' man." As a minister, King constantly assumed the irreproachable posture of an ethical reformist committed to Gandhian political efforts. When white evangelist Billy Graham urged King "to put the brakes on a little bit" in the desegregation campaign in Birmingham, the SCLC leader could use Christian doctrines to justify the necessity for continued struggle. King's famous 1963 "Letter From Birmingham Jail," was an eloquent rejection of white Birmingham clergy's appeal to halt nonviolent demonstrations.

Historical memory is selective. Most Afro-Americans now fail to recall that the support provided black activist-oriented clergy by other black church leaders was hardly unanimous. The outstanding example of this was the Reverend Joseph H. Jackson, president of the National Baptist Convention. Jackson disapproved of King's growing influence within political circles and cautioned his ministers not to become involved in the Southern Christian Leadership Conference founded in 1957. At the 1962 National Baptist Convention, Jackson singled out fellow ministers who had assisted the SCLC drive to desegregate Albany, Georgia, criticizing the futility of their efforts. "It is hypocrisy," he charged, "for a delegation to leave Chicago and go to Albany to fight segregation." Four years later, when King, Abernathy, Jesse Jackson and other black ministers followed his advice by staging a massive desegregation campaign in Chicago, Jackson issued a public statement disassociating himself from the event and peppered its unnamed instigator (King) with politely worded abuse.

KING AND THE LEFT

The success of Montgomery not only boosted the protest potential of the black church, but it affected the political relations of almost every left-of-center political group toward the black clergy. The leadership of the more conservative National Association for the Advancement of Colored People (NAACP) and Urban League, as well as King's SCLC and CORE, however, eschewed public cooperation and joint work with Marxists and socialists. In 1961, for example, the Louisville branch of the NAACP attacked Louisville's CORE for working with Carl and Anne Braden, officers in the Southern Conference Educational Fund which was "widely charged" as a communist organization. James Farmer and CORE's national leadership dealt with the Bradens most circumspectly, advising field personnel "not to accept food or lodging from them." Two years later, when black activists were confronted with a desperate shortage of lawyers in Mississippi who would take civil rights cases, the National Lawyers Guild aggressively volunteered its help to various civil rights groups. SNCC accepted the Guild's offer, but CORE's leaders rejected cooperation with the Guild, fearing that its identification as a "communist front" might damage the movement. The Reverend Adam Clayton Powell, then the most influential black elected official in the US, informed King in 1960 that he was willing to support him—on the condition that he fire Bayard Rustin, considered a leftist at that time, from his staff. In response, novelist James Baldwin charged that King "lost much moral credit ... especially in the eyes of the young, when he allowed Powell to force Rustin's resignation. King was faced with the choice of defending his organizer, who was also his friend, or agreeing with Powell; and he chose the latter course."

The explicit anticommunism of many black ministers, the NAACP and even more liberal civil rights groups existed throughout the 1940s and 50s. In 1946, the NAACP rejected cooperation with the leftist Civil Rights Congress' campaign to oust the notorious racist, Mississippi Senator Theodore Bilbo, from office, Walter White, NAACP leader, argued that "it was imperative that this [campaign] be done under non-communist auspices." In 1948, CORE's Executive Committee issued a "Statement on Communism," ordering chapters not to affiliate with leftist organizations and enacted procedures for disaffiliating chapters which had fallen under "communist domination."

In a different way, contempt for a materialist analysis was also expressed by black middle-class student radicals in the 1960s. Julius Lester wrote in 1968 that "many blacks view Marxism and communism as foreign ideologies. Young black militants do not consider Marxism relevant" since Marx "was a white man." Liberal (and anticommunist) journalist Harry Golden suggested that communists failed to attract Southern blacks for two reasons. First, "they do not depend on nor incorporate Jesus and the Gospels." Second, "the great mass of the American Negroes do not reject the existing social order, they seek only to share fully in its bourgeois blessings." More than other blacks, the clergy commonly shared an unstated antipathy for atheism in any form and possessed a class-oriented commitment to private property and black petty capitalism. The unwillingness to unite with Marxists and militant social democrats who expressed a sincere commitment to destroy racial segregation eliminated any possibility that the civil rights movement would transcend its theoretical parochialism and develop a legitimate agenda to reconstruct the political economy of America.

Legitimate criticisms of King, coming from black activists and sympathetic intellectuals, began as early as 1958. In *Presence Africaine,* Harold Cruse, a radical black intellectual, charged that King's theoretical foundations for social protest exemplified "the confusion of the Negro middle-class mind on [the] question of racial integration." For Cruse, King's assertion that the civil rights struggle would allow Negroes to lose their "racial identity" was both tragic and absurd. "It requires neither intellect, education, nor morality these days to howl for civil rights." Cruse declared, "but it does require some profundity of insight and honesty in racial matters to know what to do with civil rights after they are achieved." By late 1963, Rustin had begun to criticize King for relying too heavily upon "the tactics of lying down in the streets to prevent the movement of trucks and other forms of direct action." Rustin suggested that "heroism and ability to go to jail should not be substituted for an overall social reform program."

In 1963, black writer LeRoi Jones was perhaps the first critic to draw the historical analogy between King and Booker T. Washington, a turn-of-the-century black spokesman who accepted white supremacy and segregation. Jones noted that "Washington solidified the separate-but-equal lie, when that lie was of value to the majority of intelligent white men. King's lie is that there is a moral requirement to be met before entrance into the secular kingdom of plenty."

DISILLUSION AND REEVALUATION

With the sudden renaissance of black nationalism in the guise of Black Power, both King and his entire generation of activist ministers received a profound jolt. SNCC activist Julius Lester's *Look Out, Whitey! Black Power's Gon' Get Your Mama!* repeated Jones' denunciation of King as merely the "successor of Booker T. Washington." King's message of "love" was hypocritical, Lester declared. "What is love supposed to do? Wrap a bullet in a warm embrace? Caress the cattle prod?" For black activist veterans of the Albany, Birmingham and Selma campaigns, the spirituality and ethos of nonviolence was dead. "We used to sing 'I Love Everybody' as we ducked bricks and bottles," Lester reflected. "Now we sing: Too much love, Too much love, Nothing kills a nigger like too much love."

As for King himself, the young black nationalists had little sympathy. "As the crisis of black America deepened," Robert Allen wrote in his book *Black Awakening in Capitalist America,* King was converted into "a reluctant accomplice of the white power structure." "The white elites discovered that King was useful "to restrain the threatening rebelliousness of the black masses and the young militants." Furthermore, "King could not repudiate this role because he was convinced that the Establishment could be pushed and pressured to implement his program."

At a speech at the University of California-Berkeley in October 1966, SNCC chairperson Stokely Carmichael expressed an ambiguous respect yet deep disillusionment toward King and his goals. Carmichael admitted that King was "full of love, mercy and compassion," a man "who's desperately needed in this country. But every time I see [President] Lyndon [Johnson] on television, I say 'Martin, baby, you got a long way to go.'"

King's final years provide some parallels with the last months of the major black nationalist of the 1960s, Malcolm X. Like the former Muslim minister, King had begun to reevaluate the goals of the black struggle from the simple demand for civil rights to the pursuit of "human rights." His first public speech on the Vietnam War, given at a Virginia statewide meeting of SCLC affiliates in Petersburg in July 1965, was a mixture of anticommunism, moral suasion and passivism. "I am certainly as concerned about seeing the defeat of communism as anyone else," King stated. "But we won't defeat communism by guns or bombs or gasses. We will do it by making democracy work." He called for an immediate end to US military involvement in Southeast Asia and a "negotiated settlement even with the Viet Cong." By 1967, King was actively leading the US peace movement, addressing peace rallies and proposing concrete details for US disengagement from Vietnam. He became more concerned about the profound similarity between the oppressed material conditions of the unemployed—blacks and whites—and proposed a "Poor People's March" on Washington, DC, in October 1967.

Many of King's oldest friends rejected him, some viciously attacking his new political concerns in the media. Negro columnist Carl Rowan, who assisted King during the Montgomery bus boycott, charged that King's peace activities have "alienated many of the Negro's friends and armed the Negro's foes in both parties by creating the impression that the Negro is disloyal." Conservative representatives of the black middle class, such as Whitney Young of the Urban League, NAACP director Roy Wilkins and former socialist Ralph Bunche bitterly condemned King, as did the only black in the US Senate, Edward Brooke. Many black ministers within SCLC privately criticized King for moving too far left, and publicly separated themselves from any antiwar demonstrations and religious peace services. On April 4, 1968, King was assassinated while assisting 1,375 black sanitation workers in Local 1733 of the American Federation of State, County, and Municipal Employees, AFL-CIO, in a strike in Memphis, Tennessee. The middle-class reformer had become a militant proponent of peace, economic democracy and black working-class interests.

King's strengths and weaknesses were not his alone, but those of his social stratum, the black clergy. His moral appeals for nonviolence, racial harmony and desegregation were shared by previous generations of black middle-class reformers. His initial reluctance to emphasize economic issues, his implicit anticommunism and desire for compromise rather than confrontation with the white Establishment was also the ideology of his class.

Where King departed from his contemporaries was his recognition that black ministers as a group had to play a decisive role in the reconstruction of US civil and political society. The greatest contradiction confronting black people, the system of white supremacy, was of course the primary target of King's efforts. In the process of struggle, however, King finally concluded that the defeat of racial segregation in itself was insufficient in creating a just and decent society for all Americans. King followed the tradition of earlier black activist clergy—Henry Highland Garnet, Henry M. Turner, Nat Turner—by calling for radical and fundamental change. Without hesitation, he broke from many of his own advisers and supporters, and like Malcolm raised many public policy issues which could not be easily resolved within the existing system. Congressman Louis Stokes, chairperson of the US House Select Committee on Assassinations, believes that King was murdered because "he had begun to wake up poor people in this country, not only poor black people but also poor white people. (In) entering this dangerous area, King had to be killed." Many of King's lieutenants in the black clergy have failed to pursue King's vision. Abernathy, Hosea Williams and the brother of the martyred civil rights activist Medgar Evers, Charles Evers, endorsed the presidential candidacy of ultraconservative Ronald Reagan in 1980. Andrew Young, current mayor of Atlanta, Georgia, served as UN ambassador in the Carter administration.

Several ministers within the SCLC, including Fauntroy, have been elected to high office and Jesse Jackson's Operation PUSH captures headlines with political maneuvers which are more style than substance. As a group, King's generation has not courageously pursued the logic of his final years. Part of their current dilemma is created by their conscious, class-oriented commitment to infuse the Negro middle class into the present economic order and to perpetuate the inert politics of bourgeois reform. They are not prepared to repudiate the system which rewards their own political accommodation at the expense of the continued exploitation of black working-class and poor people.

Black ministers all too often have been content to interpret the scriptures in various ways and to preach salvation to their congregations. The real point of black faith, and the fundamental meaning of King's evolution toward more militant politics, is to change the conditions of oppressed blacks for the better. If black ministers fail to learn from their own mistakes, they may as a social stratum decline still further in the esteem of their own people. If they succeed, they may help to spark anew the moral and ethical commitment that remains essential within the struggle against racism and capitalist exploitation.

Kwame Nkrumah and the Convention People's Party

A Critical Reassessment

Kwame Nkrumah was the most outstanding member of that impressive post-World War II generation of African leaders which included Jomo Kenyatta, Patrice Lumumba, Leopold Sedar Senghor, Sekou Toure, Nnamdi Azikiwe, and Julius Nyerere. For Amilcar Cabral—probably the greatest theoretician of African libera tion—Nkrumah "was above all the strategist of genius in the struggle against classical colonialism." C.L.R. James, the noted Caribbean historian and social theorist, agrees: "Kwame Nkrumah was one of the greatest political leaders of our century. We must be on guard that his years of exile do not remove from our constant study and contemplation the remarkable achievements of the great years."[1] Even Nkrumah's most severe critics conceded that Ghana's first Prime Minister was "a man of great personal charm and warmth." Brigade Major Akwasi A. Afrifa, the Ghanaian army officer who engineered the February 1966 *coup* which overthrew Nkrumah, admitted that the deposed leader once "represented the hopes and aspirations of black people all over the world."[2]

Despite his unquestioned greatness and impressive achievements, however, Nkrumah had severe shortcomings. The history of his dramatic rise to power in 1948–51—the development of the Convention People's Party (CPP); the "Positive Action" campaign against British colonial rule; and the electoral victory of the CPP in 1951—have been frequently recounted. What are less understood are the specific internal contradictions of the CPP government from 1951 until its collapse fifteen years later, and the ambiguous chasm between Nkrumah's democratic, Pan-Africanist political vision and his authoritarian public record. This essay does not provide a general evaluation of Nkrumah's foreign policy initiatives or the extensive efforts by the US government to destabilize his government. Nor does it present a comprehensive review of the constructive achievements of the Nkrumah regime—in economic development, education, public health, and other human service areas.

The focus here is narrowly political. How did a ruling party of more than one million members—one seventh of the total population—succumb to a military coup organized by only several dozen miltiary and police officers?

In brief, Nkrumah's career in Ghanaian politics can be subdivided into three distinct phases: the national democratic mobilization against British colonialism, which gave birth to the CPP and Nkrumah's leadership, 1948–51; the years of "Tactical Action" or limited self-government, and the initial period of independence, 1951–1960; and the period of "left Nkrumaism," coming roughly between the Sekondi-Takoradi strike of 1961 and the February 1966 coup. Nkrumaism in each stage was a set of contradictory public policies, culminating into a distinct form of populist yet authoritarian rule.

THE RISE TO POWER

The successful campaign to achieve limited self-government from the British in the Gold Coast was a political achievement which can hardly be overemphasized in the context of modern African history. Basil Davidson describes these years as Nkrumah's "greatest hour. He had done what few thought possible ... The news of this went out through Africa in electrifying ripples of encouragement to all who hoped for anticolonial change." George Padmore, leading Pan-Africanist organizer and Nkrumah's political mentor, characterized the CPP's 1951 electoral victory as that of "the plebian masses, the urban workers, artisans, petty traders, market women and fishermen, the clerks, the junior teachers, and the vast farming communities of the rural areas who are the makers of Gold Coast history."[3] The CPP simply overwhelmed the conservative nationalist politicians, led by J.B. Danquah, winning 34 out of 38 legislative seats. Through a legal technicality, Nkrumah—who had been imprisoned by the colonial regime for over one year—was permitted to run in Accra, and received 22,780 out of 23,122 votes cast. About 95 percent of the urban electorate supported the CPP, and almost 80 percent of the rural vote endorsed the party. Significantly, the party's strongest support came in the working-class constituencies of Sekondi-Takoradi. The colonial governor, Sir Charles Arden-Clarke, had no choice except to release the CPP's "Party Leader" from his jail cell to form a new government. Arden-Clarke later admitted: "Without Nkrumah ... there would no longer be any faith in the good intentions of the British government and the Gold Coast would be plunged into disorders, violence, and bloodshed."[4]

In historical perspective, Nkrumah appears virtually irreplaceable as the leader of the anticolonial struggle in the Gold Coast. But as social theorist George Plekhanov once observed: "Every man of talent who actually appears, every man of talent who becomes a social force, is the product of social relations ... talented people can change only individual features of events, but not their general trend; they are themselves the product of this trend ..." In analyzing Nkrumah's role in African political history, there is a tendency to "fall victim to a sort of optical illusion," to use Plekhanov's terminology.[5] Nkrumah's social weight is projected in a "magnified form"; we tend to read history backward, and credit him with the achievements of others. But during the difficult period of political harrassment and Nkrumah's detention, the CPP was actually consolidated as a national electoral formation by dozens of dedicated nationalists. The pivotal figure here was Komla Agbeli Gbedemah, a former schoolteacher and small entrepreneur. C.L.R. James described Gbedemah in the historical role of "Trotsky leading the revolution" while Lenin was the architect of the Bolshevik party.[6] This characterization is inappropriate on at least two counts. Gbedemah was no socialist, and had little interest in Pan-Africanist politics which transcend the Gold Coast *per se*. He was a national democrat and nascent entrepreneur who instinctively comprehended that his own social class would be bound to subservience unless the British authorities were removed.

In one sense, Nkrumah's imprisonment proved beneficial to the national independence movement, because it produced local politicians who were less dependent upon Nkrumah's personal charisma and prestige. Observers on the spot fully attested to this. In 1955, Bankole Timothy noted that Gbedemah "kept the fire of the CPP burning" while Nkrumah languished in James Fort Prison. "It is also to Gbedemah's credit," Timothy added, "that he did not seek to take the leadership away from (Nkrumah), but did everything possible to stabilize the organization of the party." In the Transvolta region, editor G.K. Amegbe mobilized supporters; in Ashanti, the major leaders were Krobo Edusei, attorney Victor Owusu, and R.R. Amponsah; in the crucial industrial center of Sekondi-Takoradi, Saki Scheck published the *Takoradi Times*. These men cut across traditional ethnic boundaries, and appealed to agricultural and industrial workers, small farmers, the unemployed, and the youth. They also recognized Gbedemah's authority: as G.K. Amegbe observed, "With Kwame in jail, Gbedemah was in command and he really organized the party."[7]

But what kind of party did Gbedemah and his young comrades "organize"? A review of the Party's early documents indicates that the CPP made virtually no ideological demands of its members, other than requesting an enrollment fee of two shillings, and an annual payment of three shillings. Members could not belong to any unions or farmers' organizations "proscribed by the Party," and since members' "affiliations are apt to cause divided loyalties," Party leaders urged that "only individual membership should be encouraged." Power in the Party was already concentrated at the top rather than at the mass level. Only Party organizations "and not individual members" could submit resolutions to the Annual Delegates' Conference. Individuals or factions could be expelled by the National Executive Committee if they were members "of any other political party or of any organization whose policy is inconsistent with that of the Party," or if they supported "a candidate in opposition to the Party's official candidate." The potential dangers of authoritarian rule by the Party's elite over dissident members were not clear at this stage.[8]

Beyond a fervent commitment to achieve independence, the only ideological glue which held party leaders together was their espousal of Nkrumah as their national spokesman. They seized upon Nkrumah as a symbol to rally the African masses, and to win over reluctant sectors of the intelligentsia and middle class. This technique was not original. Several years before in Nigeria, radical nationalists used the image of Nnamdi Azikiwe to promote their cause by celebrating his birthday and by organizing a Nigerian National Church with Azikiwe its "patron saint." The remnants of the CPP followed the pattern already established by Nigeria's radical "Zilists." The CPP's constitution required party members to hold a "national holiday" on the "Life Chairman's Birthday," 18 September. Gbedemah projected Nkrumah as the nation's martyr: "Nkrumah provided the answers. If one did not know what to believe, the answer was, 'Follow Nkrumah.' If one did not know quite what to hope for, the answer was 'Follow Nkrumah.'"[9]

TACTICAL ACTION AND POLITICAL COMPROMISE

The CPP made the conscious decision to collaborate with the British administration during the period 1951–57, serving as junior partners inside the colonial regime. The party had no authority over national defense or internal security. Sensitive files were quickly removed from government offices, or "were still regarded as being fit for British eyes alone."[10] Nkrumah firmly rejected a "boycott of the existing colonial government machinery," and advocated a policy of cooperation: "Two major aims impelled this decision: the speeding up of Africanization, and the prevention of a breakdown in administration through a wholesale exodus of British officials ... It was of prime importance to us ... that we should be able to effect a smooth take-over, free from serious administrative shocks. It called for what I termed at the time 'tactical action'..."[11]

The CPP leadership had become a type of "statist elite," a political group which did not exercise full state power, but used its privileged position within the governmental apparatus to reward its supporters, to accumulate for itself, and to manipulate public policies which could eventually lead to its own consolidation as a dominant social class. It did not attempt to transform the colonial state, but to reallocate positions of authority from whites to Africans. This strategy of political cooperation was opposed by two major constituencies: first, by radical nationalists, labor union leaders and militants who belonged to the CPP, and who had favored a more aggressive, anti-colonialist policy; and by the conservative African cocoa planters, large farmers, professionals and business interests which had opposed the CPP from its origins, and viewed the populist composition of Nkrumah's government with alarm.

By April 1952, the first major bloc of CPP leaders was expelled, including two of the party's eight Central Committee members, party journalist Saki Scheck, and acting general secretary H.P. Nyemitei. Leaders of the Marxist wing of the party— lawyers Kurankyi Taylor, Trade Union Congress president Anthony Woods, and labor leader Turkson Ocran—were suspended or expelled in late 1953. George Padmore justified this "disciplinary action ... to protect [Nkrumah's] party and Government from Communist infiltration."[12] Even sympathetic observers began to question the CPP's commitment to democratic processes, and wondered about Nkrumah's plans for reviving the Pan-Africanist movement. In 1954, W.E.B. Du Bois urged Padmore and Nkrumah to accelerate plans for a major Pan-African Congress in the Gold Coast.

Padmore, however, was evasive. "We cannot do it before as we don't want to create undue alarm before we have full power in our hands." Padmore explained, "It is a skillful game of maneuvering and we cannot afford at this stage of the struggle to give the imperialists any excuse to intervene as in British Guiana. They are ready to pounce the first oppotunity we give them." Du Bois' reply was polite yet reserved. "I understand the policy of you and Dr. Nkrumah, although I am a little afraid of it. The power of British and especially American capital when it once gets a foothold is tremendous." Du Bois warned that even when "political power is in your hands," that the CPP might have to struggle with "your own bourgeoisie."[13]

Even before formal independence, there were widespread rumors of massive graft and clientage within the CPP. State revenues began to filter down into CPP regional and local offices; many government ministers accepted kickbacks from private sector contractors. Tommy Hutton-Mills, Nkrumah's Minister of Health and Labour, openly boasted: "I have now left poverty behind me forever." Civil servants, professors, and other middle strata were told bluntly that "those who joined the Party" would be "assured of promotion, wealth and influence." As evidence of CPP corruption mounted, the Party's response was to increase its public propoganda of Nkrumah as a national savior. Loyal members chanted "Nkrumah Never Dies" at rallies, to proclaim his near-immortality and omniscience. The Party Leader was the *"Osagyefo"*—*"victorious* in war," *"Oyeadeeyie"*—"one who puts things right," the "Man of Destiny," the new "Messiah," the "Teacher and Author of the Revolution."[14] For Party veterans like Gbedemah and Edusei, there was probably something unreal about these orchestrated acclamations. They established an official personality cult, elevating Nkrumah far above the party hierarchy, largely for polemical partisan reasons. But one negative feature of the cult was that Nkrumah himself had begun to believe his own publicity. By the mid-1950s, the Prime Minister became "somewhat jealous of any of his colleagues becoming increasingly popular or having increased publicity in the press." Bankole Timothy observed: "There is one thing about Nkrumah which perplexes even his closest friends. 'You can never know where you stand with him!'"[15]

The greatest challenge to Nkrumah's political authority, with the exception of the Sekondi-Takoradi strike, occurred in 1955–56, with the emergence of the opposition National Liberation Movement (NLM). The NLM drew much of its strength from the older, professional elites led by Danquah, and ethnic opposition from the Ashanti traditional leaders and farmers. But it is rarely appreciated that the NLM's most dynamic spokesmen invariably had been disillusioned followers of Nkrumah and the CPP. Victor Owusu, Kurankyi Taylor, and R.R. Amponsah all defected to the NLM; the CPP's representative in London, Joe Appiah, joined the opposition and condemned his former party as "corrupt and dictatorial." By mid-1955, 18 of the 21 members of the NLM national executive committee were former CPP members. And although the NLM's economic policy orientation was distinctly to the right of Nkrumah's populism, the opposition also succeeded in gaining some support from labor. That same year, two of the country's largest unions formed the "Congress of Free Trade Union," which promptly affiliated itself to the NLM.[16]

The July 1956 legislative elections in the Gold Coast have been interpreted as a vindication of Nkrumah and the CPP over their indigenous opponents. Superficially this seem true. In 99 contested constituencies, the CPP won 398,000 popular votes (57 percent) to the opposition's 299,000 popular votes (43 percent). The CPP received 71 seats out of a total of 106 Assembly seats. But viewed another way, the CPP's margin was not so impressive. Ex-CPP leader Victor Owusu trounced his CPP opponent, receiving 87 percent of his constituency's vote. The CPP lost heavily throughout most of the nation, except in cities and along the Atlantic coast. In those rural districts where the ruling party did well, it had been financially generous in providing government services.[17] The British granted Ghana its independence on 6 March 1957, but Nkrumah no longer exercised an overwhelming public mandate.

Between 1957 and 1960, the major elements of parliamentary democracy in Ghana were uprooted by Nkrumah. The regional assemblies created by the British prior to independence, which gave access to local grievances and constituencies, were abolished. A deportation act was passed, giving the state the power to deport any "person whose presence in Ghana is not conducive to the public good." Most severe was the "Preventive Detention Act" of 1958, which gave Nkrumah the right to imprison "certain persons for up to five years without trial." The CPP claimed that such legislation was necessary to halt "activities detrimental to the interests of state and society." Government agents who were "political appointees" replaced District Commissioners in local districts. Chief Regional Officers were fired and replaced by CPP loyalists. Opposition leaders were harrassed and imprisoned, including Amponsah and Appiah. Others fled the country. Increasingly the distinction between the ruling party and the state apparatus disintegrated. At the June 1959 CPP tenth Congress, Nkrumah declared openly: "the Convention People's Party is Ghana." John Tettegah, leader of the TUC, spelled out the fine print: "The CPP is Ghana and Ghana is the CPP ... those who sit outside the ranks of the CPP forfeit their right to citizenship in the country. For it is only within the CPP that any constructive thing can be done in Ghana."[18]

The destruction of the legal opposition meant that no viable checks existed to halt the growth of the CPP's patronage and graft network. Basil Davidson terms this process "the bureaucratic degeneration" of the CPP: "They had acquired large houses which they filled with expensive furniture and *objets d'art* of a curious and wonderful vulgarity; and here they lived, amidst a host of lackeys, hangers-on and poor relations in an atmosphere of pomp and pretentiousness ..."[19] Corruption now became a normal method of public affairs. Party-affiliated chairmen of city councils received free housing, £1800 annual salaries and an entertainment stipend of £250 annually. But this was simply the beginning. Local construction firms were expected to give funds to the party and individual leaders of government contracts; public jobs could be bought for a percentage of one's salary. The CPP, as C.L.R. James later admitted, had become a "body of stooges.... All sorts of ignoramuses, gangster-types, only had to prove their loyalty to the regime, i.e., to Nkrumah, and they could go places in the party and in the country." The corruption and bureaucratization within the state reinforced the Nkrumaist "cult of the personality." By 1960 the chief proponent of this cult was a former opposition leader, Tawia Adamafio, whom Nkrumah had rapidly advanced to the position of CPP secretary general. Through an extensive propoganda campaign, public buildings and streets were renamed for the Party Leaders. "There were the Kwame Nkrumah Markets, the Kwame Nkrumah University, the Kwame Nkrumah Leadership Training Camps.... Hymns were sung in praise of Nkrumah; and meetings began with such songs as "If you follow him, he will make you fishers of men." Adamafio's purple prose reached extremes in an essay printed in the Accra *Evening News* in May 1960: "We all are at best a small star shining only through the grace of Kwame Nkrumah, our Political Central Sun and Author of the Ghanaian Revolution. We must learn from Kwame Nkrumah's supreme modesty, humility, and simplicity of life." The primary political objective of Adamafio and his supporters was to isolate and discredit party veterans, chiefly Gbedemah.[20]

Partially because the CPP had purged its left wing, the party's level of ideological discourse was remarkably low. Nominally a "socialist" formation, the CPP had no cadre training institutes, and theoretical work within its ranks was virtually nonexistent. Perhaps the most revealing commentary here was provided by Ras Makonnen, who had first collaborated with Nkrumah in the planning of the Manchester Pan-African Congress of 1945. Coming to Ghana in 1957, he worked with Padmore's African Affairs Centre, and remained in the country until the coup. Upon arrival, Makonnen was frankly shocked by the low level of ideological development among leaders of the CPP. At independence, "nobody was asking 'What Is To Be Done'!" The CPP "elite did not know the difference between a plantation and a collective farm." The rhetoric of the CPP was "socialist." But watching the evolution of the regime from 1957 to 1966, Makonnen concluded that virtually none of the CPP leadership cared for measures to protect the material interests of workers and peasants. "You can't build socialism without socialists," Makonnen later wrote. The CPP bosses "had a simple conviction, that if there were going to be any capitalist millionaires around, then they might as well be Ghanaian ones. Some of them had acted in a helpful way with sums of money when the party was just being founded, and they saw to it that once the party was in power, they got their reward."[21] The striking testimony of Soviet leader Anastas Mikoyan confirms Makonnen's analysis. Visiting Ghana in January 1962, Mikoyan informed the world via *Tass* that Ghana under Nkrumah "had made great progress in building socialism in the country." But meeting with Nkrumah's cabinet privately, Mikoyan noted, perhaps with a smile, that "None of you are socialists." No one disagreed.[22]

The "dual degeneration of the Parliament and the Party" had several immediate social consequences. The African middle strata, those who had opposed Nkrumah since the late 1940s, essentially withdrew from public life. As James comments, "The ablest, the most qualified, and the intellectuals of finest character turned their backs on Nkrumah. Some of them, an astonishing number, went abroad and took jobs elsewhere. Those who stayed at home either devoted themselves to their professions, such as law and medicine, or did their work in the government, drew their pay and let Nkrumah govern or misgovern as he pleased."[23] The Ghanaian working class, despite the party's expulsions of the left and key trade union activists in 1953, still retained much of its loyalty to the CPP. But workers were hardly unaware that they shouldered the burden for the costs of official corruption. In Sekondi-Takoradi, the National Housing Corporation planned "two new housing estates" which were originally designed for "lower-paid workers." These apartments were allocated instead for the sexual trysts of "party big-wigs and even Accra-based MPs and their girlfriends." The CPP, the nominal "party of socialism," ratified a series of tough new laws to discipline African workers. The 1958 "Industrial Relations Act" gave Nkrumah the power to freeze TUC funds if it acted in any manner "not conducive to the public good," and the Minister of Labour could legally dissolve any union at a moment's notice. All strikes by public employees were illegal. Despite the rapid growth of TUC membership under Tettegah, workers continued to voice opposition to the regime. Forty-nine strikes occurred in 1958–59, and 50 in 1959–60. Discontent also surfaced in the cities. Ten to 15 percent of Ghana's male wage-labor force was unemployed by 1960, and over two-fifths of the unemployed lived in urban areas. Unemployment was highest among both male and female workers aged 15 to 29. Increasingly there were signs of another crisis on the social horizon; not from above, as in the abortive maneuverings of the NLM, but from below.[24]

"LEFT NKRUMAISM"

Nkrumah was fully aware of the corruption within the regime, and of the rising discontent from working class constituents. In April 1961 he announced a campaign against the Party's "bureaucratic and professional bourgeoisie." In what widely became know as the "Dawn Broadcast," the President attacked the "degrading tendency" of Party members "to create agents for collecting money," warning that such behavior "must be crushed in the most ruthless manner." He ordered civil servants to "eliminate all tendencies toward red tape-ism, bureaucracy and waste." Nkrumah condemned trade union officials for their "loose talk and reprehensible statements which do no good either to the party, to the Government or to the nation. This is not the time for unbridled militant trade unionism in our country." But Nkrumah reserved his strongest censure for the Party's hierarchy. Members of the National Assembly and Ministers would no longer be permitted to "own a business or be involved in anyone else's business, Ghanaian or foreign." No Minister, "member of a Government corporation or institution," or Government employee was permitted henceforth to make any "public statement affecting Government policy ... unless that statement has first had Presidential or Cabinet approval." A strict "limit" was to be imposed "on property acquisitions by Ministers, party officials and Ministerial Secretaries."[25] Gbedemah was demoted to Minister of Health, and other longtime party officials were attacked in the state-owned press. The semi-purge of April–May 1961 however, "did not more than tinker with the problem" of widespread graft and social inequality in Ghanaian society.[26]

When the regime ordered a 5 percent compulsory reduction in workers' wages and a regressive property tax on all homes of two rooms or more in July 1961, the schism between the neocolonial state and the working class became antagonistic. The primary center of anti-Nkrumaist militancy was in Sekondi-Takoradi. In September 1961, thousands of harbor and railroad workers staged a 17-day strike against the regime, which was popularly supported by nearly the entire Sekondi-Takoradi population. Workers criticized not only the new tax, but all of the social ills produced by the regime—the vast wage inequalities between government officials and workers, the lack of genuine worker control in their workplaces, the "excessive wealth and conspicuous consumption of politicians." St. Clair Drake and L.C. Lacy observe that "the Government saw its very existence implicitly challenged" by the Sekondi-Takoradi proletariat. Strike leaders declared that "if Parliament did not give way to the demands of the people, they would disband that body by force." The remnants of the opposition in the National Assembly, led by Victor Owusu, openly attacked the "members of the new Ghanaian aristocracy and their hangers-on ..." Labor unrest quickly spread to Kumasi and even Accra. Market women joined the strikers by providing food and other essentials. Even many soldiers sent to discipline Sekondi-Takoradi's laborers "became sympathetic" to the strike.[27]

Nkrumah's "radical" lieutenant, Adamafio, was chiefly responsible for breaking the labor unrest. Radio Ghana placed a news embargo on the strike; police and soldiers were ordered to arrest and beat labor leaders and workers. All insurgents held responsible for the strike were prohibited from ever holding union office in the future. Nkrumah described the general strike as the product of a sinister "neocolonialist conspiracy." To placate the workers, Nkrumah also initiated a thorough purge of the CPP's hierarchy, and simultaneously eliminated the few prominent opposition critics. Appiah, Owusu and Danquah were jailed without charges; also imprisoned were several opposition journalists, nineteen labor leaders, and five Sekondi-Takoradi market women. Six CPP cabinet ministers, including Gbedemah and Edusei, were ordered to resign. The regime also initiated two draconian laws to reinforce its authority. "The first imposed a fine of £500 or three years' imprisonment, or both, on anyone summarily convicted of publishing defamatory or insulting matter which might bring the president into hatred, ridicule or contempt. The second created a Special Criminal Division of the High Court to hear cases of treason, sedition, rioting and unlawful assembly, from which there would be no appeal."[28] Before Gbedemah could be arrested, he fled into exile.

The Sekondi-Takoradi strike and the fall of Gbedemah marked the acceleration of what Samir Amin terms "Nkrumaite Socialism."[29] Few leaders of the CPP remained who had been part of the pre-1951 leadership—the most prominent was Kofi Baako, who later became Nkrumah's Minister of Information and a principal ideologist of "Nkrumaism."[30] The vast majority had played insignificant roles in the Positive Action campaign; some were former members of the NLM, like Adamafio, or were too junior to have been involved one way or another in nationalist politics. Kofi Batsa, a former opposition party leader, was appointed by Nkrumah to edit *The Spark,* the CPP's "Marxist" theoretical journal. International factors, particularly the Congo crisis, the assassination of Prime Minister Patrice Lumumba, and the US-directed "Bay of Pigs" invasion of Cuba, also pushed Nkrumah to the left, to be sure. What is important to recognize is that these left Nkrumaists had absolutely no ideological commitment to socialism as it related to the democratic empowerment of the Ghanaian working class. At the peak of his power, Adamafio explained that Nkrumaist socialism could never be defined: "We are very anxious to get a Bible of Nkrumaism [but] we do not want to tie the hands of our Leader in a way that when he acts he will be accused of going against his own principles."[31]

A type of state-directed, bureaucratic "socialism" was initiated in 1961, with the nationalization of five gold mines which produced less than half of the nation's total output. The "State Mining Corporation" did not run the mines directly, but functioned as a "holding company for all of the shares taken over." British bank branches were no longer permitted to forward surplus funds to London, and were forced to lend solely inside Ghana. Still, in 1963 about half of all banking business was done by expatriate firms. A new "Seven Year Plan" was introduced for 1963–1970, which called for major increases in government spending in heavy industry and agriculture. By February 1966, 150 of the projected 600 new industrial projects were completed. To finance these ambitious projects, the state was forced to borrow funds from abroad. As Amin observed, "Interest and depreciation on the national debt took up a growing proportion of fiscal revenue: 17 percent at the fall of the regime, compared with four percent in 1960."[32] These policies followed a "left" model of socioeconomic development; but they faltered due to the ideological hostility from the civil service, which remained largely British-trained and anti-Nkrumah, and from the failure to involve workers themselves at all levels of planning. The percentage of public sector workers quickly soared: in late 1963, 39 percent of all industrial workers were employed in state-owned firms, and by the end of 1964, almost 70 percent of all wage earners were public employees.[33] But left Nkrumaists had substituted genuine workers' democracy and collective planning with a swollen state bureaucracy which was still riddled with corruption.

In September 1962, Adamafio and other left Nkrumaist leaders were arrested after being implicated in an assassination attempt against Nkrumah. Although the defendants were subsequently acquitted in court, Nkrumah overruled the decision and dismissed his own Chief Justice. From 1963 until his overthrow, Nkrumah never permitted another Ghanaian politician to attain the status of Gbedemah or Adamafio. Even in the 1950s, he had already shown a preference to recruit non-Ghanaian advisers. During the capitalist phase of Nkrumaism, the key figure in economic policy was W. Arthur Lewis, a West Indian who promoted private sector investment by multinationals. [W. Arthur Lewis won the 1979 Nobel Economics Prize.—Editor] In the 1960s, as Nkrumah became more isolated from the Ghanaian intelligentsia and from his Party leaders, he turned increasingly to other non-Ghanaians. A short list of foreign assistants and bureaucrats would include: Joseph Bognor, an Hungarian economist who advised the regime in 1962; Sir Patrick Fitz-Gerald, a Unilever Corporation executive and self-proclaimed "imperialist" who ran the largest state-owned enterprise; H.M. Basner, a former radical senator in South Africa, who served as the regime's journalist and occasional speechwriter; left British Labourite Geoffrey Bing, Nkrumah's Attorney General and liaison with the European left; Sir John Howard, head of Parkinson Howard, Ltd., and adviser on construction projects; Nigerian intellectual Sam G. Ikoku, who provided constructive criticism on an informal basis; Major General Edward Spears, an adviser on international trade and mining; and Sir Robert Jackson, an Australian, who was Nkrumah's main adviser on the Volta River Dam Project. One obvious benefit of this group was that it lacked any political constituency within the Party or society. Nkrumah could accept or reject their suggestions, depending on his own intuitions or mood. As for the "official" members of his Cabinet, their actual powers were greatly reduced. Some were "assigned errands for the President and functioned as watchdogs for the political machine." None could ever forget their personal and political vulnerability. The National Assembly had become a meaningless official organ, a curious remnant of a colonial past. The decay spread throughout the Party at all levels. As Basil Davidson comments: "Asked to embrace non-capitalist policies, eventually socialist policies, its leaders were lost in disbelief or in confusion. Active political work among ordinary members had practically ceased. . . . So little democracy did it have that its central committee was no longer elected; and the names of its members were not even allowed to be made public."[34]

It was only in the mid-sixties that the partial fruits of Nkrumaite socialism began to become evident. The state's "Program of Work and Happiness" initiated in 1962 proclaimed as its "fundamental objective" the development "of a socialist state devoted to the welfare of the masses." There was a noticeable expansion of hospitals and rural health clinics throughout the country. Five new mental hospitals, four urban polyclinics and six district hospitals were being prepared for construction at the time of the coup. A concerted effort was made in the industrial sector: the state constructed a major steelworks plant, two sugar refineries, two cocoa refineries, a meat processing plant, a glass factory and other industrial enterprises within several short years. Perhaps the greatest achievement was in education. Textbooks were free for all students, and all schooling was without charge. Over 1.2 million Ghanaian youth attended primary, middle and secondary schools by 1963. The total number of teacher-training school and university students increased from 2,100 in 1951 to 8,000 in 1963, with projected enrollments of 26,000 by 1970.[35]

Despite the regime's internal corruption and bureaucratic deformities, left Nkrumaism still represented a qualitative improvement over British colonialism. The old regime had never been democratic; the British had done little to promote educational, social welfare and economic reforms beyond their own direct needs to maintain a level of efficient social control and material exploitation. Judged by the standards of the colonial past, the CPP's government's accomplishments were substantial. But weighed against the democratic, anticolonialist visions and promises of the early 1950s, the regime's failures were immense. From the perspective of most Ghanaians, many of the massive state projects seemed irrational and illogical. The Volta Dam, a project originally promoted by Western interests, was "tragic because there was no need" for it, noted Makonnen. Only 1,600 jobs were created when the project was finished, at a cost of £75 million. During the regime's left turn, Makonnen protested the appointment of Fitz-Gerald as head of the Ghana National Trading Corporation. "This made it clear that Ghana was interested in state capitalism and not socialism. Otherwise what are you doing appointing one of the oldest United Africa hands as the manager of your nationalized sector?" Throughout the 1960s, "we had socialist talk without socialist planning," Makonnen recalled, "the worst of both worlds." Left Nkrumaists who shouted loudest "about socialism were more steeped in capitalism than the West where capitalism had undergone some reform at least ... But all that socialism meant to the ordinary people was 'funny Russian sardines, instead of the good old British brands that we knew.'" Even the director of Nkrumah's "Ideological Institute" at Winneba, Kodwo Addison, "was no socialist."[36]

The vast distance between the potential and the flawed reality of Nkrumaism was also manifested in Ghana's foreign policies. In the 1950s, "Nkrumah had been a popular symbol of African liberation," observed W. Scott Thompson. But by the time the Organization of African Unity was established in 1963, few leaders "took him seriously."[37] There were several reasons for this. Radical nationalists, well aware of the deteriorating political conditions for Ghana's proletariat, questioned Nkrumah's left-ist credentials. Ghana's criticisms of the developing East Afican Federation alienated Julius Nyerere of Tanzania, who finally denounced Nkrumah's policies as "attempts to rationalize absurdity." Ghana's initial membership in the British Commonwealth (which then still included South Africa) called into question Nkrumah's commitment in fighting apartheid. Ghana repeatedly failed to provide funds to UN-sponsored or OAU-directed programs to support African freedom fighters. The ANC, after several years of lobbying efforts, finally dismissed Nkrumah as hopeless. Conservative African leaders despised Nkrumah for different reasons. The Ivory Coast was angered by Nkrumah's financial support of the Sanwi rebels in their country. Felix Houphouet-Boigny was so hostile to Nkrumah that he succeeded in adding a clause to the OAU charter which condemned "political assassination as well as subversive activities on the part of neighboring states." Senegal reduced its total 1965 exports to Ghana to the value of £120, as Leopold Sedar Senghor bitterly attacked Nkrumah's "Pan-African Government" schemes. Hastings Banda referred to Nkrumah as an "idiot" before his own puppet parliament in Malawi; Nigerian leader Nnamdi Azikiwe deplored the death of Danquah "in a detention camp barely eight years after his country had become free of foreign domination." Even Nkrumah's closest African associate, Sekou Toure of Guinea, attacked his "ally" before the UN General Assembly, telling delegates that Africa had no need for "philosophical formulas or doctrinal theories; it needs honest cooperation ... One of the major obstacles to (unity) has been the widespread conception that it had to be formed around a single state or a single man."

Nkrumah isolated himself further by initiating or financing dissident groups, assassination attempts and various schemes against other African bureaucratic elites. In Nigeria, for example, Ghana's TUC funnelled money to underwrite the Nigerian dock workers strike in 1963, and the Ghanaian regime "dispatched arms and ammunition" to certain political factions during Nigeria's 1964 elections. In late 1965, with East German secret intelligence assistance, a new "Special African Service" was established which would "report directly to Nkrumah."[38] The great irony of the situation was that Nkrumah's call for Pan-Africanist unity was essentially correct. "The international system isolated Nkrumah on the continent." Samir Amin argues. "His Pan-Africanism was labelled 'aggressive' by his neighbors, although in fact only such a policy would have made it possible to begin solving the real problems of development."[39]

The decline of world cocoa prices initiated the final phase of the regime. The Seven Year Plan had assumed that the price of cocoa would be approximately £200 per ton from 1963–70. The US stockpiled several hundred thousand tons of cocoa as part of a coordinated effort to destabilize Nkrumah's state. The decline in cocoa revenues increased the regime's reliance on foreign loans to maintain its massive state projects. In July 1963, Ghana's outstanding credits and loans already exceeded £92 million. The regime continued to borrow heavily: £3.4 million from France for a cotton mill, £6.9 million from the Netherlands for eight merchant ships, £19 million from the British contractor Parkinson Howard; £15 million in credits from Stahl-Union of West Germany.[40] Left Nkrumaism had tried to do too much, too quickly, without developing a sufficient cadre of socialists who could implement programs with some degree of efficiency. Nkrumah recognized this, yet he felt reasonably secure. There were no coherently organized political groups capable of challenging his authority in the National Assembly, the Party, or in the streets. The only potential threat left was the military and the police. There is irony here, for the very men Nkrumah advanced into the state's agencies of coercion during their "Africanization" of the colonial apparatus were those who would topple their patron.

The Ghanaian officer corps was firmly loyal to British tradition, and was hostile to left Nkrumaism and the growing political and economic ties with the Soviet bloc. They had imprisoned the regime's critics, restored order in Sekondi-Takoradi, and buttressed the Osaygefo's authority. Publicly they praised Nkrumah; privately they viewed him as a "lunatic" and worse. For Afrifa, the President's reversal of the Adamafio court decision in 1963 was a "disgrace. The constitution itself was perverted, parliament was a mockery, the judiciary had lost its independence and the executive had become autocratic. I became Kwame Nkrumah's bitterest enemy."[41] But even in the mid-1960s, a coup could have been averted. Popular defense committees, modeled perhaps after Cuba's "Committees for the Defense of the Revolution," could have armed the workers and peasantry ideologically and militarily. State industrial projects could have promoted workers' criticisms, direction and input. But Nkrumah still feared his industrial working class, preferring to place his trust in British-trained military officers and constables, securing their allegiance with promotions and graft. When the CPP finally fell, the workers in turn failed to support Nkrumah and Nkrumaism. After the bitter experience of Sekondi-Takoradi, after the rigged elections and the deliberate dismantling of their own party, they could act no other way.

Nkrumah's central weaknesses were organizational, theoretical and personal. The CPP was never structured to lead a democratic transformation of Ghanaian society. The party used the state apparatus to consolidate itself as a new, local ruling class, which negated the empowerment of the working class. The personality cult, the rewriting of the CPP's history, the chaotic removal of prominent party leaders from office, and the suppression of the parliamentary opposition were all part of Nkrumah's general failure to link democracy with his Pan-African and nationalistic ideals. As C.L.R. James observed:

Nkrumah's great political error was this. He believed that the question of democracy was a matter between him and Danquah and Busia and Appiah and such. He never understood that democracy was a matter in which the official leaders and an opposition were on trial before the mass of the population. It is not a question of conflict between rivals for power, as so many who shout "democracy" believe ... Nkrumah was very energetic. But, overwhelmed with work, Nkrumah depended more and more upon the party and less and less upon Parliament. But here his shallow concept of democracy found him out.[42]

~

Rediscovering Malcolm X's Life
A Historian's Adventures in Living History

To the majority of older white Americans, the noted African-American leaders Malcolm X and Dr. Martin Luther King, Jr., seem as different from each other as night vs. day. Mainstream culture and many history textbooks still suggest that the moderate Dr. King preached nonviolence and interracial harmony, whereas the militant Malcolm X advocated racial hatred and armed confrontation. Even Malcolm's infamous slogan, "By Any Means Necessary!," still evokes among whites disturbing images of Molotov cocktails, armed shoot-outs, and violent urban insurrection. But to the great majority of Black Americans and to millions of whites under thirty, these two Black figures are now largely perceived as being fully complimentary with each other. Both leaders had favored the building of strong Black institutions and healthy communities; both had strongly denounced Black-on-Black violence and drugs within the urban ghetto; both had vigorously opposed America's war in Vietnam and had embraced the global cause of human rights. In a 1989 "dialogue" between the eldest daughters of these two assassinated Black heroes, Yolanda King and Attallah Shabazz, both women emphasized the fundamental common ground and great admiration the two men shared for each other. Shabazz complained that "playwrights always make Martin so passive and Malcolm so aggressive that those men wouldn't have lasted a minute in the same room." King concurred, noting that in one play "my father was this wimp who carried a Bible everywhere he went, including to someone's house for dinner." King argued, "That's not the kind of minister Daddy was! All these ridiculous clichés...." Both agreed that the two giants were united in the pursuit of Black freedom and equality.

As a child of the radical sixties, I was well ahead of the national learning curve on the King vs. Malcolm dialectic. At age seventeen, as a high school senior, I had attended Dr. King's massive funeral at Ebenezer Baptist Church in Atlanta, on April 9, 1968. I had walked behind the rugged mule-driven wagon carrying Dr. King's body, along with tens of thousands of other mourners. The chaotic events of 1968 —the Vietnamese Tet offensive in February, President Johnson's surprise decision not to seek reelection, the assassinations of both Dr. King and Bobby Kennedy, the Paris student and worker uprising that summer, the "police riot" in Chicago at the Democratic National Convention—all were contributing factors in spinning the world upside down.

By the end of that turbulent year, for the generation of African-American students at overwhelmingly white college campuses, it was Malcolm X, not Dr. King, who overnight became the symbol for the times we were living through. As leader of my campus Black student union, I re-read *The Autobiography of Malcolm X* during the winter of 1969. The full relevance and revolutionary meaning of the man suddenly became crystal clear to me. In short, the former "King Man" became almost overnight a confirmed, dedicated "X Man."

Malcolm X was the Black Power generation's greatest prophet, who spoke the uncomfortable truths that no one else had the courage or integrity to broach. Especially for young Black males, he personified for us *everything* we wanted to become: the embodiment of Black masculinist authority and power, uncompromising bravery in the face of racial oppression, the ebony standard for what the African-American liberation movement should be about. With Talmudic-like authority, we quoted him in our debates, citing chapter and verse, the precise passages from the *Autobiography,* and books like *Malcolm X Speaks, By Any Means Necessary,* and other edited volumes. These collected works represented almost sacred texts of Black identity to us. "Saint Malcolm X-the-Martyr" was the ecumenical ebony standard for collective "Blackness." We even made feeble attempts to imitate Malcolm's speaking style. Everyone quoted him to justify their own narrow political, cultural, and even religious formulations and activities. His birthday, May 19, was widely celebrated as a national Black holiday. Any criticisms, no matter how minor or mild, of Malcolm's stated beliefs or evolving political career, were generally perceived as being not merely heretical, but almost treasonous to the entire Black race.

Working-class Black people widely loved Brother Malcolm for what they perceived as his clear and uncomplicated style of language, and his peerless ability in making every complex issue "plain." Indeed, one of Malcolm's favorite expressions from the podium was his admonition to other speakers to "Make it Plain," a phrase embodying his unshakable conviction that the Black masses themselves, "from the grassroots," would ultimately become the makers of their own revolutionary Black history. Here again, inside impoverished Black urban neighborhoods and especially in the bowels of America's prisons and jails, Malcolm's powerful message had an evocative appeal to young Black males. In actor Ossie Davis's memorable words, "Malcolm was our manhood! ... And, in honoring him, we honor the best in ourselves. And we will know him then for what he was and is—a Prince—our own Black shining Prince!—who didn't hesitate to die, because he loved us so. *The Autobiography of Malcolm X,* released into print in November 1965, sold millions of copies within several years. By the late sixties, the *Autobiography* had been adopted in hundreds of college courses across the country. Malcolm X's life story, as outlined by the *Autobiography,* became our quintessential story about the ordeal of being Black in America. Nearly every African American at the time was familiar with the story's basic outline. Born in the Midwest, young Malcolm Little became an orphan: his father was brutally murdered by the Ku Klux Klan and his disturbed mother, overwhelmed by caring for seven little children, suffered a mental breakdown and had been institutionalized. Malcolm then relocated east to Roxbury and Harlem. He then became an urban outlaw, the notorious "Detroit Red," a pimp, hustler, burglar, and drug dealer. Pinched by police, "Detroit Red" was sentenced to ten years' hard labor in prison, where he then joined the Black Muslims. Once released, given the new name Malcolm X, he rapidly built the Black Muslims from an inconsequential sect to over one hundred thousand strong. But then Malcolm X grew intellectually and politically well beyond the Muslim. He decided to launch his own Black nationalist group, the Organization of Afro-American Unity. He started preaching about human rights and "the ballot or the bullet." Malcolm made a pilgrimage to the holy city of Mecca, converted to orthodox Islam, and became "El-Hajj Malik El-Shabazz." He was then acclaimed by Islamic, African, and Arab leaders as a leading voice for racial justice. Then, at the pinnacle of his worldwide influence and power, Malcolm was brutally struck down by assassins' bullets at Harlem's Audubon Ballroom. This was the basic story nearly every activist in my generation knew by heart.

A number of Malcolm X's associates and others who had known him personally published articles and books in the late sixties, which firmly established the late leader as the true fountainhead of Black Power.[1] Far more influential, however, for popularizing the Malcolm Legend was the Black Arts Movement. Poets were particularly fascinated with the magnetic, physical figure of Malcolm, as a kind of revolutionary Black Adonis. In life, towering at six feet, three inches tall and weighing a trim 175 to 180 pounds, broad-shouldered Malcolm X was mesmerizingly handsome, always displaying a broad, boyish smile, and always spotlessly well-groomed; in death, he would remain forever young. In photographs, he seemed both strong and sensitive. Poet Joyce Whitshitt captured this image of the fearless yet vulnerable model for a new Black manhood in "For Malcolm."

> ... You were the brilliant embodiment
> Of elusive manhood. Those who are less
> Negate your death and fail to acknowledge
> Righteousness felt of your logic.

Celebrated African-American poet Gwendolyn Brooks echoed similar themes and images in her ode to Malcolm:

> He had the hawk-man's eyes.
> We gasped. We saw the maleness.
> The maleness raking out and making guttural the air.
> And pushing us to walls.

One of the most popular and widely read Black nationalist poets of the period was Sonia Sanchez, who for several years was a Nation of Islam member. Sanchez's

Malcolm was less overtly the paragon of Black masculinity, than the tragic symbol of loss for what might have been, an unhealed wound that "floods the womb until I drown":

> Do not speak to me of martyrdom
> of men who die to be remembered
> on some parish day.
> I don't believe in dying
> though I too shall die
> and violets like castanets
> will echo me.
> Yet this man
> this dreamer,
> thick-lipped with words
> will never speak again
> and in each winter
> when the cold air cracks
> with frost, I'll breathe
> his breath and mourn
> my gun-filled nights.
> He was the sun that tagged
> the western sky and
> melted tiger-scholars
> while they searched for stripes.
> He said, 'Fuck you white
> man. We have been
> curled too long. Nothing
> is sacred now. Not your
> white face nor any
> land that separates
> until some voices
> squat with spasms.'
> Do not speak to me of living.
> life is obscene with crowds
> of white on black.
> death is my pulse.
> what might have been
> is not for him or me
> but what could have been
> floods the womb until I drown.

Malcolm's powerfully masculinist image was most unambiguously on full display in Amiri Baraka's (LeRoi Jones's) famous and frequently recited "A Poem for Black Hearts." Despite its blatantly homophobic final passage, Baraka powerfully projected Malcolm X as the ideal model for the perfect fulfillment of an ideal Black masculinity:

> For Malcolm's eyes, when they broke
> the face of some dumb white man. For
> Malcolm's hands raised to bless us
> all black and strong in his image
> of ourselves, for Malcolm's words
> fire darts, the victor's tireless
> thrusts, words hung above the world
> change as it may, he said it, and
> for this he was killed, for saying,
> and feeling, and being/change, all
> collected hot in his heart, For Malcolm's
> heart, raising us above our filthy cities,
> for his stride, and his beat, and his address
> to the grey monsters of the world, For Malcolm's
> pleas for your dignity, black men, for your life,
> black men, for the filling of your minds
> with righteousness, For all of him dead and
> gone and vanished from us, and all of him which
> clings to our speech black god of our time.
> For all of him, and all of yourself, look up,
> black man, quit stuttering and shuffling, look up,
> black man, quit whining and stooping, for all of him,
> for Great Malcolm a prince of the earth, let nothing
> in us rest
> until we avenge ourselves for his death, stupid animals
> that killed him, let us never breathe a pure breath if
> we fail, and white men call us faggots till the end of
> the earth.

After receding somewhat during much of the late 1970s and early 1980s, Malcolm X's cultural reputation among artists, playwrights, and musicians exploded again with the flowering of the hip-hop generation. Malcolm's cultural renaissance began with the 1983 release of Keith LeBlanc's "No Sell-Out," a 12-inch dance single featuring a Malcolm X speech set to hip-hop beat. Old School group Afrika Bambaata and the Soul Sonic Force followed in 1986 with "Renegades of Funk," declaring that both King and Malcolm X had been bold and bad "renegades of the atomic age." On its classic 1988 hip-hop album, "It Takes a Nation of Millions to Hold Us Back," Public Enemy (PE) generously sampled from Malcolm's speeches. On the song "Bring The Noise," PE took two different excerpts from a Malcolm X speech, constructing the provocative phrase, "Too Black, Too Strong." On "Party for Your Right to Fight," Public Enemy told the hip-hop nation that "J. Edgar Hoover

... had King and X set up." PE's massive popularity and its strong identification with Malcolm's image led other hip-hop artists to also incorporate Malcolm X into their own music. In 1989, the Stop the Violence Movement's "Self Destruction" album featured a Malcolm X lecture, and its companion video included beautiful murals of the Black leader as the hip-hop background for rappers. The less commercially popular but enormously talented artist Paris released "Break the Grip of Shame" in 1990, which prominently featured Malcolm's ringing indictment: "We declare our right on this Earth to be a man, to be a human being, to be respected as a human being to be given the rights of a human being in this society on this Earth in this day, which we intend to bring into existence, by any means necessary!"

As "Thug Life" and "Gangsta Rap" emerged from the West Coast and soon acquired a national commercial appeal, these artists painted Malcolm X in their own cultural contexts of misogynistic and homophobic violence. Ice Cube's 1992 "Predator," for example, sampled a Malcolm address over a beat on one cut; on another, "Wicked," Ice Cube rapped: "People wanna know how come I gotta gat and I'm looking out the window like Malcolm ready to bring that noise. Kinda trigger-happy like the Ghetto Boys." Less provocatively, KRS-One's 1995 "Ah-Yeah" spoke of Black reincarnation: "They tried to harm me, I used to be Malcolm X. Now I'm on the planet as the one called KRS." Perhaps the greatest individual artist hip-hop culture has yet produced, Tupac Shakur, fiercely identified himself with Malcolm X. On Tupac's classic 1996 "Makaveli" album, on the song "Blasphemy," he posed a provocative query:

> Why you got these kids minds, thinking that they evil while the preacher being richer. You say honor God's people, should we cry when the Pope die, my request, we should cry if they cried when we buried Malcolm X. Mama tells me am I wrong, is God just another cop waiting to beat my ass if I don't go pop?

The widespread release and commercial success of Spike Lee's 1992 biofilm "X," combined with hip-hop's celebration of Malcolm as a "homeboy," created the context for what historian Russell Rickford has termed "Malcolmology." Hundreds of thousands of African-American households owned and displayed portraits of Malcolm X, either in their homes, places of business, or at Black schools. Malcolm X by the 1990s had become one of the few historical figures to emerge from the Black nationalist tradition to be fully accepted and integrated into the pantheon of civil rights legends, an elite of Black forefathers, who included Frederick Douglass, W.E.B. Du Bois, and Dr. Martin Luther King, Jr.

As with every mythic figure, the icon of Saint Malcolm accommodated a variety of parochial interpretations. To the bulk of the African-American middle class, the Malcolm legend was generally presented in terms of his inextricable trajectory of intellectual and political maturation, culminating with his dramatic break from the NOI and embrace of interracial harmony. For much of the hip-hop nation, in sharp contrast, the most attractive characteristics of Saint Malcolm emphasized the incendiary and militant elements of his career. Many hip-hop artists made scant distinctions between Malcolm X and his former protege and later bitter rival, Louis X (Farrakhan). Some even insisted that Malcolm X had never supported any coalitions with whites, despite his numerous 1964–1965 public statements to the contrary. The hip-hop Malcolmologists seized Malcolm as the ultimate Black cultural rebel, unblemished and uncomplicated by the pragmatic politics of partisan compromise, which was fully reflected in the public careers of other post-Malcolm Black leaders, such as Jesse Jackson and Harold Washington. Despite their Black cultural nationalist rhetoric, however, hip-hop Malcolmologists also uncritically accepted the main parameters of the Black leader's tragic life story, as presented in *The Autobiography of Malcolm X*. They also glorified Malcolm's early gangster career, as the notorious, street-wise "Detroit Red," and tended to use selective quotations by the fallen leader that gave justification for their use of weapons in challenging police brutality.

The widespread sampling of Malcolm's speeches on hip-hop videos and albums, plus the popular acclaim for Lee's biopic, culminated into "Malcolmania" in 1992–1993. There were "X" posters, coffee mugs, potato chips, T-shirts and "X-caps," which newly elected President Bill Clinton wore occasionally when jogging outside the White House in the morning. CBS News at the time estimated the commercial market for X-related products at $100 million annually. The Malcolmania hype had the effect of transporting the X-man from being merely a Black superhero into the exalted status of mainstream American idol.

This new privileged status for Malcolm X was even confirmed officially by the U.S. Government. On January 20, 1999, about 1,500 officials, celebrities, and guests crowded into Harlem's Apollo Theatre to mark the issuance by the U.S. Postal Service of the Malcolm X postage stamp. Prominently in attendance were actors Ruby Dee, Ossie Davis, and Harry Belafonte. Also on hand was Harlem millionaire entrepreneur, media-mogul (and Malcolm's former attorney) Percy Sutton. The Malcolm X stamp was the Postal Service's latest release in its "Black Heritage Stamp Series." Pennsylvania Congressman Chaka Fattah, the ranking Democrat on the House of Representatives Postal Subcommittee, remarked at the festive occasion, "There is no more appropriate honor than this stamp because Malcolm X sent all of us a message through his life and his life's work." To Congressman Fattah, Malcolm X's "thoughts, his ideas, his conviction, and his courage provide an inspiration even now to new generations to come." Few in the audience could ignore the rich irony of this event. One of America's sharpest and most unrelenting critics was now being praised and honored by the same government that had once carried out illegal harassment and surveillance against him. Ossie Davis, who understood the significance of this bittersweet moment better than anyone else, jokingly quipped: "We in this community look upon this commemorative stamp finally as America's stamp of approval ..."

The Malcolm X postage stamp was the twenty-second release in the "Black Heritage Series," which had previously featured other Black heroes such as Frederick Douglass, Harriet Tubman, Martin Luther King, Jr., Mary McLeod Bethune, and W.E.B. Du Bois. The U.S. Postal Service also released a short biographical statement accompanying the stamp's issuance, noting that the retouched photographic image of Malcolm X had been taken by an Associated Press photographer at a press conference held in New York City on May 21, 1964. The statement explains that soon after this photograph was taken, that Malcolm X "later broke away from the organization," referring to the NOI, and "disavowed his earlier separatist preaching. . . ." The most generous thing one could say about this curious statement was that it was the product of poor scholarship. The photograph actually had been taken during an interview in Cairo, Egypt, on July 14, 1964. Malcolm X had publicly broken from the NOI on March 8, 1964, two months earlier than the official statement had suggested. More problematic was the U.S. Postal Service's assertion that Malcolm X had become, before his death, a proponent of "a more integrationist solution to racial problems." But none of these errors of fact and slight distortions disturbed most who had gathered to celebrate. The Malcolm X postage stamp was a final and fitting triumph of his legacy. The full "Americanization of Malcolm X" appeared to be complete.

When in 1987 I decided to write what was to have been a modest "political biography" of Malcolm X, there was already a substantial body of literature about him. By 2002, those published works had grown to roughly 930 books, 360 films and internet educational resources, and 350 sound recordings. As I plowed through dozens, then hundreds of books and articles, I was dismayed to discover that almost none of the scholarly literature or books about him had relied on serious research which would include a complete archival investigation of Malcolm's letters, personal documents, wills, diaries, transcripts of speeches and sermons, his actual criminal record, FBI files, and legal court proceedings. Some informative articles had appeared written by individuals who had either worked closely with Malcolm X or who described a specific event in which they had been brought into direct contact with the Black leader. But these reminiscences lacked analytical rigor and critical insight. What staggered the mind, however, was the literal mountain of badly written articles, the turgid prose, and various academic-styled ruminations about Malcolm X's life and thought, nearly all based on the same, limited collection of secondary sources.

There was remarkably little Malcolm X literature that employed the traditional tools of historical investigation. Few writers had conducted fresh interviews with Malcolm X's widow, Dr. Betty Shabazz, any of his closest co-workers, or the extended Little family. Writers made few efforts to investigate the actual criminal record of Malcolm X at the time of his 1946 incarceration. Not even the best previous scholarly studies of Malcolm X—a small group of books including Peter Goldman's *The Death and Life of Malcolm X* (1973), Karl Evanzz's *The Judas Factor: The Plot to Kill Malcolm X* (1992), and Louis DeCaro's *On the Side of My People: A Religious Life of Malcolm X* (1996)—had amassed a genuine "archival" or substantive database of documentation in order to form a true picture of Malcolm-X-the-man rather than the pristine icon.[2] One problem in this was Malcolm X's inescapable identification as the quintessential model of Black masculinity—which served as a kind of gendered barricade to any really objective appraisal of him. Cultural critic Philip Brian Harper has observed that Malcolm X and the Black Powerites who later imitated him constructed themselves as virile, potent, and hypermasculinist, giving weight to the false impression that racial integrationists like King were weak and impotent.[3]

Nearly everyone writing about Malcolm X largely, with remarkably few exceptions, accepted *as fact* most if not all of the chronology of events and personal experiences depicted in the *Autobiography*'s narrative. Few authors checked the edited, published "transcripts" of Malcolm X's speeches as presented in *Malcolm X Speaks* and *By Any Means Necessary* against the actual tape recordings of those speeches, or the transcribed excerpts of the same talks recorded by the FBI. Every historian worth her or his salt knows that "memoirs" like the *Autobiography* are inherently biased. They present a representation of the subject that privileges certain facts, while self-censuring others. There are deliberate omissions, the chronological re-ordering of events, and name-changes. Consequently, there existed no comprehensive biography of this man who arguably had come to personify modern, urban Black America in the past half century.

There continued to be, for me, so many unanswered basic questions about this dynamic yet ultimately elusive man that neither the *Autobiography,* nor the other nine hundred-plus books written about him had answered satisfactorily. The most obvious queries concerned his murder. Substantial evidence had been compiled both by Goldman and attorney William Kuntsler that indicated that two of the men convicted in 1966 for gunning down Malcolm at the Audubon Ballroom, Thomas 15X Johnson and Norman 3X Butler, were completely innocent. In 1977, the only assassin who had been wounded and captured at the crime scene, Talmadge Hayer, had confessed to his prison clergyman that both Johnson and Butler had played absolutely no roles in the murder, confirming that in fact, they had not even been present at the Audubon that afternoon.

There had always been whispers for years that Louis Farrakhan had been responsible for the assassination; he had been Malcolm X's closest protege, and then following his vitriolic renunciation of Malcolm, inherited the leadership of Harlem's Mosque Number Seven following the murder. Then I had to explain the inexplicable behavior of the New York Police Department (NYPD) on the day of the assassination. Usually one to two dozen cops blanketed any event where Malcolm X was speaking. Normally at the Audubon rallies, a police captain or lieutenant was stationed in a command center above the Audubon's main entrance, on the second floor. Fifteen to twenty uniformed officers, at least, would be milling at the periphery of the crowd, a few always located at a small park directly across the street from the building. On February 21, 1965, however, the cops almost disappeared. There were no uniformed officers in the ballroom, at the main entrance, or even in the park, at the time of the shooting. Only two NYPD patrolmen were inside the Audubon, but at the opposite end of the building. When the NYPD investigation team arrived, forensic evidence wasn't properly collected, and significant eyewitnesses still at the scene weren't interviewed for days, and in several instances weeks later. The crime scene itself was preserved for only a couple of hours. By 6 p.m. only three hours after Malcolm X's killing, a housekeeper with detergent and a bucket of water mopped up the floor, eliminating the bloody evidence. A dance was held in the same ballroom at 7 p.m. that night, as originally scheduled.

Perhaps I could never answer completely the greatest question about Malcolm X: if he *had* lived, or somehow had survived the assassination attempt, what could he have become? How would have another three or four decades of life altered how we imagine him, and the ways we interpret his legacy? The legion of books that he inspired presented widely different, and even diametrically opposing, theories on the subject. Virtually every group—the orthodox, Sunni Islamic community, Black cultural nationalists, Trotskyists, prisoners and former prisoners, mainstream integrationists, and hip-hop artists—had manipulated the "Black shining prince" to promote their own agendas, or to justify their causes. The enormous elasticity of Malcolm's visual image could be universally appropriated, stretching from Ice Cube's 1992 apocalyptic "predator" to being used as the template for the film character "Magneto" in the 1999 blockbuster hit, "The X-Men," illustrated the great difficulty I now confronted. Malcolm X was being constantly *reinvented* within American society and popular culture.

But the first, most original, and most talented revisionist of Malcolm X was Malcolm X himself. I slowly began to realize that Malcolm X continuously and astutely refashioned his outward image, artfully redesigning his public style and even language, to facilitate overtures to different people in varied contexts. And yet, beneath the multiple layers of reinvention, *who was he?* Was the powerful impact of his short, thirty-nine years of existence actually grounded in what he had really accomplished, or based on the unfulfilled promise of what he might have become? Malcolm X is memorialized by millions of Americans largely because of the *Autobiography,* which is today a standard text of American literature. But was Malcolm's *hajj* to Mecca in April 1964, the dramatic turning point of the *Autobiography,* the glorious epiphany Malcolm claimed it was at the time, and that virtually all other interpreters of him have uncritically accepted? Was this spiritual metamorphosis, the embracing of color blindness, and the public denouncing of Elijah Muhammad's sexual misconduct, all just part of the political price he was now prepared to pay to gain entry into the Civil Rights Movement's national leadership? Wasn't this final "reincarnation" the necessary role change for El-Hajj Malik El-Shabazz to reach inside the court of the Saudi royal family, and to gain access to the corridors of governmental power throughout the newly independent nations of Africa and Asia?

With so many unanswered questions to explore, there seemed to me to exist paradoxically a *collective conspiracy of silence surrounding Malcolm X,* an unwitting or perhaps witting attempt not to examine things too closely, to stick to the accepted narrative offered by the *Autobiography* and Lee's biopic. By not peering below the surface, there would be no need to adjust the crafted image we have learned to adore, frozen in time. We could simply all find enduring comfort in the safe, masculinist gaze of our "Black shining prince."

Historians are trained in graduate school to state only what we can actually *prove,* based primarily on archival or secondary source evidence. Information we collect from oral interviews can only be used from informed subjects, who have an opportunity to review what they've said for the record. Thus the discipline itself provides certain safeguards to interviewees and informants. Most historians, in other words, do not see themselves as investigative reporters, or would-be "cold case" investigators. Yet the skills of both seemed to me necessary in order to crack open the Malcolm X collective conspiracy of silence. Malcolm's actual legacy was dogmatically preserved and fiercely guarded by nearly everyone privy to important information pertaining to him. This was a highly unusual situation for a researcher to confront, especially considering that Malcolm X lived a very "public" existence, appearing on numerous television shows, and speaking literally at thousands of venues across the country.

When I started my biography of Malcolm X in 1987 I was then Chair of Black Studies at Ohio State University. Working with several graduate students, we began compiling photocopies of articles about Malcolm X that appeared in academic journals. We began a newspaper clipping file of more recent media coverage related to our subject (remember, these were the days before the internet and world-wide web). I knew that I would need to penetrate four principal, core areas of investigation, in order to present a really balanced and fair portrait of the man. These four broad areas were: (1) the Black organizations in which Malcolm X played a significant leadership role—the Nation of Islam, the Muslim Mosque, Inc., and the Organization of Afro-American Unity; (2) the surveillance of Malcolm X by the FBI and other governmental agencies; (3) the materials of Alex Haley, co-author of the *Autobiography,* used in preparing the book; and, of course (4) the family of Malcolm X, especially his widow, Dr. Betty Shabazz, and their access to any manuscripts, correspondence, texts or transcripts of speeches and sermons, legal documents, and odd paraphernalia. All four of these areas, for different reasons, proved to be intractable. In 1989, I accepted a professorship in ethnic studies at the University of Colorado in Boulder, and in the following academic year I organized a research team of six to ten graduate students and work-study assistants, who were dedicated to reconstructing Malcolm's life. After three hard years, we had made at best marginal headway. I then accepted my current appointment at Columbia. I had no idea at that time that another decade would elapse before I could really successfully infiltrate these four core areas of Malcolm-related investigation.

The first nearly overwhelming difficulty was the lack of a comprehensive, well-organized archive on Malcolm X. Primary source materials, such as correspondence and personal manuscripts, were literally scattered and fragmented. For some inexplicable reason, the Shabazz family had never authorized a group of historians or archivists to compile these rare documents into a central, publicly accessible repository. By my own count, as of 2003 chunks of Malcolm's core memorabilia were located at seventy-three different U.S. archives and libraries, including the Library of Congress, New York University's Tamiment Library, the Schomburg Center of the New York Public Library, Cornell University Library, Wayne State University Library, the State Historical Society of Wisconsin, Emory University Library, Howard University Library and Columbia University's Oral History Research Center. I contrasted this chaotic situation to the professionally archived life records of Dr. Martin Luther King, Jr., then at Atlanta's King Center, that would serve as the core database for historian Clayborne Carson's magnificent, 30-year-long effort, the King Papers Project. Booker T. Washington's papers, carefully archived and preserved, fill exactly 1,077 linear feet of archival boxes at the Library of Congress. Most dedicated

Malcolmologists also knew that Dr. Shabazz still retained hundreds of documents and manuscripts by her late husband in her Mount Vernon, New York home. But no one really had a clue how much primary source material there was, and whether any efforts had been made to preserve it.

I had more than a nostalgic desire to preserve memorabilia. As a historian, I also knew that all artifacts made by human beings inevitably disintegrate. Paper, left unprotected, without a climate-controlled environment and acid-free folders, "lives" only about seventy-five years. Audiotape recordings based on magnetic recording technology survive about forty years. People who had worked closely with Malcolm X and who had known him intimately would nearly all be dead in another two decades. Only the Shabazz family had the moral authority to initiate such an undertaking, to secure Malcolm X's place in history. It simply didn't make sense. Much later, in 2002, when the near-public auction by Butterfield's of a major cache of Malcolm memorabilia fetching offers of $600,000 and more came to light, I discovered that the Shabazz family had squirreled away several hundred pounds of Malcolm X–related documents and material. Maliakah Shabazz, the youngest daughter, had, without the rest of the family's knowledge, managed to pack and transport her father's materials to a Florida storage facility. Her failure to pay the storage facility's monthly fee led to the seizure and disposition of the bin's priceless contents. The new purchaser, in turn, had contacted E-Bay and Butterfield's to sell what he believed to be his property. Only a legal technicality voided the sale, returning the memorabilia to the Shabazzes.

After the international publicity and outcry surrounding the Butterfield's abortive auction, however, the Shabazzes decided to deposit their materials at the Schomburg Center in Harlem. In January 2003, the Schomburg publicly announced to the media its acquisition on the basis of a 75-year loan. I have previously written in detail about the Butterfield's abortive auction fiasco, and I had been extensively involved in the financial negotiations with the auction house and the Shabazzes on behalf of Columbia University. But what *none* of the principals, including myself, could bear to ask ourselves and the Shabazz Estate in public, is *why* had hundreds of pounds of documents, speeches, manuscripts, Malcolm's Holy Qu'ran, etc., been left deteriorating in storage in their basement *for thirty-five years?*

The intransigence of the Shabazzes forced me to contemplate negotiations with the Nation of Islam. I had written extensively, and quite critically, about Louis Farrakhan and his philosophy over a number of years. Yet during my research, I had learned that Muslim ministers like Malcolm X, under the strict authoritarian supervision of Elijah Muhammad, had been required to submit weekly reports about their mosques' activities. All sermons they delivered were audiotaped, with the tapes mailed to the national headquarters in Chicago. When I broached the possibility of examining their archives through third parties, the NOI curtly refused, explaining that they wished to "protect Dr. Betty Shabazz and her family."

Another potential avenue of biographical inquiry existed among Malcolm X's friends and associates in Muslim Mosque, Inc., and the Organization of Afro-American Unity, two groups formed in 1964, and that had disintegrated in the months after Malcolm's assassination. Here I had better luck. Prior friendships with several prominent individuals, such as actor Ossie Davis, provided valuable oral histories of their relationships with Malcolm X. Most key individuals I wanted to interview, however, were either reclusive or elusive. Some were literally "underground," and living in exile in either South America, the Caribbean, or in Africa. A few, such as writer Sylvester Leaks, cordially agreed to converse off the record, then angrily refused to be formally interviewed. Some pivotal figures such as Malcolm X's personal bodyguard, Reuben Francis, had literally disappeared months following the murder. I subsequently learned that Francis had somehow been relocated to Mexico sometime in 1966, and from then fell into complete obscurity. Lynn Shiflett, OAAU secretary and a trusted personal assistant to Malcolm X, had refused all interviews and even written contacts since 1966.

The FBI avenue of inquiry proved to be even more daunting. Despite the passage of the Freedom of Information Act, which required the Bureau to declassify its internal memoranda that required secrecy for the sake of national security, by 1994 only about 2,300 pages of an estimated *50,000 pages* of surveillance on Malcolm X was made public. Much of this information was heavily redacted or blacked out by FBI censors, supposedly to protect its informants, or to preserve "national security." For several years, a group of my student research assistants helped me to make sense of this maze of FBI bureaucratic mumbo jumbo. I learned eventually that whatever the FBI's original motives, they fairly accurately tracked Malcolm X's precise movements, public addresses and dozens of telephone calls, all without legal warrants, of course. In 1995, Farrakhan had proposed announcing a national campaign to pressure the Bureau to open up its archives about Malcolm X, and especially to release any relevant information concerning his assassination. According to Farrakhan, the Shabazz family insisted that there be no effort to force the Bureau to divulge what it knew. Friends close to the family subsequently explained to me that the memories were still too painful, even after thirty long years. A public inquiry would be too traumatic for all concerned.

Without my knowledge, historian Clayborne Carson at Stanford University was, in the early 1990s, working independently along parallel lines. He successfully annotated the FBI memoranda at that time available, publishing an invaluable reference work, *Malcolm X: The FBI File* (New York: Ballantine Books, 1995). Prior to the book's publication, however, attorneys for Dr. Shabazz expressed concerns that Carson should severely *limit* the amount of original material lifted by the FBI from Malcolm X's orations, writings, and wiretapped conversations. Thus the book that was comprised of letters and transcribed tape recordings already heavily censored by the FBI was, in effect, *censored a second time* for the purposes of not violating copyright infringement. When Black Studies scholar Abdul Alkalimat prepared a primer text, *Malcolm X for Beginners,* Dr. Shabazz threatened a lawsuit, based on the unusual legal claim that *anything* ever uttered by her late husband was her "intellectual property." Alkalimat finally consented to surrender any and all claims to royalties from the book to the Shabazz estate.

I then confronted the enigma of Alex Haley. Haley was the highest-selling author of Black nonfiction in U.S. history. His greatest achievement had been the

1976 book *Roots,* which like the co-authored *Autobiography* had become a celebrated, iconic text of Black identity and culture. Yet statements about Malcolm X made by Haley shortly before his death seemed to me strangely negative. Haley had even asserted that both Malcolm X and Dr. King were going "downhill" before their deaths.[4] Haley had placed his papers at the University of Tennessee's archives, in January 1991. Yet there remained unusual restrictions on scholarly access to his personal records. I personally visited his archives in Knoxville twice. No photocopying of any document in the Haley files is permitted, without the prior written approval of his attorney, Paul Coleman of Knoxville, Tennessee. My letters to Coleman were unanswered. When in Knoxville during my second visit, I persuaded the archive's curator to phone Coleman directly on my behalf. Attorney Coleman then explained to me over the telephone that he needed to know the *precise pages* or documents to be photocopied, *in advance!* In practical terms, scholars are forced to copy passages in pencil, by hand, from Haley's archives. This laborious model of information transferal worked well for monks in the Middle Ages, but seems inappropriate for the age of digital technology.

As luck would have it, several years before Haley's death, he had named researcher Anne Romaine as his "official biographer." Romaine was a white folksinger, trained neither as a historian nor as a biographer. Yet she was apparently diligent and serious about her work. Between the late 1980s until to her death in 1995, Romaine had conducted audiotaped interviews with over fifty individuals, some of whom covered the background to Haley's role in producing the *Autobiography.* The great bulk of Romaine's papers and research materials pertaining to the *Autobiography* were also donated to the University of Tennessee's archives. To my delight, there were absolutely no restrictions on Romaine's papers; everything can be photocopied and reproduced. One folder in Romaine's papers includes the "raw materials" used to construct Chapter Sixteen of the *Autobiography.* Here, I found the actual mechanics of the Haley–Malcolm X collaboration. Malcolm X apparently would speak to Haley in "free style"; it was left to Haley to take hundreds of sentences into paragraphs and then appropriate subject areas. Malcolm also had a habit of scribbling notes to himself as he spoke. Haley learned to pocket these sketchy notes and later reassemble them, integrating the conscious with subconscious reflections into a workable narrative. Although Malcolm X retained final approval of their hybrid text, he was not privy to the actual editorial processes superimposed from Haley's side. Chapters the two men had prepared were sometimes split and restructured into other chapters. These details may appear mundane and insignificant. But considering that Malcolm's final "metamorphosis" took place in 1963–65, the exact timing of when individual chapters were produced takes on enormous importance.

These new revelations made me realize that I also needed to learn much more about *Haley.* Born in Ithaca, New York, in 1921, Alex Haley was the oldest of three sons of Simon Alexander Haley, a professor of agriculture, and Bertha George Palmer, a grade school teacher. Haley had been raised as a child in Henning, Tennessee. As a teenager, in 1939, Haley enlisted in the U.S. Coast Guard as a mess boy. During World War II, he had come to the attention of white officers for his flair as a talented writer. During long assignments at sea, Haley had ghost-written hundreds of love letters for sailors' wives and sweethearts back at home. While Haley's repeated efforts to gain print publication for his unsolicited manuscripts failed for eight long years, his extracurricular activities gained the approval and admiration of his white superiors. By the late 1940s, Haley was advanced into a desk job; by the mid-1950s he was granted the post of "chief journalist" in the Coast Guard. After putting in twenty years' service, Haley started a career as a professional freelance writer. Politically, Haley was both a Republican and a committed advocate of racial integration. He was not, unlike C. Eric Lincoln or other African-American scholars who had studied the NOI's activities during the late 1950s, even mildly sympathetic with the Black group's aims and racial philosophy.

To Haley, the separatist Nation of Islam was an object lesson in America's failure to achieve interracial justice and fairness. As Mike Wallace's controversial 1959 television series on the Black Muslims had proclaimed, they represented "The Hate That Hate Produced." Haley completely concurred with Wallace's thesis. He, too, was convinced that the NOI was potentially a dangerous, racist cult, completely out of step with the lofty goals and integrationist aspirations of the civil rights movement. Haley was personally fascinated with Malcolm's charisma and angry rhetoric, but strongly disagreed with many of his ideas. Consequently, when Haley started work on the *Autobiography,* he held a very different set of objectives than those of Malcolm X. The Romaine papers also revealed that one of Haley's early articles about the NOI, co-authored with white writer Alfred Balk, had been written *in collaboration with the FBI.* The FBI had supplied its information about the NOI to Balk and Haley, which formed much of the basis for their *Saturday Evening Post* article that appeared on January 26, 1963, with the threatening title, "Black Merchants of Hate."[5]

I then began to wonder, as I poured through Romaine's papers, what Malcolm X really had known about the final text that would become his ultimate "testament." Couldn't I discover a way to find out what was going on inside Haley's head, or at Doubleday, which had paid a hefty $20,000 advance for the *Autobiography* in June 1963? And why, only three weeks following Malcolm X's killing, had Doubleday canceled the contract for the completed book? The *Autobiography* would be eventually published by Grove Press in late 1965. Doubleday's hasty decision would cost the publisher millions of dollars.

The Library of Congress held the answers. Doubleday's corporate papers are now housed there. This collection includes the papers of Doubleday's then–executive editor, Kenneth McCormick, who had worked closely with Haley for several years as the *Autobiography* had been constructed. As in the Romaine papers, I found more evidence of Haley's sometimes weekly private commentary with McCormick about the laborious process of composing the book. These Haley letters of marginalia contained some crucial, never previously published intimate details about Malcolm's personal life. They also revealed how several attorneys retained by Doubleday closely monitored and vetted entire sections of the controversial text in 1964, demanding numerous name changes, the reworking and deletion of blocks of paragraphs, and so forth. In late 1963, Haley was particularly worried about what he viewed as Malcolm

X's anti-Semitism. He therefore rewrote material to eliminate a number of negative statements about Jews in the book manuscript, with the explicit covert goal of "getting them past Malcolm X," without his co-author's knowledge or consent. Thus the censorship of Malcolm X had begun well *prior* to his assassination.

A cardinal responsibility of the historian is to relate the full truth, however unpleasant. In the early 1960s, the Nation of Islam had been directly involved with the American Nazi Party and white supremacist organizations—all while Malcolm X had been its "national representative." This regrettable dimension of Malcolm's career had to be thoroughly investigated, yet few scholars, Black or white, had been willing to do so. In 1998, in my book *Black Leadership* (New York: Columbia University Press, 1998), I had described Farrakhan's anti-Semitic, conservative, Black nationalism as an odious brand of "Black Fundamentalism." Farrakhan had been Malcolm's prime protege, and the question must now be posed whether Malcolm X was partially responsible for the bankrupt political legacy of Black anti-Semitism and Black Fundamentalism. The whole truth, not packaged icons, can only advance our complete understanding of the real man and his times.

The Romaine papers also had provided clear evidence that the lack of a clear political program or plan of action in the *Autobiography* was no accident. Something was indeed "missing" from the final version of the book, as it appeared in print in late 1965. In Haley's own correspondence to editor Kenneth McCormick, dated January 19, 1964, Haley had even described these chapters as having "the most impact material of the book, some of it rather lava-like."[6] Now my quest shifted to finding out what the contents of this "impact material" were. The trail now led me to Detroit attorney Gregory Reed. In late 1992, Reed had purchased the original manuscripts of the *Autobiography* at the sale of the Haley Estate for $100,000. Reed has in his possession, in his office safe, the three "missing chapters" from the *Autobiography*, which still have never been published. I contacted Reed, and after several lengthy telephone conversations, he agreed to show me the missing *Autobiography* chapters. With great enthusiasm, I flew to Detroit, and telephoned Reed at our agreed-upon time. Reed then curiously rejected meeting me at his law office. He insisted instead that we meet at a downtown restaurant. I arrived at our meeting place on time, and a half hour later Reed showed up, carrying a briefcase.

After exchanging a few pleasantries, Reed informed me that he had not brought the entire original manuscript with him. However, he would permit me to read, at the restaurant table, small selections from the manuscript. I was deeply disappointed, but readily accepted Reed's new terms. For roughly fifteen minutes, I quickly read parts from the illusive "missing chapters." That was enough time for me to ascertain without doubt that these text fragments had been dictated and written sometime between October 1963 and January 1964. This coincided with the final months of Malcolm's NOI membership. More critically, in these missing chapters, Malcolm X proposed the construction of an unprecedented, African-American united front of Black political and civic organizations, including both the NOI and civil rights groups. He perhaps envisioned something similar in style to Farrakhan's Million Man March of 1995. Apparently, Malcolm X was aggressively pushing the NOI beyond

Black Fundamentalism, into open, common dialogue and political collaboration with the civil rights community. Was this the prime reason that elements inside both the NOI and the FBI may have wanted to silence him? Since Reed owns the physical property, but the Shabazz estate retains the intellectual property rights of its contents, we may never know.

With each successive stumbling block, I became more intrigued. The complicated web of this man's life, the swirling world around him, his friends, family, and intimate associates, became ever more tangled and provocative. The tensions between these at times feuding factions, the innuendos, the missed opportunities, the angry refusals to speak on the record, the suppression of archival evidence, the broken loyalties and constant betrayals, all seemed too great. It required of me a difficult journey of many years, even to possess the knowledge of how to untangle the web, to make sense of it all. What I acquired, however, by 2003–2004, was a true depth of understanding and insight that was surprising, and much more revelatory than I had ever imagined. I finally learned that the answer to the question—why was this information about Malcolm X so fiercely protected—because the life, and the man had the potential to become much more dangerous to white America than any single individual had ever been.

Malcolm X, the *real* Malcolm X, was infinitely more remarkable than the personality presented in the *Autobiography*. The man who had been born Malcolm Little, and who had perished as El-Hajj Malik El-Shabazz, was no saint. He made many serious errors of judgment, several of which directly contributed to his murder. Yet despite these serious contradictions and personal failings, Malcolm X also possessed the unique potential for uniting Black America in any unprecedented coalition with African, Asian, and Caribbean nations. He alone could have established unity between Negro integrationists and Black nationalists inside the United States. He possessed the personal charisma, the rhetorical genius, and the moral courage to inspire and motivate millions of Blacks into unified action. Neither the *Autobiography* nor Spike Lee's 1992 movie revealed this powerful legacy of the man, or explained what he could have accomplished. What continues to be suppressed and censored also tells us something so huge about America itself, about where we were then, and where we, as a people, are now. Malcolm X was potentially a new type of world leader, personally drawn up from the "wretched of the earth," into a political stratosphere of international power. Telling that remarkable, true story is the purpose of my biography.

~

Racializing Obama

The Enigma of Post-Black Politics and Leadership

I

The historical significance of the election of Illinois Senator Barack Obama as president of the United States was recognized literally by the entire world. For a nation that had, only a half century earlier, refused to enforce the voting rights and constitutional liberties of people of African descent, to elevate a black American as its chief executive, was a stunning reversal of history. On the night of his electoral victory, spontaneous crowds of joyful celebrants rushed into streets, parks, and public establishments, in thousands of venues across the country. In Harlem, over ten thousand people surrounded the Adam Clayton Powell State Office Building, cheering and crying in disbelief. To many, the impressive margin of Obama's popular vote victory suggested the possibility that the United States had entered at long last an age of post-racial politics, in which leadership and major public policy debates would not be distorted by factors of race and ethnicity.

Obama's election almost overnight changed the negative perceptions about the routine abuses of American power that were widely held, especially across the Third World. One vivid example of the recognition of this new reality was represented by a petulant statement by Ayman al-Zawahri, the deputy leader of the Al Qaeda terrorist network. Al-Zawahri contemptuously dismissed Obama as only the "new face of America," which only "masked a heart full of hate." Al Qaeda also released a video in which former Bush Secretaries of State Colin Powell and Condoleezza Rice, both African Americans, as well as Obama, were denigrated "[in] the words of Malcolm X (may Allah have mercy on him) [as] 'house Negroes.'" Malcolm X was favorably quoted for condemning the docile "house Negro who always looked out for his master." To Al Qaeda, Obama was nothing short of a "hypocrite and traitor to his race." America "continues to be the same as ever.... "[1] Despite Obama's concerted efforts to present himself as a presidential candidate "who happened to be black," both proponents and enemies like Al Qaeda were quick to freeze his identity to the reality of his blackness, for both positive and negative reasons.

To understand the main factors that contributed to Obama's spectacular but in many ways unlikely victory, it is necessary to return to the defining "racializing moment" in recent U.S. history—the tragic debacle of the Hurricane Katrina Crisis of 2005, under the regime of President George W. Bush. It was not simply the deaths of over one thousand Americans, and the forced relocations of hundreds of thousands of people from their homes in New Orleans and across the Gulf of Mexico states-region who were disproportionately black and poor. The inevitable consequences of a natural disaster in New Orleans, a city below sea level, were not unexpected. Rather, it was the callous and contemptuous actions of the federal government—especially the Federal Emergency Management Agency (FEMA), plagued by cronyism and corruption, that directly contributed to blacks' deaths. The world witnessed on television for days the stunning spectra of thousands of mostly black and poor people stranded in New Orleans' downtown Morial Convention Center, to which FEMA's vehicles claimed it was impossible to send medical supplies, food, and fresh water, while media representatives and entertainers easily were able to drive to the center. States like Florida, that proposed to send in five hundred airboats to assist with Gulf Coast rescue efforts, were inexplicably turned away. Needed supplies such as electric generators, trailers, and freight cars stocked with food went undelivered to starving, desperate evacuees. The overwhelming collage of tragic images pointed to the enduring blight of racism and poverty as central themes within the arrangements of institutional power within the United States.[2] By mid-September, 2005, 60 percent of all African Americans surveyed were convinced that "the federal government's delay in helping the victims in New Orleans was because the victims were black." What was striking to minorities was that the overwhelming majority of white citizens remained convinced that their government was color-blind: only 12 percent of whites surveyed agreed that the government's Katrina response was racially-biased.[3]

The reality of racial injustice through governmental inaction was also reinforced among millions of black Americans by the results of the presidential elections of 2000 and 2004, both won by Republican George W. Bush. In 2000, there was substantial evidence that tens of thousands of African-American voters in Florida were deliberately excluded from exercising the franchise, through a variety of measures. Thousands of Florida voters with misdemeanor convictions, for example, were illegally barred from voting. Thousands of black voters in specific districts were inexplicably barred from casting ballots. Four years later, a similar process of black voter suppression occurred in Ohio, which Bush narrowly won over Democratic presidential candidate John Kerry.[4] To many African Americans the two controversial presidential elections and the Katrina tragedy cemented the perspective that the American system was hardwired to discriminate against the interests of people of African descent. If basic political change was possible, or even conceivable, it would probably not be through frontal assaults, similar to the bold challenges of Jesse Jackson's Rainbow Coalition presidential campaigns of 1984 and 1988. If meaningful change occurred at all, it would probably happen at the margins. Few anticipated the possibility that an African-American candidate, with relatively little experience at the national level, could capture the Democratic Party's presidential nomination, much less win election to the presidency.

II

Although the overall character of national black politics was in many respects defensive and deeply pessimistic, a growing minority trend within African-American leadership perceived the early years of the twenty-first century quite differently. For decades, prior to the early 1990s, there had been one ironclad rule in American racial politics: that the majority of white voters in any legislative municipal or Congressional district would not vote for an African-American candidate, regardless of her or his ideology or partisan affiliation. There was an omnipresent glass ceiling in electoral politics limiting the rise of all black elected officials. Blacks could be elected to Congress or as mayors of major cities only if districts held high concentrations of minority voters. In the 1980s, progressive black candidates such as Harold Washington sought to circumvent this racial barrier by constructing multiracial coalitions as the base of their electoral mobilizations, reaching out to traditional liberal constituencies.[5] Other more conservative African-American leaders, such as Thomas Bradley who had been elected mayor of Los Angeles on his second try in 1972, and Philadelphia mayor Wilson Goode in the 1980s, won whites' support by deliberately downplaying their own ethnic affiliations and racial identities. Although they espoused a pragmatic, nonideological politics that catered to local corporate interests and promoted urban concessions, even these moderate black officials could not depend on the electoral support of many whites, even in their own parties.

Political scientists first began observing the lack of reliability of pre-election polls for whites in races involving African-American candidates nearly three decades ago. In the 1982 California gubernatorial election, pre-election polls indicated that Democratic Los Angeles Mayor Thomas Bradley would easily defeat Republican challenger George Deukmejian. After Bradley narrowly lost to Deukmejian, it became evident that a significant percentage of whites who had been predicted to support Bradley had voted for the Republican.[6] This so-called "Bradley effect" was subsequently documented in dozens of elections. For example, in 1989, Virginia Lieutenant Governor Douglas Wilder, a Democrat, announced his candidacy for the state's governorship. In many ways Wilder ran a campaign similar to that of Obama, two decades later. Wilder focused on issues largely devoid of racial overtones, such as economic development, the environment, and public health. Opinion polls in the state showed Wilder maintaining a double-digit lead over a lackluster Republican candidate, Marshall Coleman. In Virginia's gubernatorial election, which Wilder managed to win, but by less than one-half of one percent of the total vote, white voters overwhelmingly had favored Coleman. Even more significantly, pollsters found that many white Virginians deliberately provided false information when revealing their voting intentions in polls. When whites were questioned about their gubernatorial preferences by a white pollster, Coleman defeated Wilder by 16 percent. But when black pollsters were used for interviews, whites favored Wilder by 10 percent over Coleman. Both the inconsistent pre-election polling information by whites and the actual election returns appear to validate the "Bradley effect."[7]

The cases of Bradley and Wilder were in many ways mirrored by the 1989 mayoral election in New York City, which was won by an African-American Democrat, Manhattan Borough President David Dinkins. As noted by Andrew Kohut, the president of the Pew Research Center, the Gallup organization's polling research on New York City's voters in 1989 had indicated that Dinkins would defeat his Republican opponent, Rudolph Giuliani, by 15 percent. Instead, Dinkins only narrowly won by 2 percent. Kohut, who worked as a Gallup pollster in that election, concluded that "poorer, less well-educated [white] voters were less likely to answer our questions," so the poll didn't have the opportunity to factor in their views. As Kohut observed: "Here's the problem—these whites who do not respond to surveys tend to have a more unfavorable view of blacks than respondents who do the interviews."[8]

By the twenty-first century, hundreds of race-neutral, pragmatic black officials had emerged, winning positions on city councils, state legislatures, and in the House of Representatives. Frequently they distanced themselves from traditional liberal constituencies such as unions, promoted gentrification and corporate investment in poor urban neighborhoods, and favored funding charter schools as an alternative to the failures of public school systems. A growing share of these new leaders were elected from predominantly white districts. In 2001, for example, according to the Joint Center for Political and Economic Studies, roughly 16 percent of the nation's African-American state legislators had won election in predominantly white districts. By 2008, out of 622 black state legislators nationally, 30 percent represented predominantly white constituencies. Between 1998 and 2008, about two hundred African Americans defeated whites for municipal and state legislative races, even in some states, such as Iowa, Minnesota, and New Hampshire, where black populations are small.[9] In November 2006, civil rights attorney Deval Patrick, employing campaign strategies drawn from Barack Obama's successful 2004 Senate bid, easily won the gubernatorial race in Massachusetts, a state with a 79 percent white population.[10]

Ideologically, this new leadership group reflected a range of divergent views on social policy. The most prominent "moderates" within this cohort included: former Tennessee Congressman Harold Ford, who is currently leader of the centrist Democratic Leadership Council; and Newark, New Jersey, Mayor Corey Booker. More ideologically "liberal" leaders in this group are: Barack Obama; New York Governor David Patterson; and Massachusetts Governor Deval Patrick. This is not to suggest that these politicians possess no strong ethnic roots or identity. All of these individuals are proudly self-identified as African Americans. But strategically, none of them pursue what could be called race-based politics. None favor or would support a Black Agenda similar to that espoused by the March 1972, Gary, Indiana, Black Political Convention. Most probably would perceive even Jesse Jackson's Rainbow Coalition campaigns of the 1980s as too narrowly race- and ethnically based, and too far to the left on economic policy.

Obama undoubtedly took most of these factors into account—the possibility of a "Bradley-Wilder effect" on whites' support of black candidates, African-American grievances surrounding the 2000 and 2004 presidential campaigns, the recent debacle of the Katrina Crisis, and the rise of the postracial politics of a new generation of black leaders—to construct his own image and political narrative essential for a presidential campaign. Early on in their deliberation process, the Obama pre-campaign group recognized that most white Americans would never vote for a black presidential candidate. However, they were convinced that most whites would embrace, and vote for, a remarkable, qualified presidential candidate who happened to be black. "Race" could be muted into an adjective, a qualifier of minimal consequence. So ethnically, Obama did not deny the reality of his African heritage; it was blended into the multicultural narrative of his uniquely "American story," which also featured white grandparents from Kansas, a white mother who studied anthropology in Hawaii, and an Indonesian stepfather. Unlike black conservatives, Obama openly acknowledged his personal debt to the sacrifices made by martyrs and activists of the Civil Rights Movement. Yet he also spoke frequently about the need to move beyond the divisions of the sixties, to seek common ground, and a post-partisan politics of hope and reconciliation. As the Obama campaign took shape in late 2006–early 2007, the basic strategic line about "race," therefore, was to deny its enduring presence or relevance to contemporary politics. Volunteers often chanted, in Hare Krishna–fashion, "Race Doesn't Matter! Race Doesn't Matter!," as if to ward off the evil spirits of America's troubled past.

Obama's strategic approach on race was indeed original, but coming at a time of hopelessness and pessimism among many African Americans, there were doubts that the young Illinois Senator could actually pull it off. To some, Obama's multiracial pedigree raised questions about his loyalties to the cause of black people. Curiously, many of those with the loudest queries were African-American conservatives and Republicans, whose own bona fides on racial matters were often under fire. For example, conservative writer Debra Dickerson, author of *The End of Blackness,* declared in January 2007, that "Obama would be the great black hope in the next presidential race, if he were actually black."[11] Journalist Stanley Crouch took a similarly negative approach, arguing that while Obama "has experienced some light versions of typical racial stereotypes, he cannot claim those problems as his own—nor has he lived the life of a black American."[12] Juan Williams, conservative commentator on FOX News, warned that "there are widespread questions whether this son of a white American mother and a black Kenyan father really understands the black American experience."[13]

As late as December 2007, roughly one-half of all African Americans polled still favored Hillary Clinton over Obama as their Democratic presidential candidate. Some of Obama's sharpest "racial doubters" were even from Chicago, his home base. Eddie Read, chair of Chicago's Black Independent Political Organization, for example, predicted that "nothing's going to happen" from the Democratic Senator's candidacy, because "he doesn't belong to us. He would not be the black president. He would be the multicultural president."[14]

Obama's ultimate victory over Hillary Clinton in the 2008 Democratic primaries began with his implacable opposition to the U.S. invasion of Iraq. Back in 2002,

Obama warned that "an invasion of Iraq without a clear rationale and without strong international support will only fan the flames of the Middle East, and encourage the worst, rather than the best, impulses of the world, and strengthen the recruitment arm of al-Qaeda." Less noticed in this speech was Obama's appeal "to make sure our so-called allies in the Middle East, the Saudis and the Egyptians, stop oppressing dissent, and tolerating corruption and inequality, and mismanaging their economies so that their youth grow up without education, without prospects, without hope, the ready recruits of terrorist cells."[15] Like Malcolm X a generation earlier, Barack Obama's entry into national politics was associated with the Islamic world.

Even before the announcement of his candidacy for president, media conservatives resorted to Islamophobia to denigrate Obama. For example, on CNN's "Situation Room," on December 11, 2006, correspondent Jeanne Moos observed darkly, "Only one little consonant differentiates" Obama versus Osama, also noting that the candidate's middle name, Hussein, was shared with "a former dictator." In early 2007, Bernard McQuirk, then the executive producer of the Don Imus Radio Show, declared on air that Obama has "a Jew-hating name." Conservative radio commentator Rush Limbaugh repeatedly referred to the candidate as "Osama Obama."[16]

Religious bigotry and intolerance, even more than traditional racism, was the decisive weapon to delegitimate Obama. The January 17, 2007, issue of *Insight* magazine, for example, claimed that Obama "spent at least four years in a so-called madrassa, or Muslim seminary, in Indonesia." Writing in the *Chicago Sun-Times,* columnist Mark Steyn then claimed that Obama "graduated from the Sword of the Infidel grade school in Jakarta."[17] On FOX News, former liberal-turned-reactionary Juan Williams argued that Obama "comes from a father who was a Muslim and all that…. Given that we're at war with Muslim extremists, that presents a problem."[18] The truth of Obama's background was that his biological father, while being raised as a Muslim, was an atheist like Obama's mother. Obama's stepfather was not deeply religious. The two elementary schools Obama attended, one Catholic, the other predominantly Muslim, were not madrassas. In 2007, CNN correspondent John Vause traveled to Indonesia, investigated the charges, and established the truth about Obama's religious and family background. Yet despite this, the "madrassa myth" linking Obama to Islamic terrorist cells continued to be promoted on television and especially over the internet.[19]

As the Democratic caucuses and primaries began, however, Obama quickly established the ability to win a surprisingly large share of whites' votes. He consistently won majorities among all voters under 30, voters earning over $50,000 annually, and college-educated voters. After the South Carolina Democratic primary, where Bill Clinton's racially insensitive remarks alienated thousands of voters, the African-American electorate swung decisively behind Obama.

The most damaging controversy involving race to erupt during Obama's quest for the Democratic presidential nomination involved the politics of faith: the media's rebroadcasting of provocative statements by the candidate's former minister, the Reverend Jeremiah Wright, of Chicago's Trinity United Church of Christ. A major center for social justice ministry in Chicago, Trinity's activist program was not unlike that of other progressive African-American churches involved in the Civil Rights Movement in the 1960s, or the anti-apartheid campaign against white South Africa during the 1980s. Yet even before the controversial videos of the Reverend Wright's speeches surfaced, some white conservatives had attempted to equate Trinity Church's theological teachings with the black separatism of the Nation of Islam. [20]

Obama's response to the Reverend Wright politics of faith controversy was a masterful address, "A More Perfect Union," delivered in Philadelphia's Constitution Center on March 18, 2008. Obama began by reminding his audience that American democracy was "unfinished" at its founding in 1787, due to "this nation's original sin of slavery." Obama declared that despite his rather unusual personal history and mixed ethnic background, "seared into my genetic makeup [is] the idea that this nation is more than the sum of its parts —that out of many, we are truly one."[21]

Obama's great strength is his ability to discuss controversial and complex issues in a manner that conveys the seeking of consensus, or common ground. His Philadelphia address reminded white Americans that "so many of the disparities that exist in the African-American community today can be directly traced to inequalities passed on from an earlier generation that suffered under the brutal legacy of slavery" and Jim Crow segregation. But he also acknowledged the anger and alienation of poor and working-class whites, people who do not live especially privileged lives, who feel unfairly victimized by policies like affirmative action. Obama criticized Reverend Wright's statements as "not only wrong but divisive, at a time when we need unity; racially charged at a time when we need to come together to solve a set of monumental problems ... that are neither black or white or Latino or Asian, but rather problems that confront us all."[22]

Another astute dimension of Obama's "A More Perfect Union" speech was his repeated referencing of U.S. racial history, while simultaneously refusing to be defined or restricted by that history. For blacks, Obama asserted, the path forward "means embracing the burdens of our past without becoming victims of our past ... it means binding our particular grievances—for better health care, and better schools, and better jobs—to the larger aspirations of all Americans."[23] In the context of electoral politics and public policy, Obama's argument makes perfect sense. In America's major cities, for example, there's no explicitly "Latino strategy" for improving public transportation, or a purely "African-American strategy" to improve public health care. Obama did not deny that racial disparities in health care, education, employment, and other areas no longer existed. But by emphasizing a "politics of hope," he implied that any real solutions must depend on building multiracial, multiclass coalitions that could fight to achieve change.

Although Obama finally secured his party's presidential nomination, religious and racial stereotypes and intolerance were again deployed by many opponents to derail his campaign. In mid-September 2008, for example, a Pew Research Center survey revealed that millions of Americans held grossly erroneous views about Obama's religious and ethnic background. Despite the extensive news coverage earlier in the year concerning the Reverend Wright controversy, and Obama's repeated affirmations about his deeply held Christian beliefs, only one-half of all Americans believed the

Democratic candidate was a Christian. Thirteen percent stated that Obama was a "Muslim," and another 16 percent claimed they "aren't sure about his religion because they've heard 'different things' about it." On a number of fundamentalist Christian radio stations, and conservative Christian websites, Obama has been described as the possible "Anti-Christ." As journalist Nicholas D. Kristof observed, "Religious prejudice is becoming a proxy for racial prejudice. In the public at least, it's not acceptable to express reservations about a candidate's skin color, so discomfort about race is sublimated into concerns about whether Mr. Obama is sufficiently Christian."[24]

What animated the fear and loathing of Obama by some terrified whites was also the recognition that America is fundamentally changing ethnically and racially. Demographically, the white majority population is rapidly vanishing. Latinos, blacks, Asians, and Native Americans combined will outnumber Americans of European descent by 2042, earlier than predicted. By 2050, racialized groups will account for 54 percent. Already, in cities like New York, Chicago, Los Angeles, and Atlanta, whites have been a "minority group" for years, but they still have exercised decisive power, especially in government and economically. So the emergence and election of a racial minority candidate like Obama was inevitable. A majority of white Americans now recognize that the traditional racial project of "white supremacy" is no longer sustainable, or even in the best interests of the nation. Nevertheless, a significant minority of whites are still dedicated proponents of both racialization and religious intolerance as central tools in the continuing perpetuation of a racist America.

III

On November 4, 2008, the U.S. electorate made its decision by electing Barack Obama its first African-American president, by a popular vote margin of 52 percent. Obama's victory rested in part on nearly unanimous (95 percent) support provided by African Americans, who voted in record numbers. Almost as impressive, however, was the broad, multiethnic, multiclass coalition the Obama forces were able to construct from Jewish voters (78 percent), Latinos (67 percent), young voters age 18–29 (62 percent), and women voters (58 percent). Obama's victory sparked hundreds, perhaps even thousands, of spontaneous street demonstrations involving millions of celebrants across the nation.

Although Obama's core constituencies provided him with the essential foundations of his triumph, equally essential was his ability to attract millions of moderate Republicans and independents, many of whom had voted for George W. Bush in 2000 and/or 2004. Throughout the 2008 campaign Obama explicitly refused to attack the Republican Party per se, focusing his criticisms either on his presidential opponent John McCain, or against the extremist right wing of the party. Obama's campaign had astutely recognized the partisan shift in voter attitudes that had taken place in the wake of disasters such as the Katrina Hurricane and the Iraq War. Obama's post-black, race-neutral rhetoric reassured millions of whites to vote for a "black candidate."

For example, according to the Pew Center for the People and the Press, in 2004, one-third of all registered voters (33 percent) identified themselves with the Republican Party, compared to 35 percent of registered voters favoring Democrats, and 32 percent claiming to be independents. In 2004, Republicans trailed Democrats in their support from 18 to 29 year olds, but only by 4 percent (29 vs. 33 percent). Republicans won pluralities over Democrats among all white registered voters (38 vs. 30 percent), voters with BA and BS degrees (38 vs. 30 percent), voters earning more than $75,000 annually (40 vs. 29 percent), white Southerners (43 vs. 28 percent), white Protestant voters (44 vs. 27 percent), and a clear majority among white evangelical Christian voters (53 vs. 22 percent).[25]

Four years later, just prior to the Democratic National Convention, the Pew Center conducted a similar national survey of registered voters and found major gains made by the Democrats in many important voter identifications. One major shift occurred among youth voters age 18–29, who favored Democrats over Republicans (37 vs. 23 percent), with another 40 percent identifying themselves as independents. Republican support in union households fell slightly, from 26 percent in 2004 to only 20 percent in 2008. Hispanics, who in 2004 had favored Democrats over Republicans, but only by a 44 vs. 23 percent margin, had become more partisanly Democratic (48 vs. 19 percent). But what was perhaps most striking was the growing defection of the intelligentsia and educated class from the Republicans. The 2008 Pew survey indicated that registered college graduates, who vote generally at rates above 80 percent, favored Democrats over Republicans (34 vs. 29 percent). For registered voters with post-graduate and professional degrees the partisan bias toward Democrats was even wider (38 vs. 26 percent, with 36 percent independents).[26]

The 2008 Pew survey also made clear that the United States, in terms of its political culture and civic ideology, had become a "center-left nation," rather than a "right-center nation," as it had been under Ronald Reagan. Sixty-seven percent of registered voters surveyed about their views on affirmative action favored such policies that had been "designed to help blacks, women, and other minorities get better jobs and education." Sixty-one percent agreed that the U.S. government should guarantee "health insurance for all citizens, even if it means raising taxes." A majority of registered voters believe that abortion should either be "legal in all cases" (18 percent), or "legal in most cases" (38 percent). Over 70 percent of those surveyed believe "global warming" is either a "very serious" or "somewhat serious problem." And over 80 percent favored "increasing federal funding for research on wind, solar and hydrogen technology."[27] This was a rationale for long-overdue governmental action, along the lines proposed by Obama, not laissez faire and the Reaganite mantra of "government-is-the-problem."

On nearly every college campus by the early fall, it became overwhelmingly clear that Obama had won the enthusiastic support of both students and faculty. In a comprehensive national survey of over 43,000 undergraduates conducted by CBS News, UWIRE and the Chronicle of Higher Education in October 2008, the Obama-Biden ticket received 64 percent vs. 32 percent for McCain-Palin. When asked to describe their "feelings about your candidate," 55 percent of the Obamabackers "enthusiastically" supported him, compared to only 30 percent of McCain's supporters. By significant margins, college students described Obama as "someone you can relate to" (64 percent), would "bring about real change in Washington" (70 percent), and "cares about the needs and problems of people like yourself" (78 percent).[28]

Although nearly one-half (48 percent) of all students surveyed had never voted in a presidential election, a significant percentage of them had become involved in one of the national campaigns, primarily through the internet. Twenty-three percent surveyed had "signed up" to be a candidate's fan on a social networking site"; 28 percent had "visited a candidate's Facebook or MySpace page"; 65 percent had browsed a candidate's official website; and 68 percent had seen a video of their favorite presidential candidate on "You Tube." Small numbers had participated in more traditional ways. Thirteen percent had volunteered to help their candidate by canvassing or by doing voter registration. Nearly one-fourth had personally attended a rally featuring their candidate, with another 31 percent recruiting friends to join their campaign.[29]

It was the conservative British newsmagazine, *The Economist,* that identified the critical "brain gap" that contributed to McCain's electoral downfall. "Barack Obama won college graduates by two points, a group George Bush won by six points four years ago," the publication noted. "He won voters with postgraduate degrees by 18 points." *The Economist* observed that Obama even carried by six points households above $200,000 annually. McCain's core constituency, by contrast, was "among uneducated voters in Appalachia and the South." In the view of *The Economist,* "the Republicans lost the battle of ideas even more comprehensively than they lost the battle for educated votes, marching into the election armed with nothing more than slogans."[30]

On the issue of racialization, the most underreported story connected with Barack Obama's presidential victory has been the disturbing spike in racial hate crimes across the U.S. On November 25, 2008, representatives of seven major civil rights groups met with the media presenting evidence of hundreds of racist incidents and hate crimes leading up to, and following, the election of Obama. These include a cross burning on the lawn of one New Jersey family, and the random beating of an African-American man on Staten Island by white teenagers, who cursed him with racial epithets and "Obama." The groups involved—the Leadership Conference on Civil Rights, the National Council of La Raza, the Asian American Justice Center, the National Urban League, the National Association for the Advancement of Colored People, the Anti-Defamation League, and the Mexican American Legal Defense and Education Fund—all condemned the recent hate crimes.

"At a time when we as a nation are celebrating our demonstrated diversity" with Obama's election, NAACP Washington D.C. Bureau Director Hilary Shelton stated, "there are unfortunately those who are still living in the past filled hatred, fear and division." Marc Morial, National Urban League Director, called upon the Justice Department to "become more aggressive in prosecuting hate crimes.... As a country, we've come a long way, but there is still more change needed."

What can be anticipated from an Obama administration, especially as it relates to the Middle East, and more broadly the Islamic world? From his major speeches on international policy, Obama deeply believes in the nationalistic, world supremacist mission of the United States. In his speech, "The American Moment," delivered at the Chicago Council of Global Affairs on April 23, 2007, Obama declared that "the magical place called America" was still "the last, best hope on Earth." He "reject[ed] the notion that the American moment had passed." The most disturbing line of Obama's address was his assertion that the U.S. had the right to launch unilateral and preemptive attacks on foreign countries, a position not unlike that of Bush and Cheney. "No president should ever hesitate to use force—unilaterally if necessary to protect ourselves and our vital interests when we are attacked or imminently threatened," Obama stated. "We must also consider using military force in circumstances beyond self-defense," Obama also argued, "in order to provide for the common security that underpins global security...."[31] This is a geopolitical worldview that directly challenges the interests of both the Third World and most Islamic nations.

In fairness, Obama never claimed to be an ideologue of the Left. He promised a post-partisan government and a leadership style that incorporated the views of conservatives and liberals alike. This political pragmatism, which is also reflected in the new, post-racial black leadership Obama represents, is a rejection of radical change, in favor of incremental reform. As Obama explained in 2006: "Since the founding the American political tradition has been reformist, not revolutionary. What that means is that for a political leader to get things done, he or she should ideally be ahead of the curve, but not too far ahead."[32] Malcolm X at the end of his life sought to overturn capitalism, not to reform it; Obama apparently seeks to achieve Keynesian changes but within our existing, market-dominated political economy.

Such criticisms in no way are intended to minimize the significance of Obama's victory, and the continuing importance of electoral politics, voting, and using all the tools of electoralism for oppressed people in the United States. The Obama victory will be of great assistance in waging the struggle for racial justice. But electoral politics is not a substitute for social protest organizing in neighborhoods and in the streets.

A new, anti-racist leadership must be constructed to the left of the Obama government, that draws upon representatives of the most oppressed and marginalized social groups within our communities: former prisoners, women activists in community-based, civic organizations, youth groups, from homeless coalitions, and the like. Change must occur not from the top down, as some Obama proponents would have it, but from the bottom up. The growing class stratification within African-American and Latino communities has produced an opportunistic, middle-class leadership elite that in many important ways is out of touch with dire problems generated by poverty, unemployment, and mass incarceration. We must reconnect the construction of leadership by addressing and solving real-world problems of racialization that challenge everyday people's daily lives. The Obama victory has the potential for creating a positive environment for achieving dramatic reforms within public policy, improving the conditions for the truly disadvantaged—but only if it is pressured to do so. Obama may be successful in standing outside the processes of racialization, but for millions of minorities, race and class inequality continue to define their lives, and only collective resistance will lead to their empowerment.

SECTION VI

*On Building a Social
Justice Movement*

Socialist Vision and Political Struggle for the 1990s

The American left seemingly stands at the margins of a whirlwind of social change, which we are witnessing throughout the world but particularly in Eastern Europe. There is a general rethinking of both Marxism and the model of Communist political and economic development derived from the writings of Lenin but radically reshaped and corrupted by Stalin and his political descendants. What does this mean in the United States, where the organized left seems at best marginal to the processes of political discourse and social change? To be taken seriously as a political force within any society, we must first take ourselves seriously. That is, despite our apparent marginality, there are mass popular constituencies that have the potential for challenging the corporate and political establishment in the 1990s. We must also rethink our commitment to the egalitarian social vision we call socialism, and find ways to articulate this perspective into specific political activities and programs in the coming decade. We must transcend the staleness of liberalism and put forward an aggressive program of democratic social change that can build the foundation of a socialist future.

We must begin by rethinking the political history of the Left in our century. The recent crisis in Marxism was prefigured by another crisis experienced by socialist parties in Europe nearly a century ago. The theoretical writings of both Marx and Engels had given the German Social Democratic party, as well as other socialist political organizations belonging to the International, a rigorous and convincing critique of the capitalist political economy. Their writings explained that the fundamental developments throughout human history were linked to class struggles, and that the task of socialists was to build a movement capable of expropriating the expropriators. Engels's works in particular drew analogies to biological evolution within natural science as depicted by Darwin. With the social evolution of human societies, human history was perceived as a progressive march from primitive societies, to feudalism, capitalism, socialism, and ultimately, communism. If the popularized version of Marxism was overly mechanistic, greatly simplifying the social contradictions within late nineteenth-century capitalism, at least it provided an analysis of the basic inequalities of daily life with which both radical intellectuals and workers could agree. By the end of the century, millions of workers from St. Petersburg to London had embraced the radical social vision of Marx. For Marx, this vision was profoundly democratic and egalitarian. Social equality and social justice could not be achieved without the abolition of classes and the democratic emancipation of workers.

The weaknesses of Marxism as a political strategy did not become apparent until the mid-1890s, with the tremendous growth of the European working-class movement. What was the appropriate strategy for achieving power within a capitalist democratic system? As we know, a gradualist approach was advanced by Eduard Bernstein and a radical strategy of class confrontation by Rosa Luxemburg of the Left. A gradualist reformist perspective eventually crystallized in the politics of European social democracy as a whole after World War I—emphasis on class collaboration rather than confrontation, advocacy of social welfare reforms that did not threaten the general hegemony of capital over labor, scrupulous adherence to electoral norms and legal procedures, and a disavowal of violent revolution.

Lenin's great accomplishment was to invigorate Marxism as a political strategy for power. He was consumed with the development of a disciplined party that would have the capacity to withstand the assaults of a hostile autocratic state and suffer mass arrests and repression while still gaining strength within the Russian working class. Instead of a broadly diverse, mass-based party, Lenin called for a tightly knit vanguard, a revolutionary elite drawn from the radicalized intelligentsia and the working class. Lenin thought that the proletariat, by itself, could scarcely go further than a trade union political consciousness, and that a highly centralized, disciplined force was essential to achieve a revolution.

Lenin's vanguard party was capable of achieving complete state power in Russia, something no social democratic formation had been able to do. There was nothing in Lenin's writings prior to 1917 to indicate that a postrevolutionary social state would have to be based on the domination of a single political party. But by 1924, the dictatorship of the proletariat had become the dictatorship of the party. By the period of Stalin's forced collectivizations in the Russian countryside, the dictatorship of the party had degenerated still further. Dissent and genuine debate within the vanguard party were impossible. The government became secondary to the ruling party; the judiciary and criminal justice system became instruments to impose the will of the party's privileged officials. Trade unions and other mass organizations degenerated. Artistic life, culture, education, and civic institutions became distorted, mirroring the narrow prerogatives of the state bureaucracy, the new ruling class. The special demands and problems of ethnic, religious, and national minorities were suppressed and their leaders eliminated or imprisoned. Revolutionary Marxists have attempted for decades to separate the political legacies of Leninism and Stalinism but only with partial success. Unquestionably, Lenin himself was profoundly democratic, and the procedure of democratic centrism permitted dissidents on important issues to express themselves without fear of retaliation. But the political practice of communism, so heavily linked to the authoritarian and repressive policies of Stalin and later Mao, still creates major difficulties for Marxists.

When American or European working people now hear the terms communism or Marxism, most may immediately think of the Berlin Wall and the hundreds of citizens from the German Democratic Republic who for years desperately attempted to escape to what they perceived to be "freedom." They may think of the policies of anti-Semitism and the suppression of national minorities; the long lines of consumers waiting for rationed goods and produce; the perks and privileges of the Communist bureaucrats who lived luxuriously at the expense of the deprived proletariat. Even more ominously, they may recall the mountain of corpses that was the chief legacy of the Pol Pot regime in Cambodia; or the victims of the Marxist-Leninist dictatorship of Menguistu in Ethiopia; or perhaps the brutal use of force sanctioned by Finance Minister Bernard Coard against Prime Minister Maurice Bishop and the popular leadership of the New Jewel Movement, which helped trigger the illegal U.S. invasion of Grenada in 1983. For all the accomplishments of regimes that call themselves Marxist-Leninist or socialist—including universal education, the improvement of health care, housing and social welfare, employment and rural development—the crimes are just as real, massive, and inescapable. The actual historical record tells us that there is nothing uniformly progressive about the historical transition from capitalism to socialism. Postcapitalist social formations can be progressive and liberating and provide a sense of empowerment to the most oppressed classes. Amilcar Cabral and Walter Rodney, to cite just two examples, were revolutionary socialists who expressed profound respect and love of humanity, a deep commitment to democratic decision-making procedures, and an opposition to narrow, dogmatic, or mechanistic applications of Marxism to their respective societies or to others. Yet many other postrevolutionary societies consolidate a type of socialism from above, negating democratic procedures and fostering the development of new social hierarchies, a state bourgeoisie which draws its authority and privileges from its monopoly of the state apparatus.

In Eastern Europe today, we are witnessing the results of the attempt to impose a dogmatic, authoritarian form of state collectivism from above. The dramatic street demonstrations and confrontations in Prague and East Berlin in the autumn of 1989 were reminiscent of the popular uprisings in 1848, when the democratic impulse confronted other conservative, autocratic regimes. These governments have been forced to liquidate the constitutional provisions for the vanguard position of the Communist party in politics, and have sanctioned the creation of opposition parties. The social upheavals in Eastern Europe illustrate the final collapse of the viability of the Stalinist model of social and political transformation. A highly centralized political formation that consists of an upper caste of privileged, powerful leaders and a lower caste of uninformed, politically semiliterate cadres, backed by the power of the military, cannot build a socialist society with democratic principles and practices. The one-party Stalinist state has inevitably degenerated into a type of authoritarian state contemptuous of civil liberties and legal due process, hostile to the existence of genuinely independent mass associations such as trade unions and farmers' organizations, censuring or expelling cadres or party officials who question or deviate from the decisions of the central committee. This form of socialism is being repudiated by the forces of history.

Despite the obvious political differences, there remain fundamental parallels between social democracy and communism as forms of socialism from above. Both have promoted extensive social engineering. The social democrats elevate into office technocrats and apolitical professionals who have little direct contact or sympathy with workers. Both have historically repudiated socialist principles in favor of power. For the social democrats to win elections within political cultures and social systems deeply rooted in individualism, materialism, and the primacy of private interests above the common welfare, they have generally jettisoned their theoretical beliefs to curry favor within the middle classes in order to get votes. From the German Social Democratic party of the early 1900s to Michael Manley's People's National party of Jamaica today, social democrats have rejected their own modest socialist agendas and moved to the right once in office. At best, these parties degenerate into a form of liberal social welfarism, guaranteeing the continuation of the capitalist market system and most of the inequities of poverty, racism, and class exploitation that exist within these social systems. Finally, like the Stalinists, many social democrats are also capable of gross violations of civil liberties and human rights, particularly against the Marxist left. One can begin with the murder of Rosa Luxemburg during the social democratic regime in postwar Germany in 1919, and continue through the murder of Walter Rodney by the agents of social democratic dictator Forbes Burnham in Guyana in 1980.

Many conservative commentators have used the events in Eastern Europe to argue that the struggle between capitalism and socialism is over, and that capitalism has won. To be sure, the Communist states are in crisis. Yet Western capitalism and imperialism are also in crisis. Capitalist social formations still experience periodic economic crisis, expressed in cycles of expansion and recession. Capitalism is a social system that creates vast disparities of wealth and privilege between those classes who own the means of production, finance, and real estate versus those who depend upon their own labor power for survival. Capitalism is still responsible for the perpetuation of racism and ethnic violence, which fractures the potential for political solidarity within workers' movements. It employs sexism to profit from the reduced wages of women in the labor force. Capitalism fosters social inequality, poverty, health-related problems, and depends on the severe exploitation of people of people of color in underdeveloped societies. As Malcolm X observed a quarter century ago: "You can't have capitalism without racism. And if you find [antiracists] usually they're socialists or their political philosophy is socialism."

Capitalist societies that are characterized by democratic elective institutions have capitalist democracy, but not genuine democracy. A genuine democracy must be identified with the elimination of class exploitation and social oppression, and the elimination of poverty, social insecurity, racism, substandard health care, and unemployment. Effective political democracy is impossible without social justice and economic equality.

Some American Communists recently have suggested that we must take from the best of both the Leninist political tradition, particularly its sharp critique of imperialism and its emphasis on political strategy, and the best of the political tradition of social democracy, such as its respect for political pluralism and civil liberties and its tolerance for diversity within the party. The argument suggests that the division of the international socialist movement after World War I and the Russian Revolution could be bridged. Already, the Hungarian and Italian Communist parties are changing their names and may soon become members of the Socialist International. But it would be a mistake to embrace a synthesis of both versions of socialism from above. We need to transcend the contradictions of both Communism and social democracy, and articulate a radical democratic vision of socialism which speaks a language that can be readily understood by the oppressed. Instead of socialism from above, we need socialism from below.

The approach of socialism from below would emphasize the necessity to develop networks of locally based progressive formations, organizations engaged in antiracist, feminist, trade union, peace, environmental, gay/lesbian rights, and/or other progressive sectors. Here the Left can play a decisive role of a social catalyst, helping to chart a new social contract to help American people to redefine the relationship between themselves and the capitalist state. What do we have a right to expect from the government? Military expenditures, which have soared to $305 billion in 1990, are destructive to the development of communities; they increase unemployment and undermine reforms in education, health care, and housing. We must establish a nonsectarian public identity to the left of traditional liberals, and call for structural change to address society's real problems. We must advocate certain socioeconomic prerequisites for full participation in a democracy, such as the human right to a job or guaranteed income, the human right not to starve in a land of agricultural abundance, the human right to clean, affordable housing, the human right to free public medical and dental care for all, the right to check the ability of corporations and businesses to move from our cities, the human right to quality public education. As socialists we need to state clearly that while capitalism promotes the unequal distribution of income, we favor programs that reverse the concentration of wealth and privileges within one social class. We must declare that environmental decisions should not be by-products of the capitalists' profit motive, but that the state must set tough and progressive goals to maintain and preserve natural resources. We must state that health and safety standards can't be held hostage to the profit imperatives of the corporations. We must insist unequivocally that the battle for racial justice is being lost; that all Americans lose when Blacks' median incomes are barely 55 percent those of whites or when Black unemployment remains above 13 percent nationally. We need to make the fundamental link between crime and poverty. In Chicago today, five out of six Black males, age 16–19 and active in the labor force, are unemployed. Black unemployment for males 20–24 years of age in Chicago is 50 percent. The real median incomes of almost all Blacks (except professionals and managers) have fallen sharply since 1979, relative to whites' incomes. Poverty and unemployment contribute to the growth of crime and drugs. There are currently 674 thousand men and women in federal and state penal institutions. The answers are not more police, prison construction, and the application of the death penalty. The termination of urban crime and drugs will come about only with the social and economic development of central cities, a domestic plan for reconstruction which can be financed by the cancellation of billions of dollars from the military budget and the allocation of funds to local groups. The Left must be in the forefront in advancing a national budget for social development and economic conversion.

The Left must continue to support the democratic struggles in El Salvador, Nicaragua, Namibia, and other Third World societies. It is in the Third World that U.S. imperialism and its agents have generated the greatest crisis. In Latin America, the Caribbean, and Africa, free-market economics has produced famine, unemployment, extreme class stratification, and social crisis. There's no triumph of capitalism in Central America, with the continuing democratic struggles of workers and peasants against the agents of foreign domination. The Left must be in the lead in the continuing struggle to overthrow the racist state of apartheid South Africa.

The Left needs to rethink its position on domestic civil rights issues, such as affirmative action. In 1989, in a series of Supreme Court decisions, affirmative action was virtually gutted. Part of this process of retrenchment can be attributed indirectly to our failure to counter the deliberate misinformation campaign of corporations and the political establishment about affirmative action. There's the popular misconception that "unqualified" women, Blacks, and Latinos were unfairly advancing at the expense of qualified candidates, who were only coincidentally white males. We were afraid to call specifically for "positive quotas," and fell back on vague formulations of nonbinding "goals and timetable," which were gradually eroded and not implemented in many institutions. The corporations now openly harass and punish workers who bring discrimination suits; legally, they have successfully attacked the entire issue of the social fairness of affirmative action by projecting the volatile concept of "reverse discrimination." The strategy of the Right is directly linked to the economic interests of the ruling class: racism and sexism are profitable. Women represent 44 percent of the labor force and receive only two-thirds of males' salaries. The median annual income of Black Americans is barely $19 thousand. We must argue that effective affirmative action never took place, because it was always underfunded and enforcement was fragmentary at best. The Left must no longer back away from the need for "positive quotas" for women and people of color within the labor force. We need to advocate federal mortgage subsidies for citizens who buy homes in racially integrated or predominantly minority communities. We should advocate the expansion of the Humphrey-Hawkins Act and the revival of the political demand for a bill guaranteeing the right to work to all who want a job and a guaranteed income for the disabled or those unable to work. Such demands should be coordinated with progressive leadership in the civil rights, feminist, and labor movements. The Left must be in the leadership in antiracist and feminist struggles.

The Left has to break from its fascination with tailending American liberalism in general and the Democratic party in particular. We need an inside-outside approach to electoral politics: a strategy that supports liberal and progressive Democrats when they run against conservatives, but develops the capacity to contest elections as independents whenever possible or feasible. If there is no fundamental difference in the politics of Republican and Democratic candidates, especially in local and state elections, we need to seriously consider working with other progressive constituencies to run candidates. But it would be dangerous to allocate most of our resources to electoral politics in the short run; in the next three to four years, the Left needs to develop a political network and structures that promote democratic resistance and socioeconomic struggle primarily at the local level. Despite Jesse Jackson and the Rainbow Coalition, the Democratic party of its own accord will never become a socialist or left social democratic party—the trend of the 1980s, if anything, illustrates that the bulk of the Democratic party is moving to the Right.

The Left must encourage constructive dialogue and ideological exchange within its own ranks, and encourage broad unity whenever possible, from Marxist-Leninists to non-Marxist socialists. We need to learn from the insights of nonsocialist activists in various social reform, environmentalist, and religious organizations in our efforts to reach broader constituencies. American socialists must cultivate a new radical identity, clearly distinct from the failed examples of Stalinism and social democracy; an identity that associates socialism with the values of social justice, pluralism, militant egalitarianism, and freedom. We have permitted the Right in this country to expropriate and distort the symbols of democratic struggle, especially the theme of human freedom. But given the rich heritage of the Afro-American liberation struggle, we should have no ambiguity about the positive and constructive value of the concept "freedom." Freedom does not have to be defined as free markets, or the freedom of the corporations to raise prices and lay off workers. Freedom can be projected as the freedom from hunger, poverty, illiteracy, unemployment, and police brutality. Freedom can be the right to think in radical ways, to call for a complete democratic social and political reconstruction of the existing social order. Freedom is essential to the struggles both to achieve and to build a democratic socialist society. As Rosa Luxemburg reminded us:

> Without general elections, without unrestricted freedom of press and assembly, without a free struggle of opinion, life dies out in every public institution, becomes a mere semblance of life, in which only the bureaucracy remains the active element ... Freedom only for the supporters of the government, only for the members of one party, however numerous they may be, is no freedom at all. Freedom is always and exclusively freedom for the one who thinks differently.

We must not fail to criticize any government or party, especially of the Left, that sanctions censorship, political imprisonment, or the violation of human rights.

Perhaps the greatest potential illusion of the American left is the belief that key elements of the socialist vision can be achieved without confrontations, conflict, or class struggle. Nothing in the social histories of oppressed people validates this gradualist perspective. The experiences of the Black freedom movement, for example, tell us that the capitalist democratic state will employ any extralegal methods including wiretapping, surveillance, income tax audits, job harassment, and even assassination. Consider the murders of Black Panther leaders Fred Hampton and Mark Clark in Chicago. If the Left ever becomes a significant force in American political life, these forms of harassment and intimidation will escalate. We have to be better prepared at some future point to anticipate another COINTELPRO (Counter Intelligence Program of the FBI) or a more sophisticated version of the Palmer raids. Make no mistake, the struggle for a radical democracy *will be a class struggle.* Remember the words of abolitionist Frederick Douglass:

> Without struggle there is no progress. Those of you who profess freedom, yet who deprecate struggle, are like those who want crops without ploughing up the ground. You want the ocean without the roar of its mighty waters. Power concedes nothing without a demand, it never did and it never will.

The struggle for socialism is protracted, and Antonio Gramsci's "war of maneuver" is not around the corner. But our socialist vision can transcend the limitations and failures of classical social democracy if we are truly committed to the struggle to uproot racism and sexism, to abolish poverty and hunger, to create jobs and social justice, and to eliminate the allocation of billions of dollars to the Pentagon. If we are truly committed, then we can anticipate a struggle. Political repression and class exploitation are not myths under capitalism; they are the essence of how power is maintained. But with a determination grounded in our collective efforts, in radical intellectual work, in cultural and political engagement, in our work as members of various protest formations, combined with constructive dialogue leading toward a national strategy of resistance and political activism, the Left can do much to achieve our vision of a just, democratic, and egalitarian society.

~

Multicultural Democracy

Who is the emerging new majority for justice and peace in the United States? It consists of 31 million African-Americans, women, men and children who have experienced slavery, Jim Crow segregation, ghettoization, poverty, high rates of unemployment and police brutality. It includes the Latino population, which is now projected to reach 35 million by the year 2000, more than double the 1980 census figure. Nearly two-thirds of the Latino population is Chicano. Like their African-American sisters and brothers, Latinos experience systemic racial and class oppression. One quarter of all Latino households are below the Federal Government's poverty line, compared to just 9 percent for whites. The average annual family income for Chicano families is only $22,200; for Puerto Rican households, $19,900. Latinos and African-Americans suffer double the rate of unemployment, and triple the rate of homelessness, than that experienced by whites.

Who is the emerging new in the U.S.? It is the Asian-Pacific American population, doubling in size over the past decade to more than 6 million people. The images of affluence and the rhetoric of the so-called "model minorities" mask the essential common ground linking Asian-Americans to other people of color. The brutal murder of Vincent Chin in Detroit and ethnic harassment of Asian people throughout the country, the efforts to undercut educational opportunities and access for Asian-Americans, and political maneuvers to divide, split, and to compromise progressive political currents in Asian-American communities link these struggles to related issues for African-Americans and Latinos.

The new emerging majority are our Arab-American sisters and brothers, at least three and one half million strong, who are subjected to political harassment, media abuse and ethnic discrimination. The FBI surveillance, interviews and intimidation aimed against Arab-American leaders during the recent U.S. blitzkrieg against Iraq parallels the forced incarceration of thousands of Japanese-Americans on the West Coast.

The new majority includes 2.2 million Native Americans who have been targeted by the U.S. government for more than two hundred years for genocide. The struggle of American Indians is simultaneously political, cultural, and spiritual; a struggle for national self-determination and sovereignty; the reclamation of the land;

and the spiritual renewal of the strength and vision of a people. And the new majority is connected inevitably with the hopes, dreams and struggles of millions of poor and working-class women and men who are white—the homeless and unemployed, the small farmers and factory workers, the students surviving on student loans and white women with children on Aid to Families with Dependent Children. We need to keep in mind constantly that 60 percent of all welfare recipients are white; that 62 percent of all people on food stamps are white; that more than two-thirds of Americans without medical insurance are white. Racial and national oppression is very real, but beneath this is an elitist dynamic of exploitation linked to the hegemony, power and privileges of corporate capitalism over labor. There is no road for the oppressed challenging the power and the dynamics of racial oppression, which does not also challenge and confront corporate capitalism.

POLITICAL PROSPECTS

What is the political future and prospects of this emerging majority? Before the end of this decade, the majority of California's total population will consist of people of color—Asian-Americans, Latinos, Arab-Americans, Native Americans, African-Americans and others. By the year 2015, the majority of the working class between the ages of twenty to forty will consist of people of color. And not long after the midpoint of the next century, no later than 2056, we will live in a country in which whites will be a distinct "minority" of the total population, and people of color will be the numerical majority. The next half century will be a transition from a white majority society to a society which is far more pluralistic and diverse, where multilingualism is increasingly the norm, where different cultures, religions, and philosophies are a beautiful mosaic of human exchange and interaction. *That* is the emerging majority.

What is a progressive agenda for the newly emerging majority? We have to be committed to the completion of the civil rights agenda—legislation which protects civil liberties and human rights, which advocates expanded "minority set-aside" programs for the development of capital formation in our communities; the passage of the 1991 Civil Rights Act which reverses six discriminatory decisions of the U.S. Supreme Court. We won't have the basis for a just society until we realize the legislative agenda of Martin Luther King, Jr.

But our responsibility is to go beyond the dream of Martin, seeking more than an integrated cup of coffee. People of color must radically redefine the nature of democracy. We must assert that democratic government is empty and meaningless without the values of social justice and multiculturalism. Multicultural political democracy means that this country was not built by one and only one group—Western Europeans; that our country does not have only one language—English; or only one religion—Christianity; or only one economic philosophy—corporate capitalism. Multicultural democracy means that the leadership within our society should reflect the richness, colors and diversity of our people. Multicultural democracy demands new types of power sharing and the reallocation of resources, to create economic and social development for those who have been most oppressed. Multicultural democracy must mean the right of all oppressed national minorities to full self-determination, which may include territorial and geographical restructuring, if that is the desire of the oppressed nation. Native Americans cannot be denied their legitimate claims of sovereignty as an oppressed nation, and we must fight for their right to self-determination as a central principle of democracy.

Multicultural democracy must articulate a vision of society which is feminist or "womanise" in the words of Alice Walker. The patterns of oppression and exploitation of women of color—including job discrimination based in gender, race and class, rape and sexual abuse, forced sterilizations, harassment and abuse within the criminal justice system, housing discrimination against single mothers with children, the absence of pay equity for comparable work, political underrepresentation, and legal disfranchisement—combine to perpetuate this subordinate status within society. No progressive struggles have ever been won for people of color throughout history without the courage, contributions, sacrifices and leadership of women. No political agenda of emancipation is possible unless one begins with the central principle of empowerment and full liberation for all women of color, at every level of organization and society. Men of color must learn from the experiences and insights of sisters of color, if they are to free themselves from their political, cultural and ideological chains which reinforce our collective oppression.

Multicultural democracy for the emerging new majority of people of color must embrace the struggle against homophobia, the fear, hatred, discrimination and oppression of lesbians and gay men. Homophobia is a form of social intolerance which has its most devastating impact upon people of color. By turning away from the concerns and political issues which motivate lesbians and gay activists in our communities, we construct vicious barriers between sisters and brothers, mothers and daughters, fathers and sons. We give comfort and support to the hate-filled, homophobic politicians and evangelical Christian charlatans who attack lesbian and gay rights. We must recognize finally that any assault against the human dignity and personal freedoms of lesbians and gays inevitably undermines the basis for all progressive politics. When a lesbian of color is denied the right to keep her child, when a gay couple cannot adopt children, or when a lesbian is refused an apartment or job, all of us are violated, all of our rights are diminished. We must certainly build political coalitions and bridges between formations and organizations of all people of color and with specifically gay and lesbian activist groups. But we must also do much more to construct bridges of genuine support, dialogue and solidarity, challenging homophobic assumptions, homophobic policies and practices at all levels of society.

ECONOMIC VISION

Multicultural democracy must include a powerful economic vision which is centered on the needs of human beings. Is it right for the government to spend billions for bailing out the fat cats who profited from the savings and loan crisis, while millions of jobless Americans stand in unemployment lines, desperate for work? Is it fair that billions are allocated for the Pentagon's permanent war economy, to obliterate the lives of millions of poor people, from Iraq to Panama, Grenada to Vietnam, while three million Americans sleep in the streets, and 37 million Americans lack any type of medical coverage? Is it a democracy when you have the right to vote, but no right to a job? Is it a democracy when people of color have the freedom to starve, the freedom to live in housing without adequate heating facilities, the freedom to attend substandard schools? Democracy without social justice, without human dignity, is no democracy at all.

The new majority for justice and peace must have an internationalist perspective. We must link our struggles domestically and locally with the battles for human rights and peace across the world. We are on the opposite side of the international barricades of Bush's "New World Order," which promises the "same old disorder": disruption, political domination and social destruction for the Third World, for working people, for the oppressed.

Multicultural democracy means taking a stand on behalf of all indigenous people, the Native Americans across the Americas, the Pacific Islands, Australia, and across the world. It means expressing our political and moral solidarity with the masses of southern Africa, the battle against apartheid led by Nelson and Winnie Mandela, the African National Congress, the multiracial trade union movement, and all the women and men of South Africa who are fighting for democracy.

The emerging multicultural majority must support all struggles for self-determination, and especially the people of Palestine. Despite years of brutal repression, the closing down of the universities, the deliberate bombing of homes, the *intifada* continues, the hope of self-determination is not extinguished, and the dream of political freedom has not died. We must learn from the courage of the Palestinian people, and extend our support and solidarity. And with this same gesture of material and moral solidarity, we embrace the masses in Central America, fighting U.S. corporate and imperialist hegemony. We find strength in the people of Cuba, standing nearly alone against the northern capitalist leviathan. The New World Order threatens the socialist revolution of Cuba, it threatens every oppressed nation and people in the Third World. Our response in pressuring the leviathan, challenging the system while inside "the belly of the beast," is our unique responsibility and our cause.

UNITY IS ESSENTIAL

Unity between progressives of color is essential if multicultural democracy is to be achieved. This doesn't mean that we minimize the difficulties inherent in such a project, the differences of perspective which exists between groups. Unfortunately, the experience of oppression does not inoculate one from being intolerant toward others. There are white lesbians and gays who are racist, and people of color who are homophobic; there are Asian-Americans who are hostile to Latinos, Latinos who are hostile to African-Americans, and African-Americans who are prejudiced against Asians. We frequently speak different languages; we have different historical experiences, religions, political ideologies and social values. But so long as these differences divide us into potentially antagonistic camps, the powers which dominate and exploit us collectively will continue to flourish. As long as we bicker against perceived grievances, maximizing our claims against each other, refusing to see the economic, political, cultural and social common ground which can unite us, we will be victimized by capitalism, sexism, racism, national oppression, homophobia, and other systems of domination. The choice is ours.

No single group has all the answers. No single group is embodied with all truth. But together, the collective path to human liberation, self-determination and sovereignty will become clear. Unity is a deliberate act of commitment, bridging the differences and emphasizing elements of common understanding. Unity must be constructed in a manner which establishes a sense of trust and shared experiences between various groups. No single group can determine all policies; no single constituency can dominate leadership; but each group must be respected and its perspectives recognized in this process.

How do we build political unity? We can begin by advocating activism which bridges differences across ethnic lines. Fighting for immigrant and refugee rights isn't a Chicano issue, or Asian-American issue, but cuts across various groups and serves our collective interests. In February, when an investigation of border violence against undocumented workers occurred in the San Diego area, participating groups included the Japanese American Citizens League, the Break the Silence on Anti Asian Violence Coalition, Los Angeles' Project on Assault Against Women, MAPA, SEIU and UE trade unionists, and the San Francisco Black Fire Fighters' Union. Unity means building coalitions with a broad, progressive perspective.

We can construct unity by pooling our resources and energies around progressive projects designed to promote greater awareness and protest among the masses of people of color. This could mean joint mobilizations against the 1992 Columbian Quincentennial. Any "celebration" of the so-called "conquest" of the Americas and the Caribbean is a gross insult to the millions of Native Americans, Latinos, Asians and Africans who died in the expansion of capitalism, the transatlantic slave trade, and colonialism. We have the opportunity to denounce 500 years of invasion, war, genocide and racism, by holding teach-ins, demonstrations, and collective protest actions. We could initiate "Freedom Schools," liberation academies which identify young women and men with an interest in community-based struggles. A curriculum which teaches young people about their own protest leaders, which reinforces their identification with our collective cultures of resistance, will strengthen our political movements. The new majority must build progressive research institutes, bridging the distance between activists and community organizers of color and progressive intellectuals who can provide the policies and theoretical tools useful in the empowerment of grassroots constituencies.

Progressives of color on college campuses must play a decisive role in the current debate on "multiculturalism" in higher education. Ideologues of the far right—such as William Bennett, former Secretary of Education in the Reagan administration—are increasingly using higher education as the vehicle for pushing back communities of color. They've reduced student grants, attacked ethnic studies programs, undermined programs for the recruitment of working-class students and students of color, and criticized courses requiring a multicultural non-Western perspective for all students. This ideological offensive against diversity and ethnic pluralism in education is the counterpart to the racist vigilante violence and harassment against people of color which is proliferating in the streets and in our neighborhoods.

We must set the contours for the debate on multiculturalism in education, and recognize this as a central political task for the 1990s. We must assert that civilizations, cultures and language patterns from Latin and Central America, from the Native American people, from Africa, the Caribbean, Asia and the Pacific, have also profoundly influenced the pluralistic American experience, and the complex and contradictory identities of its people. Multiculturalism should approach each cultural tradition among people of color with an awareness of its own integrity, history, rituals and continuity. We must recognize that the perspective of multiculturalism, the struggle to create a more democratic, pluralistic educational system in this country, is part of the struggle to empower people of color, to liberate our minds from the dependency of racist, sexist and homophobic stereotypes. Such an education seeks not just to inform but to transform.

ETHICS AND SPIRITUALITY

Finally, we must infuse our definition of politics with a common sense of ethics and spirituality which challenges the structures of oppression, power and privilege within the dominant social order. Part of the strength of the Black Freedom Movement historically was the merger of political objectives and ethical prerogatives. What was desired politically, the destruction of institutional racism, was simultaneously ethically and morally justified. This connection gave the rhetoric of Frederick Douglass and Sojourner Truth, W.E.B. Du Bois, Paul Robeson and Fannie Lou Hamer a moral grandeur and powerful vision which was simultaneously particular and universal. It spoke to the upliftment of the African-American, but its humanistic imperative reached out to others in a moral context.

Multicultural democracy must perceive itself in this grand tradition, as a critical project which transforms the larger society. It must place humanity at the center of politics. It is not sufficient that we assert what we are against; we must affirm what we are for. It is not sufficient that we declare what we want to overturn, but what we are seeking to build, in the sense of restoring humanity and humanistic values to a system which is materialistic, destructive to the environment, and oppressive. We need a vision which says that the people who actually produce society's wealth should control how it is used.

The old saying from the sixties—are we part of the solution or part of the problem—is simultaneously moral, cultural, economic and political. We cannot be disinterested observers as the physical and spiritual beings of millions of people of color and the poor are collectively crushed.

Paul Robeson reminds us that we must "take a stand," if our endeavors are to have lasting meaning. The new emerging majority must project itself not just as reforming the society at the edges in small ways, but project a program and vision of what should be and what must become reality. Can we dare to struggle, dare to build a new democracy, without poverty and homelessness; can we dare to uproot racism, sexism, homophobia, and all forms of social oppression? Can we dare to assert ourselves as an emerging multicultural democratic majority for peace, social justice, for real democracy? Let us dare to win.

~

9/11 RACISM
IN THE TIME OF TERROR

*Over the past few years I have consistently preached that nonviolence demands that
the means we use must be as pure as the ends we seek. I have tried to make clear that
it is wrong to use immoral means to attain moral ends. But now I must affirm that
it is just as wrong, or perhaps even more so, to use moral means to preserve immoral
ends.... As T. S. Eliot has said, "The last temptation is the greatest treason: To do
the right deed for the wrong reason."*
—Martin Luther King, Jr., "Letter from Birmingham Jail," April 16, 1963

I

It is still mourning time here in New York City. No matter how much time passes,
the tragedy of the terrorist attack against the World Trade Center towers will remain
brutally fresh and terribly vivid to millions of residents in this overcrowded metropolis. The horrific specter of nearly 3,000 human beings incinerated in less than 100
minutes, of screaming people free-falling more than 1,000 feet to their deaths, cannot be comprehended or even explained. For those of us who live and work here,
or for any American who loves New York City, the grief was almost overwhelming.

As I first witnessed the smoke billowing across the city's skyline, I knew that
the criminals who had obliterated the World Trade Center and part of the Pentagon
were attempting to make a symbolic political statement about the links between
transnational capitalism and U.S. militarism. But by initiating acts of mass murder,
those who plotted and carried out these crimes totally destroyed any shred of political
credibility they might have had. There can be no justification, excuse, or rationale
for the deliberate use of deadly force and unprovoked violence against any civilian
population. This was not essentially an act of war, but a criminal act, a crime against
not only the American people, but all of humanity. I immediately felt that all of

262

those who planned, financed, and assisted in carrying out these crimes had to be apprehended and brought to justice—but under the aegis of international law and the United Nations. I feared that unilateral military action by the United States might provoke new terrorist assaults against American cities and civilians.

In the days following the unprecedented terrorist attacks, some elements of the sectarian U.S. Left, including a few black activists, took the bizarre position that those who carried out these crimes were somehow "freedom fighters." These "leftist" critics implied that these vicious, indiscriminate actions must be interpreted within the political context of the oppression that gave rise to those actions. In short, the brutal reality of U.S. imperialism, including America's frequent military occupation of Third World countries, they said, somehow justified the use of political terrorism as a legitimate avenue for expressing resistance. It is certainly true that the American Left was correct to vigorously challenge the Bush administration's militaristic response to this crisis, because the unleashing of massive armed retaliation would have inevitably escalated the cycle of terror. Progressives, however, should have also affirmed their support for justice—first and foremost, by expressing our deepest sympathies and heartfelt solidarity with the thousands of families who lost loved ones in this tragedy. How can a Left that claims to defend workers' rights ignore the fact that in the World Trade Center attack an estimated 1,000 labor union members were killed; approximately 1,500 children lost a parent; and hundreds of undocumented immigrants may have also perished, but their families were unable to step forward to governmental authorities because of their illegal residence in the United States?

Political condemnation of the members of the Al Qaeda group should not, however, support their demonization, their description as "evildoers," as in the denunciations of President George W. Bush. We must denounce their actions as criminal while also resisting the Bush administration's and media's racist characterizations of their political beliefs as "pathological" and "insane." Bush's rhetoric only fed racist attacks against Middle Eastern peoples and Muslims here in the United States. Perhaps one of the most effective criticisms would be to highlight the important differences between the sectarianism of Islamic fundamentalism and the rich humanism that is central to the Islamic faith. In the eloquent words of the late Muslim intellectual Eqbal Ahmad, Islamic fundamentalism promulgates "an Islamic order reduced to a penal code, stripped of its humanism, aesthetics, intellectual quests, and spiritual devotion. It manipulates the politics of resentment and fear, rather than sharing and alleviating the oppression of the masses in the Third World."

Once again, as in my earlier discussion concerning black reparations, we must make a clear distinction between "guilt" and "responsibility." The Al Qaeda terrorist group was indeed guilty of committing mass murder. But the U.S. government was, and is, largely responsible for creating the conditions for reactionary Islamic fundamentalism to flourish. During Reagan's administration, the Central Intelligence Agency (CIA) provided more than $3 billion to finance the mujahadeen's guerrilla war against the Soviet Union's military presence in Afghanistan. The CIA used Pakistan's Inter-Services Intelligence, or secret police, to equip and train tens of thousands of Islamic fundamentalists in the tactics of guerrilla warfare.

According to one 1997 study, the CIA's financing was directly responsible for an explosion of the heroin trade in both mujahadeen-controlled Afghanistan and Pakistan. By 1985, the region had become, according to researcher Alfred McCoy, "the world's top heroin producer," supplying 60 percent of U.S. demand. The number of heroin addicts in Pakistan subsequently rose "from near zero in 1979 ... to 1.2 million by 1985." Our Pakistani "allies" operated hundreds of heroin laboratories. The Taliban regime consolidated its authoritarian rule in the mid-1990s in close partnership with Pakistan's secret police and ruling political dictatorship. And the Clinton administration was virtually silent when the draconian suppression of women's rights, public executions, and mass terror became commonplace across Afghanistan. As *The Nation* columnist Katha Pollitt observed, under the Taliban dictatorship, women could not work or attend school, had "virtually no healthcare," and could not "leave their houses without a male escort." The Bush administration's current allies in Afghanistan, the so-called Northern Alliance, are no better. As Pollitt noted, both fundamentalist groups were equally "violent, lawless, misogynistic [and] anti-democratic."

One fairly standard definition of "terrorism" is the use of extremist, extralegal violence and coercion against a civilian, or noncombatant, population. Terrorist acts may be employed to instill fear and mass intimidation or to achieve a political objective. By any criteria, Al Qaeda is a terrorist organization. Most Americans have never experienced terrorism, but we have unleashed terrorism against others throughout our history. The mass lynchings, public executions, and burnings at the stake of thousands of African Americans in the early twentieth century were homegrown, domestic acts of terrorism.

The genocide of millions of American Indians was objectively a calculated plan of mass terrorism. The dropping of the atomic bomb on Japanese cities during World War II, resulting in the fiery incineration of several hundred thousand civilians, was certainly a crime against humanity. The U.S.-sponsored coup against the democratically elected government of Chile in 1973, culminating in the mass tortures, rapes, and executions of thousands of people, was nothing less than state-financed terrorism. There is a common political immorality linking former Chilean dictator Augusto Pinochet, Osama bin Laden, and former U.S. Secretary of State Henry Kissinger: They all believed that their political ends justified their means.

II

This global tragedy has been most profoundly felt by the 8 million residents of New York City. It is difficult, if not impossible, to explain the deep emotional loss people felt and in many ways continue to feel here, the emptiness of spirit, as if one's soul has been taken. The sense of personal insecurity and civic uncertainty has permeated all things for more than a year. The sheer enormity of the crime and the media's moving presentations of the many individuals who perished and of their grief-stricken families created the image of a city united, both in its pain and its determination.

Rudolph Giuliani, who for nearly eight years had played a profoundly polarizing role as the city's aggressive, confrontational mayor, assumed overnight the image of compassionate, heroic leadership. Journalists and novelists tried to put into words the qualities that gave all New Yorkers the capacity to endure. As Roger Rosenblatt observed in the *New York Times,* "What makes the city different is a civilized wildness born of compression. Deep in their hearts, New Yorkers live comfortably with a thrilling irrationality, perhaps because the city itself is so hard to believe."

The post–September 11 image of a unified city transcending boundaries of class and color became widely and quickly popularized. Adding to the public perception of a unified city were the media's images of the faces of the 9/11 victims. Based on the countless photos reproduced in the city's newspapers and on the local all-news cable channel, it appears that the majority of those who died were either workers, people of color, and/or recent immigrants. As labor historian Joshua Freeman observed: "The September 11 attack and the response to it have once again made working-class New Yorkers visible and appreciated. Not only were the rescuers working class, but so were most of the victims.... Killed that day, along with fire, police and emergency medical workers, were accountants, clerks, secretaries, restaurant employees, janitors, security guards and electricians." Writers and intellectuals celebrated both the city's resilience and its pluralistic, multicultural character. Peruvian novelist Maria Vargas Llosa, for example, praised New York City as "a fairytale cosmopolis." Vargas poetically observed: "New York is of no man and every man: of the Afghan taxi driver who barely speaks English, the turbaned Sikh, the wok-wielding cook in Chinatown and the singer of Neapolitan songs in the restaurants of Little Italy. It is of the Dominicans and Puerto Ricans who fill streets with plena, salsa and merengue; and the Russians, Ukrainians, Kosovars, Andalusians, Greeks, Nigerians, Irish, Pakistanis, and Ethiopians who, as soon as they arrive, are turned into New Yorkers by the absorbent magic of the city."

Yet Vargas's eloquent description of the "city that never sleeps" is an illusion. Despite the newfound civic hype, the harsh reality is that this remains a bitterly divided city. American apartheid *is* strikingly and visually apparent in almost every neighborhood of New York City, and the events of September 11 have only made the racial and class stratification worse. According to the New York–based journal *City Limits,* the 2000 Census indicates that "in New York City, the ostensible capital of diversity the segregation of Asians, Latinos and black residents from white households is at virtually the same level today as it was in 1960."

Out of 331 metropolitan areas surveyed in the United States, New York City now ranks first in both Asian-white segregation and Latino-white segregation. New York's black-white residential segregation also worsened during the Giuliani years, moving from seventh overall in the 1990 Census to third place, just below Detroit and Milwaukee. New York City's Latino population doubled in the 1990s, yet the vast majority of new immigrants were concentrated in Spanish-speaking enclaves like Washington Heights and Sunset Park. As the white population became a minority group within a city that was predominantly defined by people of color, many middle- and upper-class whites retreated from any meaningful, direct interaction with segregated black communities. As *City Limits* observed, New York's children, like other children throughout the country, increasingly live their lives "in segregated neighborhoods, schools, clubs, sports teams and friendship networks."

The city's hypersegregated neighborhoods not only perpetuate distrust and social isolation behind color-coded barriers, but also obscure from public attention other major social problems reflected in the statistics of poverty and unemployment. In the immediate aftermath of 9/11, an estimated 80,000 people in the city's metropolitan area lost their jobs. About 60 percent of the jobs lost, however, paid under $23,000 per year. The largest single group of workers who became unemployed after September 11 were waiters and waitresses, numbering more than 4,200. The Fiscal Policy Institute of New York calculated that the average hourly salary of these waiters and waitresses was $7.08. The second occupation group most devastated by the World Trade Center's collapse comprised nearly 3,400 cleaning and maintenance workers who took home an average of $14.90 per hour. The next five occupations most affected were retail sales clerks (2,843 unemployed, averaging $9.15 per hour), food preparation workers (2,284 unemployed, averaging $8.90 per hour), cashiers (2,282 unemployed, averaging $7.36 per hour), housekeeping workers (1,840 unemployed, averaging $13.42 per hour), and food preparation and fast-food servers (1,718 unemployed, averaging $7.09 per hour).

Most of these individuals were employed at hotels, bars, restaurants, and private transportation companies. Only 4 percent were employed at Wall Street brokerage firms. Over four-fifths of the affected workers probably could not afford to live in Manhattan. About half lived in Brooklyn and Queens, with another 12 percent residing in the Bronx. Many of the jobs destroyed in Manhattan, in fact, were in Chinatown. The Fiscal Policy Institute's survey found that about 20 of that neighborhood's 200 sewing sweatshops went under financially. More than 1,000 members of Unite, the city garment workers union, had been fired by early November.

The vast majority of these jobless low-income workers did not benefit from the hundreds of millions of dollars donated to charities for the World Trade Center's victims. Only one-third of the jobless workers were covered by unemployment insurance, partially because in most instances, self-employed and part-time workers cannot qualify for it. As of the end of 2001, a second federal aid program, Disaster Unemployment Assistance, had extended benefits to only 2,350 jobless workers. As autumn turned into winter, New York's mostly volunteer-staffed food pantries and soup kitchens were reaching the limits of their capacity. As of November 2001, Food for Survival was supplying food for 275,000 meals a day, and City Harvest was providing another 20,000 meals—yet Joel Berg, director of the New York City Coalition Against Hunger, estimated that 30 percent of all pantries would soon have to "turn people away because they ran out of food."

Federal bureaucratic disorganization and poor planning compounded the problems of tens of thousands of families in New York City affected by 9/11. For example, the Federal Emergency Management Agency (FEMA) was charged by Congress to provide resources to needy families to cover the costs of rent or mortgages. In the first nine months of FEMAs efforts in New York City, an estimated 79,000 people contacted the agency for assistance. Less than one-half, 33,000 people, were judged to be potentially eligible for rent or mortgage assistance. Of that number, only 3,585 families received FEMA money between September 2001 and June 2002, amounting to $20.6 million, and with an average monthly payment of $1,140. Most of FEMA's case evaluators were temporary workers hired from other states who had no knowledge of the city's neighborhoods or workforce. FEMA's applications were only available in English for nine months. Not surprisingly, the rejection rate for applicants was a staggeringly high 70 percent, far higher than the rejection rates by FEMA at other disaster areas.

Politically, the net effect of 9/11 in New York City was tremendous fragmentation within the city's liberal political establishment. Throughout Giuliani's controversial administration, literally hundreds of civil-rights, labor, women's, and community-based organizations have marched, picketed, and protested. Everyone assumed that the city's public advocate, Mark Green, a well-known Upper West Side liberal, would be elected the new mayor with little difficulty. But the severe impact of 9/11 diverted the attention of community-oriented coalitions and progressive groups toward addressing more immediate political issues. Some organizations focused attention on efforts to raise public awareness about the dangers involved in the U.S. war effort in Afghanistan; others emphasized the threat to American civil liberties and constitutional rights represented by new federal antiterrorism legislation. Civil-rights organizations highlighted problems of anti-Muslim hate crimes and ethnic profiling by law enforcement officers. Grassroots activists who worked primarily on the issues of low-income people found themselves soon overwhelmed by the crises of widespread joblessness and food shortages. Individual donors and some foundations redirected funds largely to relief efforts and away from community-oriented and antiracist organizing. Very few groups dedicated to progressive change had the infrastructural capacity to engage in emergency activities while at the same time maintaining their commitments to long-term objectives.

The result, in many ways, was a sense of diffused energies, the performance of good and humanitarian activities lacking the broad, strategic vision essential for restructuring the city's power structure. At the general election in November, less than 30 percent of the city's registered voters bothered to go to the polls. In a city where registered Democrats outnumber Republicans by a margin of five to one, a novice candidate, Republican billionaire Michael Bloomberg, narrowly defeated the veteran Democratic politician Mark Green. Power remained firmly in the hands of those who owned the city, while its black and brown population slid farther into economic recession and political marginalization.

III

Did "everything fundamentally change" in the aftermath of the 9/11 attacks? Yes, there was an upsurge of public patriotism and national chauvinism, an understandable desire to "avenge" the innocent victims of the Al Qaeda network's terrorism.

Perhaps these terrible events marking the real "beginning" of the twenty-first century are, however, not a radical departure into some new, uncharted political territory, but rather the culmination of deeper political and economic forces set into motion decades before.

The core ideology of "Reaganism"—free markets, unregulated corporations, the vast buildup of nuclear and conventional weapons, aggressive militarism abroad, the suppression of civil liberties and civil rights at home, and demagogical campaigns against both "terrorism" and Soviet communism—has become central to the Bush administration's current policy initiatives today. Former President Ronald Reagan attempted to establish a national security state where the legitimate functions of government were narrowly restricted to matters of national defense, public safety, and tax subsidies to the wealthy. Reagan pursued a policy of what many economists have termed "military Keynesianism," the deficit spending of hundreds of billions of dollars on military hardware and speculative weapons schemes such as "Star Wars."

This massive deficit federal spending was largely responsible for the U.S. economic expansion of the 1980s. Simultaneously, the Soviet Union was pressured into an expensive arms race that it could not afford. The fall of Soviet communism transformed the global political economy into a unipolar world characterized by U.S. hegemony, both economically and militarily. The result was a deeply authoritarian version of American state power, with increasing restrictions on democratic rights of all kinds, from the orchestrated dismantling of trade unions to the mass incarceration of racialized minorities and the poor. By the end of the 1990s, 2 million Americans were behind bars and over 4 million former prisoners had lost the right to vote, for life. "Welfare as we know it," in the words of former President Clinton, was radically restructured, with hundreds of thousands of women householders and their children pushed down into poverty.

Behind much of this vicious conservative offensive was the ugly politics of race. The political assault against affirmative action and minority economic set-asides was transformed by the Right into a moral crusade against "racial preferences" and "reverse discrimination." Black and Latino young people across the country were routinely "racially profiled" by law-enforcement officers. DWB, "Driving While Black," became a familiar euphemism for such police practices. As the liberal welfare state of the 1960s mutated into the prison industrial complex of the 1990s, the white public was given the unambiguous message that the goal of racial justice had to be sacrificed for the general security and public safety of all. It was, in short, a permanent war against the black, the brown, and the poor.

The fall of communism transformed a bipolar political conflict into a unipolar, hegemonic New World Order, as the first President Bush termed it. The chief institutions for regulating the flow of capital investment and labor across international boundaries were no longer governments. The International Monetary Fund, the World Trade Organization, and transnational treaties such as the North American Free Trade Agreement (NAFTA) took on these roles, exercising significantly greater influence over the lives of workers in most countries than their own governments. By the year 2000, 51 of the world's 100 wealthiest and largest economies were actually corporations, and only 49 were countries. The political philosophy of globalization, termed "neoliberalism," emphasized privatizing government services and programs, eliminating unions, and applying the aggressive rules of capitalist markets to public institutions such as schools, hospitals, and even postal services. The social contract between U.S. citizens and the liberal democratic state was being redefined to exclude the concepts of social welfare and social responsibility to the truly disadvantaged.

A new, more openly authoritarian philosophy of governance was required to explain to citizens why their long-standing democratic freedoms were being taken away from them. A leading apologist for neoauthoritarian politics was former New York mayor Rudolph Giuliani. In 1994, soon after his initial election as mayor, Giuliani declared in a speech: "Freedom is about authority: Freedom is about the willingness of every single human being to cede to lawful authority a great deal of indiscretion about what you do and how you do it." As we all know, the Giuliani administration won national praise for reducing New York City's murder rate from 2,000 to 650 a year. The rate of other violent crimes also plummeted. But the social cost to New York's black, brown, and poor communities was far more destructive than anything they had known previously. The American Civil Liberties Union has estimated that between 50,000 and 100,000 New Yorkers were subjected annually to "stop-and-frisk" harassment by the police under Giuliani. The city's notorious Street Crimes Unit terrorized black and Latino neighborhoods.

Many white liberals in New York City passively capitulated to this new state authoritarianism. It is even more chilling that in the wake of the September 11 attacks, *New York Times* journalist Clyde Haberman immediately drew connections between "the emotional rubble of the World Trade Center nightmare" and Amadou Diallo, the unarmed West African immigrant gunned down in 1999 by forty-one shots fired by four Street Crimes Unit police officers. "It is quite possible that America will have to decide, and fairly soon, how much license it wants to give law enforcement agencies to stop ordinary people at airports and border crossings, to question them at length about where they have been, where they are heading, and what they intend to do once they get where they're going," Haberman predicted. "It would probably surprise no one if ethnic profiling enters the equation, to some degree." Haberman reluctantly acknowledged that Giuliani may be "at heart an authoritarian." But he added that, "as a wounded New York mourns its unburied dead, and turns to its mayor for solace," public concerns about civil-rights and civil-liberties violations would recede. Haberman seemed to be implying that the rights of individuals like Amadou Diallo are less important than the personal safety of white Americans.

As the national media enthusiastically picked up the Bush administration's mantra about the "War on Terrorism," a series of repressive federal and state laws were swiftly passed. New York State's legislature, in the span of one week, created a new crime—"terrorism"—with a maximum penalty of life in prison. Anyone convicted of giving more than $1,000 to any organization defined by state authorities as "terrorist" would face up to fifteen years in a state prison. When one reflects that, not too many years ago, the United States considered the African National Congress a "terrorist organization," it becomes apparent that the danger of being severely penalized for supporting any Third World social-justice movement has now become very real. This policy suppresses legitimate activities by U.S. citizens.

At all levels of government, any expression of restraint or caution about the dangerous erosion of our civil liberties is equated with treason. The antiterrorism bills in the New York State Assembly were passed, with no debate, by a margin of 135 to 5. The U.S. Senate, on October 12, 2001, passed the Bush administration's antiterrorism legislation by 96 to 1. The militarism and political intolerance displayed in the Bush administration's response to the September 11 attacks created a natural breeding ground for bigotry and racial harassment. For the Reverend Jerry Falwell, the recent tragedy was God's condemnation of a secularist, atheistic America. He attributed the attacks to "the pagans and the abortionists and the feminists and the lesbians" and to "the ACLU [and] People for the American Way." After a firestorm of criticisms, Falwell was forced to apologize. Less well-publicized were the hate-filled commentaries of journalist Ann Coulter, who declared: "We should invade their countries, kill their leaders, and convert them to Christianity." Similar voices of racist intolerance are also being heard in Europe. For example, Italian Prime Minister Silvio Berlusconi stated that "Western civilization" was clearly "superior to Islamic culture." Berlusconi warmly praised "imperialism," predicting that "the West will continue to conquer peoples, just as it has Communism." Falwell, Berlusconi, and others illustrate the direct linkage between racism and war, between militarism and political reaction.

Even on college campuses, there have been numerous instances of the suppression of free speech and democratic dissent. When City University of New York faculty held an academic panel that presented a variety of viewpoints about the historical and political issues leading up to the terrorist attacks, the university's chief administrator publicly denounced some of the participants. "Let there be no doubt whatsoever," warned CUNY Chancellor Matthew Goldstein, "I have no sympathy for the voices of those who make lame excuses for the attacks on the World Trade Center and the Pentagon based on ideological or historical circumstances." Conservative trustees of CUNY sought to censure or even fire the faculty involved. According to the *Chronicle of Higher Education,* hundreds of Middle Eastern college students were forced to return home from the United States as a result of widespread ethnic and religious harassment. At UCLA, Library Assistant Jonnie Hargis was suspended without pay from his job when he sent an e-mail on the university's computers that criticized U.S. support for Israel. When University of South Florida professor Sami Al-Arian appeared on television talking about his relationships to two suspected terrorists, he was placed on indefinite paid leave and ordered to leave the campus "for his [own] safety" university officials later explained. The First Amendment right of free speech, the constitutional right of any citizen to criticize policies of our government, is now at risk.

Perhaps the most dangerous element of the Bush administration's current campaign against democratic rights has been the deliberate manipulation of mass public hysteria. Millions of Americans who witnessed the destruction of the World Trade Center are still experiencing Post-Traumatic Stress Disorder anxiety and depression.

According to the Wall *Street Journal,* during the last two weeks of September, pharmacies filled 1.9 million new prescriptions for Zoloft, Prozac, and other antidepressants, a 16 percent increase over the same period in 2000. Prescriptions for sleeping pills and short-term anxiety drugs such as Xanax and Valium also rose 7 percent. The American public has been bombarded daily by a series of media-orchestrated threats focusing on everything from the potential of crop-dusting airplanes being used for bioterrorism, to anthrax-contaminated packages delivered through the U.S. postal service. People are constantly warned to carefully watch their mail, their neighbors, and one another. Intense levels of police security at sports stadiums and armed National Guard troops at airports have begun to be accepted as "necessary" for the welfare of society.

By the beginning of 2002, we began to witness "dissident profiling": the proliferation of electronic surveillance, roving wiretapping and harassment at the workplace, the infiltration and disruption of antiwar groups, and the stigmatization of any critics of U.S. militarism as disloyal and subversive. As historian Eric Foner has noted, "Let us recall the F.B.I.'s persistent harassment of individuals like Martin Luther King, Jr., and its efforts to disrupt the civil rights and anti-war movements, and the C.I.A.'s history of cooperation with some of the world's most egregious violators of human rights. The principle that no group of Americans should be stigmatized as disloyal or criminal because of race or national origin is too recent and too fragile an achievement to be abandoned now." I believe that one cannot preserve democracy by restricting and eliminating the democratic rights of any group or individual. To publicly oppose a government's policies that one believes to be morally and politically wrong, as Dr. Martin Luther King, Jr., asserted, is to express the strongest belief in the principles of democracy.

Those of us who oppose our government's course of action must clearly explain to the American people that the missile strikes and indiscriminate carpet bombings we unleashed against Afghanistan's peasants did *not* make us safer. The policies of the Bush administration actually placed our lives in greater danger, because the use of government-sponsored terror will not halt brutal retaliations by the terrorists. The national-security state apparatus we are constructing today is being designed primarily to suppress domestic dissent and racially profiled minorities, rather than to halt foreign-born terrorists at our borders. In 2000 alone, there were 489 million persons who passed through our border inspection systems. More than 120 million cars are driven across U.S. borders every year, and it is impossible to thoroughly check even a small fraction of them. Restricting civil liberties, hiring thousands more police and security guards, and incarcerating more than 1,000 Muslims and individuals of Arab descent without due process only foster the false illusion of security. The "War on Terrorism" is being used as an excuse to eliminate civil liberties and democratic rights here at home.

This "war at home" also has a profoundly racial dimension. Because U.S. democracy was constructed on institutional racism, the government has always found it difficult to present a clear, democratic argument to advance its interests in the pursuit of warfare. Instead, it relies on and manipulates the latent racism and xenophobia at all levels of society. Usually, racism is used to target external enemies, such as "Japs" during World War II. But in general, whenever the United States mobilizes militarily and goes to war, white racism goes with it hand in hand.

The extreme degree of racial segregation in New York City provides part of the explanation for the rash of hate crimes committed here after September 11. For example, in the days immediately following the attack, according to the Asian American Legal Defense and Education Fund, a Sikh man in Richmond Hill, Queens, "was assaulted with a baseball bat and shot at with a BB gun," and a "Huntington, Long Island, man tried to run down an Asian woman with his car." Arab and Muslim street vendors and store owners throughout the city experienced verbal and physical harassment and were threatened with economic boycotts. Such incidents, of course, were not confined to New York City. The New York–based South Asian American Leaders of Tomorrow (SAALT) issued a report based on more than 400 media sources documenting 645 separate incidents of hate-inspired violence against Arabs, Asians, and Muslims in the United States during the first week after September 11. These included 3 murders, 49 assaults, and 92 incidents of arson and property damage.

Those who are coded or classified by appearance, dress, language, or name, as those of Muslim or of Arab background are, have been rudely escorted off airplanes and Amtrak trains, and many have been detained without formal charges or access to attorneys. Anecdotal evidence suggests that a significant number, perhaps even the majority, of the people of color singled out for harassment as potential "terrorists" have not been Muslims or Arabs at all. In Seattle and other West Coast cities, dozens of Hawaiians, Central Americans, South Asians, and even American Indians have been subjected to verbal insults and harassment because they "appear" to be vaguely "non-American." On the East Coast, many Sikhs and Hindus have been victimized, along with non-English-speaking and non-European undocumented immigrants. Most white middle-class Americans in the so-called heartland of the country, the Midwestern states, lack both the cultural capacity and geopolitical awareness to make fine distinctions between "Muslims" and racialized others who happen to be non-Muslims.

The great exceptions to this phenomenon of new racialization in the time of terror, curiously, were African Americans. People of African descent, having lived on the American continent since 1619, occupy a unique position in the construction of white American identity and national consciousness. State power was deliberately constructed to exclude black participation; but black labor power was absolutely essential in the economic development of the nation. Black culture, moreover, contributed the most creative and original elements defining American national culture and various forms of representation.

Thus, the African American is unquestionably a recognized member of the American national household—but has never been a member of the American family. We are the Other that everybody knows. Yet there is a necessary kind of dialectical connection here, linking the false superiority of whiteness as a political and social category in the United States to the continued and "normal" subordination of blackness. Without "blacks," whiteness ceases to exist as we know it. White supremacy has difficulty imagining a world without black people, but has no reservations about the indiscriminate mass bombing of Afghan peasants, or about supporting an embargo against Iraq, which is responsible for the deaths of hundreds of thousands of Muslim children, according to international human-rights observers.

The great sociologist Oliver C. Cox understood this contradiction, the subtle distinctions between white racism, social intolerance, and xenophobia. As Cox put it: "The dominant group is intolerant of those whom it can define as anti-social, while it holds race prejudice against those whom it can define as subsocial. In other words, the dominant group or ruling class does not like the Jew at all, but it likes the Negro in his place." In a time of political terror, the "terrorist" becomes the most dangerous Other and is recognized by certain "subhuman" qualities and vague characteristics—language, strange religious rituals, unusual clothing, and so forth. The "terrorist Other" thus is presented to the white public as an uncivilized savage who has richly merited our hatred and must be destroyed to assure our safety and the preservation of the American Way of Life.

The fundamental contradiction that has always confronted black Americans during these periods of racist wars is whether or not to take advantage of this situation in order to advance up the racial and political hierarchy. I began noticing the large number of American flags, for example, displayed on the fronts of black homes and businesses. On New York City subways immediately following the attacks, I saw more blacks and Latinos wearing red, white, and blue buttons, caps, and other patriotic paraphernalia than at any other time in my memory.

Even before the devastating economic impact of 9/11, black Americans and Latinos were experiencing an economic downturn coinciding with the inauguration of the Bush administration. Between September 2000 and June 2005, African-American unemployment nationwide had increased from 7.2 percent to 8.4 percent. Latino jobless rates during the same period also rose, from 5 percent to 6.6 percent. Thousands of minority and low-income heads of household who owned homes through the Federal Housing Administration's government-insured program became delinquent in their mortgage payments. After the terrorist attacks, black jobless rates soared: 9.7 percent as of October 2002 and 10.1 percent by November 2002. Urban job-counseling centers experienced significant increases in African Americans searching for employment. In the Urban League's Job Centers in the Los Angeles area, there was a 25 percent jump in clients in 2001 "attributed mainly to Sept. 11–related job loss." A number of black-owned businesses, both in New York City and nationally, were seriously affected by the terrorist attacks. Most prominent on this list were Rice Financial Products, *Black Enterprise's* tenth-ranked investment bank, with total issues of $10 billion, which was located on the fifty-second floor of the World Trade Center's north tower; and another black investment bank, M. R. Beal and Company, ranked fourth in *Black Enterprise,* with $46.5 billion in total issues, located several blocks from the towers.

Like most Americans, African Americans were generally outraged by the terrorist attacks, and during this moment of national crisis they gave unprecedented levels of support for the Bush administration. The most widely publicized post-9/11 poll, conducted by the Gallup organization, found that 70 percent of blacks "approved of the way Mr. Bush was handling his job." Probably more accurate was the survey of the Pew Research Center, which found that 49 percent of African Americans generally supported the president, up from 32 percent prior to the attacks.

But the majority of blacks were also troubled by the exuberant hyper-patriotism of whites and the possible linkages between racism, national chauvinism, and the suppression of democratic rights. Bishop Cecil Bishop, a leader of the Congress of National Black Churches, reminded the press that "African-American people themselves have been terrorized ... [by] the killings, lynchings, hangings years back," as well as the more recent examples, such as the killing of Amadou Diallo by New York policemen. The Reverend James A. Forbes, Jr., pastor of New York's Riverside Church, called for blacks to espouse a critical "prophetic patriotism.... You will hold America to the values of freedom, justice, compassion, equality; respect for all, patience and care for the needy, a world where everyone counts." National Urban League director Hugh Price asserted that "black America's mission, as it has always been, is to fight against the forces of hatred and injustice." Price condemned the "morally repugnant notion that the need for increased security justifies racial profiling.... There is no excuse for singling out and stopping some Americans for no reason other than the color of their skin or their ethnic background or the way they dress."

The African Americans who were made to feel most vulnerable in the aftermath of the attacks were Muslims. In the early 1970s, there were only about half a million adherents to Islam in the United States, including roughly 100,000 members of the Nation of Islam. By September 2001, the American Muslim community numbered nearly 7 million, which is larger than the U.S. Jewish population. About one-third of all Muslims, more than a million, are African Americans. The most influential Muslim leader, Imam W. Deen Muhammad, is the son of the NOI's late patriarch, Elijah Muhammad. As the head of the orthodox Muslim American Society, W. Deen Muhammad has been described as "fiercely patriotic." For years, the Muslim American Society's national newspaper, the *Muslim Journal,* has featured on its cover page an American flag at the upper left corner.

Virtually all prominent Muslim religious leaders and civic representatives of the Arab-American community unconditionally condemned the attacks. Even Farrakhan denounced the criminals behind the assault as "depraved wild beasts," while at the same time urging the U.S. government to reevaluate its Middle East policies. Muslims overwhelmingly opposed U.S. military intervention in Afghanistan and favored some type of United Nations resolution to the crisis. They justly feared that the non-Muslim, white majority would aim its desire for retaliation indiscriminately, classifying all Muslims, recent immigrants and native-born citizens alike, as potential terrorists.

By the spring of 2002, many prominent African-American leaders and organizations had voiced criticisms of Bush's "War on Terrorism" and expressed concerns about the permanent deployment of U.S. troops in Afghanistan. Numbers of African-American and Latino activists participated in antiwar demonstrations and teach-ins, many led by working-class and poor people of color, that were largely ignored or unreported in the media. In San Francisco, for example, the People Organizing to Win Employment Rights (POWER) led a May Day 2002 rally and march calling for "Land, Work, and Peace." The broad range of participating organizations included the Chinese Progressive Association, the Homeless Pre-Natal Program, Hogares Sin Barreras (Housing Not Borders), and Mujeres Unidas y Activas (United and Active Women). On April 20, 2002, an estimated 80,000 people attended a Washington, D.C., protest demonstration against the Bush administration's "Permanent War on Terrorism." Significantly, at least one-third of those participating in the demonstration were Arab Americans and/or Muslims.

But the national media's attention focused exclusively on stories about the "new American patriotism," and people of color were frequently featured center stage. Blacks were reminded constantly that Colin Powell, after all, is President Bush's secretary of state, and Condoleezza Rice is his national security adviser. I also suspect that the new xenophobia was being viewed by a significant sector of African Americans as not entirely a bad thing, if jobs that had previously gone to non-English-speaking immigrants would now go to blacks. There is considerable hostility in cities such as Detroit and Houston between impoverished and working-class black urban neighborhoods and Arab shopkeepers. Blacks in 2000 voted overwhelmingly for the Gore-Lieberman ticket, while at least 40 percent of Arab Americans supported Bush-Cheney, based in part on their political and religious hostility toward Lieberman.

Part of the frustration the African-American community feels is rooted in our complicated love-hate relationship with our own country. That U.S. democracy was crudely constructed on the mountain of black bodies destroyed by centuries of enslavement, segregation, and exploitation is abundantly clear to us. Yet there is also that knowledge, gleaned from our centuries-old struggle for freedom, that the finest ideals of American democracy are best represented by our own examples of sacrifice. This was undoubtedly behind W.E.B. Du Bois's controversial editorial, "Close Ranks," which endorsed African-American participation in the U.S. war effort during World War I. It is important to remember, however, that immediately after World War I ended, the "Red Summer" of 1919, during which hundreds of African Americans were lynched, beaten, and even burned at the stake, erupted. Most African Americans understood, however, that we cannot overturn the structural racism against us if we accommodate or compromise with war and racism against others.

IV

The bombing campaign against the people of Afghanistan may be described in future history books as "The United States Against the Third World." The launching of high-tech military strikes against a feudal peasant society did little to suppress global terrorism and only eroded American credibility in Muslim nations around the world. The question, repeatedly asked in the U.S. press in the days after 9/11, "Why do they hate us?" can only be answered from the vantage point of the Third World's widespread poverty, hunger, and economic exploitation.

The U.S. government cannot engage in effective multilateral actions to suppress terrorism because its behavior illustrates its thinly veiled contempt for international cooperation. The United States owed $582 million in back dues to the United Nations, and it paid up only when the 9/11 attacks jeopardized its national security. Republican conservatives demanded that the United States be exempt from the jurisdiction of an International Criminal Court, a permanent tribunal established at The Hague, Netherlands. For the 2001 United Nations–sponsored World Conference Against Racism in South Africa, the U.S. government authorized the allocation of a paltry $250,000, compared to more than $10 million provided to conference organizers by the Ford Foundation. For three decades, the United States refused to ratify the 1965 United Nations Convention on the Elimination of Racism. Is it any wonder that much of the Third World questions our motives? The carpet bombing of the Taliban seems to Third World observers to have less to do with the suppression of terrorism than with securing future petroleum-production rights in Central Asia.

The U.S. media and opinion makers repeatedly went out of their way to twist facts and to distort the political realities of the Middle East by insisting that the Osama bin Laden group's murderous assaults had nothing to do with Israel's policies toward the Palestinians. Nobody else in the world, with the possible exception of the Israelis, really believes that. Even Britain, Bush's staunchest ally, cited Israel's intransigence toward negotiations and its human-rights violations as having contributed to the environment for Arab terrorist retaliation. In late September 2001, during his visit to Jerusalem, British Foreign Secretary Jack Straw stated that frustration over the Israeli-Palestinian conflict might create an excuse for terrorism. Straw explained: "There is never any excuse for terrorism. At the same time, there is an obvious need to understand the environment in which terrorism breeds." Millions of moderate and progressive Muslims who sincerely denounced terrorism were nevertheless frustrated by the extensive clientage relationship the United States has with Israel, financed by more than $3 billion in annual subsidies. They want to know why the United States has allowed the Israelis to relocate more than 200,000 Jewish settlers—half of them after the signing of the 1993 peace agreement—to occupied Palestine.

How did terrorist Osama bin Laden gain loyal followers transnationally, from northern Nigeria to Indonesia? Perhaps it has something to do with America's massive presence—in fact, its military-industrial occupation—of Saudi Arabia. In the past two decades, U.S. construction companies and arms suppliers have made over $50 billion in Saudi Arabia. As of late 2001, more than 30,000 U.S. citizens were employed by Saudi corporations or by joint Saudi-U.S. corporate partnerships. ExxonMobil, the world's largest corporation, signed a 2001 agreement with the Saudi government to develop gas projects worth between $20 billion and $26 billion. Can Americans who are not orthodox Muslims truly appreciate how spiritually offensive the presence of 5,000 U.S. troops in Saudi Arabia is for them?

There is a clear link between 9/11 and the shameful political maneuvering committed by the United States at the United Nations World Conference Against Racism held in Durban, South Africa, only days before the terrorist attacks. There, the U.S. government opposed the definition of slavery as "a crime against humanity."

It refused to acknowledge the historic and contemporary effects of colonialism and racial segregation on the underdevelopment and oppression of the non-European world. The majority of dark humanity is saying to the United States that racism and militarism are not the solutions to the world's major problems.

If the fundamental challenge of U.S. democracy in the twenty-first century is that of "structural racism," then at an international level, the central problem of the twenty-first century is the growth of "global apartheid." The wealth and resources of all humanity are unequally divided, and warfare and systemic forms of violence are employed to preserve that gross inequality. According to a United Nations Human Development Report in 1998, the world's 225 wealthiest individuals had a combined net wealth of $1 trillion, which was equal to the combined income of the planet's most impoverished 2.5 billion people. One-half of the people currently living on earth, slightly more than 3 billion individuals, exist on the equivalent of $2 or less per day. About 1.3 billion people survive on less than $2 each day. The overwhelming majority of those 3 billion people live in Africa, Asia, and Latin America. For them, globalization is nothing less than a new phase of racialization on a global scale.

Terrorism is frequently the tool of the weak. A global superpower that possesses overwhelming material resources and armaments can afford the luxury of buying off its Third World opponents, or overthrowing unfriendly governments, through covert action and the collusion of local elites. A classical mixture of fraud and force is preferable because it maintains the facade of democratic procedures and processes. But for extremist fundamentalists in the Third World, terror is a cheap, low-tech alternative for striking back. The American people must understand what the black and brown world already knows: The threat of terrorism will not end until a new global dialogue is established that constructively works toward the elimination of the routine violence of poverty, the violence of disease, the violence of hunger. Global apartheid is essentially only a form of violence.

To stop the extraordinary violence of terrorism, we must stop the daily violence of class inequality and poverty. To engage in the struggle for justice—to find new paths toward reconciliation across the boundaries of religion, culture, and color—is the only way to protect our cities, our country, and ourselves from the terrible violence of terrorism. Without justice, there can be no peace.

A year after 9/11, Afghanistan remained occupied territory, as will be the case into the foreseeable future. The Western donor nations pledged $4.5 billion in economic aid to the devastated nation, but only one-third of the promised aid had been delivered after one year. More than half the country's population of 27 million had directly benefited from humanitarian aid such as food shipments or housing resettlement. Hundreds of local schools, hospitals, and health clinics had been rebuilt or newly constructed. Yet an unknown number of Afghani citizens, perhaps thousands, were killed or maimed by the "friendly fire" of U.S. forces. More than 1.5 million refugees had reentered the country from Pakistan in 2002, most of whom were living in intolerable conditions.

What I have also learned from the experience of being near Ground Zero on 9/11 is the simple truth that sometimes, even for intensely political people, "politics" is not enough. No political ideology, no crusade, no belief in a virtuous cause, can justify the moral bankruptcy of terror. Yet, because of the military actions of our own government, any claims to moral superiority have now disintegrated, in the minds of much of the black and brown world. The American bombings have indeed destroyed the ruthless Taliban regime, but in the process the lives of innocent civilians were also lost. Martin Luther King, Jr., possibly, would have admonished us for using "moral means to preserve immoral ends." We were, and are, politically and morally right to oppose the violence of terrorism. But by employing the tools of violence and repression, we blur the brutal boundaries between the killers and the victims. We must share history's terrible judgment of common responsibility, making sinners of us all. As T. S. Eliot observed seven decades ago:

> Because these wings are no longer wings to fly
> But merely vans to beat the air
> The air which is now thoroughly small and dry
> Smaller and dryer than the will
> Teach us to care and not to care
> Teach us to sit still.
> Pray for us sinners now and at the hour of our death
> Pray for us now and at the hour of our death.
> —T. S. Eliot, "Ash Wednesday," 1930

The Political and Theoretical Contexts of the Changing Racial Terrain

At the first Pan-African Conference held in London in August 1900, the great African-American scholar, W. E. B. Du Bois, predicted that "the problem of the twentieth century is the problem of the color line—the relation of the darker to the lighter races of men in Asia and Africa, in America and the islands of the sea." Today, with the tragic and triumphant racial experiences of the twentieth century behind us, we may say from the vantage point of universal culture that the problem of the twenty-first century is the problem of "global apartheid," the construction of new racialized ethnic hierarchies, discourses, and processes of domination and subordination in the context of economic globalization and neoliberal public policies. Within the more narrow context of the United States, the fundamental problem of the twenty-first century is the problem of "structural racism": the deeply entrenched patterns of socioeconomic and political inequality and accumulated disadvantage that are coded by race and color and are consistently justified in public and private discourses by racist stereotypes, white indifference, and the prison industrial complex.

African political scientist and anthropologist Mahmood Mamdani has observed that, beginning with the imposition of European colonial rule in Africa, "race was the central organizing principle of the development of the modern state." This also holds true for the U.S. In the United States, racial identities were, more than anything else, politically constructed. That is, racial identities were legally sanctioned categories, supported by the weight of the courts, political institutions, organized religion, and custom, and they were reinforced by deliberate and random acts of violence. Thus, the African American became the permanent reference point for the racialized *other* within political and civil society. To be Black was to be excluded from the social contract that linked white citizens to the state through sets of rights and responsibilities.

After more than a century of Black civic and political exclusion, the early American colonies, even before the American Revolution against the British and the consolidation of the new federal system of a United States in 1787, were structured such that the centrality of race was the main organizing principle of power. Marxist sociologist Nicos Poulantzas first used the phrase *the relative autonomy of the state* to describe the indirect and interactive dynamics between political institutions and the economic structures of private ownership and production within liberal democratic societies. That is, for Poulantzas, the modern state was not, as some traditional Marxists once interpreted it, simply the dictatorship of a capitalist ruling class. Poulantzas suggested that the capitalist state itself was the site of extensive contestation, group negotiation, and conflict reflecting a disconnection between average citizens and the modes and relations of production. But I suggest that we must go further than Poulantzas; I argue that the power dynamics of all modern states are organized around the central principle of race.

Structural racism creates its own distinctive political materiality, its hierarchies and patterns and relations of power. Thus, the modern racist state may be organized around many different types of economies, including those defined by private markets as well as those of state collectivism. We should interrogate state power as an organizing principle on its own.

For nearly four hundred years, two very different political narratives have evolved to explain the nature of U.S. democracy, how the American nation-state was founded, and the character of the social contract between the American people and the state. For most white Americans, U.S. democracy is best represented by values such as personal liberty, individualism, and the ownership of private property. For most African Americans, the central goals of the Black freedom movement have always been equality and self-determination: the eradication of all structural barriers to full citizenship and full participation in economic relations and other aspects of public life, and the ability to decide, on their own collective terms, what their future as a community with a unique history and culture might be. For Black Americans, freedom was always perceived in collective terms, as something achievable by group action and capacity building. Equality meant the elimination of all social deficits between Blacks and whites as well as the eradication of cultural and social stereotypes and patterns of social isolation and group exclusion generated by white structural racism over several centuries.

The current debate regarding Black reparations reflects this central conflict over the nature of U.S. democracy and whether a deeply racialized and class stratified society can be transformed. Many who support Black reparations believe that racial peace can be achieved only through social justice—coming to terms with the ways America and, broadly, even Western civilizations have related to people of African descent. As Marcus Garvey scholar Robert Hill of UCLA observed recently, the campaign for Black reparations is "the final chapter in the five-hundred year struggle to suppress the transatlantic slave trade, slavery, and the consequences of its effects."

STRUCTURAL RACISM: HISTORY AND EVOLUTION

Historically, the United States has witnessed two great struggles to achieve a truly multicultural democracy, struggles that have centered on the status of African Americans. The First Reconstruction (1865–1877) ended slavery and briefly gave Black men voting rights, but failed to provide meaningful compensation for two centuries of unpaid labor. The promise of "forty acres and a mule" was, for most Blacks, a dream deferred. The Second Reconstruction (1954–1968), or the modern Civil Rights Movement, outlawed legal segregation in public accommodations and achieved major legislative victories such as voting rights. But these successes paradoxically obscure the tremendous human costs of historically accumulated disadvantage that remain central to Black Americans' lives.

The disproportionate wealth that most white Americans enjoy today was first constructed from centuries of unpaid Black labor. Many white institutions, including Ivy League universities, insurance companies, and banks, profited from slavery. This pattern of white privilege and Black inequality continues today, decades after legal segregation was ended. For example, so-called "equity inequity"—the absence of Black capital formation—is a direct historical consequence of America's structural racism. One in three Black households actually has a negative net wealth. In 1998, the typical Black family's net wealth was $16,400, less than one-fifth that of white families. Black families are denied home loans at twice the rate of whites. Blacks are frequently forced to turn to predatory lenders who charge outrageously high home mortgage rates.

In the labor force, Blacks remain the last hired and first fired during recessions. For example, during the 1990–1991 recession, African Americans suffered disproportionally. At the Coca-Cola Company, 42 percent of employees who lost their jobs were Black; at Sears, Roebuck & Co., the number was 54 percent. Black workers usually have less job seniority and fewer informal networks of friends and relatives who could aid hiring and job retention.

In regard to health, Blacks have significantly shorter life expectancies, partly because of racism in the health establishment. Blacks are statistically less likely than whites to be referred for kidney transplants or early-stage cancer surgery. Blacks are about twice as likely as whites to lack health insurance.

In criminal justice, African Americans constitute only about 14 percent of all drug users, yet are 35 percent of all drug arrests, 55 percent of drug convictions, and 75 percent of prison admissions for drug offenses. Among juveniles arrested and charged with a crime, Black youths are six times more likely than whites to be sentenced to prison.

RESISTANCE STRATEGIES

How have African Americans responded to the evolving domains of this structural racism? In terms of racial counterhegemonic approaches, the Black American community over the course of 150 years has developed three overlapping protest strategies—integration or racial assimilation, Black nationalism or Black separatism, and what feminist anthropologist and my co-author Leith Mullings and I have termed *transformation*. Integrationist movements sought full democratic rights and interracial assimilation within the existing institutions of society. Integration called for the desegregation of public accommodation, schools, and residential patterns, as well as more equitable Black representation throughout the class structure. Black nationalism was premised on the pessimistic (or realistic) notion that most white Americans' prejudices were relatively fixed, that meaningful racial reforms were impossible in the long run. What was required was the construction of strong Black-owned institutions, businesses, and schools, an emphasis on Black cultural awareness and group consciousness, and frequently a strong identification with Africa. Transformationalism, or Black radicalism, focused on the link between racial oppression and class exploitation, calling on a redistribution of wealth as being key in dismantling racism. Transformationists attempted to construct strategic coalitions across racial boundaries, focusing on issues of socioeconomic inequality and the day-to-day violence perpetuated by poverty.

Each of these three strategies had strengths and weaknesses. Integrationists placed too much faith in the American capitalist class's commitment to liberal democracy, and social fairness, and tended to believe that racism was rooted in ignorance, rather than cold, deliberate exploitation. Black nationalists perhaps underestimated how "American" Black Americans really are—how African Americans as a people share many of the same economic values, political aspirations, and cultural practices as white Americans. Strategies of Black entrepreneurial capitalism along segregated racialized markets cannot work, particularly in a period that has seen the rise of global markets and transnational corporations. Transformationists may have unduly emphasized class conflict as the driving force in social history and underestimated the psychological and cultural factors that justified and perpetuated white power and privilege.

As UCLA legal scholar Cheryl Harris observed over a decade ago, in a racialized social hierarchy, whiteness is essentially a form of private property. The state is organized around the processes of what can be termed *racial accumulation.* Such accumulation of racial benefits occurs with whites' higher salaries, superior working conditions, lower rates of unemployment, higher rates of home ownership, greater access to professional and managerial positions, and average life expectancies that are seven years longer than those of Black Americans. White Americans have benefited from nearly four hundred years of accumulated white privilege, which is reflected in vast disparities in material resources and property between racial groups.

The challenges of the current political situation in the U.S. differ in several significant respects from those that gave rise to the mass movement against Jim Crow segregation. In our political system, both major parties have, to varying degrees, moved significantly to the ideologically right. Reaganite Republicans and so-called New Democrats alike now adhere to neoliberal, procorporate policies. The extreme right has waged a twenty-year war against all public sector institutions, pushing for the privatization of public schools, health care services, public transportation, public housing, and other government-funded programs. Closely related to this privatization campaign are the concerted efforts to bust labor unions. Today's Democrats look and sound similar in many respects. In terms of criminal justice, the nation's prison population grew by seven hundred thousand during President Bill Clinton's administration and now exceeds two million. On any given day, the U.S. now has approximately 5.4 million individuals under criminal jurisdiction—either in prisons or jails, on probation, parole, or awaiting trial. More than 4.3 million Americans, of whom 1.7 million are Black, have permanently lost the right to vote because of prior felony convictions. In 1994, government funding for Pell grants that assisted prisoners seeking college training was eliminated.

In the context of racial policy, the retreat from the civil rights agenda continues to accelerate—in our courts, state legislatures, and in Congress. Affirmative action programs such as minority-economic set-asides and race-based academic scholarships, which were endorsed by many Republicans thirty years ago, are now routinely described in our media as examples of "racial quotas." Within the African American community, however, there is some uncertainty about what steps should be taken to respond to this conservative political assault. A number of Black religious leaders endorsed the Bush administration's faith-based initiatives, a push to encourage churches, mosques, and synagogues to provide social services—a trend that actually threatens to undermine publicly funded social services for the vast majority of poor and working people. Even local leaders of the NAACP and some Black elected officials have endorsed school vouchers and other proposals to reallocate scarce public funds to private educational corporations. We must acknowledge that there exist growing divisions within Black America, which is fragmented by social class and income, age, political affiliations, and other divisions.

In this time of global apartheid, Western democratic states increasingly construct authoritarian and elitist barriers to popular participation and decision making. Privatization in such societies organized around racial hierarchies becomes nothing less than a new racialization. In the United States, more than 30 percent of all African Americans are employed by the public sector. Any significant decline in government employment will have disproportionately been imposed on the growing but still fragile Black middle class.

The ultimate goal of the antiracist movement should be the delegitimization and destruction of the idea of *race* itself. Social scientists now agree that race is socially constructed, that it has no biological or genetic validity. This does not mean racial consequences aren't starkly real: Embedded in the way race functions in society are the concepts of hierarchy and oppression. The social processes of racialization involve the realities of domination and subordination, which inevitably culminate in social conflict. Or as reggae artist Bob Marley once sang, "Until the color of a man's skin is of no more significance than the color of his eyes, me say war." The difficult challenge, of course, is how do we get there?

MARGINALIZED AND EXPLOITED: BLACK-ASIAN BONDS

First, scholars who study ethnicity and race, especially as they relate to modes of state power, should contribute to a richer theoretical and historically grounded understanding of diversity. Instead of just celebrating diversity, we must theorize and interrogate it and actively seek the parallels and connections between peoples of various communities. Instead of merely talking about race, we should popularize the public's understanding of the social processes of racialization, that is, how certain groups in U.S. society have been relegated to an oppressed status, by the weight of law, social policy, and economic exploitation.

This oppression has never occurred solely within a Black-white paradigm. Although slavery and Jim Crow segregation were decisive in framing the U. S. social hierarchy, with whiteness defined at the top, and Blackness at the bottom, people of African descent have never experienced racialization by themselves. As historian Gary Okihiro has observed, the 1790 Naturalization Act defined citizenship only for immigrants who were "free white persons." Asian immigrants who were born outside the U.S. were largely excluded from citizenship until 1952. U.S. courts constantly redefined the rules determining who was white and who was not. For example, as Okihiro observes, Armenians were originally classed as Asians and thus were nonwhite, but legally became whites by a 1909 court decision. Syrians were white in court decisions in 1909 and 1910; they became nonwhite in 1913 and became white again in 1915. Asian Indians were legally white in 1910, but nonwhite after 1923. Historians such as David Roediger and Noel Ignatiev illustrate how a series of ethnic minorities, such as the Irish and Jews, experienced racialization, but scaled the hierarchy of whiteness.

Let me provide an example of the richness of a comparative approach to the study of racialized ethnicity. Any critical study of the complex, multilayered relationship between Asians and Blacks in the United States must begin with the historical background of Asia's extensive interactions with Africa and its people. Historians have long established the links of economic trade between China and eastern Africa bordering the Indian Ocean. Islam created a transnational faith community that extended from what is today Senegal to Indonesia. The political, economic, and cultural interactions between Arabs and Africans are represented, for example, by both the Kiswahili language, on one hand, and the oppressive east African slave trade, developed over many centuries, on the other. One also finds parallels and connections between Asians and Africans in the development of the Americas and Caribbean societies. About 15 million Africans were involuntarily transported as chattel slaves to the western hemisphere between the years 1550 and 1870. People of African descent, working in sugarcane fields from Bahia, northeast Brazil, to the South Carolina and Georgia coasts, constructed cultures, traditions, and societies that drew from their African past and reflected their new material conditions and social realities. Similarly, European colonialism and imperialism were responsible for the derogatorily labeled "coolie trade," the coerced migrations of Chinese and Indians into Africa, the Caribbean, and the Americas. As ethnic studies scholar Lisa Yun observes, sometimes the same ships that were used to transport enslaved Africans across the notorious Middle Passage of the Atlantic were later utilized to bring these Asian workers across the Pacific. For the slave, coerced Asian laborer, and non-European indentured worker, the physical conditions of exploitation were often indistinguishable.

The construction of Asian diasporas created new societies: the Cape Malays of the Western Cape Colony, South Africa; the Indian communities of Natal, South Africa; the Indians of Uganda, Kenya, and Tanzania; the Indian communities of Trinidad and Guyana; the Chinese laborers who built the railroads from the Pacific across the mountains in the western U.S. in the mid-nineteenth century; and the Japanese agricultural workers of Hawaii. Asian and African peoples share common histories of slavery and indentured servitude, of physical exploitation, political disfranchisement, social exclusion, and cultural marginalization. Despite the obvious differences between these groups in their cultures and languages of origin, the Asian and African diasporas broadly overlap each other, with complex and often remarkable patterns of assimilation and shared struggles for freedom.

W. E. B. Du Bois's famous 1915 essay, "The African Roots of the War," documenting European colonial expansion as the driving force behind World War I, is echoed in the revolutionary writings of Sun Yat-sen and Ho Chi Minh. Mohandas Gandhi brought nonviolent civil disobedience and the philosophy of satyagraha, *soul force,* to the struggle against racism in South Africa, and Martin Luther King Jr., adopting Gandhi's model to the conditions of the U.S. South, helped launch the Montgomery bus boycott in 1955. The political project of Third World nonalignment in the aftermath of World War II was essentially an Asian-African collaboration, uniting Sukarno of Indonesia, India's Nehru, Kwame Nkrumah of Ghana, and Gamal Abdel Nasser of Egypt. Both Malcolm X and later Muhammad Ali, in different ways, became heroes in the Afro-Asian and Islamic worlds. The struggles by non-European peoples against French colonialism link Vietnam with Algeria and both with the Haitian revolution of Toussaint L'Ouverture. Hip-hop and reggae are as integral within the popular youth cultures of Seoul and Tokyo as they are in Kingston, Brixton, South Central Los Angeles, and Harlem. So when we discuss multicultural study with an emphasis on Asians and Blacks, it is essential to start first with our profound interactions and parallel developments from a historical and comparative approach, and then consider areas of group conflict and possible divergence within that historical framework.

REPRODUCING CATEGORIES OF DIFFERENCE

Historically, oppressed groups frequently—and often unconsciously—defined themselves by the identity boundaries that were superimposed by dominant groups. Jean-Paul Sartre once referred to this social dynamic as "overdetermination." Oppressed people living at the bottom of any social hierarchy are constantly encouraged to see themselves as the other, as individuals who dwell outside of society's social contract, as subordinated categories of marginalized, fixed so-called minorities. Frequently, oppressed people have utilized these categories and even terms of insult and stigmatization, such as *nigger* or *queer,* as a site of resistance and counterhegemonic struggle.

This kind of oppositional politics tends to anchor individuals to narrowly defined, one-dimensional identities that essentially are invented by others. For example, how did African people become known as *Black,* or in Spanish, *Negro?* Europeans launching the slave trade across the Atlantic four hundred years ago created the terminology as a way of lumping together in one category the peoples of an entire continent—one with tremendous variations in language, religion, ethnicity, kinship patterns, and cultural traditions. Blackness, or the state of being Black, was completely artificial; *no people* in Africa call themselves *Black.* Blackness exists only as a social construct in relation to something else, something it is not. That "something else" became known as *whiteness.* Thus, Blackness became a totalizing category relegating other identities—ethnicity, sexual orientation, gender, class affiliation, religious traditions, kinship affiliations—to secondary or even nonexistent status.

In other words, those who control or dominate hierarchies, whether through their ownership of the means of production or through their domination of the state, have a vested interest in manufacturing and reproducing categories of difference. An excellent recent example of this occurred in the United States in 1971, when the U.S. Census Bureau invented the *Hispanic* category. At that time, the category was imposed on a population of nearly twenty million people who represented widely divergent and often contradictory nationalities, racialized ethnic identities, cultural traditions, and political affinities: Spanish-speaking Black Panamanians of Jamaican or Trinidadian descent; Argentines of Italian or German descent; anti-Castro, white upper-class Cubans in Miami's Dade County; impoverished Mexican American farm workers in California's Central Valley; and Black Dominican working-class people in New York City's Washington Heights. Despite this enormous range of humanity, the state had named them as one category of other. That act of naming created its own materiality for these groups, as it does for oppressed groups in general. Government resources, economic empowerment zones, and affirmative action scholarships are in part determined by who is classified as *Hispanic* and who is not. Identities may be situational, but when the power and resources of the state are used to categorize groups under a "one-size-fits-all" designation, the life chances of individuals who are defined within these categories are largely set and determined by others.

REVITALIZING PROTEST

Scholars who are involved in social change projects must also focus on capacity building: How do we begin to rebuild resistance organizations and their protest capacity within Black, Latino, Asian/Pacific Island, and other racialized and immigrant communities? Part of this effort must be frankly defensive, the construction of racialized minority-based institutions to provide goods and services, educational and childcare resources, and health clinics that must be able to flourish with little or no government funding.

Nongovernmental organizations such as neighborhood associations and comprehensive community initiatives potentially enhance the ability of disadvantaged groups to realize their specific, objective interests. We need new approaches to combat what Angela Davis describes as "civic death," the legal marginalization and civic disempowerment that has become so widespread that it threatens to negate not only the Voting Rights Act of 1965, but also threatens, in effect, to void the Fifteenth Amendment of the U.S. Constitution, which granted Black males the right to vote.

To revitalize the African American social protest movement, we must also break with the idea that the electoral arena is the only place where politics takes place. Voter registration and mobilization are, of course, crucial tools in the struggle for Black empowerment. But electoral politics, by itself, cannot transform the actual power relations between racialized, oppressed minorities and the white majority. New tactical protest approaches that use creative political confrontations by mass constituencies of African Americans must be initiated. Black political history, moreover, provides several successful models of mass collective mobilizations around issues of public policy.

One excellent example was A. Philip Randolph's Negro March on Washington Movement of 1941. This mobilization, the first of its kind, was established outside the formal organizational structures of such civil rights groups as the NAACP. Like Garvey's Universal Negro Improvement Association, it was largely if not exclusively an all-Black movement. It advanced a specific set of public policy objectives that pointed toward the ultimate elimination of legal Jim Crow segregation. The Negro March on Washington focused its energies not on persuading white liberals to support racial reforms. Instead, it emphasized action by the Black masses through town hall–style meetings and protest demonstrations. It linked the issues of the most oppressed sectors of the Black community to the organized efforts of Black unions and more progressive Black middle-class organizations.

Randolph's intervention forced President Franklin Roosevelt to issue Executive Order 8802, declaring that "there shall be no discrimination in the employment of workers in defense industries or government because of race, creed, color or national origin." Roosevelt also established the Fair Employment Practices Committee. Because of Executive Order 8802, more than one-quarter million African Americans were hired in defense industries during World War II. The Negro March on Washington created a new political environment of Black militancy that directly contributed to the creation of the Congress of Racial Equality in 1941 and to the unprecedented growth of the NAACP, increasing its membership from fifty thousand in 1940 to over two hundred thousand by 1945.

The demand for Black reparations may have the same potential for transforming the national public-policy discourse on race relations as the Negro March on Washington Movement did sixty years ago. Randolph's 1941 movement brought together young leftist intellectuals such as Ralph Bunche with Black trade unionists, constructing a multiclass, Black-identified coalition that espoused both a long-term vision—the complete dismantling of Jim Crow segregation and the democratic access of Negroes to all levels of American society and public life—and short-term objectives, such as the end of racial exclusion in hiring at wartime industries and the outlawing of racially segregated units in the U.S. military. The reparations campaign must approach the challenge of breaking apart the leviathan of American structural racism in a similar way. We must clearly set out the long-term objective, the realization of a truly multicultural, pluralistic democracy without the barriers of race, class, and gender. At the same time, we must focus specifically on immediate, realizable reforms that are necessary to achieve as first steps in a broad counterhegemonic democratic movement.

POOR AND FEMALE: STARK PATTERNS

We must also consider the intersections of race with gender, sexuality, and class. For decades, Black feminists have made the effective theoretical observation that institutional racism does not exist in a gender vacuum, that structures of domination and social hierarchy reinforce each other across the boundaries of identity. In practical political terms, from day-to-day experiences working with multiethnic communities, we can observe how gender, sexuality, and class intersect with structural racism.

For example, Andrea Smith, a Native American pacifist and activist, wrote in the journal *Color Lines* (Winter 2000) that in the 1970s, as many as 30 percent of all Puerto Rican women, and 25–40 percent of American Indian women were sterilized without their consent. Smith also cited statistics showing that "women of color are 64 percent of the [U.S.] female prison population and serve longer sentences for the same crime[s] as do white women or men of color." The Women of Color Center in Berkeley, California, issued a remarkable report, *Working Hard, Staying Poor: Women and Children in the Wake of Welfare Reform,* that graphically illustrates the intersectionalities of oppression. As of 1998, African Americans, who represent 12.5 percent of the U.S. population, comprise 26.4 percent of all poor people. Latinos comprise 23.4 percent of those below the federal government's poverty line. Although only 8.2 percent of all non-Hispanic whites are poor, 12.5 percent of all Asians and Pacific Islanders are below the poverty line.

Immigrants are 50 percent more likely to be poor than the native born. In female-headed households with children, the statistics are much worse: 21 percent of all non-Hispanic white female-headed households were poor in 1998, compared to 46 percent of African Americans and 48 percent of Latinas. Within two years of the abolition in 1998 of Aid to Families with Dependent Children, 50 percent of Mexican American former welfare recipients in Santa Clara, California, reported food shortages as had 26 percent of all Vietnamese women in the city. In Wisconsin, one out of three Hmong women recipients had run out of food at some point during a six-month period. A 1998 study in San Francisco of immigrant households whose food stamps had been cut found that 33 percent of all immigrant children were experiencing moderate to severe hunger. Antiracist politics that do not acknowledge the profound connections of gender, sexuality, and class with race cannot develop a language that speaks to the vast majority of the world's oppressed people.

CROSSING BORDERS: COMMON STRUGGLES

The future politics of racialized ethnicity must also address transnational contexts. The Black freedom movement in the U.S. must reorient itself in a period of globalization and transnational corporations toward the anti-racist struggles being waged internationally. White supremacy in the U.S. has always tried to reinforce political parochialism among the African American people, encouraging Blacks to perceive themselves in isolation from the rest of the racialized nonwhite world. Those Black revolutionary activists and progressive social reformers who advocated internationalist perspectives on Black liberation—Du Bois, Paul Robeson, King, Angela Y. Davis, and Malcolm X, among others— were invariably perceived to be the most subversive and threatening to the established order. Yet in the age of globalization, there can be no *national* solution to the problem of structural racism. As the power of nation-states declines relative to the growth of transnational capital, individual counterhegemonic political projects confined to one narrow geographic area will lack the theoretical and organizational tools to transform their societies.

More than fifty years ago, representatives of the non-European world met at Bandung, Indonesia, to initiate the nonaligned movement, articulating an agenda independent of the capitalist West and the Communist states. As theorist Samir Amin suggested last year in Durban, South Africa, the central task before us is the renaissance of an "Afro-Asian [and Latino] front," capable of challenging the global apartheid supported by international bodies like the International Monetary Fund (IMF), World Trade Organization (WTO), and the World Bank.

The twenty-first century truly began—politically, socially, and psychologically— with two epochal events: the World Conference Against Racism held in Durban, South Africa, last summer and the terrorist attacks of September 11, 2001, which destroyed the World Trade Center towers and part of the Pentagon. These events were directly linked to the political economy of global apartheid, to the crystallization of new transnational hierarchies of racialized otherness, and to new expressions of power and powerlessness.

At Durban, the Third World, led primarily by African Americans and African people, attempted through diplomacy to renegotiate their historically unequal and subordinate relationships with Western imperialism and globalized capitalism. Reparations were seen by Black delegates at Durban as a necessary precondition for the socioeconomic development of the Black community in the U.S., as well as in African and Caribbean nation-states. September 11 was another type of renegotiation—but this was one of terror, a violent statement by fundamentalist Muslims demanding an end to the economic and political subordination of Arab peoples by American imperialism. Both events challenged, literally and symbolically, the United States' almost completely uncritical support for Israel; to some extent, they were expressions of solidarity with the Palestinians' struggle for self determination. The aftermath of both events left the U.S. government more politically isolated from the African and Islamic worlds than ever before.

Although the traumatic events of September 11 have pushed the Black reparations issue temporarily into the background in the United States, the reality is that U.S. and Western European imperialism ultimately will be forced to acknowledge the legitimacy and necessity of at least a limited reparations agreement. This movement also has international implications that link to issues of redress for colonialism: U.S.

policy makers will undoubtedly attempt to solidify their problematic relationships with African and Caribbean countries to preclude any possible strategic coalition between those nations and more radical Islamic states. The price for their diplomatic cooperation may be debt forgiveness and financial aid to assist in development projects. If African countries are successful in renegotiating their debt payments, such assistance may well be seen as compensation—whether implicit or explicit—for those nations' histories of colonial exploitation and slavery. In that case, the granting of some program of Black reparations in the U.S. also becomes more likely.

"WHY DO THEY HATE US?"

The recent bombing campaign against the people of Afghanistan will likely be described in future history books as the "U.S. Against the Third World." The launching of military strikes against Afghan peasants does nothing to suppress terrorism and only erodes U.S. credibility around the world. The question frequently posed in the media today, "Why Do They Hate Us?," can only be answered from the vantage point of the Third World's widespread poverty, hunger, and economic exploitation. These are the new frontiers for the interrogation of the racialized other in the context of global apartheid.

The United States government cannot engage in effective multilateral actions to suppress terrorism because it has repeatedly illustrated its complete contempt for international cooperation. The United States owed $582 million in back dues to the United Nations, and it paid up only after the September 11 attacks jeopardized its national security. Republican conservatives still demand that the United States should be exempt from the jurisdiction of an International Criminal Court, a permanent tribunal now being established at The Hague, Netherlands. For the 2001 World Conference Against Racism, the U.S. government authorized the allocation of a paltry $250,000, compared to over $10 million provided to conference organizers by the Ford Foundation. Since the 1970s, the U.S. has had an explicit policy of subsidizing terrorist movements against radical democratic and socialist governments—such as Renamo in Mozambique against the Frelimo government. For three decades, the U.S. refused to ratify the 1965 United Nations Convention on the Elimination of Racism.

Is it any wonder that much of the Third World questions our motives? The carpet-bombing of the Taliban seems to many observers to have less to do with the suppression of terrorism and more to do with securing future petroleum production rights in central Asia.

The official U.S. delegation at Durban rejected the definition of slavery as "a crime against humanity." It refused to acknowledge the historic and contemporary effects of colonialism, racial segregation, and apartheid on the underdevelopment and oppression of the non-European world. The world's subaltern masses represented at Durban sought to advance a new political discussion about the political economy of global apartheid— and the United States insulted the entire international community. Should we therefore be surprised that Palestinian children celebrate in the streets of their occupied territories when they see televised images of our largest buildings being destroyed? Should we be shocked that hundreds of protest marches in opposition to the U.S. bombing of Afghanistan took place throughout the world?

The majority of dark-skinned humanity is saying to the United States that racism and militarism are exacerbating the world's major problems. Transnational capitalism and the repressive neoliberal policies of structural adjustment represent a dead-end for the developing world. We can only end the threat of terrorism by addressing constructively the routine violence of poverty, hunger, and exploitation that characterizes the daily existence of several billion individuals on this planet. Racism is, in the final analysis, only another structural manifestation of violence. To stop the violence of terrorism, we must stop the violence of xenophobia, racialization, and class inequality. To struggle for peace, to find new paths toward reconciliation across the international boundaries of religion, culture, and color is the only way to protect our cities, our country, and ourselves from the violence of terrorism.

GLOBAL ANTIRACISM: TWO APPROACHES

The World Conference Against Racism may be judged by history to have represented a dramatic turning point toward the construction of a global antiracism. But to create practical, democratic instruments of social advocacy and capacity building—community-centered institutions that can make real changes in the material conditions and contexts of the lives of peoples of color—we must acknowledge two ideological tendencies within this antiracist current: a liberal, democratic, and populist tendency and a radical, egalitarian tendency. Both were present throughout the Durban conference, and they made their presence felt in the deliberations of the nongovernmental organization panels and in the final conference report. They reflect two very different political strategies and tactical approaches in deconstructing processes of racialization.

The liberal democratic tendency focuses on a discourse of rights, calling for civic participation, political enfranchisement, and the capacity building of institutions to promote civic empowerment and multicultural diversity. This impulse seeks the reduction of societal conflict through the sponsoring of public conversations and multicultural dialogues. It seeks not a rejection of economic globalization, but its constructive engagement, with the goal of building political cultures of human rights. The most attractive quality of this liberal perspective is its commitment to multicultural social change without resorting to violence.

The radical egalitarian tendency of global antiracists promotes a discourse about inequality and power. It seeks the abolition of poverty, the realization of universal housing, health care, and educational guarantees across the non-Western world. It is less concerned with abstract rights and more concerned with concrete results. It seeks not political assimilation in an old world order, but the construction of a new world from the bottom up.

These tendencies, which exist both in the United States and throughout the world in varying degrees, now define the ideological spectrum within the global antiapartheid struggle. Scholars and activists alike must contribute to the construction of a broad front bringing together both the multicultural liberal democratic and radical egalitarian currents representing globalization from below. New innovations in social protest movements will also require the development of new social theory and new ways of thinking about the relationship between structural racism and state power.

~

Interview with Former Jamaican
Prime Minister Michael Manley

Marable: One of the most important political figures of the 20th century, without any question, is the former Prime Minister of Jamaica, Michael Manley. Michael Manley for decades has represented one of the most brilliant and significant figures representing progressive social and democratic change, not only for the Caribbean but throughout the world. And so in this dialogue over the next few minutes, we'd like to explore Prime Minister Manley's personal insights into Jamaica's social and political history, the politics of Jamaica and the post–World War II era, and most significantly, his perspectives, philosophically and politically, on the future of democratic socialism, the future of the world. Historians of Jamaica have written frequently about the nature of Jamaican society, its complexity. One of the things that historians have focused on is what they term "social conservatism." And by this they mean such factors as race, and religion, which have served to deflect greater trade union awareness or political consciousness among many people. I'd be interested in learning your own perspective about Jamaican society, the society in which you grew up, during the late Colonial period. And what was the role of race or factors such as race in that society? And how do they have an impact upon the politics and the culture of Jamaica?

Manley: May I back up at the start to the way the question is formulated. Which really takes us at the point of departure, an assumption of social conservatism. I suppose that if a society that objectively suffers from very serious mal-distribution of wealth, very serious gaps between wealth and poverty, and which has, you might say, at a superficial glance, a lot of the characteristics that you would associate with explosiveness, perhaps even leading to revolutionary potential. If that society is not revolutionary, and has never taken to that sort of thing, has never responded to that sort of thing, then that is prima facie suggestion that it must be conservative. So let's accept that that is so, if we define it in that way. I think that we should start with an idiosyncrasy about the Jamaican racial patterns, very much idiosyncratic if you compare it, say, with the United States experience in the black struggle. In that there is not in Jamaica, a natural solidarity between all people of color. That you do not get a sharp dichotomy between a white superstructure, or upper class, and the rest. What you do get is a very complex set of racial gradations, where white and near-white very often regard themselves as being the same, where a brown (quote, unquote) middle class is very much itself, and where you have the so-called black masses. I suspect something like that may be beginning to evolve in the United States now as I look at some of your television programs, or who your new heroes are. [laughter] I suspect that is happening. But I must say, I've always been very struck by the fact that Jamaican politics have been substantially influenced by this.

For example, when our nationalist movement started in 1938, you had an interesting phenomenon, where one personality called Bustamante became a sort of labor leader himself, a white man. Became the labor leader of the black workers. And another person, coincidentally my father, who was a Rhodes scholar, a brilliant intellect, idealistic socialist, etc., formed a political party that was meant to unite the nation in the drive for independence. And it was very interesting to see how the white Bustamante was a deeply conservative person, rather as George Meany was a conservative, if I might draw a quick American parallel, To watch how Bustamante could unite the black workers into a uniform hatred and fear of the brown middle class, and was able to suggest that the movement for national independence was really the creature of brown middle class ambition, and had nothing of benefit for the black masses. And in one stroke Bustamante was able to split the nationalist movement in two. And deflect the majority of the black masses from an interest or concern with independence. And directed their whole attention, all of their psychic energy went into the struggle for wages, better take-home pay, so on and so forth, So that you saw this complex racial factor at work.

Now let me trace it back. I suspect that you really can find it in the niche of slave society. Let's dissect slave society as we knew it in the Caribbean. The slave labored in the field. There was the attractive nubile woman slave. The slave master would take that to bed, and there would be the brown offspring. That woman slave probably became the house slave, and eventually concubine, and so on and so forth, And from that union sprang the overseers, the bookkeepers, of the sugar estates. Later on in the century, the professionals, the lawyers, the civil servants. So that deep in slave and post-slavery history, there is an objective reason for the distrust of the black formerly slave masses for the brown freed overseer thing. And of course, as so often happens, the person who escaped by concubinage and its product from the field slave experience had to put all the distance in the world between him or herself and that from which the mother had sprung. So that often you got the most brutal oppression by the overseer who was a brown person as I have described. So that is where I think you got the genesis of this enormous complexity, which apparently is not yet a factor in American race relations.

Marable: Well, historically, it has been a factor, that had been declining over about a century and a half. As a follow-up to this question, what's striking me is that historically if one looks at the most radical or the most—the strongest advocates of profound social change, whether they've called themselves socialists or nationalists or communists or whatever—not just in Caribbean society but in the United States—or throughout world history—have frequently come from the relatively privileged middle strata. It's precisely that strata that can produce daughters and sons who have access to higher education, who have a greater sense of the politics and economic dynamics of the world, and who can target inequalities or inequities within their own societies. And so you get this kind of curious contradiction of relative privilege, not absolute, but relative privilege, within this middle-class society, but a radicalism that comes from it. Because it's been denied full democratic rights.

Manley: Granted. But what has always struck me as interesting about Jamaicans is the ability that one political process had to use the dichotomy between what you describe by the educated and by extension politically conscious middle class, is to be able to exploit mass resentment, black mass resentment, so as to tear apart a progressive movement. I don't know if that's common in other parts of the world. My reading doesn't suggest that it is widespread. It's very strong in early Jamaican political history. Anyway, it's interesting. That would half-explain an element in our social conservatism as it affected the political process. As you could not assume a uniting around progressive objectives. And to this day, Jamaican politics still are partly conditioned by the dynamic between these two poles, as I'm sure you know.

Turning to the religious factor, I suppose that you could argue that a very religious church-conscious society as Jamaica is, was, and always will be, is probably led by that to perhaps a greater tendency to acceptance of difficulty on earth.

Marable: Or delayed gratification.

Manley: I am quite certain quotations at this point [laughter].

On the other hand, a very interesting thing. I have often thought myself that because, for instance, a certain type of Baptist experience was very strong in post-slave Jamaican experience, that one of the reasons why Jamaica has taken very naturally to democratic process and is not much given to acceptance of authoritarianism is that it has a deep tradition of the community going to the church meeting and discussing issues, and being accustomed for the majority to rule. And Jamaicans have taken, really like ducks to water, to democratic process. They are naturally very democratic. And accept being on the losing side of democracy with amazing good nature.

Marable: One of the things that is striking, also, about Jamaican history, is the origins of the labor movement, and economists have written that during the post-emancipation period, one of the chief characteristics of the labor process is what one sociologist has called "spreading out work." In other words, a high percentage of the labor force is trapped in low-paying jobs for short period of time. And that because you had a large rural peasantry, it could be brought into the process of production, and then shift out, Labor-intensive types of production. And so in effect, that kind of dynamic spreading outward, of using unemployment in effect is a very calculated tool of suppressing working class dissent and organization. This is a real difficulty in that type of society in organizing labor movement. And so what I'm wondering is, how labor movement from your standpoint was able to develop into such a powerful vehicle in Jamaica with the eruption in 1938?

Manley: Because I think the people who make the analysis that you describe really completely misunderstand the nature of Jamaican society.

Marable: That's fair enough, but ...

Manley: That is almost a guarantee that [laughter]

Manley: I think that is a very superficial application of certain social theories to the situation, I don't think that that's what happened at all. I think that the reality is something like this: (1) Of course in a society at that stage of economic development, it was a labor-intensive society, labor-intensive economy. Of course there was massive unemployment, And to the extent that wages were depressed, the depression was reflecting the objective reality of labor intensivity. You cannot pay very high wages in a product that has to sell competitively in the world market. If you have to employ a tremendous number of people. Because that is the technology currently employed, as is bound to be the case. To suggest that the level of the wages was conditioned by the strike-breaking force that you could bring in from the mountains, that is just not true. I can't think of any Jamaican strike in 50 years that was ever broken. What they misunderstand is the depth of class solidarity in Jamaica. What they don't understand is that if you have a sugar estate strike and I was involved in conflicts over the years, you could never persuade a member of the unemployed to cross the line. That would be to betray their task. And none ever did. So there could never be an objectively valid argument made for the level of the wages being conditioned because critical strikes were broken by strike-breakers from the unemployed. That's why I leapt on it, because I recognize nonsense when I hear it. [laughter]

On the other hand, there was fact that thousands of workers were doing what maybe three or four tractors could do, and of course you're going to have the effect of that, and it had terrible effects on standards. What was also interesting, perhaps more interesting, and really was professional consequence of being a small country, and created great difficulty in the labor movement, still does, is that the size of the operation and for the maximum potential membership, makes it extremely difficult to build unions around occupations, around industries. Because the number of people in the industry is small, therefore the overhead costs—various support, clerical, analytical, all the others—are just prohibitive. And so what Jamaica and a lot of the Caribbean did was to evolve a very rational response to that, which was to have the blanket union which had its sugar section, its manufacturing section, etc. Where one set of people probably negotiated for many industries, and one set of clerks kept the records for many industries. But it did have this effect of lessening the sensitivity of the union to the particular needs of particular industries. It tended to get a rather global solution, rather global-type contracts, global-type grievance procedures, etc. So that was a weakness.

The other factor which Israel got, but not much any more, is that in the early days the close association of two major union blocks, with the two rival political parties, now that was a problem. Because that split the working class along political lines, not with the unemployed, but just among members. And for quite a while that was a complicating factor in Jamaican unionism. By the beginning of the '60s, professionals who spent their lives in it, like myself and others, came to the conclusion this was nonsense. And we began to build bridges across the political divide. And now you have a surprisingly united labor movement, although some still have a nominal allegiance to one political party or another. But common sense has tended to bring them together.

Marable: Now I'm familiar with the history of the evolution of Jamaica's political system. The evolution of the two parties, with the formation of the People's National Party under your father, and then the formation of the conservative Jamaican Labor Party. But I'd like to hear a little about your own interpretation of the similarities and differences between the two founders of Jamaica's modern political system. And how the character of the parties, in part, reflected that leadership during the 1930s and 1940s.

Manley: That is very difficult, because one is my father and the other is a distant cousin. But I'm more objective about my distant cousin than about my father, obviously. Let me think.

They shared a commitment to peaceful political process. That's very important.

Marable: Both were influenced by the political culture that you're talking about.

Manley: They're both very much products of the whole English political tradition. They took to parliamentary democracy like ducks to water. They were very happy with a parliament. Both were confronted with a defeat: one took it with grace and the other always had something unkind to say about the other. That was big—they shared things in common. They had the same values in total, but they had absolutely different personalities. Bustamante was a classic charismatic populist leader, a formidable personality, deeply conservative instincts. He's a guy who really was a deep royalist and very much felt the queen was properly the head of everything—the empire, if not the world. Resisted the independence movement for years because it didn't really suit his political agenda. First favored federation, then smashed it up quite conveniently. Some would say opportunistic, others would say pragmatic. Take your pick. Depends on your perspective. Was an absolute authoritarian. He brooked no dissent whatsoever with his movement. And that has conditioned the party that he left behind him, which is very much formed with the leader.

Marable: That's what I'm alluding to.

Manley: And the reason it's really quite amazing, given the recent evidence. A group of people either challenged his leadership or to ask him to discuss a more participatory style. And he, virtually with all the authority of a pope, excommunicated them. The only reason why they're not out of the party is that they won't go. He can't find a formal reason for declaring them "non-Christians" you know, so they're sort of excommunicated within the vault. And that is because they just wanted to discuss with him style of leadership. And he is very much—Bustamante was like that. So you had a party that tends to be ideologically conservative in terms of policy, of no particularly fixed [?] in terms of commitment. It's hard to put your finger on what, other than what would win votes at that moment in time. Echoes of that I'm sure are familiar in this country. But essentially authoritarian.

The other one was the classic intellectual idealist. And I use both words advisedly. Because to him you would come to a set of principles about organization, or democracy, about national interests, whatever, by an intellectual route. But deep concern for what you thought was right and wrong. And where you would then create structures, policies and everything else, that reflected serious commitment. You might be right or wrong, that's irrelevant. But the process was idealistic, intellectual. And that was really quite an extraordinary political organization for a small, new country that is deeply conscious of its constitution, of its democratic processes, that you have to determine policy by debate and consensus. That will not act if action does not have the imprimatur of executive authority, duly debated and voted. And is really, I suspect, a lot more democratic than many conservative movements in the political spectrum in the rest of the world. And that reflected this extraordinary difference in their personalities and outlook. So one was a nationalist, one was a democratic socialist of admittedly a very pragmatic kind, but still very idealistic. One saw regional cooperation as an imperative, and devoted his life to trying to establish a federation, because that was the right thing to do. And yet when challenged, was the one who said, "Well, I'm going to let the Jamaican people vote in a referendum." Because that was the democratic principle. So they were very different.

Marable: I remember, at least the story, of the very important vote that occurred. And I remember Eric Williams's response, that 10 minus 1 equals nothing. And that much of the history of the Caribbean was decided in that very decisive vote. And it was not a smashing defeat. Could have changed the course of history for not just Jamaica, but for the entire region. How do you look back—I mean this isn't a part of this, but I just thought about this—how do you look back at that election and the personalities that were contending then?

Manley: Well, I see two things. Of course my father has been criticized for being over-idealistic. That he should have toughed it out. Well I've seen a lot of other people tough out things in history, and we're looking at some current catastrophes because they did. People that would not be sensitive to democratic reality, wouldn't allow it to express itself. His own view was that if you try to force a people very conscious of their sovereignty, into a thing that they really did not want, that although you felt it was for their good and correct, etc., that what—he often discussed this with me. So I'm not theorizing, I'm telling you what I know about the man. That we were very close. And his feeling was that you might get away with toughing it out, and saying, "Well we have a federal constitution, that's it!" But his argument was that if you do that, then you're going to create within your society an unending source of tension, contradiction, difficulty, with the drop of a pin. If there is a quarrel within the federation, there'll be forces to mobilize and keep the country in seething discontent. And he felt better be democratically surgical. If you win, then you have popular authority and you proceed. If you lose, then it was not meant to be at that time. And that you will be sorry if you try to force it to happen by the use of temporary power. And I think he was absolutely right. He has done nothing in his life that I more respected than that wisdom. And when I look at Yugoslavia, and I look at a lot in Africa, I think they are confirming the wisdom of a very serious man.

Marable: Your father was willing to take …

Manley: not defeat.

Marable: Even though historically the position that he took was, at least in my own view, in the view of a lot of scholars, historically was imperative for the region. And the region has suffered since then because of that defeat.

Manley: And we have no way of knowing if it would have happened otherwise. His own view is that Bustamante would have won an election and smashed it up. And I think he's right. And don't get me wrong. It's not that we didn't fight to win. I have never fought a harder election than fighting with him and few others to try to persuade the Jamaican people to vote for it. And we lost. But, you know, you can argue it both ways. But that's my own residual view.

Since then, putting it all together another way, with economics—god knows, that's difficult enough! [laughter]

Marable: Well, I think that your father, and, in a different way, C.L.R. James are going to be proven right historically, in the long run. Because if you look at what's happening in Europe, you look at what's happening with the North American Accords, the whole trend of economic and political integration throughout the world is the dominant trend at this time.

There are several events that have happened in your political life that a lot of people have written about, and at least to me as a historian, that I've always wanted to ask you about. And since I'm holding you captive for a few minutes, let me ask you a few of these questions. You can respond either briefly or at length, or whatever your pleasure is. One of the events that people have written a great deal about in different ways, that your voice of clarity might help to clarify how you saw this, as a leader and participant, were the events that happened in the early 1950s. In the Jamaican labor movement and politically with the PNP. The National Workers' Union was formed—in part, this came about because of the conflict between the people's national party and the trade union congress. And I guess what I'd like to know is your own interpretation of the process, and the factors that you feel are most important in understanding the political dynamics and the tensions within the labor movement, and politically in the party, and among progressives in Jamaica in the early 1950s.

Manley: All right. I think that you have to distinguish an international context from a local context, Because they were interconnected, And each throws a different light on what happened. It so happens, if you think back, that that particular split which ripped our movement apart in a soul-searing kind of away, in 1952, was happening at a time when the world was finally establishing and accepting the east-west divide. By then the consolidation of Soviet power had occurred. You were by then well into the Cold War. By then the world labor movement, which had been WF to you, had split into the World Federation which went the straight hard-line Communist way, and the international confederation of free trade unions which was going broadly everything from a Walter Reuther ... everything else was in that. All the so-called democratic aligned unions were in it. Now the TUC, which was the Trade Union affiliated group to the People's National Party, had quite a group of strong socialists. They were intent to this day and I think currently, democratic sources, in the leadership, And they were part of the WFTU. Now inside Jamaica, by then there was tremendous propaganda beginning to generate about socialism, as happens all over the world. And tarring it with the brush of communism. And traditional vague alliances between some kinds of socialism, so kinds of communism, were part of the natural political culture of the time. But as the Cold War begins to harden, all this now becomes very, very dramatic, difficult politics. Just "what side are you on?" "can you really build bridges?" and so forth and so on. And the quarrel inside the People's National Party developed partly because the leftists, who were all democratic socialists, but leftists, felt why should they smash their allegiance with the WFTU because of the Cold War forming? Whereas the more right-wing pragmatists said, "But you're crazy? How can you do this and expose yourself to be tarred with a pro-communist, communist-leaning brush?" So the quarrel starts. And really part of the quarrel had this kind of ideological root—they weren't so much quarreling about what they believed in, but who their friends should be. And who they should have the right to have as friends? Do you get the distinction?

In due course this becomes incorporated within what quite separately was a power struggle. Because it so happened that the group of people were more the moderate rightists, and a group of people the other side, were genuine contenders for power and influence within the PNP, with sharp personality conflicts and difficulty. So in the end, it was discovered that the leftists at some point a few years before, had been using some elements of Marxist teaching in a political education process. And the conservatives made sure that that information got to the press. Sound familiar? And so the minute it got into, you might say, the public domain, it could no longer be contained as a minor internal political party squabble. It now was a major matter of national focus and attention. And the minute that happened, the truth is that it was impossible to sweep this issue under the carpet. And so that in the end there was an inquiry, it was established that they really had been doing a bit of Marxist teaching and so on and so forth. And although they were avowedly not Marxists themselves, they were eventually expelled. One interpretation is that it was a power struggle. Another interpretation is that it was a power struggle that had to end in a certain way as a matter of political survival in the climate of the time.

Marable: One of the things that's most striking about the 1952 struggle inside of the PNP is that 20 years later you come to power in your own right, as prime minister of the first term that you held. And within about 18 months it's very clear—and here I'm speaking as an American, as an outsider—but it was very clear to the rest of the world, that you were articulating not a path that representing totalitarianism or what was projected upon the Castro government from the outside—that is, the Communist model—but rather a democratic and yet very profoundly socialistic program of development. I just was re-reading the Thirteen Principles of Democratic Socialism that came out in November 1974. Many people see that as a major turning point, not just as in the history of the party, but as an effort to articulate a democratic and socialist path for development in the Third World. And I wondered if you could talk about what went on between the time you were elected to the time that this very landmark piece came out?

Manley: Well, I think two things are important. One is that in 1967 in the last election that my father fought, and very narrowly lost, he in fact campaigned on a much more socialist program than anything that we ever—

Marable: I know people ignore that.

Manley: They ignore that immediately. Because by now he's a national hero, he's an icon, and therefore everybody makes him whatever they want him to be. So the right, he really was slightly to the right of Attila the Hun, and so on. But that's what happens to icons.

Marable: Yes, they did that to King in the United States.

Manley: Absolutely. [laughter] Can I talk a few words about this? If it really is Jamaica you're talking about? This is of world interest, but is of Jamaican interest. He felt by 1961—he made a profound speech in 1961 in which he stated that the attempt to follow the Puerto Rican model of development had failed in all the social objectives that were valid for him and for the People's National Party. A tremendous speech about the widening gap between the rich and poor and all the things that we know are classically associated with the industrialization by invitation type of U.S. bootstrap model. And when he lost that election, he set about to try to re-work the thinking of the PNP, which had become very moderate, very middle-of-the-road. I was part of a group of young Turks, intellectuals, whatever, whom he set to work under him to do a complete re-think. And when we fought that election in '67 we lost, but it was on a very radical platform. And I felt that one of the things that had happened is that he had projected a government program without first getting a political party to think through in depth. You know, it was all duly voted—but we had not really gone into the bowels of the party, to get them to try and understand why this change in policy. And so when our time came, after he retired and I won an election for the leadership, I felt two things. One, that you could not put forward a radical program of change without deep internal party process. Because you just tear your own party apart. They wouldn't understand what you're talking about. So we deliberately campaigned on a program of change, but without too much detail. Partly we didn't have the time to think of too much detail. But I was determined to pick up from where I felt my father left off. And go into the party with it, and try and re-think the whole question of ideology. So that what comes out in '74 is not some chance thing. It's years of process, debate and thought, which the journalists just conveniently sweep into a snippet of five minutes of history. As if you could do that in five minutes of history, God help us.

The other thing of course that had changed profoundly was the nonaligned movement had come into existence. Third World consciousness was now a reality. When my father was an activist, these things were just barely—they were just surfacing at the tip of international social consciousness. And I grew up very much more within that atmosphere. Very much more determined that Jamaica must now realize it can't solve its problems alone. It's got to find its fellow creatures in a world process. It's got to have an outward-looking foreign policy. And of course the nonaligned movement was there, so that when we articulate all of that is after years of internal party process, and by a time when we had now directed the party to think in terms of foreign policy.

Marable: Let me interject. I'm approaching this as a historian, not a political organizer.

Manley: Listening to your questions, that is clear.

Marable: Okay. Fair enough. One of the things that's striking about Jamaica in the late '60s that also occurred was the whole growth of a black power group. The demonstrations that occurred at MONA campus around Walter Rodney's expulsion from the country. The very first book I ever read of Walter was the pamphlet, "Groundings with My Brothers," that came out of a whole series of lectures to working-class people in Jamaica. What was the impact—

Manley: Tremendous impact.

Marable: I should finish this up. I also knew several other activists who came out of that process, and who joined the PNP in the early 1970s. So that's one of the questions I'm having—what was that impact upon the party?

Manley: Tremendous. In this sense, again trying to respond in a historical way. That the very forces that had led my Dad looking at it analytically in the late '50s, just begin to sense the social failure of a strategy then being employed. By the forces that were creating greater and greater mass resentment, at last spilling out into black consciousness. By now Malcolm X has happened, and other tremendous things are happening in the United States and the world. The African Liberation Process is now a reality, and we've got independent nations. Nkrumah has happened, etc. So all those things converge in an explosion of consciousness among young black intellectuals. And they are partly reflective of the dynamics. And themselves influence the dynamics of the time.

Marable: How did those events affect or influence your own development politically?

Manley: To the extent that one is a part of the total social milieu, to the extent that one was oneself always driven by only one imperative in my life, egalitarianism. Nothing else has really driven me. How do you create a world of more equal opportunity—how do you create empowerment? Is what I've been about. Even when I didn't even know the phrase. That's what I thought I was doing! As a person who has had a totally undeviating inner personal emotional commitment about life. I am responding to the same forces as everybody else. I look around and I see massive investments of Jamaica and less and less percentage of the people being educated, less and less opportunity happening. More and more concentration of wealth, etc. So I am a product of the same forces, responding to the same failures and the same stimuli. And being stimulated like Rodney. I was a unionist, you know. I've been to trenches of wage negotiations. It's a marvelous thing to sit down with some of the young kids like Rodney and the rest of them, and hear them think. Things that unionists don't always have the time to do.

Marable: Why don't we do a break here and change tape?

Manley: That's a great idea!

[side comments around coffee machine, etc.]

Marable: Let's cover a few events that happened during your administration, the first administration in Jamaica, in the 1970s. One of the most controversial things, at least from the standpoint of the United States, that occurred was in 1975, when you had a state visit to Cuba, and then Castro returned the visit to Jamaica, two years later. This has frequently been cited as a pivotal reason for the deterioration of relations between the United States and Jamaica. And so I have two questions:

First, how would you characterize your relationship with not just Fidel, but with the Cuban Revolution over the years, as you've seen it unfold? And then secondly, how do you characterize the tensions that evolved between the United States and Jamaica over the Cuba issue?

Manley: Can I back up for absolute clarity, and state that when I was a student at the London School of Economics, I sorted out once and for all what was my fundamental location in the political spectrum. And it is not subject to change in response to pressure or inference. And at that stage I sorted myself out as belonging to that category of political activists, thinkers, whatever, who are totally committed to democratic process in the sense of the widest involvement of people in decision-making. Secondly, I myself concluded at that time that I rejected democratic centralism and any attempt to set up a sort of bureaucratized centrally directed society. For many reasons I thought that was wrong, and won't work. Thirdly, I came to the conclusion that although there's a tremendous role for state activity—perhaps in the economy and always in all sorts of things—that the idea of the elimination of private initiative and involvement in the economy was an error. Now those were settled when I was a student. I just look with a sort of dismay at people who have since felt that because Castro is my friend, which he still is, that that could change my fundamental commitments about social, economic and political organization. Let's put that on the record.

Now, Cuban Revolution. I was part of many, many people who were horrified by Batista's Cuba. What Cuba had become. Among other things, a stamping ground for the Mafia, Murder, Inc., all the other criminals who had it as their breeding ground. And was very, very excited at the thought of this popular revolution. And could not help but be impressed by one of the most extraordinary personalities of this century. Whatever happens to him, he is one of the most extraordinary personalities of the 20th century. So that I begin with the tremendous feeling of "Thank God, somebody is going to rip this place apart and shake it up and give it a fresh start. Thank God, somebody is going to talk to Cuban nationalism, Cuban pride and all these things." And that remains about the main feeling that I have about Castro.

As he evolved into his explicit Communist position, I remember thinking with a certain regret, "Gosh, I wish he hadn't gone that way." Because of my own private convictions, but very much feeling that other countries have to evolve their own route for themselves. And with a feeling that there was massive popular support for what he was doing. And that, therefore, fine. That's the way they go, that's their business. What I then watched was something that many people have watched. His ability to mobilize a country, his ability to give a country pride, his ability to give young people a sense of place, his ability to concentrate the finest performance of applied resources in education and health in the entire Third World. Nothing can touch it. And I thought, "Boy. Whatever his ideology, he's putting it to some good purposes. And he's really transforming a country," One then also looked at the huge pressures generated on Cuba by the United States, and while understanding why they were doing that, from their perspective, wondering how far they were driving him into an entrenched radicalism of position to survive. So that you watched the dialectical process with a sort of dismay and horror, wondering how much would have gone that way without that? And vice versa. You know, so one looked at all of that, So that for instance—am I boring you with this? Because it really did cause a lot of trouble, and it causes incredible misunderstanding ...

In coming to office, I didn't have a particular clear view of how Jamaica might relate to Cuba, but Cuba I noticed by then was becoming quite a dynamic force in the nonaligned movement, was taking strong positions over Third World trade and economic issues. And I began to think, you know, he seems to be committing Cuba in foreign policy to things very much of concern to us. And the relationship with him began when he invited me to fly with him and Forbes Burnham, to the Algiers nonaligned summit. We sat up and talked. And I was very impressed by his huge intellect, his grasp of world affairs. What came across as a very real humanism, concern for poverty, things of that sort. And a sense of humor. And an enormous sophistication. I mean, I have watched Castro sit down with the entire church leadership of Jamaica, and dazzle them on the subject of St. Thomas Aquinas. Probably knew more about Aquinas than they did. You know, he's a dazzling scholar. And a person of immense intellectual accomplishment, so naturally I thought, "Boy, he is all he is cracked up to be. This is really quite a guy." Because people with a mind interest me. And so—our relationship started then, which was really restricted to common positions in international issues. And common positions in the nonaligned movement.

The U.S. didn't like that. And I constantly tried to explain to them that, you know, we are not Communist. We are not involved in that aspect of the thing. But surely we have a right to make common cause in sugar prices and things of this sort. As a sovereign nation. They were uneasy with it. I tell you what really caused it. It had nothing to do with going to Cuba. Tell you exactly what caused the trouble between the U.S. and ourselves. To me, the anti-apartheid struggle is sacred. There is nothing Michael Manley will not do to help that struggle. And we watched the emergence of the front-line states, and we watched how South Africa began the destabilization program that virtually wrecked, and still wrecks Mozambique. And has put to the sword Zambia, my good friends in Tanzania. All they have suffered at South Africa's hands. Come Southwest Africa, the beginning of the Namibia independence movement. And comes the moment when South African troops strike north from Namibia to smash Angola. Because it's very important to them strategically to try and destroy the legitimate but leftist government of Angola. Cuba is invited by Augustino Netto to come to their defense, because he already was helping them with education and a little bit of training of his guerrilla forces into the regular army, etc. And in one of the historic decisions and one in which history is going to absolve him again, mark my words, Castro agreed. And sent his army into Angola. He did not go at Moscow's behest. In fact, Moscow was mad as hell about it. Because they were into the strategic arms limitations treaty—they weren't into nothing about black independence. Look at Russia today. Are they into black independence? Now that they don't respond to Castro?

And he really, in a sense, bluffed them into supporting him, by saying, "You can't let me down, I'm your prize exhibit in the West for Communism." And Kissinger asked me personally not to support Cuba's presence in Angola when it came to a vote in the United Nations. He sat in the Government House in Jamaica where I had him to lunch, right after he married that nice lady, Nancy. Came to honeymoon, and he asked me. He would have probably done it if I hadn't had him to lunch. And I remember explaining to him—because you know, what Jamaica did at that time was felt to be important. Still is, in some ways. A little country, but with influence. And I remember explaining to him that I could not give such an undertaking, because our interpretation was that he was defending Angola from South African troops, and that it was very important to the whole dynamic of the liberation struggle in southern Africa.

Marable: And it's been shown that Unita was simply a front for South Africa.

Manley: A stooge. An animal. He's just a traitor. A mercenary is also over Africa. We attended the famous OAU meeting when Africa unanimously voted, every African state, supported Cuba. And I sent a message and said, "I'm sorry, we're voting for Cuba, but please, it is not an act of hostility to America. It is a pursuit of a duty to the anti-apartheid struggle." Well, I tell you, within 14 days the number of CIA operatives in Jamaica was doubled. Within 14 days James Reston, who was the famous stalking horse of the *New York Times,* had me down as a wide-eyed dangerous Castro stooge. I was transformed! [laughter] I said, "when did I become so important from this little island?" Reston wrote five articles about me. And that's when it all began. I was punished. For supporting Cuba in Angola. That's what really caused it. And if I had to do it tomorrow, I'd do it again. I might not bother sending the message this time, because that obviously didn't help. And after that, until Carter came to office, it was grief. We were negotiating $100 million line of credit with Washington, with good prospects. It just disappeared. To say that they got us is an understatement. So I think that's what really caused and of course, I will admit that in my own case, being of a rather defiant nature, and you know, with my trade union background. I didn't take it lying down. And I think I was wrong to allow that explicit hostility to provoke me into responses which in my more mature incarnation, I might avoid.

Marable: But in effect, what happened with that decision is that you underwent in the West literally a character assassination. Because there's no other word for it.

Manley: (laughing) They did a good job.

Marable: Because there was a real concerted effort to distort who you were, to distort your ideology, and to identify you with a political movement, communism, which you were not identified with at all. Yet it's a massive kind of historical distortion.

Manley: It really was. [laughter] ... promoting democratic processes, private sector development. You know at the very time they were doing it, we were drafting laws to guarantee foreign investment security in Jamaica—it teaches you the whole difference in politics. Which I learnt, I suppose, too late in life. The difference between perception and reality. That what people perceive in politics is sometimes far more important than the reality. Nobody bothers with the reality of Michael Manley, the PNP, all that we were doing, the laws we were passing, what they were about, etc. The assiduous effort to cultivate foreign capital to come to Jamaica. Which communist does that, for God's sake? And scrupulous observance of foreign capital's rights in

Jamaica. But to identify with Cuba in Angola—that's perception. You have to be a bad man to do that! So everything else became irrelevant. And I said, "What are you guys talking about?" And they nailed me, "Didn't you support him? Didn't you vote in the UN?" Of course I did. Next question.

Marable: Now some scholars have used the term to describe the election of 1980 as a kind of electoral coup in which you not only had to contend with the forces of an opposition party in a democratic process, but that the United States took a very active role in destabilization of your country. Now, before I talk about the 1980 election, I need to talk also about another event that happened that was very significant in the second term of your administration. And that was the whole relationship with the International Monetary Fund. This was another thing that got a great deal of play and attention in the United States in the media, and in the Western media. If you could capsulate just briefly the basic problems that you encountered with the IMF in your negotiations. I recall that in 1977, in April, you accepted very harsh terms for a loan to address the balance of payment situation. Then toward the end of your second administration, there was a reversal of your position vis-à-vis the IMF. How would you characterize those very murky and very complicated negotiations with IMF, and in retrospect, how do you see the IMF issue as having an impact on the election in 1980?

Manley: First of all, I didn't have a reversal of position about the. IMF, because I signed an agreement then and I signed an agreement later. I certainly learnt that it's a waste of time to attack them too consistently, because sometimes they will just tighten the screw on you. And if you have no alternatives, that's just silly. But a lot of things I think about in capsule: the criticism that I still have of the IMF is that starting with a very monetarist ideological position, it confuses two things constantly. On the one hand, its correct insistence on financial prudence and care that you cannot live indefinitely with budget deficits. And all that is perfect; nobody except an idiot any longer questions that that is true, though the first time it hits you, you're going to get a sense of shock at what they're demanding that you do in return for the foreign exchange support without which your country will sink. We dealt with them because we had got to a point in foreign exchange where we were finding it hard to finance penicillin for hospitals. And that can concentrate the mind wondrously, if you cannot put penicillin in your hospitals. You ought to try that some time. And so we had no choice but to deal with them, because there was no one else to change. The error they make is in trying to compress the process of adjustment into so tight a time frame, that your economy can't respond. Very often a compression of a deficit is sucking the man out of the society. It is drying up working capital, etc. And then you say to an economy, "You must find a way to grow with less means, within one year, or at most, two. So that you no longer need the heavy strictures." So you're then in a catch-22. You're caught inside a contradiction. What they should do and still should do is be iron-hard on fiscal discipline. And nobody became more fiscally disciplined than me once I put my mind to it. And I really began to think about what was involved. But say, if you will be truly disciplined, take a five-year period to slowly work through your development programs, and we will support you with the resources that you need, as the reward for your discipline. They don't do that. And so what they have is a series of failure where people have no choice but to accept the discipline which is correct; then have to try to go through the structural adjustment in maybe 24 months, which no economy can do. Then find at the end of the 24 months you're still in a crisis but you can't produce your way out of it. And so you go round and round and round.

Now, what would I do differently? I can't begin to tell you what I would do differently. The great error that I made was—two things. An over-reliance on what the state could do in economic increment, in creating incremental economic capacity. I grossly over-rated what the state could do. And tried to use the state as an economic machine, as a form of short-cut to development. And I'd learnt that I was wrong. And I've never been afraid to say so, "I was wrong." The other thing that I did was to fail to make an adequate connection between perceptional problems that could arise from the ideology of your concern for the masses, for poverty, equality, for your foreign policy, and its effect on the mind of the private sector. The truth is that while working with the private sector, and almost begging them to invest and produce, and assuring them that we really saw them as a critical part of the engine of development, they looked at the state activity and saw a threat. And they looked at the egalitarian ideology and perceived a threat. And looked at the foreign policy, and perceived a threat. And so they just down downs, and became part of the problem instead of part of the solution.

Marable: There was, in effect, a kind of capital strike.

Manley: And as one accustomed to strikes from the other side, I understood! When I look back at it all, I said, "My God, you know, you really have to re-think this. That if you could pull it off with the state, then you might regard the private sector as marginal. But you don't want them to be marginal, because they are part of your philosophy of a mixed economy anyway." So second time around I didn't change over the IMF. What I changed over was how to elaborate a total strategy that would not frighten the private sector, that would find other ways to development than over-reliance on the state. But most important—you know, this is the big thing, Manning, that I really learnt. And it's all to do with the future of socialism. I don't think socialism is going to have a future until it commits itself to a re-interpretation of its ideas in action.

Marable: What do you mean?

Manley: What I mean precisely by that is this: what is socialism about? The great Arthur Lewis of Princeton once summed it up so succinctly. He said, "Socialism is about equality." Period.

Marable: Yes, That is exactly what it is about.

Manley: That is what it's about. Now, for a long time we thought that the way to deal with the transformation of power relations in this society could only be accomplished with state as activist, that is state intervening in the economy. More and more I found my mind working was to go back to another root of my thinking, which is about participative democracy, Which is about how you could transform power equations, power relations in society. Workers themselves became owners. As well as stuff we're working on now in Jamaica. Has a heavy emphasis on trying to get workers as strong shareholders within their own concerns. Get them into unit trust that they have the kind of concerns that doesn't have shareholding so that they become part of the beneficial ownership of this society. And as to use ownership as the means to equality. By getting out of the Thatcherite trap, into what is really a socialist articulation of equality through ownership. Thatcher could never do this because Thatcher would go as far as wanting her low and middle class to own British Airways, but the thought of a worker owning British Airways was anathema to her, because she's a creature of her class attitude. In my own view, if you can see the state as the catalyst of this kind of transformation—the catalyst in education, the catalyst in promoting small business groups of cooperatives, this, that, the other—I think the road has to lead to a huge cooperative ferment of ownership in the society. And if we can get that going, I think we're going to make the right irrelevant.

Marable: Now that you've gone off in this direction—I'm glad you did, because now I'm thinking about what's the role—if that's the future of socialism in that kind of context, let's try to flesh that out a bit. What would be the role of say a progressive tax policy, or taxation policy, in the context of society, say a government that might be committed to greater worker ownership and participation in the economy?

Manley: We're only just beginning to experiment with it in Jamaica. But we're doing, for instance, already we're having whole sections of tax exemption. If a worker will re-invest in shares, there's a tax benefit. If a company will try and help finance share ownership for the employees, that's a tax credit. So you use tremendous tax relief technique to support and encourage and create incentive for investment in this kind of democratization of ownership.

You see, to me it's a parallel thing. I think you have to do two things. And if you can get back into the idea of participation and equality, equality drives you to opportunity and changing of the relations of power, participative democracy, democratic socialization, deepen democracy seat as a participatory rather than a four-year voting phenomenon. Okay. The other thing that we try to work on, and I hope my heirs and successors pursue it, is to find ways to link democratization and industry. Democratization and communities. Of trying to find ways to set up community councils so that you get whole neighborhoods and communities into a decision-making process at levels that are denied them where you're dealing with a sophisticated remote state. So that what I think the future has to be is all about participation. And that creates a clear difference of message, of strategy, of everything, from the way the conservative sees it. The conservative has latched on to the fact that the state is a clumsy instrument, and in many cases has grown too big and inefficient and beyond the capacity to pan out. So the right has got a classic ease to understand, and can appeal to every person who's tried to get a pension claim from this big bureaucracy and gets angered because it doesn't come back in time. They have a heck of a lot of stuff going for them. And they've played it with great skill.

What we need to do is to completely reverse it. Decentralize. Bring whatever can be brought into the reach of the people, including ownership.

Marable: This sounds more like—and I think that politically or historically, this sounds more like the kind of small c communist model of what the early utopian socialists talked about with small c communism. In other words, small units largely self-sufficient in which the socialist ideal is found in the empowerment of families and neighborhoods and communities, and that the state is not looked at as the be-all and end-all of sustenance for the neighborhood, but rather simply as a catalytic agent for where the real action is, which is at the neighborhood level, or the community level. Is that what you're really for?

Manley: Well, there's an extent to which there is a connection. But that is not a realistic prescription in the modern state, The modern state is of necessity concerned with large industries, very highly technical industries, etc. And you can't bring a sort of neighborhood small c, small s anything. Communalism is a more appropriate word. You can't bring that to bear on the large aggregates that are the major part of the modern state. But those large aggregates are what create the remoteness of power and the sense of powerlessness. Therefore, my view is since you can't reverse that, you can't turn that back. Or you're going to have inefficient non-competitive economy. You have to have a highly efficient aluminum industry, communication industry, But it does not have to rest upon an assumed dichotomy between those who work for it and those who draw dividends from it. That is the dichotomy that I think needs to be closed, be bridged. And I think the minute you do that, I think you have a far more rational society.

Marable: There are models among democratic socialist societies that have part of the way tried to articulate this vision that you're talking about. Are there any societies that we can point to that have tried to move down this road?

Manley: Well, all the Scandinavian societies have done a lot. I mean, I think that they remain the best model we have. I've always thought so. I think that starting with Sweden and to some extent now, Norway, and Holland to a lesser extent, Denmark, I think you have a very, very correct model. Granted that everybody has their own culturality, their own history, their own stage of economic development. But I think the extent to which they have tried to develop society, in a tri-partite mold—government, labor, employer—are part of a national family. That have to talk to each other and work things out. To the extent that they have encouraged strong worker participation and ownership in management decisions, and committee involvement, I think they have the answer. You see, I'll tell you what's interesting. Already you are driven by distress in Detroit to a correct solution. The UAW will now get into worker ownership with General Motors, etc. But not because of a positive response to an ideological configuration for the future.

Marable: But because of a crisis.

Manley: Because of crisis.

Marable: It's being deposed.

Manley: I want that more to be an axiom of action.

Marable: We only have a little bit of time, but there are several things that struck me that might be very interesting to hear your response to. I have a short list of about seven or eight people, who were politically at one level or another in the 1970s and the early 1980s, very influential, either in the Caribbean or in U.S. policy or European policy. And so I'd like you to give me, respond to these political personalities that you've encountered, and give me your brief impressions about them—pro, con or in between. The first you've already talked a little bit about. That's Henry Kissinger. If you had to summarize your relationship with him, or his character in 50 words or less, what would you say?

Manley: I think he was a person with a very strong view of world politics, which you can trace back to Machiavellian [?] and etc., in which he saw the world as safest in the hands of big battalions that could be moved around like the Queen on a chess board, or if you really stretch it, perhaps the castle. But we pawns must know their place. And this is a highly able brilliant man, enormously agile mind and a strong grasp of the world. But a very powerful and clear philosophy about how he thought it should work. And what angered him about Cuba was here was this arrogant little pawn, striding across the Atlantic. Not even on a right angular past, but diagonally—to Angola. Cuba! And he nearly went crazy. Because he thought if a pawn acts like a queen, where is there any order in the world? [laughs] But also a very humorous and charming man.

Marable: Charming?

Manley: I've met him since and found that in his own dry way, if you meet him socially, he can be very charming. I don't mean that he would change what he's thinking. But he has a sense of humor.

Marable: The thing that strikes me about Kissinger—I remember in undergraduate school, reading a biography he wrote of Metternich.

Manley: Did he? Is that so.

Marable: That's right. And his whole study—well, it was on the congress of 1815, and the whole dynamics in Europe, and the setting up the Metternich system that ruled until the revolutions of 1848. And the thing that strikes me about Kissinger consistently is that there is a radical separation between politics and morality. And what strikes me, frankly, about your politics, is the merger of the two.

Manley: Well, I wish I'd thought to put it that way myself. Thank you. [laughter] Who doesn't trace that back to Machiavelli? Actually, Machiavelli in the popular myth. But Machiavelli as I understood him, I think that's the real intellectual route to Kissinger.

Marable: That's right. What about Zbigniew Brzezinski?

Manley: I only met him a little bit, very casually. I know that he was the one who discouraged Carter from coming to a mini-summit that I held in Jamaica about the new international economic order. In fact, Carter might have come, but Brzezinski advised him not to. So I had a rather, shall we say, slightly negative view of him, at that point, though I didn't know him particularly. I met him afterwards and had a TV debate with him once, a discussion, really, not a debate. And he said a very interesting thing. I was discussing with him what I think is going to be a very big place in history for Carter, as the first American president who tried to come to terms with pluralism in the world. In a very interesting way, very positive role in Africa in many ways that we won't discuss now. And I was talking about all this, and my admiration for this aspect of Carter. And he said a very interesting thing, that he thought that Carter had one of the finest minds, and finest grasps of the world of anybody of his contemporaries, but that what he lacked was the capacity to communicate what he understood. And he drew on Roosevelt. Saying that Roosevelt took America through enormous changes. But he had such a gift of communication, of exposition. In a way that the people could understand. That he carried America in some amazing directions. We later saw another great communicator carry America all the way back over the same terrain, in reverse. Through communication. And I was very struck by that. But I didn't know him.

Marable: What about your relations with Carter?

Manley: Well, we get on very well now. Because we don't really have —you know, Cuba's not between us any longer. So we get on fine. I find him an extremely engaging personality. There's a quiet modesty about him that is nice. I think he is a genuinely moral man. I was always struck by the fact that my great friend Julius Nyerere went and saw him once about Zimbabwe during the struggle with Ian Smith's Southern Rhodesia, for the freedom of Zimbabwe. And put into his mind at that time and sanctions against Southern Rhodesia and all that were very much the thing. And put into his mind the simple understanding that what Zimbabwe was about wasn't power, economics, but the right of one person to have a vote. And how he saw the coin drop in Carter's mind. And, my God. When Bishop Muserere tried to betray the liberation movement in Zimbabwe, and the U.S. Senate to lift sanctions, because there seemed to be a settlement, and Maggie Thatcher was off on her charger accepting the settlement, newly elected in Britain, Carter vetoed it. And held the sanctions, because he never forgot one conversation with Nyerere about one person, one vote. And that told me a lot about that man's moral stature.

Marable: The interesting thing about Jimmy Carter is that—and many people don't know this outside of the United States—that in 1970 when he ran for governor the first time—well, the second time, this time successfully—in effect his running mate, his unofficial running mate, was the then-governor of Georgia, Lester Maddox. Lester Maddox was one of the notorious racists in the United States. But as soon as Carter got elected, he gave a historic speech from the capitol building in Georgia, denouncing racism, and saying that "with my election" the Jim Crow era of the South in Georgia is now ended. That in effect he broke with a very long historic tradition of southern racism.

Manley: I didn't know that story. A deeply moral man.

Marable: That's right.

Manley: And playing a tremendous role, you know.

Marable: Well, moving from a rather positive note to a rather negative note, perhaps is your relations with Margaret Thatcher.

Manley: Well, with Thatcher, you have to first of all admit things you have to admit. She is one of the most brilliant people that's ever been in 20th-century politics. A sharp mind. She is like a rapier in debate. A woman of fierce inner ideological conviction, and without whom what claim to intellectual respectability such as it might be, could Reagan have? You know, she really was the philosopher of the rampant radical right. And she clothed Reagan in her own intellectual respectability, as indeed she did Helmut Kohl. So you have to give her that. This is a formidable woman. And has probably had a deeper influence on English politics than almost any other individual in this century. And a lot of what she stood for I have no quarrel with. A lot of the privatization that she tried to do, as I said earlier, I can make sense of, because she wanted little people to get into the thing. But where she parted company with any social ethics that I can respect is that she had this total blind spot about workers. Workers were bad people. To be kept in their place and kept down. So she could never think as I did, of a participatory democratic model of ownership because to her, the workers mustn't have any shares. That's a line they must not cross; they must know their place. Also she was very negative about apartheid. And not always honest about it. She sometimes would play tricks in conferences, once in my presence. Pretending that we're all coming to accommodation with South Africa, because that would play well in the headlines back home. This was in Kuala Lumpur. And in fact, nothing like that had happened. So she was a very ruthless politician, who could play very ruthlessly about what she said and did. And also as a tactician, I found that she was very—you know, once it was within her broad sort of philosophical framework, she really could be quite naughty. Well, I suppose politicians tend to be like that, most of them. So I think she's a mixed bag. But what she has done is play havoc with English education. Sound familiar? Play havoc with many social developments in England, sound familiar? Play havoc with the health system. Play havoc with the inner cities. Sound familiar? Same, same story. England has paid a high price for her, in some respects.

Marable: There are three people from the Caribbean that I would benefit from having brief comments about. One was on the political scene, and who emerged in the 1950s, Forbes Burnham.

Manley: Boy, that's a tough question. Burnham was one of the cleverest men I ever met. And I knew him almost all my life, because ironically when I was a student, he used to babysit for me. I knew him back from them.

Marable: Now, this is the question. Several people have told me that Burnham, from very reliable sources, was in the Communist Party when he was in England, during that time. Have you heard anything about this?

Manley: No, if that is so, I did not know it. And I knew him well enough that he used to—he would babysit for me sometimes. As young married students with a young baby my parents liked to get out occasionally. And he was very nice, he'd come and babysit. And before I was through the door he would be on the phone to his girlfriend. Which was standard student fare, you know. So I never heard that. What I know is that when he went out to Ghana, and he and Jagan set up the PPP, that he very soon—although the PPP was, you might say, a Communist party, by calling itself that, that he quickly broke with Jagan because he thought Jagan was naive and unrealistic.

Marable: That's the public interpretation. But what many people say is that actually Burnham recognized, given what had happened in the Gold Coast, with Nkrumah, that it made far more sense in dealing with the whole dynamics of Whitehall, that there had to be a break with the Communists. And that he came to that realization—

Manley: Yes, but the Communist he broke with was Jagan.

Marable: But in effect, if it is true . . .

Manley: I agree with that interpretation. But I never heard that he was a communist. You ask me, was he a member of the Communist Party? And I had not heard that. I cannot say it's not so, but I didn't know it if it was. But I mean, we knew him as a radical leftist. That he and a whole group of Ghananese they always were in a quarrel with us Jamaicans, because we were very much more what we now call democratic socialists, and they were so radical socialists that they were far more what you may as well have called communist.

Marable: But Jagan, did he exhibit any kind of tendencies, in his personality, toward totalitarianism in this time? Or say in the 1950s, when you knew him?

Manley: No, I don't think Jagan had the kind of personality that would have made him totalitarian at all.

Marable: I'm sorry, not Jagan, but Burnham.

Manley: Burnham. Well, I don't know that Burnham was ever what you'd call a totalitarian. What I know is that Burnham was a guy with a very cynical view of both power and how you acquire it and keep it. The great problem with Burnham—Burnham, you have to give credit for his immense ability. You have to give him credit for his energy and organizing strength. You have to give him credit for the iron consistency of his stand with the nonaligned movement, and over black issues. Magnificent, uncompromising about apartheid. He would take any lick in the world and never compromise those things. But over power internally. He was a cynic. He thought that anybody who wants power and lasted was naive. He'd tell anybody so.

Marable: But that means that he never was . . .

Manley: There's a difference between totalitarian which connotes a lot of things about how you organize the state. And whether you are willing to play tricks with an election because you're involved to make sure [?] to get you out.

Marable: As he did in 1968.

Manley: Over and over and over again.

(talking over, laughing)

Marable: Arguably since 1964.

Manley: I blame Jagan as much as him. When I was faced with that danger in Jamaica, I brought it to an end by refusing to take part. Denouncing it as a fraud and saying, "I won't take part in it. If you're going to do it by crooked means, have it," In 1983. What Jagan did, was over and over and over, would go screaming into the election, "I think this is cooked." Would lose the election and come out and say, "We wuz robbed!" like somebody fighting in boxing. And everybody would say, "Well, if you knew you were going to be robbed, why did you take part in the election?"

Marable: So in effect, what you're suggesting is, is that there's a kind of rather odd marriage between the two political leaders?

Manley: No, I don't think so. I think by then they were well and truly divorced. [laughter]

Marable: I don't mean that literally.

Manley: No, no, I don't even know how to accept that metaphorically.

Marable: In a sense they were connected into a process.

Manley: They started out in a process. And to the end they had a symbiotic relationship with each other. _____ said, "You know, they were weird." They had a weird chemistry. And maybe that's why Jagan couldn't bring himself to just boycott an election. If he had, he might have created a crisis and something might have changed. I'm only saying that I don't think it is really accurate to put Burnham in the totalitarian camp. He was very heavy into the state and the economy; he was very heavy into racial control, Because the black vote is the only vote he could depend on, in a highly polarized Indian black society. And he was quite ruthless, that his army would be black, and black-led and loyal. That his bureaucracy would be black and black-led and loyal. That his party would be controlled by the population he could trust with a certain token presence of Indians.

Marable: But in effect that's a kind of party state government marriage that . . .

Manley: True.

Marable: There was no democratic government for two decades.

Manley: Oh, no, there was not a legitimate democratic government.

Marable: Exactly.

Manley: That is true. Whether he took it so far as to create what you would call a totalitarian state, a la Mussolini, I don't think that's true.

Marable: I don't know if I would go as far as Mussolini, but maybe I've been too influenced by Walter Rodney in this.

Manley: You know, Rodney had his own radical and often quite valid perspective. But I think that Rodney overstated a lot of things. Borne out of his Ghanese frustration. Rodney was a very idealistic person. And he would have started with a deep disgust for Burnham's pragmatic/cynicism. Because he was a pragmatic cynic. Who had strong convictions which he never departed from. That's why you can't just dismiss Burnham like that. He is more significant than that. And he was a strong regionalist. Very strong supporting regional integration and so on. So you have to be respectful to his strengths.

Marable: There are two other people from the Caribbean that I wanted your comments on. One is Eric Williams.

Manley: Well—boy, now, that's a story. Eric starts out, obviously, as one of the great intellectuals of Caribbean history, you know. Still arguably our finest economic historian. He has produced many classic works that will live forever. He, you cannot think—if Trinidad didn't have Eric Williams, they'd have had to invent him. He was The Man who could bring that polyglot cynical calypso society into seriousness and unity. And he did something completely incredible. That he did because he not only had immense intellectual stature—he was beholden to nobody. He was the rebel radical that Oxford wouldn't give a degree to, and had to cross the Atlantic to get his degree. He was anti-imperialist, anti-colonialist, he had stature! And he had Trinidadian savagery of tongue. Eric Williams in the early days, in Woodford Square, where he went to lash whoever he wanted to lash. He did it with a Trinidadian style that you have to go to S___ to hear. So he had this ability to use his great intellect, and direct it in the vernacular that the Trinidadians understood, which made him an effective communicator. And they admired him as their greatest product. There was somebody, this little guy, he would just turn the hearing aid down so he wouldn't hear what you said, and he was about four foot nothing, you know? [laughter] But he was a formidable man. Later on, I suppose as happens to a lot of people, I think that he eventually got such a total dominance over the society, the bureaucracy, the state, the government, that it became almost inefficient. You know, it's not that power corrupted, because he never was corrupt. He was totally indifferent to money and all that stuff. But I think in the end he began to suffer a hardening of the arteries that you get when one person is dominant for too long in one place.

Marable: It was already 1970 with the black power revolts—that was in a real sense, I think, historically, an event that indicated that perhaps his time on the scene had come and gone. And yet he would remain in power for a number of years after that.

Manley: Yes, because nobody would ever go against him. He remained in power in the later years almost by default. But he was a very formidable man, very complex personality, actually.

Marable: I've saved the last person, the most complicated person perhaps, at least in historical terms, to last—Maurice Bishop. There's almost literally a cottage industry that's developed in England and the United States, assessing and reassessing the Grenadian Revolution, because of the role of the United States in ending it. But I'd like to know what your impressions were, at least relations were, with Maurice, Let me prefigure this. When can you recall the first time, meeting Maurice Bishop? When was that?

Manley: I think it was one of the times when he came to our party conference. Our PNP conference has all the progressives from all over the continent.

Marable: That's when we first met, actually.

Manley: Correct. And he came to one of those and I met him and I was very impressed with his intensity and his obvious sincerity and stuff like that. You know, he made a good impression on me, and became a friend. I always regarded him as a friend. A person I liked very much, admired very much, thought had very great courage, great capacity to articulate a defiance on the one hand, and a concern for egalitarianism and for the masses and for people on the other, and I think he was very sincere about those things. And I think he deserved an awful lot better than the people around him.

You must have read the minutes of the last year of the executive committee. I mean, talk about Marxist p____ridity. They were _____. The whole Cord faction. And I don't dislike Cord at all, don't get me wrong, And I'm very glad nothing's going to happen to him, and he may well be right when he says he wasn't in the business of killing Bishop. I'm ready to believe Cord Bernard when he says that. But the mental level of the executive that surrounded Maurice, it just beggars description. They were into just games. "Your tendencies are p.b.—petty bourgeois." All these little catch phrases, you know. Nonsense. And the way that they, in a sense, isolated him, with their preoccupation with these nonsense issues in the last year, I think it's one of the saddest things I've ever read. I find it really sad.

Now there are some who say that he should not have bypassed the party to such an extent, with the setting up of the mass[?] organizations among women and farmers, etc. But would have done better to confront them within the party. Who am I to say? I was too far away to know. I hear it as an argument. And there may be something in that. If you have your mass movements, they should be very much the creature of your patty, so they represent an organic extension, and not a threat. As we never allow, if we can avoid it, to have in the PNP. We try always to make sure they are part of an organic whole. Now whether that was his fault or their fault, who am I to say? They claim it was his fault, and I think it was largely their fault, because I think they were just so inflexible. So that one feels very sad about. I myself question if any of this would have happened if he had just held an election and wiped out the opposition,

Marable: Had he held an election any time in the first two years, he would have won a landslide victory.

Manley: Landslide! And the whole history would have been different. Now how far—I don't know the answer to this. And I don't know who does know it. How far he didn't hold the election because he was himself flirting with notions of democratic centralism and that whole configuration, or how far because they were flirting with that, and wouldn't allow him to hold an election, I don't know. You might know. I don't happen to know. If it was him, then I blame him for a serious error of judgment. Because I myself, more than once, said, "You know, why don't you hold an election?" And he would always say to me, "Well, we're working on it. We have to get a constitution ready." This, that and the other. Whether this is Maurice or the snake skidding in front of me, or because he had something else that was worrying him, I never found out. But none of that would have happened if he'd had an election.

Marable: We only have about one minute left. In the one minute, the big question that I have is, does socialism have a future?

Manley: Absolutely. No question.

Marable: Why are you convinced?

Manley: Because there has to be a place for human aspiration expressed in terms that incorporate everybody in mankind's dream. And the concept that there has to be a politics of activism, for the realizing of a dream that includes everybody, rather than a favored few. That cannot die, will never die, and socialism will be reborn in a new dynamic which I think is going to be very participatory, very much rooted in its greatest strength, which is democratic.

Marable: Thank you. Thank you very much.

Notes

SECTION II

NOTES FOR "ANATOMY OF BLACK POLITICS"

1. Andrew Young, "Why I Support Jimmy Carter," *The Nation* 222 (April 3, 1976).
2. "Turning Up for the Vote," *Focus* 4 (October, 1976).
3. Arthur Miller, Warren E. Miller, Alden S. Raine, and Thad A. Brown, "A Major Party in Disarray: Policy Polarization in the 1972 Election," in Richard G. Niemi and Herbert Weisberg, *Controversies in American Voting Behavior* (San Francisco, 1976) p. 190. Whites supported Nixon by a margin of 68 percent to 32 percent.
4. "Let Them Eat Words," *The New Republic* 177 (September 17, 1977).
5. Oliver W. Cromwell, "Black Voter Participation," *Focus* 5 (January, 1977).
6. "Black House Members Re-elected," *Focus* 4 (November, 1976).
7. Paul Abramson, *Generational Change in American Politics* (Lexington, Mass., 1975) pp. 51-70.
8. *Sacramento Observer* (December 9, 1976).
9. *Cleveland Call and Post* (November 20, 1976).
10. Eddie N. Williams, "Black Impact on the 1976 Elections," *Focus* 4 (November, 1976).
11. J.K. Obatala, "How Carter Should Pay His Debt." *The Nation* 223 (November 27, 1976).
12. "Publisher's Foreward," *The Review of Black Political Economy* 7 (Fall, 1976) pp. 3-4.
13. *The New Republic* 175 (October 23, 1976); 176 (May 14, 1977); 177 (July 2, 1977); all sources listed as editorials.
14. "Let Them Eat Words." *The New Republic*.
15. About 55 to 60 percent of all black adults vote in a presidential year. In off-year congressional, state, and city contests, black voting seldom rises above 40 percent.
16. Ronald Walters, "Strategy for 1976: A Black Political Party," *Black Scholar* 7 (October, 1975) p. 13.
17. Alfred E. Osborne, Jr., "A Note on Black Economic Well-Being in the North and West," *The Review of Black Political Economy* 7 (Fall, 1976) pp. 85-92.
18. Herrington J. Bryce, "Are Most Blacks In the Middle Class?" *Black Scholar* 5 (February, 1974) pp. 32-33.
19. Arthur Tolson, "Historical and Modern Trends in Black Capitalism," *Black Scholar* 6 (April, 1975) pp. 9-12.
20. Theodore Cross, *Black Capitalism* (New York, 1969); Robert L. Allen, *Black Awakening in Capitalist America* (Garden City, N.Y., 1969) p. 156.
21. John H. O'Connell, Jr., "Black Capitalism," *The Review of Black Political Economy* 7 (Fall, 1976) pp. 67-84.

22. Jon Frappier, "Chase Goes to Harlem: Financing Black Capitalism," *Monthly Review* 28 (April. 1977) p. 33.

23. Waltraud M. Kassarjian, "Blacks as Communicators and Intrepreters of Mass Communication," *Journalism Quarterly* (Summer, 1973), pp. 285-291.

24. Robert Axelrod, "Communication," *American Political Science Review* 68(1974) pp. 718-19; *Statistical Abstract of the United States* (Washington, D.C., 1973) p. 379.

25. Alfred E. Osborne, Jr., "A Note on Black Economic Well-Being in the North and West."

26. Eugene Smolensky. "Poverty, Propinquity and Policy," *Annals of the American Academy of Political and Social Science* 409 (September, 1973) pp. 120-124.

27. Official unemployment rates for Mississippi are currently 5.5 percent. When one includes (1) all workers who have stopped looking for work, (2) involuntary part-time workers, and (3) full-time workers whose incomes are below the official poverty level, the "subemployment index" for rural Mississippi amounts to 42 percent. Richard J. Margolis, "Redlining Rural America," *The New Leader* 60 (August 15, 1977) pp. 13-14.

28. Robert S. Browne, "Economics and the Black Community," *Review of Black Political Economy* 5 (Spring, 1975) p. 309.

29. Cathy Sedwick and Reba Williams, "Black Women and the Equal Rights Amendment," *Black Scholar* 7 (July-August, 1976) pp, 24-29.

30. Jodie T. Allen, "The Food Stamp Program: Its History and Reform," *Public Welfare* 35 (Summer, 1977) p. 33.

31. Lester M. Salamon, *Black-Owned Land: A Profile of a Disappearing Equity Base* (Durham, N.C., 1974).

32. Robert Browne, "Black Land Loss: The Plight of Black Ownership," *Southern Exposure* 2 (Fall, 1974) pp. 112-115.

33. Gilbert H. Caldwell, "Black Folk in White Churches," *The Christian Century* (February 12, 1969), p. 34. One important example of this is Dr. Nathan Wright, a black organizer of the initial Black Power Planning Conference in 1966, who also was executive director of the Department of Urban Work of the Episcopal Diocese of Newark, New Jersey. Wright's brother, Benjamin Wright, served as Market Development Manager for Clairol and later used his influence to obtain corporate support for subsequent Black Power meetings. The Wrights and other religious/business leaders encouraged large industries to create "a front for channeling black militancy into the arms of the corporate capitalists." Robert Allen, *Black Awakening in Capitalist America* pp. 161-165.

35. The complex and crucial relationship between the church and state within advanced capitalism has been ignored generally by most American socialists. One indication of the church's economic power is revealed in statements of corporate assets for 1975. The Southern Baptist Convention, a predominantly white denomination with over 12,400,000 members, recorded greater assets ($6 billion vs. $5.8 billion) and a larger number of paid employees (54,150 vs. 53,100) than Dow Chemical, one of the largest corporations in America. The United Methodist Church recorded assets for 1975 greater than the assets of the Columbia Broadcasting System, Coca-Cola, J.P. Stevens, Texas Instruments, and Burlington Industries *combined.* Jim Sessions, "Protestant Power and Wealth," *Southern Exposure* 4 (1976) pp. 83-87.

36. Frantz Fanon, "The Negro and Hegel," *Black Skin, White Masks* (New York, 1967) pp. 216-222.

37. William R. Morris, "Housing: Segregation's Last Stand," *HUD Challenge* (April, 1977).

38. Thomas Bodenheimer, "The Poverty of the State," *Monthly Review* 24 (November, 1972) pp. 7-18.

39. Dorothy Buckton James, "The Limits of Liberal Reform," *Politics and Society* 2 (Spring, 1972) pp. 309-322.

40. Ron Walters, "Strategy for 1976: A Black Political Party," p. 16.

41. John Conyers, "Toward Black Political Empowerment: Can the System be Transformed?" *Black Scholar* 7 (October, 1975) p. 5.

42. Jeffrey M. Elliot, "Interview with Julian Bond," *Negro History Bulletin* 39 (September/October, 1976) pp. 608-609.

43. Mari Evans, *I Am A Black Woman* (New York, 1970) pp. 91-92.

44. The conservative reaction in the aftermath of a massive social movement to change society is not a unique human event, but a permanent feature in the dialectic of social transformations. The concept "Thermidor" expresses the historical inability of social activists to realize their political agendas and their tendency to compromise with the old order for important concessions. See my "Thermidor and Revolution," in *Moving On,* to be published in autumn, 1977.

45. Robert L. Allen, *Black Awakening in Capitalist America,* p. 274.

NOTES FOR "REAGANISM, RACISM, AND REACTION"

1. "New U.S. Policy on Job Bias Draws Anger in House Panel," *New York Times* (September 27, 1981).

2. Howell Raines, "Blacks Shift To Sharper Criticism on Civil Rights," *New York Times* (July 26, 1981); Howell Raines, "Reagan Sends Mixed Signals on Civil Rights," *New York Times* (July 16, 1981); Cheryl M. Fields, "Administration Moves to Ease Federal Anti-Bias Regulations," *The Chronicle of Higher Education* (September 2, 1981).

3. "Budget Ax Rips Welfare Families," *Guardian* (October 7, 1981).

4. Robert Pear, "U.S. Acts To Shrink School Lunch Size For Poor Children," *New York Times* (September 5, 1981).

5. A.S. Young, "Blacks Give Reagan All-Time Low Ranking," *Charleston Chronicle* (August 15, 1981).

6. Gordon Crovitz, "Black Community Reviews Life with Reagan," *Wall Street Journal* (September 4, 1981).

7. NAACP Asserts Reagan Budget Profits the Rich at Expense of Poor," *New York Times* (April 14, 1981).

8. Joyce Daniels Phillips, "Reaganomics Call For Values," *Jackson Advocate* (September 17-23, 1981).

9. Crovitz, "Black Community Reviews Life with Reagan."

10. Ivory Phillips, "Reaganism, Americanism and the Future," *Jackson Advocate* (September 17-23, 1981).

11. Bureau of the Census, *Characteristics of Household and Persons Receiving Noncash Benefits: 1979* (Washington, D.C.: U.S. Department of Commerce, 1981).

12. "America's Restructured Economy," *Business Week* (June 1, 1981).

13. Thomas Weisskopf, "The Current Economic Crisis in Historical Perspective," *Socialist Review,* II (May-June, 1981), p. 36.

14. "A Sudden Change in the Climate—the Economy," *Business Week* (May 25, 1981); "Why the Middle Class Supports Reagan," *Business Week* (May 18, 1981).

15. "Feeling the Pinch at $90,000 a Year," *Newsweek* (May 25, 1981).

16. "A Disquieting Rise in Past-due Mortgages," *Business Week* (May 25, 1981).

17. Karen W. Arenson, "A Debt of $1 Trillion: Its Effect on Economy," *New York Times* (September 30, 1981).

18. Franklin Williams, "A Pall Over Civil Rights," *Milwaukee Courier* (August 1, 1981).

320 Notes to Reaganism, Racism, and Reaction

19. Sam Bowles, "The Trilateral Commission: Have Capitalism and Democracy Come to a Parting of the Ways?" URPE, *US Capitalism in Crisis* (New York: Union for Radical Political Economics, 1978).

20. Manning Marable, *Blackwater: Historical Studies in Race, Class Consciousness and Revolution* (Dayton: Black Praxis Press, 1981), pp. 160-161.

21. Lee A. Daniels, "The New Black Conservatives," *New York Times* (October 4, 1981); Nathan Wright, Jr., "Dilemma of Black Republicans," *Pensacola Voice* (May 30-June 5, 1981).

22. See Colin Campbell, "Conservative Economist Rides With Reagan Tide," *New York Times,* (September 18, 1981).

Sowell's unbridled sycophancy was strikingly revealed in an October 12, 1981, interview in *U.S. News and World Report*. Beneath a large portrait of slaves laboring in the cotton fields, Sowell stated, "Blacks who suffered from slavery also suffered from its aftermath, in that many became hypersensitized against menial jobs. That's tragic." Sowell asserted that racial discrimination plays only a minor role "in holding back ethnic groups in America." Sowell's bankruptcy as a social theorist is matched only by his ability to debase himself as the witless tool of racist reactionaries.

23. "Top Black Reagan Appointees Honored At Hill Reception," *Pensacola Voice* (June 6-12, 1981); "White House Names Minority Liaisons," *Civil Rights Update* (May 1981), p. 4.

24. Lee A. Daniels, "The New Black Conservatives."

25. Tony Brown, "NAACP Shuns Denver Blacks, Part II," Fort Lauderdale *Westside Gazette* (August 30, 1981).

Another prominent fellow traveller is Percy Sutton, former attorney for the family of Malcolm X and past Manhattan Borough president. At the San Francisco conference of black conservatives, Sutton attacked the "environmental movement" and praised the federal deregulation of corporations. Reagan's policy of urban enterprise zones, a massive corporate rip-off of taxpayers and inner city residents, received Sutton's endorsement with one qualification. "Free enterprise zones" will work, he declared, only if the state "[gave] us a lot [more] policemen." "Percy Sutton Calls For Help To 'Help Ourselves'," *Milwaukee Courier* (June 13, 1981).

26. Frank Elam, "Marchers Back Voting Rights," *Guardian* (May 6, 1981); "3000 March in Montgomery," *Guardian* (August 19, 1981).

Jackson also led a major march in Natchez, Mississippi, on May 31, 1981, in support of the Voting Rights Act. "Natchez March Begins Struggle," *Jackson Advocate* (June 4-10, 1981). Julian Bond hosted a black conference on the significance of the Voting Rights Act in Jackson, Mississippi, on October 10, while Yolanda King, Martin's daughter, led a rally of over one thousand people to defend a group of poor black workers attempting to organize in Tylertown, Mississippi, on October 3, 1981. "Bond in Jackson for Voting Confab," and "Mass March At Tyler-town," *Jackson Advocate* (October 8-14, 1981).

27. "Bond Accuses Greensboro Police of 'Negligence,' " *Atlanta Constitution* (October 3, 1981).

28. William Serrin, "Labor Group Girds For Capital Rally," *New York Times* (September 18, 1981); Seth S. King, "240,000 in Capital Rally For Protest of Reagan Policies," *New York Times* (September 20, 1981).

29. William Raspberry, "Coke Deal: Reciprocity Rather Than Generosity," *Miami Times* (September 3, 1981).

30. Ibid.; and "Coke Covenant Brings King Followers Back Together," *Miami Times* (September 3, 1981).

The black brahmins joined forces once more when Ralph Abernathy, a prominent supporter of Reagan in 1980, and "Daddy" King endorsed the mayoral candidacy of Andrew Young in

Atlanta, Georgia. Carole Ashkinaze, "Abernathy Endorses Young," *Atlanta Constitution* (October 3, 1981).

31. Tony Brown, "The newest twist in the Coke Deal," *Pensacola Voice* (September 26-October 2, 1981).

32. Sheila Rule, "Black Caucus in Capital Works to Develop Communal Leadership," *New York Times* (September 30, 1981).

33. Gus Savage, syndicated column, *Pensacola Voice* (September 26-October 2, 1981).

34. Reginald Stuart, "Georgia Blacks Join Battle on Legislative Redistricting," *New York Times* (September 28, 1981); Vernon Jarrett, "Black Democrats turn to the Republicans for help," *In These Times* (September 16-22, 1981).

The attitude of white Reaganites toward the Black Old Guard leadership was one of bitter denunciation. Richard Richards, Reagan's personal selection as national GOP chairperson, complained that his party did not win many black votes because of "the so-called civil rights leaders, [and] the black ministers." Richards attacked Benjamin Hooks by name, stating that "the NAACP hasn't been our friend at all," and declared that Reagan and other Republican politicians would go "around, through; and over" traditional black leaders, to win a conservative black constituency. Adam Clymer, "Black Leaders Criticized by GOP Chairman," *New York Times* (September 20, 1981).

35. Kwame Nkrumah, *Class Struggle in Africa* (New York: International Publishers, 1970), p. 56.

36. Hanes Walton, *Black Politics* (Philadelphia: J.B. Lippincott, 1972), pp. 60-64.

37. Draft Document, Substitute Motion written by Ron Daniels, New Orleans Convention of the National Black Political Assembly, August 23, 1980. Also see Manning Marable, "Toward a Black Political Party: Report on the New Orleans Convention," *Moving On* (November/December, 1980), pp. 17-21.

38. Draft Document, "Preamble of the National Black Independent Political Party," written by Black Party Steering Committee, Philadelphia, November, 1980.

SECTION III

NOTES FOR "BLACK POLITICS AND THE CHALLENGES FOR THE LEFT"

1. Michael Oreskes, "Black Candidate in Virginia: Campaign Is Not a Crusade," *New York Times,* 3 November 1989. Also see B. Drummond Ayres, Jr., "Black Virginia Politician Takes Run at History," *New York Times,* 16 April 1989; and Tom Wicker, "Drama in Virginia," *New York Times,* 3 November 1989.

2. James Zogby, "Dinkins Has Locked Arab Americans Out of His Campaign," *City Sun,* 18–24 October, 1989; Celestine Bohlen, "Arab Group Says Dinkins Shunned Their Bid to Help," *New York Times,* 19 October 1989; and Howard Kurtz, "Arab Americans in New York Say Mayoral Nominees Spurn Support," *Washington Post,* 16 October 1989.

3. Immediately following his election, Wilder urged Democrats to move to the right ideologically and programmatically. Democratic presidential campaigns must support the "values of the overwhelming majority of the people in this country," including the "free enterprise system" and "holding the line on taxes." See Robin Toner, "Enter the Mainstream, Wilder Tells Democrats," *New York Times,* 14 November 1989.

SECTION IV

NOTES FOR "TUSKEGEE AND THE POLITICS OF ILLUSION"

1. Ralph Ellison, *Invisible Man* (New York, 1949).
2. Stokely Carmichael and Charles V. Hamilton, *Black Power: The Politics of Liberation in America* (New York, 1967), p. 122.
3. *Ibid.,* p. 126.
4. The history of Macon County is explored in a special issue of *Alabama Historical Quarterly,* 18, (Summer, 1956). Louis Harlan provides a good, brief treatment of the deal which founded Tuskegee Institute in *Booker T. Washington, The Making of a Black Leader, 1856–1901* (New York, 1972), pp. 113–115.
5. In the Alabama election of 1892, the registered white voters cast 53 percent of their votes for the Populists, 27 percent for the Democrats and 20 percent did not vote. Blacks voted 49 percent for the Democrats, 14 percent for the Populists and 36 percent did not vote. The total statewide Populist vote was 47.6 percent. J. Morgan Kousser, *The Shaping of Southern Politics: Suffrage Restriction and the Establishment of the One-Party South, 1880–1910* (New Haven and London, 1974), pp. 4142.
6. *Tuskegee News,* November 4, 1976; Kevin P. Phillips, *The Emerging Republican Majority* (Garden City, New York, 1969), pp. 209–232.
7. Handy Williamson and Noel A.D. Thompson, *An Economic Study of the Alabama Black Belt* (Tuskegee Institute, Alabama, 1975), p. 104.
8. U.S. Department of Commerce, *Census of Agriculture* (Washington, D.C., 1972).
9. U.S. Department of Commerce, *Census of Population, 1970* (Washington, D.C., 1972).
10. *Ibid.,* Williamson and Thompson, *An Economic Study, passim.*
11. Harlan, *Booker T. Washington, op. cit.,* pp. 171–175.
12. Stokely Carmichael and Charles V. Hamilton, *Black Power,* p. 133.
13. The Black academic elites' median salary is several thousand dollars higher than that of the majority of rural whites and working class blacks, but it is not in most repects an overwhelming, annual income. By both regional and national standards, faculty salaries at Tuskegee Institute are rather low. The median Tuskegee faculty salary for the 1975–76 academic year was $12,500, compared to $16,600 at nearby Auburn University and $13,800 at Alabama A&M. Instructor's salaries at Tuskegee Institute averaged $10,000 during the last academic year. Considering that the average yearly cost of living for a family of four in the nonmetropolitan South for the year 1975 was estimated by the federal government to be $19,800, Tuskegee's academic elite do not have significant surplus capital for major investments outside of food, education, clothing, shelter, transportation and a minimal amount for conspicuous consumption. These figures also provide an explanation for the lack of a taxation base for increased governmental services and higher bureaucratic costs and salaries which the Ford administration became noted for. See the *Bulletin of the American Association of University Professors* (Summer, 1976).
14. One is constantly reminded of Booker T. Washington's joke about Macon County's political economy: "I went to the black belt of the South, inhabited almost exclusively by Negroes and mules." The entire physical culture of the population, black and white, is rooted in the soil: even today, many Tuskegeeans cultivate sizeable vegetable gardens in their backyards. The town itself is barely a generation removed from a rugged, agricultural economy and the plantation itself.
15. A critical discussion on the relationship between political society, and especially electoral political institutions, and civil society is presented in Antonio Gramsci, "State and Civil Society," in *Selections from the Prison Notebooks* (New York, 1973), pp. 206–276.

16. *Tuskegee News*, April 17, 1969; *the Model Cities Experience: Tuskegee, Alabama., 1968–1975* (Tuskegee, 1975).

17. Letters to the Editor, *Montegomery Advertiser-Alabama Journal,* January 30, 1977.

18. *Tuskegee News,* July 15, 1976.

19. *Tuskegee News,* August 5, 1976. In most Southern small towns, the, black ministerial elite has served as the black intelligentsia as well as the central political vehicle for the entire black community. This has not been true for Tuskegee, because of the existence of a well educated, academic black petty bourgeoisie strata. Relations between town and gown blacks were always at best rocky, even during the pre-Populist period. As early as 1884, one local black minister of the A.M.E.Z. Church, the Reverend P.J. McFintosh, referred sarcastically to Tuskegee Institute as "the beacon light on yonder hill, kept in a blaze by $3,000 annually poured into the furnace by a Southern legislature." *Tuskegee News,* September 25, 1884.

20. *Tuskegee News,* August 5, 1976.

21. *Tuskegee News,* August 12, 1976.

22. *Tuskegee News,* August 26, 1976.

23. *Tuskegee News,* December 30, 1976.

24. *Tuskegee News,* February 10, 1977; *Tuskegee Voice,* February 12, 1977.

25. *Tuskegee News,* February 24, 1977.

26. *Tuskegee News,* March 3, 1977.

27. *Tuskegee News,* January 20, 1977. Since the middle fifties, Governor George Wallace attempted to identify his political interests with the interests of Tuskegee Institute. Wallace achieved his initial national exposure by refusing to desegregate the University of Alabama, on the grounds that state assisted institutions like Tuskegee Institute already existed for young black students. Marshal Frady, *Wallace* (New York, 1975).

28. Tuskegee News, January 14, 1977.

29. *Tuskegee News,* September 8, 1977.

30. Joseph Jones to Emmett J. Scott, May 14, 1914; Jones to Scott, May 18,1914; Jones to Scott, June 29, 1914; Scott to Jones, August 13,1914; Jones to Scott, September 24, 1914. Cpy of "Weekly Report on Mahogany," no date but probably 1914; letter to Directors of Company discussing the amount of stock Africans should be permitted to purchase, May 14, 1915; Scott to Jones, May 18, 1915. All letters are in the Booker T. Washington Collection, Container 9, Library of Congress, Washington, D.C.

31. Charles W. Chappelle to Jones, no date; Jones to Scott, August 15, 1915; August 17, 1915; August 25, 1915. Letters are in the Washington Collection, Container 9, Library of Congress.

32. *Tuskegee News,* December 16, 1976; "Baxley Rules Reed out," The *Tuskegee News,* October 27, 1977.

33. Tuskegee Voice, March 5, 1977.

34. Stan Voit, "Money misuse chard made," *Tuskegee News,* November 34. Stan Voit, "Money misuse charge made," *Tuskegee News,* November 24, 1977.

35. Stan Voit, "Audit explains school money," *Tuskegee News,* November 24, 1977.

36. "Charges Dropped, but Amerson, Young and Baxley keep talking." *Tuskegee News,* December 1, 1977.

37. Stan Voit, "Police didn't have total banking," Editorial, *Tuskegee News,* October 27, 1977.

38. "Commodores, Tuskegee musicians to be honored on Saturday," *Tuskegee News,* June 23, 1977.

39. "The Way I See It," *Tuskegee News,* October 27, 1977. 40 Arnold S. Kaufman, "Murder in Tuskegee: Day of Wrath in Model.

40. Arnold S. Kaufman, "Murder in Tuskegee: Day of Wrath in Model Town," *The Nation* (January 31, 1966), 119.

41. Carmichael and Hamilton, Black Power, p. 143.

42. *Ibid.,* p. 144.

43. Frantz Fanon, Introduction, *Peau Noire,* masques blanks (Paris, 1952).

NOTES FOR "THE LAND QUESTION IN HISTORICAL PERSPECTIVE"

1. John Hope Franklin, *From Slavery to Freedom* (New York: Alfred A. Knopf, third edition, 1969), p. 398. This essay defines the Blackbelt as those counties in Georgia, Alabama, Mississippi, South Carolina, and Louisiana that contained a percentage of black people in excess of 50 percent of the county's total population and dependent upon cotton as their primary agricultural product between 1865 and 1910. In 1880, about 5.5 million people lived in the Blackbelt, including 3 million black people. These counties produced 4.1 million bales of cotton in 1880, about three-fourths of the South's total production.

2. Peter Kolchin, *First Freedom: The Responses of Alabama's Blacks to Emancipation and Reconstruction* (Westport, Conn.: Greenwood Press, 1972), pp. 10-11.

3. *Ibid.,* pp. 12-19.

4. *Ibid.,* p. 16.

5. W.E.B. Du Bois, *Black Reconstruction in America, 1860-1880* (New York: Russell & Russell, 1935), p. 434; Lawanda Cox, "Promise Land for the Freedman," *Mississippi Valley Historical Review,* 45 (December 1958), pp. 418-440. A Marxian perspective of southern blacks' desires for land after Reconstruction is presented in Manuel Gottlieb, "The Land Question in Georgia during Reconstruction," *Science and Society,* 3 (Summer 1939), pp. 356-388.

6. Peter Camejo, *Racism, Revolution and Reaction, 1861-1877: The Rise and Fall of Radical Reconstruction* (New York: Monad Press, 1976), p. 52.

7. Herbert Aptheker, ed., *A Documentary History of the Negro People in the United States* (New York: Citadel Press, 1951), pp. 627, 633-636.

8. Du Bois, *Black Reconstruction,* p. 431. For many years, Du Bois was interested in rural economic development in the South. As early as 1893, while a doctoral student at the University of Berlin, Du Bois had composed a paper on the subject, "Die Landwirtschaftliche Entwickelung inden Sudstaaten der Vereinigten Staaten." Du Bois to the Trustees of the John F. Slater Fund, December 6, 1893, in Herbert Aptheker, ed., *The Correspondence of W.E.B. Du Bois, vol.* 1 (Amherst, Mass.: University of Massachusetts Press, 1973), pp. 26-27.

9. Lerone Bennett, Jr., *Black Power, U.S.A.: The Human Side of Reconstruction, 1867-1877* (Chicago: Johnson Publishing Company, 1967), p. 332.

10. Franklin, *From Slavery to Freedom,* p. 312.

11. Bennett, *Black Power, U.S.A.,* p. 331.

12. Ladd Haystead and Gilbert C. Fite, *The Agricultural Regions of the United States* (Norman, Oklahoma: Oklahoma University Press, 1950), pp. 110-111.

13. Du Bois, *Black Reconstruction,* p. 508.

14. C. Vann Woodward, *Origins of the New South, 1877-1913* (Baton Rouge, La.: Louisiana State University Press, 1951), p. 205.

15. Roger Ransom and Richard Sutch, *One Kind of Freedom: The Economic Consequences of Emancipation* (New York: Cambridge University Press, 1977), pp. 77-80.

16. August Meier and Elliott Rudwick, *From Plantation to Ghetto* (New York: Hill & Wang Press, revised edition, 1976), pp. 171-172, 173; Kolchin, *First Freedom,* p. 41-42; Joseph D. Reid, Jr., "Sharecropping as an Understandable Market Response," *Journal of Economic History,* 33 (March 1973), pp. 106-130; Joseph D. Reid, Jr., "Sharecropping in History and Theory," *Agricultural History,* 49 (April 1975), pp. 426-440. One of the earliest histories of tenancy is E.A. Goldenweiser and Leon Truesdell, *Farm Tenancy in the United States* (College Station, Tex.: Texas A & M University Press, 1921). Influential studies on sharecropping during the Great Depression include Charles S. Johnson, Edwin R. Embree, and W.W. Alexander, *The Collapse of Cotton Tenancy* (Chapel Hill, N.C.: University of North Carolina Press, 1935), and David Eugene Conrad, *The Forgotten Farmers* (Urbana, Ill.: University of Illinois Press, 1965).

17. Eugene D. Genovese, *Roll, Jordan, Roll: The World the Slaves Made* (New York: Pantheon Books, 1974), p. 322.

18. Du Bois, *Black Reconstruction,* p. 510.

19. Haystead and Fite, *The Agricultural Regions of the United States,* p. 106.

20. Gunnar Myrdal, *An American Dilemma* (New York: Harper & Brothers, 1944), p. 233. Cotton's central place in the South's economic history is reviewed in Gavin Wright, "Cotton Competition and the Post-Bellum Recovery of the American South," *Journal of Economic History,* 34 (September 1974), pp. 610-635; David L. Cohn, *The Life and Times of King Cotton* (New York: Oxford University Press, 1956).

21. Guano is a substance consisting largely of seafowl excrement or cannery waste. Marl is a sandy, loose earth deposit, containing a large amount of calcium carbonate ($CaCO_3$).

22. Cottonseed is the seed of the cotton plant. When crushed, it makes a rich oil which is sometimes used in the preparation of protein meal.

23. On fertilization in southern agriculture, see Eugene D. Genovese, *The Political Economy of Slavery* (New York: Pantheon Books, 1965), pp. 90-95, and Rosser H. Taylor, "The Sale and Application of Commercial Fertilizers in the South Atlantic States," *Agricultural History,* 21 (January 1947), pp. 46-52. Common antebellum agricultural practices and problems in farming are the subject of Keith Aufhauser's essay, "Slavery and Scientific Management," *Journal of Economic History,* 33 (December 1973), pp. 811-823.

24. J.L. Fowler and L.L. Ray, "Response of Two Cotton Genotypes to Five Equidistant Spacing Patterns," *Agronomy Journal,* 69 (September-October 1977), p. 733.

25. Genovese, *The Political Economy of Slavery,* pp. 96-97.

26. Ransom and Sutch, *One Kind of Freedom,* p. 185.

27. *Ibid.,* pp. 150-154; Stephen J. DeCanio, "Cotton 'Overproduction' in Late Nineteenth Century Southern Agriculture," *Journal of Economic History,* 33 (September 1973), pp. 608-633.

28. Ransom and Sutch, *One Kind of Freedom,* pp. 182-185.

29. *Ibid.,* pp. 300-305.

30. *Ibid.,* pp. 140-148; Glenn N. Sisk, "Rural Merchandising in the Alabama Black Belt, 1875-1917," *Journal of Farm Economics,* 37 (November 1955), pp. 705-715.

31. Jack T. Kirby, *Darkness at the Dawning: Race and Reform in the Progressive South* (Philadelphia: Lippincott, 1972), p. 8.

32. Ransom and Sutch, *One Kind of Freedom,* pp. 190-191. The position of black people within the total capitalist economic structure is presented in Robert Higgs, *Competition and Coercion: Blacks in the American Economy, 1865-1914* (New York: Cambridge University Press, 1977).

33. Monroe Work, *Negro Year Book and Annual Encyclopedia of the Negro* (Tuskegee Institute: Tuskegee Institute Press, 1912), pp. 22, 168, 176, 177, 178. The emergence of the black entrepreneur within the South is skillfully documented in Du Bois' essay, "The Economic Revolution in

the South," in Booker T. Washington and W.E.B. Du Bois, *The Negro in the South* (Philadelphia: G.W. Jacobs & Co., 1907).

34. Ransom and Sutch, *One Kind of Freedom,* p. 30.

35. Work, *Negro Year Book,* pp. 17, 110, 114-118; Kirby, *Darkness at the Dawning,* p. 173. The Morrill Act of 1890 created segregated schools for black agricultural students in seventeen states. Interestingly enough, this racist legislation has never been changed, and existing legislation affecting black agricultural education has been "codified upon it. In 1971, for example, of the $76.8 million in U.S. Department of Agriculture funds which were allocated to agricultural colleges in the states which established segregated school systems, 95.5 percent of the funds went to white schools; $28.8 million marked for agricultural research and forestry research in 1971 was received by white southern colleges; not one penny was granted to black colleges that year for research. See David Dyar Massey, "The Federation of Southern Cooperatives: Hard Times and High Hopes," *Southern Exposure,* 2 (Autumn 1974), p. 41.

36. Louis R. Harlan, Booker T. Washington, *The Making of a Black Leader* (New York: Oxford University Press, 1972), p. 130.

37. Kirby, *Darkness at the Dawning,* p. 171.

38. Booker T. Washington, "How to Build a Race," Sunday night lecture *Tuskegee Student,* 12 (October 20, 1898), pp. 3-4. Copy in Tuskegee Institute Archives, Tuskegee Institute.

39. August Meier, *Negro Thought in America, 1880-1915* (Ann Arbor, Mich.: University of Michigan Press, 1963), pp. 139-140, 148.

40. Woodward, *Origins of the New South,* pp. 132, 135.

41. Richard A. Straw, "The Collapse of Biracial Unionism: The Alabama Coal Strike of 1908," *Alabama Historical Quarterly,* 37 (Summer 1975), p. 93.

42. Booker T. Washington, "The Best Labor in the World," *Southern States Farm Magazine,* 5 (January 1898), pp. 496-498. Copy in the Booker T. Washington Papers, Container 864, Library of Congress, Washington, D.C.

43. Richard T. Ely and George S. Wehrwein, *Land Economics.* (New York: Macmillan, 1910), p. 205.

44. Work, *Negro Year Book,* pp. 163, 167, 180.

45. Meier and Rudwick, *From Plantation to Ghetto,* p. 233.

46. George Brown Tindall, *The Emergence of the New South* (Baton Rouge, La.: Louisiana State University Press, 1967), p. 33.

47. Clara Eliot, *The Farmer's Campaign for Credit* (New York: Appleton, 1927), p. 156.

48. Arthur M. Ford, *Political Economics of Rural Poverty in the South* (Cambridge, Mass.: Ballinger Publishing Company, 1973), p. 20; Robert Browne, "Black Land Loss: The Plight of Black Ownership," *Southern Exposure,* (Autumn 1974), p. 11.

49. Tindall, *The Emergence of the New South,* pp. 33-34; Eliot, *The Farmer's Campaign for Credit,* pp. 156-160.

50. John Kenneth Galbraith, "The Farm Problem and Policy Choices," in Edmund S. Phelps, et al., *Problems of the Modern Economy* (New York: Norton, 1966), p. 151; Arthur S. Link, "The Cotton Crisis, the South and Anglo–American Diplomacy," in J. Carlyle Sitterson, ed., *Studies in Southern History* (Chapel Hill, N.C.: University of Carolina Press, 1957), pp. 122-138; Theodore Saloutos, *Farmer Movements in the South, 1865-1933* (Berkeley, Calif.: University of California Press, 1960), pp. 238-248.

51. Robert R. Moton to I .F. Duggar, September 13, 1916; Carl Vrodman to Robert R. Moton, October 4, 1916, both letters in the Robert Russa Moton General Correspondence, Container 7, Tuskegee Institute Archives, Tuskegee Institute.

52. Monroe N. Work, *Negro Year Book 1918-1919* (Tuskegee: Tuskegee Institute Press, 1919), p. 368.

53. Ransom and Sutch, *One Kind of Freedom,* pp. 172-174.

54. Haystead and Fite, *The Agricultural Regions of the United States,* p. 112.

55. Hanes Walton, Jr., *Black Republicans. The Politics of the Black and Tans* (Metuchen, N.J.: Scarecrow Press, 1975), pp. 81-84.

56. On black politics in Alabama between 1890 and World War I, see Sheldon Hackney, *Populism to Progressivism in Alabama* (Princeton, N.J.: Princeton University Press, 1969) and Mary Tucker, "The Negro in the Populist Movement in Alabama, 1890-1896, Master's thesis, Atlanta University, 1957.

57. Work, *Negro Year Book, 1918-1919,* p. 374.

58. Carter G. Woodson, *A Century of Negro Migration* (New York: Associated Publishers, 1918), p. 169.

59. Haystead and Fite, *The Agricultural Regions of the United States,* pp. 123, 128.

60. *Ibid.,* p. 116. As late as 1940, only 21.7 percent of all farms in Mississippi owned tractors.

61. Ransom and Stitch, *One Kind of Freedom,* p. 196.

62. Paul M. Sweezy, *The Theory of Capitalist Development* (New York: Monthly Review Press, 1942), pp. 272-273.

SECTION V

NOTES FOR "A. PHILIP RANDOLPH AND BLACK AMERICAN SOCIALISM"

1. Irwin Silber, "Randolph: What was his Role?" *Guardian* (May, 1979).

2. Jervis Anderson's biography, *A. Philip Randolph: A Biographical Portrait* (New York, 1972), examines the black socialist's personal and political life. There are two excellent sources on the Brotherhood of Sleeping Car Porters: William H. Harris' recent study, *Keeping the Faith: A. Philip Randolph, Milton P. Webster, and the Brotherhood of Sleeping Car Porters* (Urbana, Chicago and London; 1977), and Brailsford R. Brazael, *The Brotherhood of Sleeping Car Porters: Its Origin and Development* (New York, 1946). Theodore Kornweibel's Ph.D. dissertation, "The *Messenger* Magazine, 1917–1928" (Ph.D. dissertation, Yale University, 1971), examines Randolph's early years as a political activist.

The list of popular and scholarly articles published about Randolph or his role in the black Movement are almost endless. See, for example, L.W. Thomas, "Three Negroes Receive 1964 Presidential Freedom Medal," *Negro History Bulletin* (December, 1964), pp. 58–59; M. Kempton, "A. Philip Randolph," *New Republic* (July 6, 1963), pp. 15–17; Arna Bontemps, "Most Dangerous Negro in America," *Negro Digest* (September, 1961), pp. 3–8; John Henrik Clarke, "Portrait of an Afro-American Radical," *Negro Digest* (March, 1967), pp. 16–23; A. Morrison, "A. Philip Randolph: Dean of Negro Leaders," *Ebony* (November, 1958), pp. 102–104.

3. Philip S. Foner, *Organized Labor and the Black Worker, 1619–1973* New York, 1974), pp. 129–135.

4. *Ibid.,* pp. 169–172.

5. *Ibid.,* pp. 164–166, 171–172.

6. *Ibid.,* pp. 147–160.

7. J. Anderson, *A. Philip Randolph,* pp. 32, 50, 51, 52.

8. *Ibid.,* pp. 76–77; W. Harris, *Keeping the Faith,* pp. 28–29. In 1944 Randolph commented that his "extensive reading of Socialist literature" was one of the "fundamental forces that had shaped his life." The Socialist Party theorists and authors he named included Morris Hillquit, Algernon Lee, Norman Thomas, Frank Crosswaith and Eugene V. Debs. Until 1964, when he

voted for Lyndon Johnson, he had consistently endorsed the Socialist Party ticket. J. Anderson, *A. Philip Randolph,* p. 343.

9. J. Anderson, *A. Philip Randolph,* pp. 79–82.

10. *Ibid.,* pp. 48, 59.

11. Editorial, "Some Negro Ministers," *Messenger* (March, 1920), p. 3.

12. J. Anderson, *A. Philip Randolph,* p.25. Randolph stopped attending church within a year after his arrival in Harlem in 1911. But in December, 1957, the Reverend Richard Allen Hildebrand, an AME minister in Harlem received a request from Randolph to become a member of his church. Randolph seldom attended, if ever; nevertheless, he probably rested somewhat easier with the spiritual knowledge that he was a member.

13. J. Anderson, *A. Philip Randolph,* pp. 97–98.

14. *Ibid.,* pp. 107–109.

15. "The Bolsheviki," *Messenger* (January, 1918), p. 7.

16. "The Russian Triumph," *Messenger* (March, 1920), pp. 3–4. Randolph's mechanistic, economic determinism is evident in his faulty commentary on the Bolsheviks and the coming U.S. revolution. "The Government of the United States ... is located in Wall Street. When the large combinations of wealth—the trusts, monopolies and cartels are broken up ... a new government will then spring forth just as the Soviet Government was an inevitable consequence of the breaking up of the great estates of Russia and assign the land to the peasants, and the factories to the workers. It is as impossible to have a political machine which does not reflect the economic organization of a country, as it is to make a sewing machine grind flour." "The Negro Radicals," *Messenger* (October, 1919), p. 17.

17. Editorial, Messenger *(September, 1919), pp. 9–10.*

18. J. Anderson, A. Philip Randolph, *pp. 92–96.*

19. "When British Capitalism Falls," Messenger *(March, 1920), p. 3.*

20. One of DuBois' most controversial prowar editorials was "Close Ranks," published in the July, 1918, issue of the *Crisis.* He argued, "Let us, while this war lasts, forget our social grievances and close our ranks shoulder to shoulder with our white fellow citizens and the allied nations that are fighting for democracy."

21. Chandler Owen, "The Failure of the Negro Leaders," Messenger *(January, 1918), p. 23.*

22. Randolph. W.E.B. Dubois," Messenger *(July, 1918), pp. 27–28; Editorial,* Messenger *(March, 1919), pp. 21–22.*

23. W.E.B. DuBois, "Socialism is Too Narrow for Negroes," *Socialist Call* (january 21, 1912); DuBois, "A Field for Socialists," *New Review* (January 11, 1913), pp. 54–57; DuBois, "Socialism and the Negro Problem,' *New Review* (February 1, 1913), pp. 138–141. This does not mean that DuBois disavowed socialism. In May, 1914, DuBois joined the editorial board of the Socialist Party's journal, *New Review.* His criticisms of some Socialist's explicitly racist platforms in the South did not lessen his intellectual commitment to socialist economic goals.

24. W.E.B. DuBois, "The Black Man and the Unions," *Crisis* (march, 1918).

25. W.E.B. DuBois, "The African Roots of the War," *Atlantic Monthly (May, 1915), pp. 707–714.*

26. W. E. B. DuBois, "The Reward," Crisis (*26. W.E.B. DuBois, "The Reward,"* Crisis (*September, 1918).*

27. W.E.B. DuBois, "The World Last Month," Crisis *(March, 1917).*

28. W.E.B. DuBois, Crisis *(September, 1917), p. 215.*

29. W.E.B. DuBois, "The Negro and Radical Thought," *Crisis* (July, 1921). DuBois' attitude toward the Bolshevik revolution warms as Randolph's wanes. See DuBois' "Opinion" on Russia, *Crisis* (December, 1925), where he states, "We should stand before the astounding effort of Soviet Russia to reorganize the industrial world with an open mind and listening ears."

30. "The Crisis of the *Crisis,"Messenger* (July, 1919), p. 10.

31. J. Anderson, *A. Philip Randolph*, pp. 100–101; *Ibid.*, p. 10.

32. "A Record of the Darker Races," *Messenger (September,* 1920), pp. 84–85; Owen, "The Failure of the Negro Leaders," p. 23.

33. J. Anderson, *A. Philip Randolph*, pp. 115–119.

34. "W.E.B. DuBois," *Messenger* (July, 1918), p. 27.

35. J. Anderson, *A. Philip Randolph*, p. 122.

36. Ibid., pp. 122–123; Tony Martin, *Race First: The Ideological and Organizational Struggles of Marcus Garvey and the Universal Negro Improvement Association* (Westport, Connecticut, 1976), pp. 9–10. On the Garvey Movement, also see Amy Jacques-Garvey editor, *The Philosophy and Opinions of Marcus Garvey,* Volumes I and II, Reprinted (New York, 1977).

37. Martin, *Race First,* p. 182. After Harrison's newspaper, *The Voice,* closed in 1919, Garvey offered him a position on the *Negro World.* During 1920–1921 Harrison was "joint editor" of the paper. *Martin, Race First,* p. 92.

38. "A Negro Party," *Messenger* (November, 1920), pp. 130–131.

39. Martin, *Race First,* p. 320.

40. "The Garvey Movement: A Promise or a Menace," *Messenger* (December, 1920), p. 171. Throughout the entire history of the *Messenger* one finds an anti-nationalist bias. Randolph and Owen even took the extreme position that the greatest danger to U.S. socialism and the trade union movement was not the racist, conservative white worker, but the Negro! "Negroes must learn to differentiate between white capitalists and white workers," the editors declared. Since they do not, "this makes the Negro both a menace to the radicals and the capitalists. For inasmuch as he thinks that all white men are his enemies, he is inclined to direct his hate at white employers as he is to direct it at white workers." In the *Messenger's* opinion, the only hope was for organized labor to "harness the discontent of Negroes and direct it into the working-class channels for working-class emancipation." "The Negro—A Menace to Radicalism," *Messenger* (May-June, 1919), p. 20.

41. *Ibid.,* p. 170–172.

42. Editorial, *Messenger* (November, 1922), p. 523.

43. Editorial, *Messenger* (July, 1922), p. 437.

44. A. Philip Randolph, "The Only Way to Redeem Africa," *Messenger* (January, 1923), p. 568–570, and (February, 1923), p. 612–614. DuBois' comments against the Garvey organization were provocative. He defended the *Negro World* against Attorney General Palmer's attacks during the Red Summer of 1919, and in late 1920 described Garvey as "an honest and sincere man with a tremendous vision, great dynamic force, stubborn determination and unselfish desire to serve." In 1921, he admitted that the "main lines" of the U.N.I.A.'s activities "are perfectly feasible." It was only in 1922 and 1923, when Garvey began to consider the Ku Klux Klan as a potential ally to the black liberation movement, that DuBois registered his strongest denunciations. See "Radicals," *Crisis* (December, 1919); "Marcus Garvey," a two-part essay in *Crisis* (December, 1920) and (January, 1921); "Back to Africa," *Century Magazine* (February, 1923), pp. 539–548.

45. J. Anderson, *A. Philip Randolph*, p. 82.

46. Harold Cruse, *The Crisis of the Negro Intellectual* (New York, 1967), pp. 45, 75. At its peak in 1921, the A.B.B. had 2,500 members in 56 chapters throughout the country. It demanded th right for black self defense, "absolute race equality," a "free Africa" and political suffrage. In many respects, its platform was strikingly similar to the agendas of Malcolm X's Organization of Afro-American Unity, over forty years later. See "Cyril Briggs and the African Blood Brotherhood," W.P.A. Writers' Project Number 1, Schomberg Collection, New York Public Library.

47. *Ibid.,* p. 46.

48. The final break between the black Marxist-Leninists and Social Democrats does not come

in early 1919, as many have suggested, but much later. As late as mid–1920 Briggs was a participant in Randolph's Friends of Negro Freedom. Martin, *Race First,* p. 320.

49. "The Menace of Negro Communists," *Messenger* (August, 1923), p. 784. The division between black socialists and Communists tended to be along ethnic as well as political lines. Cruse observes that "after 1919, the split among Negro Socialists tended to take a more or less American Negro vs. West Indian Negro character. The Americans, led by Randolph, refused to join the Communists, while the West Indians—Moore, Briggs and Huiswoud—did." There were several exceptions; Fort-Whiteman, an American, joined the Communists. It is interesting to note that Cruse does not fully discuss the fate of Harrison, a revolutionary socialist who abandoned the Socialist Party because of its racism and never joined the Marxist-Leninists; a black nationalist who nevertheless did not wholeheartedly embrace the Garvey phenomenon. His primary concerns were generating independent black political activity and developing a greater race-consciousness among all socialists. See H. Cruse, *The Crisis of the Negro Intellectual,* p. 118.

50. DuBois, "Socialism and the Negro," *Crisis* (October, 1921).

51. DuBois, "Socialism and The Negro," *Crisis* (October, 1921), p. 245; DuBois, "The Class Struggle," *Crisis* (August, 1921), p. 151.I.DuBois, "Communists Boring into Negro Labor," *New York Times* (January 17, 1926), pp. 1–2.

52. Emmett J. Scott, "The Business Side of a University," *Messenger* (November, 1923), p. 864. Early in its career, the *Messenger* was not reticent in its denunciations of Moton. "Moton has neither the courage, education or the opportunity to do anything fundamental in the interest of the Negro," Randolph declared in 1919, "He counsels satisfaction, not intelligent discontent; he is ignorant of the fact that progress has taken place among any people in proportion as they have become discontented with their position .. .." "Robert Russa Moton," *Messenger* (July, 1919), p. 31.

53. "High Types of Negro Business Men," *Messenger* (January, 1925), p. 21.

54. Samuel Gompers," *Messenger* (March, 1919), p. 22; "Why Negroes Should Join the I.W.W.," *Messenger* (July, 1919), p. 8; and "Unionizing of Negro Workers," *Messenger* (October, 1919), pp. 8–10.

55. "The Knowledge Trust," *Messenger (may,* 1925), pp. 197, 209.

56. "Black Persons in Selected Professional Occupations, 1890–1970;" "Percent of Persons 5 to 20 Years Old Enrolled in School;" and "Illiteracy in the Population 14 Years Old and Over for Selected Years," in U.S. Department of Commerce, Bureau of the Census, *The Social and Economic Status of the Black Population in the United States: An Historical View, 1790–1978* (Washington, D.C., 1979), pp. 76, 89, 91.

57. Brazeal, *The Brotherhood of Sleeping Car Porters,* p. 40. At this time, Randolph also began a modest effort within the A.F.L. to drum up support for the Brotherhood's position against Pullman. See Randolph, "Case of the Pullman Porter," *American Federationist* (November, 1926), pp. 1334–1339.

58. *Ibid.,* p. 18; J. Anderson, *A. Philip Randolph,* p. 140. Crosswaith eventually became a member of New York City's Housing Authority, appointed by Mayor Fiorello LaGuardia, in the early forties. Earlier he had been a leading political opponent of Marcus Garvey, and revolutionary Socialist Party theorist.

59. J. Anderson, *A. Philip Randolph,* pp. 171–174; Harris *Keeping the Faith,* pp. 76, 78–79, 91–92. It is significant to note that DuBois had anticipated Randolph's interest in the porters by at least a decade. In a brief essay for the *New York Times,* DuBois suggested that the porters should organize as a union and strike for higher wages and better working conditions. See DuBois, "The Pullman Porter," *New York Times* (March 16, 1914), p. 5.

60. Robert L. Vann, conservative black editor of the Pittsburgh *Courier,* argued that "the company will not deal with (Randolph) because of his history as a socialist. It is known that American capital will not negotiate with socialists." *Courier* (April 14, 1927). A more fundamental reason

was provided by one lower level Pullman boss to his black employees: "Remember, this is a white man's country, white people run it, will keep on running it, and this company will never sit down around the same table with Randolph as long as he's black."

61. Harris, *Keeping the Faith*, p. 110; Foner, *Organized Labor and the Black Worker*, pp. 183–184.

62. Harris, *Keeping the Faith*, p. 110; Foner, *Organized Labor and the Black Workers*, p. 185.

63. Harris, *Keeping the Faith*, p. 112.

64. *Ibid.*, pp. 113, 114.

65. Foner, Organized Labor and the Black Worker, *p. 184.*

66. J. Anderson, *A. Philip Randolph*, pp. 204–205. It should be noted as well that after 1928 Randolph remained "the dominant figure" in the Brotherhood, but no longer wielded "absolute power." Webster demanded and won the right to have all major union decisions made within the Brotherhood's Policy Committee, which he chaired. Historian William H. Harris describes Randolph as the union's "national black leader," whereas Webster was "a union organizer. Randolph thought in wider terms; he saw the problem of blacks in the totality of American society, whereas Webster thought mainly of the porters and of finding ways to improve their conditions at Pullman."

67. Ralph J. Bunche, "A Critical Analysis of the Tactics and Programs of Minority Groups," *Journal of Negro Education*, (1935), pp. 308–320; Ralph J. Bunche, "The Programs of Organizations Devoted to the Improvement of the Status of the American Negro," *Journal of Negro Education*, (1939), pp. 539–50; A. Philip Randolph, "The Trade Union Movement and the Negro," *Journal of Negro Education*, (1936), pp. 5458; Walter Green Daniel, "A National Negro Congress," Journal of Negro Education, (1936); A. Philip Randolph, "Why I Would Not Stand for Re-Election as President of the National Negro Congress," *American Federationist* (July, 1940), pp. 24–25.

68. J. Anderson, *A. Philip Randolph*, p. 254.

69. *Ibid.*, pp. 254–255.

70. *Ibid.*, pp. 241–261.

71. See August Meier and Elliot Rudwick, *From Plantation to Ghetto*, Revised Edition (New York, 1970).

72. On the question of Malcolm, we confront again the inconsistencies of Randolph pertaining to black nationalism. According to one source, Randolph was "a friend and admirer of Malcolm" even during his years as minister of Harlem's temple number seven of the Nation of Islam. In 1962, Randolph invited him to serve on the Committee on Social and Economic Unity, a multiethnic coalition in Harlem. When several conservative black ministers threatened to leave when Malcolm arrived, Randolph replied that he would leave immediately if he was denied a voice on the committee. See Anderson, *A. Philip Randolph*, pp. 13–14.

73. Harold Cruse's discussion of Rustin is in his book, *Rebellion or Revolution* (New York, 1968).

74. Harold Cruse, *The Crisis of the Negro Intellectual* (New York, 1967), p. 65.

75. W.E.B. DuBois, "The Field and Function of the Negro College,' in Herbert Aptheker, ed., *The Education of Black People, Ten Critiques, 1906–1960* (New York, 1973), pp. 95–96.

NOTES FOR "KWAME NKRUMAH AND THE CONVENTION PEOPLE'S PARTY"

1. Basil Davidson, *Black Star: A View of the Life and Times of Kwame Nkrumah* (New York: Praeger, 1974), p. 13; and C.L.R. James, "Kwame Nkrumah: Founder of African Emancipation," *Black World*, Vol. 21 (July 1972), p.4.

2.   Akwasi A. Afrifa, *The Ghana Coup: 24th February 1966* (London: Frank Cass, 1966), p. 121. For Nkrumah's perspective on the coup, see Kwame Nkrumah, *Dark Days in Ghana* (New York: International Publishers, 1968).

3.   Davidson, *Black Star,* pp. 85, 89.

4.   Dennis Austin, *Politics in Ghana* (London: Oxford University Press, 1964), pp. 140-141, 150.

5.   George V. Plekhanov, *Fundamental Problems of Marxism* (New York: International Publishers, 1975), pp. 168-17L

6.   C.L.R. James, *Nkrumah and the Ghana Revolution* (Westport, Conn.: Lawrence Hill, 1977), p. 139.

7.   Bankole Timothy, *Kwame Nkrumah: His Rise to Power* (London: George Allen and Unwin, 1955), p. 111; Austin, *Politics in Ghana,* pp. 84-85, 114-115, 120, 129, 268; and David Apter, *Ghana in Transition* (New York: Atheneum, 1963), p. 172.

8.   Apter, *Ghana in Transition,* pp. 200-201; and Austin, *Politics in Ghana,* pp. 140-141.

9.   Chinweizu, *The West and the Rest of Us* (New York: Vintage, 1975), pp. 135-136; Kwame Nkrumah, *Revolutionary Path* (New York: International Publishers, 1973), p. 71; and Apter, *Ghana in Transition,* p. 173.

10.   Davidson, *Black Star,* pp. 85, 92.

11.   Kwame Nkrumah, *Africa Must Unite* (New York: International Publishers, 1970), pp. 87-88.

12.   George Padmore, *Pan-Africanism or Communism* (New York: Doubleday, 1971), p. 319.

13.   George Padmore to W.E.B. Du Bois, December 3, 1954; and Du Bois to Padmore, December 10, 1954, in Herbert Aptheker, ed., *The Correspondence of W.E.B. Du Bois, Volume III* (Amherst, Mass.: University of Massachusetts Press, 1978), pp. 373-375.

14.   T. Peter Omani, *Kwame Nkrumah* (New York: Africana Publishing Corp., 1972), pp. 2, 60-61.

15.   Timothy, *Kwame Nkrumah,* pp. 173, 180.

16.   Austin, *Politics in Ghana,* pp. 267-268; Nkrumah, *Revolutionary Path,* pp. 117-118; and Robert E. Dowse, *Modernization in Ghana and the USSR* (London: Routledge and Kegan Paul, 1969), pp. 23, 29.

17.   Austin, *Politics in Ghana,* pp. 340-353.

18.   Omani, *Kwame Nkrumah,* pp. 50-53, 55; Henry L. Bretton, *The Rise and Fall of Kwame Nkrumah: A Study of Personal Rule in Africa* (New York: Praeger, 1966), p. 48; and Austin, *Politics in Ghana,* p. 31, 242, 380-384. Background sources on the evolution of Ghana's political institutions and legal systems include: William B. Harvey, *Law and Social Change in Ghana* (Princeton: Princeton University Press, 1966); Martin Staniland, *The Lions of Dagbon: Political Change in Northern Ghana* (Cambridge: Cambridge University Press, 1975); Leslie Rubin, *The Constitution and Government of Ghana* (London: Sweet and Maxwell, 1961); Thom Kerstiens, *The New Elite in Asia and Africa: A Comparative Study of Indonesia and Ghana* (New York: Praeger, 1966); and Robert Pinkney, *Ghana Under Military Rule, 1966-69* (London, Methuen, 1972).

19.   Davidson, *Black Star,* pp. 179, 210.

20.   C.L.R. James, *At the Rendezvous of Victory* (Westport, Conn.: Lawrence Hill, 1984), pp. 178-179; Omani, *Kwame Nkrumah,* pp. 84-85; Apter, *Ghana in Transition,* p. 287; Austin, *Politics in Ghana,* pp. 383, 405; and W. Scott Thompson, *Ghana's Foreign Policy, 1957-1966* (Princeton: Princeton University Press, 1969), p. 112.

21.   Thompson, *Ghana's Foreign Policy,* p. 14; and K.J. King, ed., *Ras Makonnen: PanAfricanism From Within* (London: Oxford University Press, 1973), pp. 222-223, 238.

22.   Thompson, *Ghana's Foreign Policy,* p. 186.

23.   James, *At the Rendezvous of Victory,* p. 178.

24. Richard D. Jeffries, "Populist Tendencies in the Ghanaian Trade Union Movement," in Richard Sandbrook and Robin Cohen, eds., *The Development of an African Working Class: Studies in Class Formation and Action* (Toronto: University of Toronto Press, 1975), p. 263; and Tony Killick, "Labor: A General Survey," in Walter Birmingham, I. Neustadt, and E.N. Omaboe, eds., *A Study of Contemporary Ghana: Volume 1, The Economy of Ghana* (London: Allen and Unwin, 1966), pp. 143-144, 146-147.

25. Nkrumah, *Revolutionary Path,* pp. 151-159.

26. Davidson, *Black Star,* p. 175.

27. Jeffries, op. cit., pp. 261-280; St. Clair Drake and L.C. Lacy, "Government Versus the Unions: The Sekondi-Takoradi Strike, 1961," in G. Carter, ed., *Politics in Africa,* (New York: Harcourt, Brace, 1966), pp. 68, 99; and Omani, *Kwame Nkrumah,* p. 90. Sekondi-Takoradi exploded for several other reasons. It had a relatively small petty bourgeois strata locally; 90 percent of the earnings in the city came from wage labor, a much higher rate than in Accra (67 percent) or Kumasi (22 percent). Unemployment was at least 12 percent in 1961.

28. Austin, *Politics in Ghana,* p. 35; and Owusu, *Kwame Nkrumah,* pp. 88, 91-92.

29. Samir Amin, *Neo-Colonialism in Africa (New* York: Monthly Review Press, 1973), p. 244. Other economic studies on Ghana include: Philip J. Foster, *Ghana and the Ivory Coast: Perspectives on Modernization* (Chicago: University of Chicago Press, 1971); Josephine F. Milburn, *British business and Ghanaian independence* (Hanover, N.H.: University Press of New England, 1977); and Peter C. Garlick, *African traders and economic development in Ghana,* (Oxford: Clarendon Press, 1971).

30. Baako's metaphysical definition of Nkrumaist socialism was "a non-atheistic philosophy" which is "modeled or adapted to suit the conditions and circumstances of Africa ... Nkrumaism is not a religion, but it preaches and seeks to implement all that true religion teaches. I can safely therefore describe Nkrumaism as applied religion ... It seeks to realise its socialist aims amid the legacies of colonialism and yet, in the process, never sacrificing its African character and heritage." See Omari, *Kwame Nkrumah,* pp. 194-195.

31. Thompson, *Ghana's Foreign Policy,* pp. 48, 155, 165-175, 195, 258, 284-86.

32. Killick, "Mining" and "The Monetary and Financial System," in Birmingham, Neustadt, and Omaboe, eds., A *Study of Contemporary Ghana: Volume I,* pp. 251,264,294-296; and Amin, *Neo-Colonialism in Africa,* p. 246.

33. Bretton, *The Rise and Fall of Kwame Nkrumah,* p. 106.

34. Apter, *Ghana in Transition,* p. 77; Thompson, *Ghana's Foreign Policy* pp. 21, 23, 272, 293; Davidson, *Black Star,* pp. 185-186; and Bretton, *The Rise and Fall of Kwame Nkrumah,* pp. 110-111.

35. Nkrumah, *Revolutionary Path,* pp. 394-413; and Omani, *Kwame Nkrumah,* p. 112.

36. King, ed., *Pan-Africanism From Within,* pp. 223, 245-253; and Amin, *Neo-Colonialism in West Africa,* p. 245. Makonnen adds: "There were only a handful of socialists in Ghana—the socialist boys, or the Socialist Six, as people used to call us." The "Socialist Six" were *Evening News* editor Eric Heymann, Cecil Forde and T.D. Baffoe of the *Ghanaian Times,* CPP ideological secretary K. Akwei, Finance Minister Kwesi Amoaka-Atta, and Makonnen.

37. Thompson, *Ghana's Foreign Policy,* pp. 332-333.

38. Ibid., pp. 24-43, 307, 328, 333, 350, 353, 386-387.

39. Amin, *Neo-Colonialism in West Africa,* p. 249.

40. Omari, *Kwame Nkrumah,* pp. 109, 114.

41. Afrifa, *The Ghana Coup,* pp. 114-115, 122. There is considerable evidence that Nkrumah planned to eliminate his potential rivals in the military during 1966. Three weeks before the coup, Nkrumah spoke before the National Assembly on the problem of coups d'etat in Africa: "The duty of the armed forces is to defend and support the Civil Government, and not to overthrow it ... it has no political mandate and its duty is not to seek a political mandate ... The substitute of a

military regime or dictatorship is no solution to the neo-colonialist problem." Nkrumah, *Revolutionary Path,* pp. 370-371.

42. James, *At the Rendezvous of Victory,* pp. 177-178.

NOTES FOR "REDISCOVERING MALCOLM X'S LIFE"

1. Immediately following Malcolm X's assassination, several individuals who had worked closely with the fallen leader sought to document his meaning to the larger Black freedom struggle. These early texts include: Leslie Alexander Lacy, "Malcolm X in Ghana," in John Henrik Clarke, ed., *Malcolm X: The Man and His Times* (New York: Macmillan, 1969), pp. 217–255; Ossie Davis, "Why I Eulogized Malcolm X," *Negro Digest,* Vol. 15, no. 4 (February 1966): 64–66; Wyatt Tee Walker, "On Malcolm X: Nothing But A Man," *Negro Digest,* Vol. 14, no. 10 (August 1965): 29–32; and Albert B. Cleage, Jr., "Brother Malcolm," in Cleage, *The Black Messiah* (New York: Sheed and Ward, 1968), 186–200.

The advocates of Black Power subsequently placed Malcolm X firmly within the Black nationalist tradition of Martin R. Delany and Marcus Garvey, emphasizing his dedication to the use of armed self-defense by Blacks. Amiri Baraka's essay, "The Legacy of Malcolm X, and the Coming of the Black Nation," in LeRoi Jones, *Home: Social Essays* (New York: William Morrow, 1966), pp. 238–250, became the template for this line of interpretation. Following Baraka's Black nationalist thesis were: Eldridge Cleaver, "Initial Reactions on the Assassination of Malcolm X," in Cleaver, *Soul On Ice* (New York: Ramparts, 1968), pp. 50–61; James Boggs, "King, Malcolm, and the Future of the Black Revolution," in Boggs, *Racism and the Class Struggle: Further Pages from a Black Worker's Notebook* (New York: Monthly Review Press, 1970), pp. 104–129; Cedric Robinson, "Malcolm Little as a Charasmatic Leader," *Afro-American Studies,* Vol. 2, no. 1 (September 1972): 81–96; and Robert Allen, *Black Awakening in Capitalist America* (Garden City, N.Y.: Anchor/Doubleday, 1970), especially pages 30–40.

2. The best available studies of Malcolm X merit some consideration here. Although originally written more than three decades ago, *Newsweek* editor/journalist Peter Goldman's *The Death and Life of Malcolm X* (New York: Harper and Row, 1973), still remains an excellent introduction to the man and his times. Well-written and researched, Goldman based the text on his own interviews with the subject. Karl Evanzz's *The Judas Factor: The Plot to Kill Malcolm X* (New York: Thunder's Mouth Press, 1992), presents a persuasive argument explaining the FBI's near-blanket surveillance of the subject. Evanzz was the first author to suggest that NOI National Secretary John Ali may have been an FBI informant. Louis A. DeCaro has written two thoughtful studies on Malcolm X's spiritual growth and religious orientation: *On the Side of My People: A Religious Life of Malcolm X* (New York: New York University Press, 1996); and *Malcolm and the Cross: The Nation of Islam, Malcolm X and Christianity* (New York: New York University Press, 1998). DeCaro graciously agreed to be interviewed in 2001 for the Malcolm X Project at Columbia.

The field of religious studies has also produced other informative interpretations of Malcolm X. These works include: Lewis V. Baldwin, *Between Cross and Crescent: Christian and Muslim Perspectives on Malcolm and Martin* (Gainesville: University of Florida, 2002); a sound recording by Hamam Cross, Donna Scott, and Eugene Seals, "What's up with Malcolm? The real failure of Islam" (Southfield, Michigan: Readings for the Blind, 2001); Peter J. Paris, *Black Religious Leaders: Conflict in Unity* (Westminster: John Knox Press, 1991).

3. Philip Brian Harper, in his book *Are We Not Men? Masculine Anxiety and the Problem of African-American Identity* (New York: Oxford University Press, 1996), argues that the simplistic stereotypes of King and his courageous followers as being "non-masculine" and "effeminate" and

leaders such as Malcolm X and Stokely Carmichael as "super-masculine, Black males" became widely promulgated. "The Black power movement," Harper observes, was "conceived in terms of accession to a masculine identity, the problematic quality of those terms notwithstanding" (p. 68).

4. In an extraordinary interview with writer Thomas Hauser, Alex Haley stated that he had "worked closely with Malcolm X, and I also did a *Playboy* interview with Martin Luther King during the same period, so I knew one very closely and the other a little." Based on his knowledge of both men, he had concluded that they had "both died tragically at about the right time in terms of posterity. Both men were ... beginning to decline. They were under attack." In Haley's opinion, Malcolm, in particular, "was having a rough time trying to keep things going. Both of them were killed just before it went really downhill for them, and as of their death, they were practically sainted." See Thomas Hauser, *Muhammad Ali: His Life and Times* (New York: Touchstone/ Simon and Schuster, 1991), p. 508.

5. Alfred Balk had contacted the FBI in October 1962, seeking the Bureau's assistance in collecting information about the Nation of Islam for the proposed article he and Haley would write for the *Saturday Evening Post*. The Bureau gave Balk and Haley the data they requested, with the strict stipulation that the FBI's assistance not be mentioned. The Bureau was later quite pleased with the published article. See M.A. Jones to Mr. DeLoach, FBI Memorandum, October 9, 1963, in the Anne Romaine Papers, Series 1, Box 2, folder 16, University of Tennessee Library Special Collections. Also see Alfred Balk and Alex Haley, "Black Merchants of Hate," *Saturday Evening Post* (January 26, 1963).

6. On January 9, 1964, Haley wrote to Doubleday Executive Editor Kenneth McCormick and his agent, Paul Reynolds, that "the most impact material of the book, some of it rather lava-like, is what I have from Malcolm for the three essay chapters, 'The Negro,' 'The End of Christianity,' and 'Twenty Million Black Muslims.'" See Alex Haley to Kenneth McCormick, Wolcott Gibbs, Jr., and Paul Reynolds, January 19, 1964, in Annie Romaine Collection, the University of Tennessee Library Special Collection.

NOTES FOR "RACIALIZING OBAMA"

1. Mark Mazzetti and Scott Shane, "Al Qaeda Offers Obama Insults and a Warning," *New York Times,* November 20, 2008.

2. See Manning Marable and Kristen Clarke, eds., *Seeking Higher Ground: The Hurricane Katrina Crisis, Race, and Public Policy Reader* (New York: Palgrave Macmillan, 2008).

3. CNN, *USA Today,* and Gallup poll on Hurricane Katrina Attitudes, September 13, 2005; and Desiree Cooper, "Outrage, Carrying Mix in Katrina Response," *Detroit Free Press,* September 15, 2005.

4. See Michael Powell and Peter Slevin, "Several Factors Contributed to 'Lost' Voters in Ohio," *Washington Post,* December 25, 2004; and Jamal Watson, "Blacks File Lawsuit in Ohio, Claim Disenfranchisement in Election," *Amsterdam News,* December 16–22, 2004.

5. See Manning Marable, "How Washington Won: The Political Economy of Race in Chicago," *Journal of Intergroup Relations,* 11, no. (2) (Summer 1983): 56–81.

6. See Raphael J. Sonenshein, "Can Black Candidates Win Statewide Elections," *Political Science Quarterly* (Summer 1990).

7. See Judson Jefferies, "Douglas Wilder and the Continuing Significance of Race: An Analysis of the 1989 Gubernatorial Election," *Journal of Political Science,* 23 (Summer 1995): 87–111.

8. Andrew Kohut, "Getting it Wrong," *New York Times,* January 10, 2008.

9. Rachel L. Swarns, "Quiet Political Shifts as More Blacks are Elected," *New York Times,* October 13, 2008.

336 Notes to Racializing Obama

10. On Deval Patrick, see Scot Lehigh, "Patrick's Stunning Victory," *Boston Globe,* September 30, 2006; and Kirk Johnson, "In Races for Governor, Party May Be Secondary," *New York Times,* November 4, 2006.

11. Debra Dickerson, "Color-blind," *Salon,* January 22, 2007, www.salon.com/opinion/feature/2007/ 01/22/obama.

12. Stanley Crouch, "What Obama Isn't: Black Like Me," *New York Daily News,* November 2, 2006.

13. John K. Wilson, *Barack Obama: His Improbable Quest* (Boulder: Paradigm Publishers, 2008), 57–58.

14. Peter Wallsten, "Would Obama Be 'Black President'?" *Los Angeles Times,* February 10, 2007.

15. Paul Street, *Barack Obama and the Future of American Politics* (Boulder: Paradigm Press, 2008), 156–159.

16. Wilson, *Barack Obama,* 93–94.

17. Ibid., 95–96.

18. Ibid., 96–97.

19. Ibid., 98–99.

20. Ibid., 73–74.

21. Barack Obama, "A More Perfect Union," March 18, 2008, Philadelphia, Pennsylvania.

22. Ibid.

23. Ibid.

24. Nicholas D. Kristof, "The Push to 'Otherize' Obama," *New York Times,* September 22, 2008.

25. "A Closer Look at the Parties in 2008," Report of the Pew Research Center for the People and the Press, August 22, 2008.

26. Ibid.

27. Ibid.

28. Elyse Ashburn, "Poll: Students Less Engaged Than Thought," A1, A25–A27; and CBS News, UWIRE, and the Chronicle, "College Students and the Presidential Election," *Chronicle of Higher Education,* 55, no. (10) (October 31, 2008), A28–A29.

29. Ibid.

30. "Lexington: Ship of Fools," *The Economist* 389, no. 8606 (November 15, 2008).

31. Street, *Barack Obama and the Future of American Politics,* 156–160.

32. Ken Silverstein, "Obama, Inc.: The Birth of a Washington Machine," *Harper's* (November 2006).

Credits

SECTION I: ON RACE AND RACIALIZATION

"Introduction: The Prism of Race," in *Beyond Black and White: Transforming African-American Politics,* 1–10. London, New York: Verso, 1995.

"History and Black Consciousness: The Political Culture of Black America," in *Beyond Black and White: Transforming African-American Politics,* 216–229. London, New York: Verso, 1995.

"On Being Black: The Burden of Race and Class," in *Blackwater: Historical Studies in Race, Class Consciousness, and Revolution,* 69–77. Dayton, Ohio: Black Praxis Press, 1981. Published originally as "Beyond the Race-Class Dilemma: Toward a Black Politics," *The Nation,* vol 232 (April 11, 1981) 417, 429–433. Used by permission of *The Nation*

SECTION II: ON BLACK PROTEST AND POLITICS: THE 1970S AND 1980S

"Anatomy of Black Politics," *Review of Black Political Economy,* vol. 8, no. 4 (Summer 1978), 368–383. Also published in Marable, *From the Grassroots: Essays Toward Afro-American Liberation,* 25–40. Boston: South End Press, 1980.

"Reaganism, Racism, and Reaction: Black Political Realignment in the 1980s," *The Black Scholar,* vol. 13, no. 6 (Fall 1982), 2–15. Used by permission of *The Black Scholar.*

"The Unfinished Revolution," *New Statesman* [London], vol. 107, no. 2756 (January 13, 1984), 17–19.

"Africa Links," *New Statesman,* vol. 109 (April 5, 1985), 22–24.

"Black Politics in Crisis," *The Progressive,* vol. 51, no. 1 (January 1987), 18–23. Reprinted by permission of *The Progressive* magazine. www.progressive.org.

SECTION III: ON BLACK PROTEST AND POLITICS: THE 1990S TO THE PRESENT

"Black Politics and the Challenges for the Left," *Monthly Review,* vol. 41, no. 11 (April 1990), 22–31.

"Eurocentrism vs. Afrocentrism: The Impasse of Racial Politics," *Democratic Left,* vol. 18, no. 3 (May–June 1990), 14–15.

"A New Black Politics," *The Progressive,* vol. 54, no. 8 (August 1990), 19–23. Reprinted by permission of *The Progressive* magazine. www.progressive.org.

"Black America in Search of Itself," *The Progressive,* vol. 55, no. 11 (November 1991), 18–23. Reprinted by permission of *The Progressive* magazine. www.progressive.org.

"African-American Empowerment in the Face of Racism: The Political Aftermath of the Battle of Los Angeles," *Black Collegian,* vol. 23, no. 1 (September/October 1992), 91–96.

"After the March," *New Statesman,* vol. 27 October 1995, 14–18. (An analysis of the 1995 Million Man March)

"Facing the Demon Head On: Race and the Prison Industrial Complex," in *The Great Wells of Democracy: The Meaning of Race in American Life,* 147–163. New York: Basic Civitas.

SECTION IV: ON THE SOUTHERN QUESTION

"Tuskegee and the Politics of Illusion in the New South," *The Black Scholar,* vol. 8, no. 7 (May 1977), 13–24. Used by permission of *The Black Scholar.*

"The Land Question in Historical Perspective: The Economics of Poverty in the Blackbelt South, 1865–1920," in Leo McGee and Robert Boone, eds., *The Black Rural Landowner—Endangered Species: Social, Political, and Economic Implications,* 3–24. Westport, CT: Greenwood Press, 1979. Also published in *Blackwater: Historical Studies in Race, Class Consciousness, and Revolution,* 53–68. Dayton, Ohio: Black Praxis Press, 1981.

"The Tchula Seven: Harvest of Hate in the Mississippi Delta," *WIN Magazine,* vol. 18, no. 18 (October 15, 1982), pp. 18–22. Reprinted by permission of *WIN Magazine*

SECTION V: ON BLACK LEADERSHIP

"A. Philip Randolph and the Foundations of Black American Socialism," *Radical America,* vol. 14, no. 3 (May–June 1980). Reprinted in James Green, ed., *Workers' Struggles, Past and Present: A "Radical America" Reader,* 209–233. Philadelphia: Temple University Press, 1983. Courtesy of the Center for Digital Scholarship, Brown University Library.

"King's Ambiguous Legacy," *WIN Magazine* (Workshop in Nonviolence), vol. 18, no. 7 (April 15, 1982), 15–19. Reprinted by permission of *WIN Magazine*

"Kwame Nkrumah and the Convention People's Party: A Critical Reassessment," *TransAfrica Forum,* vol. 3, no. 4 (Summer 1986), 19–36.

"Rediscovering Malcolm X's Life: A Historian's Adventures in Living History," *Souls,* vol. 7, no. 1 (Winter 2005), 20–35.

"Racializing Obama: The Enigma of Post-Black Politics and Leadership," *Souls,* vol. 11, no. 1 (January-March 2009), 1–15.

SECTION VI: ON BUILDING A GLOBAL JUSTICE MOVEMENT

"Socialist Vision and Political Struggle for the 1990s," *Rethinking Marxism,* vol. 3, nos. 3–4 (Fall-Winter, 1990), 27–36.

"Multicultural Democracy," *Crossroads,* no. 11 (June 1991), 2–7.

"9/11 Racism in the Time of Terror," in *The Great Wells of Democracy: The Meaning of Race in American Life*, 293–317. New York: Basic Civitas.

"The Political and Theoretical Contexts of the Changing Racial Terrain," *Souls*, vol. 4, no. 3 (Summer 2002), 1–16.

Interview with Former Jamaican Prime Minister Michael Manley, unpublished manuscript, 1992.

Index

Abernathy, Ralph David, 24, 40, 72–73, 195, 197, 200

Adamafio, Tawia, 207, 209, 210, 213

Adams, Lewis, 140, 141, 144, 148

Addison, Kodwo, 212

Affirmative action, 8, 9, 17, 24, 38, 43, 49, 52, 73, 94, 104, 105, 109, 111, 121, 190, 283; Coca-Cola and, 53; condemnation of, 51, 70; corporate, 110; ending, 44–45, 71, 268; initiation of, 18; non-enforcement of, 82; social fairness of, 252; support for, 50, 87

Afrifa, Akwasi A., 201

Agriculture, 58, 143, 153, 157, 159, 160, 161, 162, 166

Ahmad, Eqbal, 263

Aid to Families with Dependent Children (AFDC), 45, 170, 256, 288

Al-Arian, Sami, 270

Al Qaeda, 232–33, 237, 263, 264, 267–268

Al-Zawahri, Ayman, 232

Ali, Muhammad, 285

Alinsky, Saul, 93

Alkalimat, Abdul, 227

Allen, Robert, 43, 199

Amegbe, G. K., 203

American Federation of Labor (AFL), 177, 178, 179, 186, 187, 190, 192

Amerson, Lucius, 151

Amin, Samir, 209, 210, 212–213, 289

Amponsah, R. R., 203, 205, 206

Andrews, Jim, 171

Anti-Semitism, 25–26, 95, 97, 103–104, 105, 106, 121, 230, 249

Antiracism, 101, 267, 288, 289, 291–292

Apartheid, 15, 65, 87, 167, 238, 252, 265, 277, 279, 283, 289, 290, 292, 312, 313; battle against, 62, 66, 67, 258; economic/political support for, 67

Appiah, Joe, 205, 206, 209, 214

Arden-Clarke, Sir Charles, 202

Arrington, Richard, 57

Asante, Molefi Kete, 12, 88, 89, 90

Ashe, Arthur, 63

Autobiography of Malcolm X, The (Malcolm X and Haley), 216–217, 221, 223, 224, 225, 228, 229, 230, 231

Azikiwe, Nhamdi, 66, 201, 204, 212

Baako, Kofi, 209

Bagnall, Robert W., 179

Baker, Ella, 8

Baldwin, James, 197

Balk, Alfred, 229

Banda, Hastings, 212

Bankhead, John H., 162

Banks, Charles, 161

Baraka, Amiri (LeRoi Jones), 198, 218 219

Barlow, David, 132–133

Barry, Marion, 57, 72, 85, 95, 97

Basner, H. M., 210

Batista, Fulgencio, 303

Batsa, Kofi, 209

Baxley, Bill, 150, 151

Belafonte, Harry, 63, 221

Bennett, L. Roy, 195

Bennett, William, 259

Bentsen, Lloyd, 85

Berg, Joel, 266

Berlusconi, Silvio, 270

Bernard, Cord, 315

Bernstein, Eduard, 180, 248

Berry, Mary Frances, 63

Bethune, Mary McLeod, 221

Bevel, James, 72–73, 196

Biden, Joe, 240

Biko, Steve, 67

Bilbo, Theodore G., 168–169, 197

Bin Laden, Osama, 264, 276

Bing, Geoffrey, 210

Bishop, Cecil, 274

Bishop, Maurice, 249, 315

Blac, Fred, 52

Black community, 12, 16, 23, 33, 37, 40, 42, 55, 62, 71–72, 82, 92, 99, 145, 281; defining, 11, 109; Democratic party and, 39, 57, 69;

Black community *(continued)*
deterioration of, 93; healing by, 111, 121; politics of, 13, 36, 68; social character of, 17; socioeconomic development of, 289
Black nationalism, 12–14, 17, 19, 20, 24, 49, 56, 85, 88, 92, 124, 125, 183–184, 185, 190, 192, 193, 198–200, 217, 220, 224, 230, 231, 281, 282
Black Panther Party, 23–24, 119, 121, 253
Black Power, 9, 23–24, 25, 50, 57–58, 67, 74, 87, 94, 98, 101, 140, 144, 145, 146, 152, 191, 192, 194, 198, 216, 217, 222
Black Reaganism, 24, 44, 50–52, 56, 70, 72, 76
Blackness, 17, 20, 28, 216, 233, 284, 286; definition of, 16, 101; function of, 7, 19; redefining, 10, 27; subordination of, 272
Blanchard, James J., 70
Bloomberg, Michael, 267
Blydens, Edward Wilmot, 7
Bognor, Joseph, 210
Bond, Christopher, 34
Bond, Julian, 43, 53, 54
Booker, Corey, 235
Braden, Anne and Carl, 197
Bradley, Melvin L., 45, 51, 70
Bradley, Thomas, 83, 234, 235
Breaux, John B., 74–75
Briggs, Cyril V., 14, 176, 184
Bronstein, Alvin J., 135
Brooke, Edward, 50, 68, 199
Brooks, Arthur L., 140, 141, 144
Brooks, Gwendolyn, 217
Browder, Earl, 178
Brown, John, 29
Brown, Ron, 85
Brown, Tony, 52
Brown v. Board of Education (1954), 50, 55, 106–107, 194
Browne, Robert S., 35
Brzezinski, Zbigniew, 310
Buchanan, John H., 194
Bunche, Ralph, 188–189, 199, 287
Burleson, Albert, 181
Burnham, Forbes, 250, 304, 312, 313, 314
Burns, Arthur, 36
Bush, George H. W., 94, 114, 115, 117, 258, 268
Bush, George W., 108, 239, 241, 242, 268, 275; criticism of, 271, 274; denunciations by, 263; electoral fraud and, 233
Buthelezi, Chief Gatsha, 64
Butler, Norman 3X, 223
Byrd, Harry F., 55
Cabral, Amilcar, 21, 28, 201, 249
Caldwell, Gilbert, 42
Camejo, Peter, 154

Campbell, Grace, 176
Candler, Asa G., 162
Capitalism, 10, 26, 45, 49, 55, 88, 118, 165, 186, 198, 212, 247, 249, 251, 289; black, 34, 39, 54, 60, 82, 92, 282; corporate, 18, 43, 108, 256; expansion of, 41, 50–51, 252, 259; overturning, 242; racism and, 250, 259; restructuring, 44–48; transnational, 262, 291
Carmichael, Stokely (Kwame Toure), 23–24, 52, 139, 140, 152, 191, 199
Carson, Clayborne, 225, 227
Carter, Jimmy, 35, 46, 108, 142, 166–167, 305; black vote for, 33, 34, 36, 40, 41, 57; centrist policies of, 61; relations with, 310–311
Carthan, Eddie, 170–171
Carver, George Washington, 178
Cary, Mary Ann Shadd, 88
Castro, Fidel, 300, 303, 304, 305
Chavis, Benjamin, 17, 55, 120, 121–122, 125
Cheney, Dick, 242, 275
Cheney, Felmer, 96
Chin, Vincent, 255
Civil liberties, 66, 76, 251, 256, 267; violation of, 250, 268, 269, 271
Civil rights, 9, 23, 38, 49, 52, 63, 66, 73, 81, 82, 84, 98, 144, 171, 197, 252, 267; agenda, 71, 256, 283; economic development and, 70; legislation, 42, 45, 50, 62, 74, 121; struggle for, 55, 145, 198; suppression of, 71, 268, 269, 271; trade unionism, 188–193
Civil Rights Act (1964), 17, 74, 98, 110, 115
Civil rights movement, 4, 16, 24, 34, 37, 55, 61, 75, 82, 87, 95, 106, 119, 148, 152, 166, 175, 191, 194, 195–196, 229, 236, 252, 281; African-American churches and, 238; aggressive, 71; Democratic Party and, 40; leadership of, 224; March on Washington Movement and, 90; ministers and, 40–41; repudiation of, 51; rural, 41–42
Clark, Kenneth, 22, 23, 24
Clark, Mark, 253
Class, 19, 30, 277, 287, 288, 295; social, 4, 90, 110, 283; race and, 23, 24–25, 122; struggle, 27, 182–188, 185, 254
Clay, William, 34
Cleaver, Eldridge, 24, 73, 135
Clinton, Bill, 124, 132, 221, 237, 264, 282–283; Omnibus Crime Bill and, 123; welfare and, 268
Clinton, Hillary, 236–237
Coard, Bernard, 249
Coca-Cola, 42, 53–54, 162, 281
Cohen, Richard, 109
Coleman, Marshall, 234, 235
Coleman, Paul, 228
Coleman, William T., 50

Commoner, Barry, 36
Communism, 88, 185, 197, 198, 249, 250–251, 270, 294, 299–300, 304, 308, 309; democracy and, 199; fall of, 268; social democracy and, 251
Communist Party, 85, 175, 176, 177, 178, 184, 249, 312, 313
Compton, James, 45–46
Congress of Racial Equality (CORE), 38, 60, 73, 74, 191, 196, 197, 287
Congressional Black Caucus, 13, 43, 44, 54, 60, 63, 68, 95, 99–100
Connor, Bull, 57, 196
Conover, Ted, 127–128
Convention People's Party (CPP), 201, 202, 203, 204, 205, 206 207, 208, 209, 211, 213
Conyers, John, 43
Coulter, Ann, 270
Cox, Oliver Cromwell, 25, 273
Crenshaw, Kimberle, 98
Crime, 9, 42, 59, 95; drug, 130, 281; poverty and, 251; violent, 129, 130
Cross, Theodore, 38
Crosswaith, Frank W., 176, 187, 189
Crouch, Stanley, 236
Cruse, Harold, 175, 184, 192, 193, 198
Culture, 20 272, 279, 291; black, 10, 28, 39, 92, 106, 192, 272, 282; racism and, 29
Cummings, James, 50
Cuomo, Mario, 103, 127
Dale, Johnny, 170–171
Daniels, Ron, 55, 85
Danquah, J. B., 202, 205, 209, 214
Darwin, Charles, 247
Daugherty, Harry M., 185
Davidson, Basil, 202, 206, 211
Davis, Angela Y., 120, 286, 289
Davis, Ossie, 216, 221, 227
Davis, Philip J., 52
De Jongh, James, 103
Debs, Eugene V., 180, 181
DeCaro, Louis, 222
Dee, Ruby, 221
Delany, Martin, 71, 88
Dellums, C. L., 187, 189
Dellums, Ronald V., 34, 72
Democracy, 58, 67, 195, 275, 287, 295, 307; building, 261; communism and, 199; economic, 20, 107; multicultural, 20, 256, 257, 258, 260, 280, 292; multiracial, 15; parliamentary, 297; preserving, 49, 271; social justice and, 258
Democratic Party, 49, 81, 82, 92, 106, 142, 148, 183, 234, 240; AFL-CIO and, 94; blacks and, 3, 27, 36, 37, 39, 40, 43, 57, 59, 60, 68, 69; centrism of, 61; civil rights and,

40, 74; Jackson and, 59–60, 69, 86, 94, 98; Rainbow Coalition and, 69, 108; reform of, 17, 77, 93, 97
Denton, Jeremiah, 74
Des Verney, W. H., 186, 187
Desegregation, 5, 21, 35, 39, 40, 41, 50–51, 67, 72, 76, 87, 88, 92, 106, 142, 151, 159, 167, 197, 200; campaign for, 169, 194, 195, 196; out-migration after, 143; political issue of, 42
Deukmejian, George, 234
Diallo, Amadou, 269, 274
Dickerson, Debra, 236
Dinkins, David, 83, 84, 91, 105, 235
Discrimination, 3, 5, 8, 15, 16, 23, 45, 88, 117; employment, 93, 190, 287; experiences of, 11; housing, 257; racial, 12, 13, 24, 81, 90, 100, 115, 189; reverse, 109, 252, 268; social, 7
Dole, Elizabeth, 51
Dole, Robert, 94
Domingo, W. A., 179, 183
Donahue, Thomas R., 65
Douglass, Frederick, 13, 52, 88, 89, 91, 106, 135, 220, 221, 254, 260
Drake, St. Clair, 209
Du Bois, W.E.B., 12, 20, 66, 90, 92, 111, 154, 156, 175, 179, 182, 183, 187, 193, 220, 221, 260, 285, 289; Afrocentrism and, 89; black community and, 11; class struggle and, 185; on color line, 22, 279; desegregationist agenda of, 88; double consciousness and, 89; Pan-Africanism and, 67, 204; political economy and, 191; on political power, 205; popular coalition and, 189; racism and, 182; "Talented Tenth" and, 186; World War I/ blacks and, 275
Duggin, Thelma, 51, 70
Dukakis, Michael, 85, 108
Dunbar, Paul Lawrence, 4
Easton, J.W.H, 183
Echols, Ezra, Jr., 150–151
Economic development, 5, 21, 43, 70, 82, 88, 100, 159, 171, 252, 296
Education, 36, 43, 55, 68, 71, 100, 114, 129, 148, 159, 211, 251, 291, 295; differences in, 109; multiculturalism and, 259, 260; poor, 51; prison, 132; quality, 84, 141; spending on, 18, 131; Third World, 303; universal, 249
Edusei, Krobo, 203, 205, 209
Eizenstat, Stuart, 109
Eliot, T. S., 262, 278
Ellison, Ralph, 139
Ely, Richard T., 161–162
Employment, 58, 81, 99, 114, 117, 195; discrimination in, 93, 190, 287
Engels, Friedrich, 247

Equality, 28, 66, 88, 98, 99, 107, 112, 136, 280; economic, 54, 191, 250; struggle for, 9, 20

Ethnicity, 15, 16, 19, 20, 99, 112, 192, 232, 234, 283; racialized, 284, 288–289

Evans, Mari, 43

Evanzz, Karl, 222

Evers, Charles, 200

Evers, Medgar, 8, 118, 200

Exploitation, 117, 291; class, 14, 40, 250, 254; economic, 11, 90, 170, 275, 284, 290

Falwell, Jerry, 64, 270

Fanon, Frantz, 24, 25–26, 29, 42, 152, 192

Farmer, James, 197

Farrakhan, Louis, 84, 92, 104, 122, 123, 125, 226; anti-Semitism of, 230; Black nationalism of, 230; homophobia of, 120; Jackson and, 97, 124; Malcolm X and, 221, 223, 227; Million Man March and, 230; NOI and, 121; September 11th and, 274; voter registration and, 124

Fattah, Chaka, 221

Fauntroy, Walter, 63, 64, 196, 200

Ferraro, Geraldine, 96

Fite, Gilbert C., 156, 164

Fitz-Gerald, Sir Patrick, 210, 211

Fitzwater, Marlin, 114

Flake, Floyd, 117

Fletcher, Art, 50, 72

Foner, Eric, 271

Foner, Philip, 177

Forbes, James A., 274

Ford, Gerald R., 33, 35

Ford, Harold, 34, 235

Ford, Henry, 178

Ford, Johnny, 146, 147, 148, 150, 151; election of, 142, 144; federal grant and, 145

Ford, Sharkey, 170

Fort-Whiteman, Lovett, 184

Foster, Luther, 148

Foster, Wilbur F., 140, 141, 144

Foster, William Z., 178

Francis, Reuben, 227

Freeman, Joshua, 265

Freud, Sigmund, 22

Friedman, Milton, 50, 51

Fuller, Howard, 57

Galbraith, John Kenneth, 162

Gandhi, Mohandas K., 190, 285

Gangi, Robert, 127

Garnet, Henry Highland, 88, 89, 200

Garret, Thaddeus, 51, 70

Garrison, William Lloyd, 29

Garvey, Marcus, 7, 14, 52, 59, 71, 88, 92, 177, 182, 183, 185, 192, 280, 287; black community and, 11; popular coalition and, 189; popularity of, 184

Garveyism, 12, 88, 175, 176, 183, 184, 185, 187

Gasper, Phil, 123

Gates, Henry Louis, 12

Gbedemah, Komla Agbeli, 203, 204, 205, 207, 208, 209, 210

Genovese, Eugene D., 156

Gergen, David R., 45

Gershman, Carl, 22, 23, 24

Gingrich, Newt, 122

Giuliani, Rudolph, 83, 235, 265, 267, 269

Glenn, John, 61

Goetz, Bernard, 73, 105

Golden, Harry, 198

Goldman, Peter, 222, 223

Goldstein, Matthew, 270

Goode, Wilson, 234

Goodman, Andrew, 29

Gore, Al, 275

Graham, Billy, 196

Gramsci, Antonio, 27, 254

Gray, Kevin, 108

Gray, Lloyd Douglas, 168

Gray, William, 85, 95, 97

Green, Mark, 267

Green, William, 178, 186, 188

Gregory, Dick, 95

Grey, Fred, 149

Grimke, Archibald, 185

Guinier, Lani, 98

Gunn, Wendell Willkie, 51

Haberman, Clyde, 269

Hacker, Andrew, 133

Haig, Alexander, 24

Haley, Alex, 69, 227–228; Malcolm X and, 225, 228, 229–230; youth of, 228–229

Haley, George, 69

Haley, Simon Alexander, 228

Hamer, Fannie Lou, 7, 8, 20, 135, 260

Hamilton, Charles V., 52, 139, 140, 152

Hampton, Fred, 253

Hargis, Jonnie, 270

Harper, Philip Brian, 222

Harrington, Michael, 36, 93

Harris, Cheryl, 282

Harris, Thomas A., 143

Harris, William H., 188

Harrison, Hubert H., 14, 179, 183

Hart, Gary, 63, 76

Hatcher, Richard, 53

Hawkins, Augustus, 45

Hayer, Talmadge, 223

Hayes, John Edgar, 170

Haygood, Tony, 146

Haystead, Ladd, 156, 164
Health care, 15, 44, 47, 55, 84, 93, 100, 249, 251, 291, 312; racism and, 281; Third World, 303; universal, 20, 74, 81, 121
Hegel, G.W.F., 27, 42
Henry, Aaron, 169
Hill, Robert, 280
Hillquit, Morris, 181
Ho Chi Minh, 285
Holland, Kenneth, 34
Holtzclaw, W. H., 160
Hooks, Benjamin, 36, 53, 60, 66
Hoover, J. Edgar, 219–220
Horton, Willie, 115
Houphouet-Boigny, Felix, 212
Housing, 15, 42, 81, 93, 121, 249, 251, 258; affordable, 99; public, 61, 62, 68, 74, 100, 110, 116, 282; substandard, 8
Howard, Sir John, 210–211
Huckaby, Jerry, 34
Huiswood, Otto, 184
Hulett, A. W., 168
Human rights, 111, 119, 132, 199, 253, 256, 273; CIA and, 271; violation of, 64, 250, 276
Hutchings, Phil, 191
Hutton-Mills, Tommy, 205
Hynes, Charles, 105
Ice Cube, Malcolm X and, 220, 224
Identity, 108; Afrocentric, 14; black, 19, 20, 28, 92, 107; cultural, 20, 66; ethnic, 15, 386; racial, 9, 10, 11, 16, 198, 234, 279; radical, 253; white, 272
Ignatiev, Noel, 284
Ikoku, Sam G., 211
Inequality, 7, 13, 117, 122; black, 22, 281; class, 122, 243, 277, 291; political, 279; racial, 12, 20, 58, 122, 136, 243; social, 19, 20, 208, 250; socioeconomic, 279, 282
Innis, Roy, 38, 73, 74
Integration, 12, 13, 91–92, 110, 111, 117, 231, 281, 282; economic, 299; racial, 24
International Monetary Fund (IMF), 62, 268, 289, 306, 307
Iron and Steel Corporation (ISCOR), 65
Jackson, Deal, 162
Jackson, George, 119, 135
Jackson, Jesse, 36, 40, 52, 53, 61, 62, 68, 72, 82, 88, 93, 107, 108, 125, 196; anti-Semitism of, 104; campaign of, 57, 81, 83, 85–86, 91; Democratic Party and, 59–60, 69, 86, 94, 98; desegregation and, 197; Dinkins and, 84; Farrakhan and, 97, 124; King and, 197; Latino community and, 100; Malcolm X and, 221; NOI and, 97; PUSH and, 53; Rainbow Coalition and, 17, 63, 69, 96–97, 105, 121,

233, 235, 253; responsibility, and, 75; South Africa and, 63
Jackson, Joseph H., 196–197
Jackson, Maynard, 53
Jackson, Sir Robert, 211
Jacobs, Harold, 103
Jacobs, John F., 60
James, C.L.R., 21, 203, 206, 207, 213–214, 299
Javits, Jacob, 50
Jeffries, Leonard, Jr., 12, 14, 103, 104, 105
Jenrette, John, 34
Jews, 25, 26, 63, 94; relations with, 103, 105–106
Jim Crow, 5, 8, 14, 16, 26, 75, 81, 82, 93, 98, 107, 117, 136, 141, 165, 166, 177, 178, 181, 189, 191, 194, 238, 255, 282, 284, 287, 311; battling, 76, 118, 190, 195; impact of, 13; nostalgia for, 76; political etiquette of, 6
Johnson, Cyrus, 52
Johnson, J. J., 147
Johnson, John H., 54
Johnson, Lyndon B., 36, 76, 114, 192, 199, 215–216
Johnson, Paul B., Jr., 169
Johnson, Thomas 15X, 223
Jones, Joseph, 149
Jordan, Vernon, 36, 53, 54, 59
Jordan, Winthrop, 28
Kaufman, Arnold S., 151–152
Kautsky, Karl, 180
Kean, Thomas H., 69, 95
Kennedy, Edward, 64
Kennedy, John F., 24, 192
Kennedy, Robert F., 63, 216
Kenyatta, Jomo, 201
Keough, Donald R., 53
Kerensky, Alexander, 182
Kerry, John, 233
Key, V. O., 171
Keyes, Robert, 35
Keynes, John, 49
King, Coretta Scott, 52, 53, 60, 72
King, Martin Luther, Jr., 8, 20, 24, 53, 59, 63, 72, 73, 75, 91, 97, 106, 107, 119, 121, 148, 152, 190, 196, 220, 221, 256, 278, 285, 289, 301; assassination of, 118, 199, 200, 216; black nationalism and, 199; civil rights movement and, 194; on communism/democracy, 199; desegregation and, 197; FBI and, 271; Left and, 197–198; legacy of, 195; Malcolm X and, 199, 200, 215, 216, 219, 222, 225, 228; March on Washington and, 57; prominence of, 41; quote of, 126, 262; strengths/weaknesses of, 199–200; Vietnam War and, 191
King, Martin Luther, Sr., 33
King, Mel, 81

King, Rodney, 9, 113, 114, 116, 117
King, Yolanda, 215
Kissinger, Henry, 304–305, 310
Kloosterboer, W., 26
Koch, Ed, 83, 84
Kohl, Helmut, 311
Kohut, Andrew, 235
Kolchin, Peter, 154
Kristof, Nicholas D., 239
Ku Klux Klan, 27, 59, 67, 73, 153, 167, 178, 195, 217
Kun, Bela, 181
Kunstler, William, 223
Labor, 18, 26, 28, 29, 76, 192, 252, 272, 281, 295, 296, 299
Lacy, L. C., 209
Lafayette, Bernard, 196
Lancaster, Burt, 126
Lance, Bert, 36
LaRouche, Lyndon, 73
Lawson, James, 72, 196
Leadership, 39, 41, 49, 51, 5254, 59, 71, 74, 118, 136, 194
Leaks, Sylvester, 227
LeBlanc, Keith, 219
Lee, Spike, 8, 220, 231
Left, 77, 248, 253, 263; civil rights and, 252; political history of, 247; as social catalyst, 251
Left Nkrumaism, 21, 202, 208–214
Lenin, Vladimir, 181, 182, 203, 247, 248
Lester, Julius, 103, 197, 198, 199
Leventhal, Nathan, 84
Levin, Michael, 104
Lewis, Arthur, 307
Lewis, John, 72
Lewis, W. Arthur, 210
Lieberman, Joe, 275
Lifsh, Yosef, 104–105
Limbaugh, Rush, 237
Lincoln, C. Eric, 229
Locke, Alain, 188
Logan, Rayford, 189
Long, Huey, 59
Loury, Glenn, 70, 71, 72, 76, 99
L'Overture, Toussaint, 285
Lowery, Joseph E., 52, 53, 63
Lucas, William, 69–70
Lumumba, Patrice, 201, 209
Luxemburg, Rosa, 248, 250, 253
Lynch, Bill, 84
Lynch, Leon, 65
Maddox, Lester, 73, 311
Madison, Joe, 54
Makonnen, Ras, 207, 211, 212
Malcolm X, 8, 14, 17, 21, 24, 71, 97, 107, 118–119, 121, 135, 136, 191, 192, 232, 285,

289, 302; anti-Semitism of, 230; assassination of, 217, 223–224; biography of, 222, 225; black masculinity and, 216, 218–219, 222; black nationalists and, 217; Black Power and, 217; capitalism and, 242, 250; described, 217–218; Farrakhan and, 221, 223, 227; Haley and, 225, 228, 229–230; Islamic world and, 237; King and, 199, 200, 215, 216, 219, 222, 225, 228; legacy of, 216, 220–221, 224, 225, 231; NOI and, 220, 222, 225, 231; racism and, 250; silencing, 224–225, 231
Mamdani, Mahmood, 279
Mandela, Nelson, 15, 62, 63, 258
Mandela, Winnie, 258
Manley, Michael, 250, 293, 304, 305
Mao Zedong, 248
Marable, James, 4, 6, 8
Marable, Joshua, 8
Marable, June, 4
Marable, Malaika, 8, 9
Marable, Morris, 163
Marable, Sojourner, 8–9
March on Washington (1963), 17, 57, 70–71
March on Washington (1983), 63, 68
Marcuse, Herbert, 24
Marley, Bob, 283
Marx, Karl, 22, 179, 180, 182, 192, 198, 247, 248
Marxism, 88–89, 175, 176, 177, 178, 197, 198, 247, 248, 249, 253
McCain, John, 239, 240, 241
McCarthy, Eugene, 76
McCormick, Kenneth, 229, 230
McCoy, Alfred, 264
McGee, James, 4
McGee, Michael, 95–96
McGovern, George, 36, 76
McKay, Claude, 182
McKissick, Floyd, 38
McQuirk, Bernard, 237
McZier, Arthur, 51–52
Meany, George, 191, 294
Meese, Edwin, 50
Meier, August, 190, 196
Menguistu, 249
Mikoyan, Anastas, 207
Miller, John, 52, 196
Miller, William Robert, 196
Million Man March, 120–121, 122, 124, 230
Mitchell, Parren, 36
Mondale, Walter, 61, 63, 74, 108, 176
Montgomery bus boycott, 53, 54, 63, 194, 199, 285
Montgomery, Isaiah T., 167
Moon, Sun Myung, 73
Moore, Henson, 75

Moore, Mildred, 146
Moore, Morris "Dad," 187
Moore, Richard B., 184
Moos, Jeanne, 237
Morial, Marc, 241
Morris, William R., 42
Morrow, Edward P., 187
Moton, Robert Russa, 163, 182, 186
Moynihan, Daniel Patrick, 23, 103–104, 116, 176
Muhammad, Elijah, 14, 52, 224, 226, 274
Muhammad, W. Deen, 274
Mullings, Leith, 12, 281
Multiculturalism, 103, 256, 257, 258, 280, 287, 292; education and, 259, 260
Murphy, Carl, 185
Murray, Charles, 99
Muserere, Bishop, 311
Myrdal, Gunnar, 29, 156
Nasser, Gamal Abdel, 285
Nation of Islam (NOI), 14, 21, 95, 120, 121, 122, 217, 229, 230, 238, 274; American Nazi Party and, 230; Jackson and, 97; Malcolm X and, 220, 222, 225, 231; negotiations with, 226; voter registration and, 124
National Association for the Advancement of Colored People (NAACP), 12, 13, 17, 42, 49, 53, 54, 60, 61, 94, 96, 98, 120, 125, 140, 169, 179, 181, 182, 189, 191, 197, 199, 241, 283; alternative federal budget by, 46; Chavis and, 121–122; corruption/patronage and, 122; criticism of, 51; desegregationist agenda of, 88; Garvey and, 185; growth of, 287; Reagan and, 52; Tuskegee students and, 144
National Urban League, 13, 60, 69, 121, 241, 274
Native Americans, 101, 112; genocide against, 255–256, 264; harassment of, 272
Negro March on Washington Movement (1941), 70, 175, 176, 189, 190–191, 192, 193, 195, 287
Neoconservatism, 24, 44, 75
Neoliberalism, 87, 269, 279, 291
Newman, Constance, 52
Newton, Huey P., 14
Nichols, Bill, 148
Nixon, E. D., 195
Nixon, Richard M., 24, 46, 50, 129, 142, 145; black capitalism and, 34, 38
Nkrumah, Kwame, 54, 66, 285, 302, 312; assassination attempts against, 210; CPP and, 201, 202, 206; criticism of, 205, 213–214; cult of the personality of, 206–207; detention of, 203; Pan-African Congress and, 204; Pan-Africanist vision of, 201, 212–213; rise of, 202–204

Nunn, Sam, 85
Nyemitei, H. P., 204
Nyerere, Julius, 201, 212, 311
Obama, Barack, 240; campaign of, 234, 235, 236, 239; election of, 232, 233, 241, 242; Islamic world and, 237; racialization and, 241, 243
Obatala, J. K., 35
Ocran, Turkson, 204
Okihiro, Gary, 284
Osborne, Alfred E., 37
Owen, Chandler, 179, 180, 181, 182, 183, 185, 192
Owens, Major, 73, 74
Owusu, Victor, 203, 205, 206, 209
Padmore, George, 202, 204, 205, 207
Palin, Sarah, 240
Palmer, Bertha George, 228
Pan-Africanism, 201, 202, 203, 204, 212–213
Parenti, Christian, 134
Parker, Anthony, 107
Parker, J.A.Y., 51
Parks, Rosa, 63, 149, 194–195
Pataki, George, 127
Patrick, Deval, 235
Patterson, David, 235
Patterson, T. T., 187
Percy, Alexander, 168
Percy, Charles, 50, 168–169
Perlik, Charles A., 65
Perry, Dudley, 148, 150
Pettiford, W. R., 159
Phillips, Joyce Daniels, 46
Pickard, William, 51
Pickens, William, 179, 182, 185
Pierce, Samuel, 50
Pinochet, Augusto, 264
Plekhanov, George, 202–203
Pol Pot, 249
Pollitt, Katha, 264
Poulantzas, Nicos, 280
Poverty, 4, 34, 87, 90, 105, 116, 122, 125, 159, 233, 242, 250, 253, 254, 255, 261, 266, 268, 277, 282, 288; abolition of, 291; black, 24, 39, 40, 68, 166; crime and, 251; crisis of, 95; Third World, 275, 290; violence of, 291
Powell, Adam Clayton, 197
Powell, Colin, 124, 232, 275
Price, Hugh, 274
Prisons, 135; blacks and, 59, 133; building, 123, 131, 133; juvenile, 133; spending on, 131, 133; visiting, 126–129
Progressive movement, 83, 85, 86, 93, 189, 295
Protest, 52, 62; revitalizing, 286–288; social, 67, 69, 81, 85, 88, 95, 96, 198, 287, 292
Quayle, Dan, 113, 116

Race, 10, 16, 21, 27, 232, 283, 287, 288; burden of, 11, 19, 30; class and, 23, 24–25, 122; perverse logic of, 21; prism of, 5, 6, 7, 8, 9; reality of, 3, 11; reframing debates on, 17; social conservatism and, 293; as social construction, 15; as social force, 9; unequal relations and, 9; violence and, 117–119
Racial separatism, 17, 19, 89, 97, 238, 281
Racialization, 241, 243, 272, 277, 283, 284, 289, 290, 292
Racism, 7–8, 11, 12, 22, 23, 25, 27–28, 44, 55, 60, 81, 95, 114, 117, 182, 192, 233, 250, 252, 254, 261, 271–272, 273; black, 100; capitalism and, 250; challenging, 7, 14, 90, 151, 200, 282; economics of, 166; health care and, 281; institutional, 10, 12, 26, 91, 109, 260, 288; legal system and, 115; manifestations of, 13; militarism and, 272, 277, 291; patriotism and, 274; political economy of, 145; small manifestations of, 8; society/culture and, 29; structural, 131, 135, 275, 277, 279, 280–281, 289, 292; upsurge in, 168–169; war and, 270; white, 25, 27, 29, 145, 160, 165, 194
Rainbow Coalition, 76, 81, 85, 101, 107–108, 124; Jackson and, 17, 63, 69, 96–97, 105, 121, 233, 235, 253
Randolph, Asa Philip, 70, 181, 182, 183, 184, 195, 287; activism of, 179; black nationalism and, 190, 192; criticism of, 175–176, 188; death of, 176, 191; economic determinism and, 193; Garvey and, 185; influence of, 175; legacy of, 177; militant pacifism and, 180; opposition to, 185; political life of, 176–177; Pullman porters and, 186; socialism and, 180; strike and, 187–188; Vietnam War and, 191
Randolph, James, 180
Randolph, Lucille, 179
Ransom, Roger, 157, 159
Raspberry, William, 53
Ravitch, Diane, 103
Read, Eddie, 236
Reagan, Ronald, 44–45, 50, 51, 87, 240, 311; blacks and, 24, 46, 62, 64, 72; Buthelezi and, 64; campaign of, 129; capitalism and, 48; election of, 62–63, 67; endorsing, 200; FmHA and, 167; national security state and, 268; social policies of, 45, 46; white Southerners/Christians and, 62; working-class support for, 74
Reaganism, 18, 44–45, 49, 50, 69, 71, 82, 87–88, 122; core ideology of, 268; emergence of, 56; opponents of, 53; social crisis generated by, 81; social devastation of, 84
Reaganomics, 44, 45, 52, 58; failure of, 450; understanding, 46–47

Reed, Gregory, 230, 231
Reed, Thomas, 147, 148, 150
Republican Party, 81, 180, 183, 239; support for, 34, 60, 240; votes for, 34
Reston, James, 305
Reuther, Walter, 299
Rice, Condoleezza, 232, 275
Rickford, Russell, 220
Riff, Michael, 103
Robb, Charles, 85
Robbins, Ira, 135
Robertson, Pat, 70
Robeson, Paul, 20, 260, 261, 289
Robinson, Leo, 65–66
Robinson, Randall, 63
Rockefeller, Nelson, 50
Rodney, Walter, 21, 101, 249, 250, 302, 314
Roediger, David, 284
Romaine, Anne, 228, 230
Roosevelt, Franklin D., 33, 45, 311; Executive Order 8802 and, 287; March on Washington and, 190; welfare capitalism and, 189
Roots (Haley), 69, 228
Rosenthal, A. M., 105
Rowan, Carl, 199
Rudwick, Elliott, 190
Rustin, Bayard, 36, 60, 93, 177, 191–192, 195, 197, 198
Sanchez, Sonia, 217–218
Sartre, Jean-Paul, 285
Savage, Gus, 54, 95
Savimbi, Jonas, 73
Sawyer, Eugene, 102
Scheck, Saki, 203, 204
Schlesinger, Arthur, Jr., 36
Schultze, Charles, 36
Schuyler, George S., 180
Schwerner, Michael, 29
Scott, Emmett J., 149, 186
Seale, Bobb, 135
Segregation, 4–5, 6, 14, 16, 19, 38, 57, 82, 91, 92, 93, 98, 109, 117, 140, 144, 149, 160, 170, 198, 238, 255, 265, 266, 275, 281, 282, 284, 287; contemporary effects of, 277; crimes of, 9; *de facto/de jure*, 26, 142, 164; encountering, 8; outlawing, 106–107; racial, 10, 14, 15, 76, 82, 136, 167, 178, 200, 272, 277, 290; residential, 265; rise of, 66
Sekondi-Takoradi strike (1961), 202, 203, 205, 208, 209, 213
Self-determination, 16, 55, 56, 119, 182, 193, 255, 257, 258, 259, 289
Senghor, Leopold Sedar, 201, 212
Shabazz, Attallah, 215
Shabazz, Betty, 222, 225, 226, 227, 231
Shabazz, Maliakah, 226

Shakur, Tupac, 220
Shanker, Albert, 176
Shapiro, J. Salwyn, 179
Shelby, Richard C., 74
Shelton, Hilary, 241
Shiflett, Lynn, 227
Shuttlesworth, Fred, 196
Silber, Irwin, 176
Simpson, O. J., 9, 124
Sindab, Jean, 66
Slavery, 10, 11, 117, 155, 156, 170, 255, 275, 280, 281, 284, 285, 286, 290, 294; blackness and, 28; as crime against humanity, 276, 290; end of, 106–107, 115
Slotnick, Barry, 105
Smith, Andrea, 288
Smith, Ian, 311
Smith, William French, 59
Social change, 20, 86, 87, 90, 177, 247, 249, 253, 289, 291, 293, 294
Social democracy, 55, 74, 83, 89, 176, 250, 251, 253
Social justice, 60, 136, 248, 250, 253, 254, 256, 258, 261, 270, 280
Social welfare, 36, 43, 68, 69, 122, 211, 248, 249, 250, 269
Socialism, 86, 186, 193, 208, 210, 212, 247, 249, 250, 299, 300, 307, 308; democratic vision of, 251; faith in, 75; future of, 316; struggle for, 254
Socialist Party, 86, 118, 177, 181, 183, 184, 193; Randolph and, 176, 179, 180, 182
Southern Christian Leadership Conference (SCLC), 63, 72, 191, 194, 195, 196, 197, 199, 200
Sowell, Thomas, 50, 51, 52, 70, 72, 99
Spears, Edward, 211
Stalin, Joseph, 247, 248
Stalinism, 88, 89, 93, 248, 250, 253
Stedman, Seymour, 181
Steele, C. K., 196
Stennis, John C., 169
Steyn, Mark, 237
Stockman, David, 45
Stokes, Louis, 200
Straw, Jack, 276
Student Nonviolent Coordinating Committee (SNCC), 57, 72, 144, 170, 191, 196, 197, 198, 199
Sukarno, 285
Sullivan, Leon, 24, 54, 64, 65
Sun Yat-sen, 285
Sutch, Richard, 157, 159
Sutton, Percy, 221
Sweezy, Paul, 165
Takaki, Ronald, 100

Taliban, 264, 276, 278, 290
Taylor, Henry Louis, Jr., 93
Taylor, Kurankyi, 204, 205
Teasdale, Joseph, 34
Terrorism, 118, 153, 268, 269, 271; blacks and, 273–274; breeding, 276; domestic acts of, 264; global, 275; mass, 264; military strikes and, 290; political, 263; suppressing, 276, 290; threat of, 277, 291; violence of, 277, 278, 291
Tettegah, John, 206, 208
Thatcher, Margaret, 308, 311
Thomas, Clarence, 121
Thomas, Norman, 180, 191
Thompson, W. Scott, 212
Thurman, Wallace, 179–180
Thurmond, Strom, 141
Timothy, Bankole, 203, 205
Tindall, George B., 162
Tisdale, Charles, 169
Tolson, Arthur, 38
Tonry, Richard, 34
Toote, Gloria E. A., 51
Totten, Ashley, 186, 187, 188
Toure, Sekou, 201, 212
Trotsky, Leon, 181, 182, 203
Trotter, Monroe, 181
Truman, Harry, 141
Truth, Sojourner, 260
Tubman, Harrriet, 221
Turner, Henry M., 200
Turner, Nat, 200
Tuskegee Institute, 71, 144, 148, 149, 150, 151, 160, 163, 177, 186; creation of, 140, 141, 143; statue at, 139
Unemployment, 8, 15, 23, 34, 51, 74, 90, 95, 116, 122, 124, 170, 208, 242, 252, 253, 256, 258, 266, 296; black, 36, 40, 47, 58, 59, 75, 249, 251, 255, 273, 282; Latino, 273; non-white, 58; rate of, 118, 255
Urban League, 36, 53, 59, 61, 191, 197, 199, 273
Usry, James, 69, 95
Vargas Llosa, Maria, 265
Vause, John, 237
Venable, Abraham, 52
Violence, 56, 123, 277, 279, 291; black, 87, 105, 114, 118, 215; border, 259; collective, 118; criminal, 102, 129, 130; hate-inspired, 272; institutional, 114, 118; mass, 162, 196; political, 168; prisoner, 128; racist, 59, 114, 117–119, 260; radical, 113; systemic, 13, 277; terrorism, 277, 278; vigilante, 100
Vivian, C. T., 196
Voit, Stan, 147
Voting Rights Act (1965), 45, 53, 74, 82, 115, 134, 287

Walker, Alice, 257
Walker, W. O., 50
Walker, William, 35
Walker, Wyatt Tee, 196
Wallace, Charles, 146, 150
Wallace, George, 10, 129, 142, 148, 151, 169
Wallace, Mike, 229
Walters, Ronald, 37, 43
Washington, Booker T., 9, 52, 54–55, 71, 82, 92, 149, 159, 160, 162, 176, 177, 178, 181, 183, 186, 191, 195; accommodationism and, 72; agricultural development and, 161; black community and, 11; black economy and, 161, 165; capitalist alliance and, 177; King and, 198; lecture by, 160–161; papers of, 225; popular coalitions and, 189; Randolph and, 191; statue of, 139
Washington, Denzel, 8
Washington, Harold, 46, 57, 81, 83, 221, 234
Washington, Roy: lynching of, 168
Waters, Maxine: on riots/rebellions, 113
Webber, George William ("Bill"), 128, 136
Webster, Milton, 187, 188
Wehwein, George S., 161–162
Weisskopf, Thomas, 47
Welfare, 39, 44, 49, 71, 84, 99, 170, 250, 268
West, Cornel, 107
Whelan, Jim, 95
White, Walter, 185, 189, 197
White, William, 179
Whitehead, Willie, 146

Whitshitt, Joyce, 217
Wilder, Douglas, 84, 95, 234, 235; election of, 83, 91, 96–97
Wilkins, Roy, 12, 199
Williams, Eddie N., 35
Williams, Eric, 298, 314
Williams, Franklin, 49
Williams, Hosea, 40, 53, 72, 200
Williams, Joslyn, 65
Williams, Juan, 236, 237
Williams, Ron, 150
Williams, Walter, 51, 70, 76
Wilson, Margaret Bush, 54
Wilson, William Julius, 23, 24, 109
Wilson, Woodrow, 175, 180, 182
Wonder, Harry, 63
Wood, Virgil, 196
Woods, Anthony, 204
Woodson, Carter G., 164
Woodson, Robert, 70, 71
Woodward, C. Vann, 155
World Trade Center: attack on, 262, 263, 269, 270, 273, 289; victims of, 263, 266
Wright, Jeremiah, 237–238
Wright, Nathan, Jr., 52, 72
Young, Andrew, 33, 34, 35, 40, 53, 57, 61, 72, 96, 196, 200
Young, Coleman, 60
Young, Whitney, 199
Yun, Lisa, 284

About the Author and Editor

Manning Marable is the M. Moran Weston and Black Alumni Council Professor of African American Studies at Columbia University, where he is also professor of history and public affairs. Among his many influential books is *Malcolm X: A Life of Reinvention* (Viking 2011). Dr. Marable is a frequent commentator for such media as CNN, the History Channel, PBS, NBC's *Today Show, Tavis Smiley,* BET, the *Charlie Rose Show,* BBC, and Al Jazeera.

Russell Rickford has selected the essays for this volume and provides an engaging introduction to Marable's writings. Assistant Professor of History at Dartmouth, he is the author of a biography of Dr. Betty Shabazz, Malcolm X's wife, and a forthcoming book on African-American liberation schools during the black power era.